NARRATIVITY IN BIBLICAL AND RELATED TEXTS
LA NARRATIVITÉ DANS LA BIBLE ET LES TEXTES APPARENTÉS

BIBLIOTHECA EPHEMERIDUM THEOLOGICARUM LOVANIENSIUM

CXLIX

NARRATIVITY IN BIBLICAL AND RELATED TEXTS

LA NARRATIVITÉ DANS LA BIBLE ET LES TEXTES APPARENTÉS

EDITED BY

G.J. BROOKE AND J.-D. KAESTLI

LEUVEN UNIVERSITY PRESS

UITGEVERIJ PEETERS
LEUVEN

2000

BS
521.7
.N37
2000

ISBN 90 5867 068 6 (Leuven University Press)
D/2000/1869/64
ISBN 90-429-0877-7 (Peeters Leuven)
D/2000/0602/82
ISBN 2-87723-504-1 (Peeters France)

All rights reserved. Except in those cases expressly determined by law,
no part of this publication may be multiplied, saved in an automated data file
or made public in any way whatsoever
without the express prior written consent of the publishers.

Leuven University Press / Presses Universitaires de Louvain
Universitaire Pers Leuven
Blijde-Inkomststraat 5, B-3000 Leuven-Louvain (Belgium)

© 2000, Peeters, Bondgenotenlaan 153, B-3000 Leuven (Belgium)

PREFACE

This collection of essays derives from the joint symposium organized by the Centre for Biblical Studies, University of Manchester, and the Institut Romand des Sciences Bibliques, Université de Lausanne, in May 1996. The symposium was held in the Department of Religions and Theology in the University of Manchester. In addition to staff members from both the University of Manchester and the University of Lausanne, the speakers included staff from other universities and colleges, as well as some postgraduate students.

The symposium was the fourth in a series of joint symposia which have been held alternately in Lausanne and Manchester. The earlier symposia have already been published: Christopher M. TUCKETT (ed.), *Luke's Literary Achievement: Collected Essays* (Journal for the Study of the New Testament Supplement, 116), Sheffield, Sheffield Academic Press, 1995; Daniel MARGUERAT (ed.), *Le déchirement: Juifs et chrétiens au premier siècle*, Geneva, Labor et Fides, 1996; Adrian H.W. CURTIS and Thomas RÖMER (eds.), *The Book of Jeremiah and Its Reception / Le livre de Jérémie et sa réception* (BETL, 128), Leuven, Peeters-Leuven University Press, 1997.

We are grateful to the Universities of Lausanne and Manchester for the financial support which made this symposium both possible and very enjoyable. Especially we are grateful to the University of Manchester Research Support Fund for assistance with the costs of preparing this collection of essays for publication. We are also grateful to Sylvie Janin and Catherine Franc for assistance with the translation of the English abstracts. Peeters as well as the Editor of the series *Bibliotheca Ephemeridum Theologicarum Lovaniensium* have been very helpful in encouraging this volume forward.

George J. BROOKE
Manchester

Jean-Daniel KAESTLI
Lausanne

CONTENTS

Preface VII

Introduction XI

The Old Testament

1. Jean-Daniel Macchi (Genève)
   Les interprétations conflictuelles d'une narration (Genèse 34,1–35,5; 49,5-7) 3

2. Thomas C. Römer (Lausanne)
   La narration, une subversion. L'histoire de Joseph (Gn 37–50*) et les romans de la diaspora 17

3. Bernard S. Jackson (Manchester)
   Law, Wisdom, and Narrative 31

4. Roger Tomes (Manchester)
   "Come and See my Zeal for the Lord": Reading the Jehu Story 53

5. John Applegate (Salford, UK)
   Narrative Patterns for the Communication of Commissioned Speech in the Prophets: A Three-Scene Model 69

The New Testament

6. J. Martin C. Scott (Edinburgh)
   Jesus Walking on the Sea: the Significance of Matthew 14,22-23 for the Narrative Development of the Gospel . . 91

7. F. Gerald Downing (Chorley, UK)
   Markan Intercalation in Cultural Context 105

8. Andrianjatovo Rakotoharintsifa (Antananarivo, Madagascar)
   Les séjours de Jésus à Béthanie au-delà du Jourdain selon le chronotope de l'Évangile de Jean 119

9. Christopher M. Tuckett (Oxford)
   Pilate in John 18–19: a Narrative-Critical Approach . . . 131

10. Martinus C. DE BOER (Amsterdam)
    The Narrative Function of Pilate in John 141

11. Daniel MARGUERAT (Lausanne)
    The God of the Book of Acts 159

III. RELATED TEXTS

12. George J. BROOKE (Manchester)
    Joseph, Aseneth, and Lévi-Strauss 185

13. Jean-Daniel KAESTLI (Lausanne)
    L'usage du narratif dans le *Testament de Joseph* 201

14. Helen K. BOND (Edinburgh)
    The Literary Function of Pontius Pilate in Josephus' Narratives 213

15. Steve NOLAN (Manchester)
    Narrative as a Strategic Resource for Resistance: Reading the *Acts of Thecla* for its Political Purposes 225

16. Kate COOPER (Manchester)
    Matthidia's Wish: Division, Reunion, and the Early Christian Family in the Pseudo-Clementine *Recognitions* 243

17. Pierluigi PIOVANELLI (Ottawa)
    The Miraculous Discovery of the Hidden Manuscript, or the Para-Textual Function of the Prologue to the *Apocalypse of Paul* 265

INDEX OF AUTHORS 283

INDEX OF BIBLICAL REFERENCES 291

INDEX OF CLASSICAL SOURCES 303

INTRODUCTION

A generation or more ago historical criticism of the Bible was largely dominated by redaction criticism in which it was supposed that the most suitable understanding of a biblical composition was to be had through the close reading of the final form of the text, a close reading which would reveal at least some of the principal intentions and purposes of the actual author or editor and so enable an objective reading of the written product. Much has happened in the last thirty years to show that in addition to the many solid benefits which historical criticism has brought for the better appreciation of the biblical and other ancient texts, there are many additional ways of reading texts of any kind which greatly enhance their significance.

Two methodological innovations have become profitable resources for the textual analyst. On the one hand, based on developments in semiotics and the appreciation of the structures of language, there has been much attention to how language works, particularly as a key element in communication. On the other hand, based on developments in the reading of non-canonical texts in the secular disciplines of literary studies and comparative literature, there has been attention to the literary dimension of biblical texts. These two innovations have come together in particularly fruitful ways in narrative criticism. Narrative criticism has already produced a vast literature, but for those less familiar with its chief characteristics an up to date introduction to its principal features together with essential bibliography can be found in the recent book by Daniel Marguerat and Yvan Bourquin, *Pour lire les récits bibliques* (Paris, Les Éditions du Cerf, 1998), now translated into English as *How to Read Bible Stories: An Introduction to Narrative Criticism* (London, SCM Press, 1999). Since the innovative discourses of narrative criticism have been carried on almost exclusively in French and English, the studies collected here in both languages allow for a profitable dialogue through their very juxtaposition. The reader will find here a wealth of interpretative detail illumined at every stage by recent methodological developments.

Overall this collection of essays on the broad theme of narrativity is not an attempt to produce a comprehensive assessment of where narrative criticism has reached after two or more decades of application in biblical studies. Rather this collection puts together seventeen specialist studies, each of which is based on the research strengths of its author and seeks to address a particular topic through issues with which narrative criticism is often concerned. Thus, the collection is not a forced reading of material to fit a previously determined intellectual schematization of what the analysis of narrative should contribute to the better understanding of texts. Yet, in surprising and stimulating ways this collection as a whole makes a distinctive contribution to the better appreciation of how attention to various aspects of narrative analysis intriguingly provides fresh insight into what many texts might have been and may still be about. As a collection, the essays tackle a large number of methodological issues, not in an artificial or hypothetical way, but as keys for furthering the understanding of whole texts or compositions, either in their historical dimension as artefacts of the past, or in terms of their ongoing significance, objects to be appropriated somehow nowadays. In this way the methodologies visible in these essays are not straightjackets encouraging forced readings, but liberating tools.

Because there was no attempt to encourage the contributors to this volume to address particular methodological concerns, the essays have not been grouped according to any kind of systematic approach to the topic of narrativity. In a methodologically neutral way, the essays have rather been arranged in the three artificial categories determined by the bounds of canonicity; so there are three sections, one devoted to the Old Testament or Hebrew Bible, one to the New Testament, and one to related non-canonical literature. In fact the essays could have been grouped in rather different categories which would have spoken more eloquently about the concerns of narrative criticism, but since some of the studies belong in more than one category, it has been decided to present them in a more traditional artificial arrangement. However, something of the categories into which the various contributions to this collection might have been put can be expounded in this introduction to give the reader some guide to the richness of what is on offer in this book as a contribution to the topic of narrativity.

The three basic categories of narrative criticism are the categories of the author, of the message and of the reader. Within each category there are many interpretative and methodological issues which need to be sharpened. With regard to the author a distinction needs to be made between the actual or real author or authors who exist apart from the text and the implied author who is discernible through the way in which the text is put together, through the authorial choices which are visible in the end product. The discovery of the real author or authors for most ancient texts is a largely hypothetical exercise, though it has played an enormous part in much historical criticism which has been concerned with arguing that the purpose of a literary composition of any sort can be determined principally by searching the mind of the real (if reconstructed) author. As far as authorship is concerned narrative criticism is more concerned with the discovery of the author that the text implies, and even that author can also be one step removed from the actual narrator of the text.

Subtlety is also required in the handling of the narrative message. All kinds of literary criticism have become concerned to discuss separately the content of any message from the way in which it is delivered, to distinguish the signified from the signifier. In some traditional applications of form criticism the opposite has been the case: to argue that the structure of a text is directly determined by its subject matter and vice versa. Narrative analysis has shown that such a direct association of form and content is not always helpful and certainly inhibits the exploration of the development of literary genres. In its appreciation of the way in which authors create the world of the narrative, the ways in which they link actions together causally, and the ways in which time plays a part, narrative criticism expounds the multifarious ways in which a subject can be encoded in a narrative form for delivery to the reader.

As with the author, so narrative criticism has enabled much greater precision concerning who might be the receiver of the narrative message, the reader. Whereas historical criticism has been primarily concerned with the discovery of the first readers and hearers of the composition and whereas theological interests have encouraged texts to be read in certain ways by those readers with a particular commitment towards them, narrative criticism has shifted the focus towards two different kinds of reader. The first is the reader implied by the text who is largely constructed by the text and addressed by it; such a reader is the one who is supposed by the author to be able to appreciate and realize the meanings of the text. The second is any other reader of the text who stands outside the supposed contract between the author and the implied reader. Such free readers, any of us, bring all their own luggage of reading strategies when they come to a text, ancient or modern. Narrative criticism, an appreciation of narrativity, can provide additional strategies for anybody's reading of the text.

The studies in this collection relate to such a description of narrativity and narrative criticism in a large number of ways. In what follows here a few aspects of their analytical concerns will be described in relation to the wider enterprise of narrative criticism. This will provide the reader with some orientation to the collection without exhausting in any way the contributions these studies make to their chosen topics.

(a) Author. While historical criticism has been concerned to establish information about actual authors and their historical circumstances, narrative criticism has also paid attention to implied authors. The implied author is to be discerned in and through the text. The identification of the implied author will depend on how particular narrative strategies are used.

Thomas Römer's essay on the Joseph cycle begins from the point of view of the story's autonomy and basic literary unity as reflecting circumstances of Egypt in the Persian period. Römer is concerned to use such a dating of the story as a reading strategy whereby the chief characteristic of the narrator of the Joseph narrative is subversion. The implied author makes the Joseph narrative strangely subversive of the dominant exilic view emanating from the Jewish community of Babylon, namely that the exile was brought about by a foreign king and that the best theological strategy for survival was one of exclusivist behavior based in claims of divine election. Read in this light the Joseph cycle becomes the narrator's political statement from the Egyptian Jewish community of how it was fellow-Israelites who should be held responsible for the exile and that the most suitable response to exile was not attention to divine election and exclusivism but the proclamation of the universal God to whom all could have access. As an exemplary detail the tone of Gen 43,32 on how Jews and Gentiles eat apart is noted as an ironic challenge to the practice of kashrut. In its present context in Genesis the Joseph narrative takes on other purposes, though it retains something of its subversive voice. Through redating and relocating the narrator of the narrative, Römer has been enabled to reread the subject matter and the manner of its discourse in fresh ways.

Whereas in Römer's essay attention is paid to the narrator of what might be constructed as an original form of the Joseph narrative, the contribution by Roger Tomes gives due place to the later editorial items in the story of Jehu and considers the final form of the text as itself a reading of an earlier story. Thus Tomes builds on the work of historical critics who have isolated what is later editorial activity, with a tendency to discount it, by insisting that the reading of the story embedded in its final form needs to be heard from the point of view of its own implied author. Its perspective is to be found above all in 2 Kings 9,7-10a in which the divine purpose is made plain: Jehu is to strike down Ahab's house so that Yahweh may avenge on Jezebel the blood of his servants the prophets. But Tomes takes delight in also pointing out not only the suitable place of the material which is often regarded as secondary, but also how and why it is organized and presented as it is. It is as if the early reader who has become the narrator wanted to provide his own readers with reading strategies as they read the reworked story. In assessing the story line of the Jehu narrative in this way, Tomes suggests that a reading which allows for the construction of a later implied author allows the narrative to retain an overall coherence. Whereas the problems modern readers have had with the narrative have generally been explained through proposing multiple editorial layers or even the juxtaposition of incompatible sources, Tomes suggests a solution to the apparent unevenness of the narrative which is far more satisfactory at the same time as being more respectful of the text as it stands.

Helen Bond's study of Pilate in the writings of Josephus is a cameo which pays attention to how an actual author may present similar material differently in two separate narratives because of a change in his circumstances. She argues that in Josephus' two principal works the portrayal of Pilate in both cases is determined by the apologetic purposes of the author and the rhetorical devices which are used to convey his intentions. In neither work is there anything much which might be clearly associated with the historical figure of Pilate.

Pierluigi Piovanelli's discussion of the Prologue of the *Apocalypse of Paul* raises questions from a very different angle about what can be known about authors. The Prologue is an artificial device to encourage readers to believe that the actual author of the *Apocalypse* was Paul himself. As a pseudepigraphical piece it is the clearest example one can obtain of narrative asserting an implied author, since authorship is its subject matter. Piovanelli suggests that the success of the narrative can be measured by the way in which the majority of the manuscript tradition for the *Apocalypse of Paul* does not include the Prologue; the work was widely accepted as by Paul and after a while needed no Prologue to authenticate it. Augustine and Sozomen writing not long after the appearance of the *Apocalypse* denounced it as inauthentic. Beyond the discussion of the significance of the Prologue for authorship Piovanelli also suggests that the *Apocalypse* is significant in itself as a prime example of how the transformation of Christianity into the official religion of the Roman Empire produced reformulated doctrine in a wide variety of genres, including narratives such as the *Apocalypse of Paul*.

(b) Message. Working with the insights of the structural analysts, many recent interpreters of narrative have paid special attention to the way in which the content of narrative is put together. Several contributions to this collection pay attention to this matter.

In the first section of the book, the detailed contribution by Bernard Jackson argues that it is possible to discover an association between law and wisdom at a popular, oral stage providing that one introduces a consideration of narrative into the equation. He proposes that the later formal differentiation between law and wisdom and the absence of narrative context came about in the transformation by various professionals of the oral into the written form. There are, nevertheless, sufficient examples in other biblical written traditions of the narrative illustration of legal matters in a proverbial way to suggest that the original vehicle for most of such material at the oral stage was narrative. Legal statements are not simply a sum of facts, listed and declared in some way. The grammar of the discourse of much legal material presupposes a story, though that story is not necessarily presented now in a readily recognizable narrative form. Jackson's attention to narrative in the oral stage of wisdom-laws illuminates both the subject matter of such wisdom-laws and the likely discourse through which such wisdom-laws were originally conveyed, perhaps primarily for didactic purposes.

Just as Bernard Jackson is able to suggest a reconsideration of much of the generic labelling of developing legal and wisdom traditions, so John Applegate's essay is really an argument that many earlier form-critical readings of commissioned speeches in the prophets have perhaps been heading in a false direction because they have not taken sufficient account of the narrative element in the wider overall context. Applegate rediscovers the narrative framework of many of these commissioned speeches in the literary prophets and in so doing does not only provide suitable literary contexts for the consideration of such commissioned speeches, but also argues that it is only through taking account of the narrative framework that the truly interactive character of such commissioned speeches can be recognised. Attention to narrative provides a surprising redrawing of the genre in terms of the prophetic process which has ramifications for how all authoritative speech may best be understood. In an intriguing way causality and time, essential ingredients of story, are added to the views of the world contained in the commissioned speeches, to suggest that all such speech is in need of narrative redefinition if it is to be appreciated properly.

Both Jackson and Applegate in very different ways are making distinctive contributions to genre analysis. The same can be said for the essay by Gerald Downing. He subjects the method of the discourse of several sections of Mark's Gospel to comparative literary analysis. In several places Mark sandwiches one narrative within another. Though usually there is mutual illumination in this practice, in most instances the stories could just as well have stood by themselves. Downing investigates some aspects of the character of causality and sequence in these intercalations and searches for comparative material to illuminate the practice. Somewhat surprisingly he finds virtually nothing similar in comparable literature and so he poses the question whether such a narrative discourse strategy, effectively introduced by Mark, could be one of the significant characteristics which might distinguish the Gospel narratives in some measure from other ancient lives.

In a slightly different vein, Andrianjatovo Rakotoharintsifa suggests that the narrative analysis of the Fourth Gospel may have placed too much attention on the widely recognised elements of story-telling, especially temporal sequencing. As a corrective to much of the narrative analysis of the Gospel he proposes that topography also plays an important part. For example, Samaria and Transjordan are the locations of faithful witness to the person of Jesus, Galilee is the place of discipleship, even if it is somewhat imperfect, and Judaea is the home of hostility towards Jesus. More particularly in his convincing analysis of Bethany across the Jordan in the Fourth Gospel, Rakotoharintsifa argues that it is there above all that the witness of John concerning Jesus in John 1,19-28 is fulfilled in John 10,40-42. Attention to place as well as time is significant for appreciating the specificity of the spatio-temporal dimension of the Gospel's christology. Attention to all the dimensions of the narrative message thus has significant theological implications.

(c) Reader. Some of the essays in this volume are concerned not so much with what their narrative subject may say about the author, implied or otherwise, or how the message may be construed, but with the way in which the implied reader can be best indicated.

Jean-Daniel Macchi's analysis of the violation of Dinah (Gen 34,1-35,5) and Jacob's curse of Simeon and Levi (Gen 49,5-7) offers much by way of detailed interpretation of the textual units themselves. A significant part of his interpretation of the principal problem of the text, concerning whether the action of Simeon and Levi is approved or disapproved (as especially in Jacob's curse) derives from his understandings about the implied readers of the story. For Macchi the implied reader of the final version of the story in which approval is given to Simeon and Levi are those who are being instructed against intermarriage; but the implied reader of an earlier version of the story, still discernible in Genesis 34, seems to accept intermarriage as entirely natural and to provide a sharp criticism of the Levites. Both sets of readers could belong happily in the post-exilic period when an intermarrying majority was being challenged by a more restrictive levitical view. The text of Gen 34,1-35,5 thus reflects the conflicting ideologies of two groups, though it is the group which supports the hard line of Levi and Simeon which has the last word. Macchi also considers the modern feminist reader's position, but notes that although this has provided for sympathetic portraits of Dinah, it has distracted attention from the political struggles amongst the text's implied readers.

George Brooke's essay deals with a perennial problem in the reading of the narrative of *Joseph and Aseneth*: to whom was it addressed? By deploying a fresh reading strategy derived from the insights of cultural anthropology he is able to suggest that the scholarly concern to locate the implied reader exactly as either Jewish men intending to marry out or Gentile women intending to marry Jewish men misses the overarching purpose of the narrative. Through recognizing and naming the universal polarities in the narrative, Brooke is able to show that the purpose of the narrative should not be construed with reference to a very narrowly defined readership in mind. Rather the story of the patriarchal figure who married out is told in such a way that any reader should learn from it that Judaism is the very apogee of culture and all things Gentile are in need of transformation from their raw state. Clearly *Joseph and Aseneth* handles the figure of Joseph very differently from that suggested by Römer in his analysis of the Joseph narrative in Genesis.

(d) Author-Message-Reader. Some of the essays in this volume make contributions to their subject matter which cannot be so readily linked to just one aspect of narrative criticism, whether it concerns author, message or reader.

In a contextual reading of Matthew's Gospel's retelling of the story of Jesus walking on the sea (Matt 14,22-33), Martin Scott shows how the narrative firstly discloses the identity of the implied author, that he is intent upon focusing the meta-narrative of Israel's salvation history on Jesus, secondly has a particular discourse strategy in describing the status and authority of the figure of Jesus himself, and thirdly reveals some of the character of its implied readership who are in need of reaffirming their understanding of what it means for Jesus to be Son of God and of coming to terms with the ambiguous nature of their own discipleship. In paying attention to the methodological opportunities of narrative criticism Scott is able to read the Matthean story in a more thoroughgoing manner than any redaction critic.

In a pair of essays on the same topic Christopher Tuckett and Martinus de Boer show how slightly different understandings of implied author, discourse strategies, and implied readers, can lead to different conclusions about how best a particular narrative should be understood in its ancient setting. They discuss the portrayal of Pilate in the passion narrative of the Fourth Gospel. Tuckett argues that John shows no sympathy at all for the figure of Pilate, revealing his true nature as one who is opposed to all that Jesus stands for and all that is of God. Tuckett's interpretation is based in large part on his construal of John as implied author and his theological concerns, especially with kingship. The discourse strategy which Tuckett highlights is irony: in the story line Pilate is the instigator of the ultimate blasphemy of the Jews' denial of their heritage and their God and this is made plain in the way that in his stubbornness and mocking jests he becomes unwittingly the vehicle for the expression of profound truth.

De Boer on the other hand suggests equally forcefully that Pilate is an uncomprehending, unbelieving and reluctant participant in the events leading to Jesus' death. Like Tuckett, de Boer insists that the principal discourse strategy surrounding the description of Pilate's actions is terrible and tragic irony, but the difference of interpretation for de Boer seems to arise from another direction. Whereas Tuckett spends some considerable time in his analysis working on the implied author of the passage and searching the passage and its wider Gospel context for clues about his intentions, de Boer makes several references to the implied readers of the narrative. From the perspective of such readers it is the author's concern to demonstrate precisely why it was necessary for Jesus to be labelled "king *of the Jews*". The Gospel agenda is to play off the Jews against their real king and so to encourage the allegiance of the reader. In all this de Boer explains how the reader is not lead to believe that Pilate is implicated in the events in the same way as the Jews are; it is the Jews who actively sought to do away with Jesus for supposed blasphemy, not a matter which Pilate either as narrative character or real life governor could have appreciated. Between them Tuckett and de Boer show intriguingly that narrative criticism does not necessarily provide all the neat answers for which modern readers are looking; emphasis on different aspects of narrativity produces different and sometimes irreconcilable understandings of the narrative itself.

The image of God in the Book of Acts is the subject of the contribution by Daniel Marguerat who sets about investigating the interplay between the narrator, the message and the readers which narratology has highlighted. As the contributor to this volume who has written and reflected more than any other on the benefits of narrative criticism, Marguerat's essay is especially important for the way it names the various parts of his investigation with the appropriate technical terms of narrative criticism. Here are incisive insights into how the narrator in the Book of Acts refers to God: he uses narrative (extradiegetic) language when God manifests himself by a mediation which in effect conceals him and he uses discursive (intradiegetic) language when God is named as an agent of history. Marguerat's detailed analysis of the roles that God plays in the narrative of Acts allows him to distinguish between divine interventions which are programmatic (preceding events), performative (accomplishing things), or interpretative (following events to justify or explain them). In all this the reader is encouraged to recognize that God comes to the world through the words of his messengers; to learn about God, there is no other way than to read the story of his messengers. However, in so doing readers find their own freedom to deny the significance of what they read strangely protected; readers only become part of the view of the world which is offered in salvation history if they enter into the salvific logic narrated in the book. Whatever response readers might make, the narrative of Acts reassures them that the divine irony of it all is that God integrates even the actions of his enemies within his purposes. Through attention to one topic Marguerat displays masterfully the benefits of a close narrative reading of the text.

In a slightly different vein, the essays by Jean-Daniel Kaestli on the *Testament of Joseph*, by Steve Nolan on the *Acts of Paul and Thecla*, and by Kate Cooper on the Pseudo-Clementine *Recognitions* and related texts all consider how their respective narrative messages convey morality, ideology, or values of one sort or another from author to reader.

Jean-Daniel Kaestli investigates how the structure of the *Testament of Joseph* interweaves two biographical narratives (*TJos* 3-9, 11-16) within the parenetic body of the composition. In particular he is concerned to address the question of the literary relationship of the two narrative passages to one another. Through careful attention to various details in both narrative sections Kaestli concludes that the two passages belong to the same editorial hand and that their differences are most easily explicable through attention to how the different biblical sources upon which each section depends have been developed. Thus *TJos* 3-9 is not a continuous novelistic narrative, but a series of eleven haggadic scenes elaborated for homiletic purposes as the incidents portrayed carry their message from narrator to reader: Joseph is an archetype of endurance firstly in resisting the multiple advances of a woman and secondly through accepting his unjust imprisonment. Likewise in the second narrative section, there is a series of incidents, each of which exemplifies Joseph's love for his brothers. In Kaestli's contribution there are indications of what is clear also in Jackson's essay, that narrative is a principal way of presenting material for didactic purposes.

Nolan's analysis of the *Acts of Thecla* is an attempt to show how the questions of deviance and struggle posed by Foucault unlock two possible political readings of the narrative which have significance for how the implied authors and readers are construed. The first is a reading which seeks to preserve male privilege and takes Thecla as the catalyst for the struggle between a male apostle and the state in which women's oppression is maintained; anything said positively about Thecla is to be understood on a spiritual level. The second is a reading which precisely challenges such a viewpoint by portraying Thecla herself as a creative resource for resistance which is represented by what happens to her body. Nolan's use of Foucault to provide a reading strategy reveals the ambiguities of this narrative composition and shows why it may have had such wide appeal. By resisting the temptation to argue that one reading is right, the other wrong, Nolan puts a fresh perspective on many of the contributions to this collection. Narrative criticism, based on whatever strategy, is not primarily about the correct reading of texts, but about discerning the range of possibilities enshrined in narratives which are multivalent because authors have deliberately compiled them to have a wide appeal.

Cooper's discussion of the Pseudo-Clementine *Recognitions* is a comparative assessment of some ancient romances. Cooper asserts that the Pseudo-Clementine Books are sufficiently replete with typical genre conventions that their apologetic purpose is readily discernible. Most especially these conventions are visible in the characterizations of Peter, Clement and Matthidia. Like the ethical and pastoral advice of the New Testament's Pastoral Epistles and the Letters to the Colossians and Ephesians the *Recognitions* assert the importance of blood kinship as the basic ingredient of social solidarity. Having set the apologetic in a broad framework of early Christian literature Cooper is able to conclude that there were several options for how the family was to be viewed in the multi-cultural society of the Roman Empire. The narrative of the *Recognitions* argues for one view which its author tries to pass on to its readers.

To say more by way of introduction might detract from the enjoyment of these varied studies, each of which makes its own contribution to its chosen subject matter and in each of which, as part of the whole, there is food for thought for those concerned more broadly with narrativity in all its several aspects.

George J. BROOKE
Manchester

Jean-Daniel KAESTLI
Lausanne

THE OLD TESTAMENT

1

LES INTERPRÉTATIONS CONFLICTUELLES D'UNE NARRATION (GENÈSE 34,1–35,5; 49,5-7)[*]

Dans la délicieuse bande dessinée d'Hergé *L'affaire Tournesol*, Tintin tombe sur un article de journal concernant l'arraisonnement d'un avion syldave par la chasse bordure. Sur deux colonnes, on trouve les communiqués émanant des deux parties. La version bordure commence par «"Notre espace aérien a été violé" déclare le gouvernement de Szohod», alors que le compte rendu de la version syldave s'ouvre par «"Inqualifiable agression pleksziste" dit-on à Klow»[1]. Cette anecdote, décrite sur le mode humoristique par Hergé, nous rappelle à quel point un événement peut être interprété de manière radicalement différente en fonction du milieu qui le décrit.

Bien qu'il ne doive pas être considéré comme la narration d'un événement historique, l'épisode de l'enlèvement de Dina joue littérairement un rôle semblable. La narration peut être interprétée de manière radicalement opposée, suivant que l'on considère normal le mariage de Dina et de Sichem ou que l'on cherche à justifier le massacre des Sichémites.

À Sichem comme à Plekszy-Gladz, remonter à l'événement originel n'est finalement pas la question déterminante. Ce sont les interprétations littéraires qui en ont été faites – et dont témoignent la diachronie biblique – qui nous sont accessibles, et c'est l'idéologie qu'elles véhiculent qui vont retenir notre attention.

Unité et (in)cohérence

L'épisode décrivant l'enlèvement de Dina (Gn 34,1-31, auquel il faut en tout cas ajouter 35,5) forme une petite unité parfaitement indépendante du cadre narratif du cycle de Jacob. Elle apparaît de manière relativement abrupte à l'intérieur du livre de la Genèse. On remarque ainsi que Gn 35,1 pourrait fort bien constituer la suite de 33,20. Les seuls passages qui présupposent ce texte sont d'une part Gn 30,21, un ajout per-

---

[*] Le contenu de cet article, rédigé antérieurement, a été réutilisé dans ma thèse de doctorat: J.-D. MACCHI, *Israël et ses tribus selon Genèse 49* (OBO, 171), Fribourg-Göttingen, Éditions Universitaires – Vandenhoeck & Ruprecht, 1999, p. 54-80.

[1]. HERGÉ, *L'affaire Tournesol*, version originale 1956, p. 43, case 2.

mettant d'insérer Dina dans le récit de naissance des douze fils de Jacob[2] afin de préparer le terrain pour Gn 34,1, et d'autre part les reproches adressés à Siméon et Lévi en Gn 49,5-6. Ce dernier texte est difficilement dissociable de cette narration. En effet, l'association de Siméon et Lévi n'apparaît dans aucune autre tradition vétérotestamentaire[3]. De plus, au niveau thématique, la violence dont parle Gn 49,5-6 ne peut que rappeler celle de Gn 34 et la malédiction proférée en 49,7 semble difficilement compréhensible indépendamment de Gn 34. Il semble donc clair à la fois que les deux textes entretiennent un rapport étroit entre eux et qu'ils peuvent être considérés comme l'expression d'une ou plusieurs traditions indépendantes du reste de la Genèse.

Pourtant, l'ensemble Gn 34,1-31; 35,5; 49,5-7 ne peut guère être considéré comme l'oeuvre d'un auteur unique ayant travaillé d'un seul jet. La description précise de la violence figurant en 49,6b, avec sa bipolarité «homme» אִישׁ et «taureau» שׁוֹר, correspond mal au massacre suivi d'un pillage décrit en Gn 34,25-29, au cours duquel les animaux ne sont pas éliminés. En outre, Gn 34 comporte plusieurs irrégularités. On constate la présence de protagonistes différents aussi bien dans le camp sichémite que dans le camp israélite. Au verset 6 l'orateur sichémite est Hamor, alors qu'au verset 11 c'est Sichem. Du côté de Jacob, on constate que le patriarche a un rôle relativement effacé à côté de ses fils; parmi ces derniers on distingue Siméon et Lévi, auteurs de la première attaque (vv. 25-26), et l'ensemble des «fils de Jacob», protagonistes du reste du récit. On trouve deux attaques distinctes de la ville de Sichem: aux vv. 25-26 Siméon et Lévi massacrent les mâles, Hamor, Sichem, et reprennent Dina; aux vv. 27-29, les fils de Jacob pillent la ville et emportent du butin. Au niveau de la thématique générale du récit, on a un mélange entre le thème du viol de Dina et celui plus général des intermariages. Enfin, il est difficile de savoir si le massacre des Sichémites est jugé positivement (Gn 34,31; 35,5) ou négativement (Gn 34,30; 49,5-6).

2. La présence de Dina s'inscrit mal dans Gn 29,31-30,24. À la différence des autres enfants de Jacob, on ne trouve aucune considération sur l'étymologie de son nom. Sur le caractère secondaire de Dina, voir entre autres M. NOTH, *Das System der zwölf Stämme Israels* (BWANT, 4/1), Darmstadt, Wissenschaftliche Buchgesellschaft, 1966, p. 9; C.H.J. DE GEUS, *The Tribes of Israel. An Investigation into some of the Presuppositions of Martin Noth's Amphictyony Hypothesis* (Studia Semitica Neerlandica, 18), Assen – Amsterdam, Van Gorcum, 1976, p. 70; C. WESTERMANN, *Genesis. Teilband 2. Genesis 12-36.* (BK, I/2), Neukirchen-Vluyn, Neukirchener Verlag, 1981. La question se pose en termes similaires pour Gn 46,15.

3. Si l'on excepte évidemment les listes tribales, dans lesquelles le plus souvent les deux tribus se suivent. Voir en particulier le récit de naissance des douze fils de Jacob (Gn 29,31-30,24).

Tour d'horizon de la recherche

Sans revenir en détail sur les solutions proposées par l'exégèse historico-critique de ce chapitre[4], on peut *grosso modo* tracer les grandes lignes suivantes.

On retrouve très souvent la distinction entre deux sources, l'une impliquant le personnage de Sichem et l'autre celui d'Hamor[5]. Cependant Gn 34 permet difficilement de reconstituer deux récits complets, à la fois indépendants et cohérents, ce qui tend à rendre cette solution difficilement crédible.

Les solutions alternatives proposées traitent souvent le corps du récit (vv. 1-24) différemment de sa finale (vv. 25-31). Dans le corps du récit, plusieurs auteurs s'attachent à défendre l'unité de l'ensemble[6]; d'autres, tout en maintenant l'existence de deux versions distinctes, attribuent leur liaison à un stade prélittéraire[7]; enfin, des exégètes ont soutenu l'idée que la version «Hamor» constituait le résultat du retravail d'une couche de base[8]. Quasiment tous les exégètes[9] considèrent que la finale, contrairement au corps du texte, a subi au moins une relecture. Le débat se fo-

---

4. Pour plus de détails on se reportera aux excellents travaux de A. DE PURY, *Genèse XXXIV et l'histoire*, in *RB* 76 (1969) 5-49, pp. 5-9.15-19.29-30 et P. KEVERS, *Étude littéraire de Genèse XXXIV*, in *RB* 87 (1980) 38-86, pp. 40-47

5. C'est la solution retenue par la critique classique, et notamment défendue par J. WELLHAUSEN, *Die Composition des Hexateuchs und der historischen Bücher des Alten Testaments*, Berlin, de Gruyter, 1963³, pp. 314-322; H. GUNKEL, *Genesis* (Göttinger Handkommentar zum Alten Testament, 1), Göttingen, Vandenhoeck & Ruprecht, 1901; O. EISSFELDT, *Hexateuch-Synopse. Die Erzählung der fünf Bücher Moses und des Buches Josua mit dem Anfange des Richterbuches*, Leipzig, J.C. Hinrichs, 1922; O. PROCKSCH, *Die Genesis* (KAT, 1), Leipzig, A. Deichertsche Verlagsbuchhandlung, 1924² & ³, pp. 199-204.543-549; WESTERMANN, *Genesis 12-36* (n. 2).

6. J. PEDERSEN, *Israel. Its Life and Culture, Vol. 1, I-II*, London – Copenhagen, G. Cumberlege – P. Branner, 1926, pp. 521-523; H. EISING, *Formgeschichtliche Untersuchung zur Jakobserzählung der Genesis*, Emsdetten, Verlagsanstalt Heinr. & J. Lechte, 1940, pp. 295-316; E. NIELSEN, *Shechem. A Traditio-Historical Investigation*, Copenhagen, G.E.C. Gad, 1955, pp. 241-259 soutiennent la cohérence de tout le texte. KEVERS, *Étude littéraire* (n. 4), pp. 47-72 se prononce pour la cohérence de 1-26 exception faite de deux ajouts, le v. 13b et la mention de Siméon et Lévi au v. 25. E. OTTO, *Jakob in Sichem. Überlieferungsgeschichtliche, archäologische und territorialgeschichtliche Studien zur Entstehungsgeschichte Israels* (BWANT, 110), Stuttgart et al., Kohlhammer, 1979, pp. 170-175 défend l'existence d'une unité de base formée de 34,1*.2-25aα.27-29. Cf. aussi J. VAN SETERS, *Prologue to History. The Yahwist as Historian in Genesis*, Louisville, Westminster – John Knox, 1992, p. 278, pour qui seuls les vv. 5, 7b et 13b sont secondaires en 1-26.

7. C'est la solution de S. LEHMING, *Zur Überlieferungsgeschichte von Gen 34*, in *ZAW* 70 (1958) 228-250, pp. 238-243, et DE PURY, *Genèse XXXIV* (n. 4), pp. 27-28 pour ce qui concerne la plus grande partie du récit (pour les ajouts Siméon-Lévi, cf. *infra*).

8. C'est en particulier le cas de A. KUENEN, *Dina en Sichem*, in *Theologisch tijdschrift* 14 (1880) 257-281; M. NOTH, *Überlieferungsgeschichte des Pentateuch*, Stuttgart, W. Kohlhammer, 1966³, p. 31, n. 99; E. BLUM, *Die Komposition der Vätergeschichte*

calise autour de deux points. D'une part, lorsque la question du rapport entre les deux récits de conflit est résolue de façon diachronique, c'est généralement le second (vv. 27-29) qui est considéré comme secondaire[10]. D'autre part, Lehming a observé que la mention de Siméon et Lévi était relativement mal ancrée dans le récit et il la considère comme une adjonction secondaire à partir de Gn 49,5-7[11]. Ceci signifierait que les deux tribus auraient été ajoutées aux בְּנֵי־יַעֲקֹב primitifs au v. 25, en même temps que l'ensemble du v. 30 (et que le v. 31 qui en dépend). En outre, il faut relever que E. Blum, bien qu'il ne tienne pas la mention de Siméon et Lévi pour secondaire au v. 25, n'en considère pas moins comme tel le v. 30[12].

GN 34 ET 49,5-7: PERSPECTIVE GLOBALE ET DIACHRONIQUE

Les remarques que nous venons de faire sur l'état de la recherche montrent qu'en dépit d'observations fort pertinentes sur ce texte, aucun consensus ne se dégage vraiment; or, en prenant comme point de départ les liens qui unissent Gn 34 et Gn 49, il est possible de sortir de l'impasse.

(WMANT, 57), Neukirchen-Vluyn, Neukirchener Verlag, 1984, pp. 214-216. N. WYATT, *The Story of Dinah and Shechem*, in *UF* 22 (1990) 433-458 constitue un cas particulier; il va beaucoup plus loin (trop loin) en postulant trois relectures d'un texte de base formé des vv. 1*.2*.3*.11*.12.14*.18*.19.26*.

9. À part les défenseurs de l'unité complète cités à la note 6 (PEDERSEN, EISING, NIELSEN).

10. C'est notamment l'avis de NOTH, *Überlieferungsgeschichte des Pentateuch*. (n. 8), p. 31, n. 99 (sauf le v. 29) et de VAN SETERS, *Prologue to History* (n. 6), p. 278. À l'opposé, OTTO, *Jakob in Sichem* (n. 6), pp. 170-175, considère 25aß-26 comme secondaires. Sur ce point, toute distinction diachronique est cependant rejetée en bloc par BLUM, *Die Komposition der Vätergeschichte* (n. 8), p. 215 (cf. aussi LEHMING, DE PURY, *supra* note 7).

11. Cf. LEHMING, *Zur Überlieferungsgeschichte* (n. 7), pp. 228-237. Sur ce point, cet auteur a été suivi par DE PURY, *Genèse XXXIV* (n. 4); ID. *La ville dans les traditions patriarcales de la Genèse*, in F. BRÜSCHWEILER et al. (éds.), *La ville dans le Proche-Orient ancien* (Cahiers du CEPOA, 1), Leuven, Peeters, 1983, pp. 219-229, spéc. 225; OTTO, *Jakob in Sichem* (n. 6); KEVERS, *Étude littéraire* (n. 4), p. 43.85; ID., *Les 'fils de Jacob' à Sichem*, in C. BREKELMANS et J. LUST (éds.), *Pentateuchal and Deuteronomistic Studies. Papers Read at the XIIth IOSOT Congress Leuven 1989* (BETL, 94), Leuven, University Press-Peeters 1990, pp. 41-46, spéc. 42; N.K. GOTTWALD, *The Tribes of Yahweh. A Sociology of the Religion of Liberated Israel 1250-1050 B.C.E.*, London, SCM Press, 1979, p. 373, n. 213. En revanche, la position de Lehming est rejetée par A.H.J. GUNNEWEG, *Leviten und Priester. Hauptlinien der Traditionsbildung und Geschichte des israelitisch-jüdischen Kultpersonals* (FRLANT, 89), Göttingen, Vandenhoeck & Ruprecht, 1965, pp. 48-51; H. STRAUSS, *Untersuchungen zu den Überlieferungen der vorexilischen Leviten*, Bonn, Rheinische Friedrich-Wilhelms-Universität, 1960, pp. 118-120.

12. BLUM, *Die Komposition der Vätergeschichte* (n. 8), pp. 216-219. Voir plus loin.

Relecture favorable au massacre

On observe que les deux textes, si on les lit de manière synchronique, semblent contradictoires. En Gn 49, la violence de Siméon et de Lévi est jugée de manière totalement négative et conduit à la condamnation de 49,7; au contraire, le texte de Gn 34 sous sa forme actuelle, en dépit d'un fil narratif qui devrait conduire logiquement à une telle condamnation, cherche sans cesse à rendre acceptable le massacre des Sichémites. On y trouve en effet une justification explicite du mensonge aussi bien que du massacre, exprimée par une formule similaire qui insiste sur l'impureté (טמא Pi'el) subie par Dina «leur soeur» (vv. 5aα, 13b et 27b). Le verset 7b souligne lourdement le caractère illicite de l'acte de Sichem. Le verset 31 laisse le dernier mot à l'auto-justification de Siméon et Lévi. En outre, Gn 35,2.4 semblent chercher à inscrire le récit de Gn 34 dans le cadre de la lutte contre les idoles; enfin, en 35,5 c'est Dieu lui-même qui va protéger les fils de Jacob des conséquences néfastes envisagées par 34,30. Ces indices textuels tendent à montrer qu'une main est venue corriger l'image négative de l'action militaire menée contre Sichem que véhiculait auparavant Gn 34 et 49[13].

La seconde attaque de Sichem (vv. 27-29) doit probablement appartenir également à une couche secondaire. On remarque d'emblée qu'il y a une rupture évidente entre le v. 26 et et le v. 27. Au v. 26, Siméon et Lévi sortent de la ville après avoir massacré les mâles, tandis qu'au v. 27 les autres frères y entrent à nouveau pour la piller. La mention des tués (חללים) présuppose clairement les v. 25-26[14].

Le pillage décrit en 34, 27-29 contredit, en tout cas partiellement, la mutilation des taureaux décrite en 49,6b puisqu'au v. 28 le gros bétail (בקר) est emporté comme butin. En revanche, la description du massacre de Sichem aux vv. 25-26 s'harmonise fort bien avec Gn 49,6b. En 34,25b on trouve la phrase ויהרגו כל־זכר «ils tuèrent tous les mâles»; or זכר peut désigner à la fois les mâles humains et les mâles animaux. De plus, la présentation du raid au v. 25 comme un massacre gratuit, sans butin, est encore soulignée par les reproches formulés en 49,6b: au meurtre des hommes s'ajoute la mutilation volontaire des taureaux

---

13. Cet aspect de la démonstration s'accorde partiellement, entre autres, avec des observations de BLUM, *Die Komposition der Vätergeschichte* (n. 8), pp. 216-223 (gloses en 5aα, 13b et 27b; 34,30 et 35,5 retravail «D»; 34,31 serait plus ancien, p. 222 n. 60) et de VAN SETERS, *Prologue to History* (n. 6), p. 278 (secondaire: vv. 5.7b.13b.27-29.31).

14. Cf. notamment KEVERS, *Étude littéraire* (n. 4), p. 53. La modification du TM en «malades», חלים, proposée sans appui textuel par BHS, par H. GUNKEL, *Genesis* (n. 5) et par WESTERMANN, *Genesis 12-36* (n. 5), vise à permettre de considérer les vv. 27-29 comme la suite du v. 24.

(וּבִרְצֹנָם עִקְּרוּ־שׁוֹר), acte de guerre purement barbare et qui, dans l'optique d'un pillage (qui est celle de Gn 34,27-29), serait contre-productif.

Cet aspect barbare des actes de Siméon et Lévi est souligné en outre par le vocabulaire utilisé en 49,6b. En effet, l'association de l'«homme» אִישׁ avec le «taureau» שׁוֹר[15] est une caractéristique du vocabulaire utilisé pour décrire le massacre des ennemis «voués à l'interdit» (חרם Hif). En Jos 6,21, 1 Sam 15,3 et 22,19, אִישׁ ouvre la liste des humains tués et שׁוֹר celle des animaux qui subissent le même sort[16]. Les actes qui sont reprochés à Siméon et Lévi en Gn 49,6 font donc allusion à une extermination sans butin, conforme à Gn 34,25[17].

Il faut dès lors s'interroger sur les raisons de l'adjonction des versets 27-29. Ces trois versets décrivent l'intervention et le pillage de Sichem par les «fils de Jacob» après que Siméon et Lévi en sont ressortis (v. 26)[18]. Cette adjonction permet d'associer les autres frères à l'action de Siméon et Lévi. Par ce moyen, l'auteur invite à porter un regard favorable sur le massacre des Sichémites, dont la «responsabilité» incombe à tout Israël. Il s'inscrit ainsi dans la droite ligne des corrections tendant à justifier la colère des frères, comme les versets 7b, 5aα, 13b; les deux derniers versets utilisent d'ailleurs une terminologie semblable à celle du v. 27b, en particulier avec l'utilisation du vocabulaire de la «souillure», טָמֵא.

On pourrait certes considérer Gn 34,30 comme une préparation à la condamnation de Siméon et Lévi en 49,5-6; mais, comme l'a bien montré E. Blum[19], les motivations des reproches adressés aux deux protagonistes sont très différentes de Gn 49. En 34,30, ce n'est pas l'acte qui est critiqué mais ses conséquences possibles, qui sont d'ailleurs immédiatement annulées, en 35,5, par l'affirmation de la protection divine. On

---

15. אִישׁ et שׁוֹר figurent dans le même verset en Gn 49,6; Ex 21,28.29.33.35.37; 22,9; Lv 17,3; 27,26; Jos 6,21; 1 Sam 14,34; 15,3; 22,19; Es 66,3.

16. En outre, on retrouve en Jos 6,21, 1 Sam 15,3 et 22,19 le vocabulaire du passage par le fil de l'épée, לְפִי־חֶרֶב, ainsi que la mention de l'âne, חֲמוֹר, présents en Gn 34,25-26.

17. Néanmoins, contrairement à Jos 6,21, 1 Sam 15,3 et 22,19, Gn 34,25 ne parle pas de l'extermination des femmes et des autres animaux. L'utilisation du terme רָצוֹן, «volonté», en Gn 49,6b fait peut-être allusion à ce côté atypique du massacre de Sichem, l'initiative personnelle des deux protagonistes étant ainsi mise en évidence.

18. KEVERS, *Étude littéraire* (n. 4), pp. 59-61, a montré que cette énumération du butin se rapproche du langage de textes tardifs comme 1 Chr 5,21; 2 Chr 28,8 et surtout Nb 31,7-10. D'autre part, ce pillage est conforme au droit de la guerre exprimé en Dt 20,14

19. BLUM, *Die Komposition der Vätergeschichte* (n. 8), pp. 216-217. Il se fonde principalement sur le vocabulaire de 34,30, qu'il juge dtn/dtr, et sur le fait que ce verset constitue un élément narratif surajouté (la crainte des habitants du pays, qui n'entre pas en ligne de compte dans la trame principale), qui implique un nouveau rebondissement et nécessite l'ajout de 35,5.

peut ainsi admettre que l'auteur de 34,30 cherche à expliquer le pourquoi de la colère de Jacob exprimée en Gn 49,5-7, tout en montrant immédiatement son caractère non fondé (34,31; 35,5).

Nous proposons donc de considérer Gn 34,27-31 et 35,2.4-5 comme des adjonctions secondaires, provenant de la même main que les versets 5, 7b, 13b et probablement aussi 23. L'ensemble vise à réhabiliter l'attitude de Siméon et de Lévi

Le problème de la malédiction de Siméon et surtout de Lévi proférée en Gn 49,5-7 à la suite des événements de Gn 34 a beaucoup préoccupé le judaïsme intertestamentaire. Les réponses tendent, comme c'est le cas dans la couche secondaire de Gn 34, à justifier le massacre[20].

Le problème est de savoir pourquoi les prêtres bénis par Dieu peuvent être maudits par Jacob, et ce pour une faute qui, pour beaucoup, ne doit pas être considérée comme telle puisqu'il s'agit de séparer les Israélites des nations. On peut penser que l'auteur des adjonctions tendant à justifier Siméon et Lévi est issu d'un milieu vivement opposé aux mariages mixtes (dès lors, le massacre des Sichémites lui semble normal). Ce type de problématique, tout comme la réponse particulièrement intransigeante qui y est apportée, n'est pas sans rappeler les positions d'une partie de la communauté judéenne postexilique, dont on trouve la trace dans les livres d'Esdras et de Néhémie.

La première version du texte

On peut maintenant s'interroger sur le contenu du texte de Gn 34 et 49 avant l'adjonction que nous venons de discerner. Gn 34 devait se terminer au verset 26. Le fil conducteur de la narration fait apparaître Siméon et Lévi sous un jour extrêmement défavorable. Aux vv. 2-3, Sichem couche certes avec Dina, la fille de Jacob, mais cet acte n'est pas présenté comme un viol.

Il faut s'arrêter ici à un problème de traduction. Le premier aspect à prendre en compte tient au fait que le verset 3 insiste sur l'amour de Sichem pour Dina.

---

20. Voir en particulier Jdt 9,2-4; *Jubilés* 30 et *Testament de Lévi* 5-6. Cf. A. STANDHARTINGER, *"Um zu sehen die Töchter des Landes". Die Perspektive Dinas in der jüdisch-hellenistischen Diskussion um Gen 34*, in L. BORMANN, K. DEL TREDICI et A. STANDHARTINGER (éds.), *Religious Propaganda and Missionary Competition in the New Testament World. Essays Honoring Dieter Georgi* (NT.S, 74), Leiden – New York – Köln, Brill, 1994, pp. 89-116; T. BAARDA, *The Shechem Episode in the Testament of Levi. A Comparison with Other Traditions*, in J.N. BREMMER et F. GARCÍA MARTÍNEZ (éds.), *Sacred History and Sacred Texts in Early Judaism. A Symposium in Honour of A.S. van der Woude* (CBET, 5), Kampen, Kok Pharos, 1992, pp. 11-73; J. KUGEL, *The Story of Dinah in the Testament of Levi*, in HTR 85 (1992) 1-34; R. PUMMER, *Genesis 34 in Jewish Writings of the Hellenistic and Roman Periods*, in HTR 75 (1982) 177-188.

3 וַתִּדְבַּק נַפְשׁוֹ בְּדִינָה בַּת־יַעֲקֹב וַיֶּאֱהַב אֶת־הַנַּעֲרָ וַיְדַבֵּר עַל־לֵב הַנַּעֲרָ

«Son être s'attacha à Dina la fille de Jacob. Il aima la jeune fille et il parla au coeur de la jeune fille».

Le verset précédent (34,2) décrit l'action incriminée de la façon suivante:

2 וַיַּרְא אֹתָהּ שְׁכֶם בֶּן־חֲמוֹר הַחִוִּי נְשִׂיא הָאָרֶץ וַיִּקַּח אֹתָהּ וַיִּשְׁכַּב אֹתָהּ וַיְעַנֶּהָ

«Sichem, fils d'Hamor le hivite chef du pays la vit»; on trouve ensuite une série de trois verbes. Les deux premiers verbes, «prendre» לקח dans un sens sexuel, et «coucher avec» שכב, n'ont en soi aucune connotation de contrainte.

Le dernier verbe du verset 2, ויענה, vocalisé par le TM comme un Pi'el (וַיְעַנֶּהָ), est souvent traduit par «violer»; mais il doit plutôt être compris dans le sens d'«humilier» et vise à connoter une relation sexuelle honteuse car socialement illégitime[21]. Ce verbe permet ainsi d'introduire la problématique du rétablissement de la légitimité de la relation entre les deux jeunes gens par le rituel de la circoncision. On peut même se demander si ויענה ne doit pas être compris dans un sens proche de «il cohabita avec elle» ou «il fit l'amour avec elle». Cette forme peut dériver du verbe «habiter» עון (Ex 13,22), signification qui est aussi appuyée par עֹנָה* dans le sens de «cohabitation» (Ex 21,10)[22].

En fait, de nombreux exégètes ont retenu une interprétation impliquant la notion de viol[23]. C'est notamment le cas de l'exégèse féministe, qui s'est abondamment interrogée sur les conséquences de ce fameux «viol de Dina»[24]. Le massacre des Sichémites a ainsi pu être interprété comme un acte de suprême respect à l'égard de la Femme. Alors que les fils de Jacob, et Jacob lui-même, étaient prêts à vendre la jeune fille violentée au violeur désormais amoureux, Siméon et Lévi se sont opposés à la culture «machiste» du temps pour défendre leur soeur envers et contre tout.

---

21. Ce point a bien été montré par L.M. BECHTEL, *What if Dinah is not Raped? (Genesis 34)*, in *JSOT* 62 (1994) 19-36, pp. 23-27, sur la base de l'usage du verbe en question en Dt 22,23-29 et 2 Sam 13,11-14.

22. Ce point a été relevé par WYATT, *The Story of Dinah* (n. 8), pp. 435-436.

23. Voir la liste établie par BECHTEL, *What if Dinah* (n. 21), n. 2.

24. Cf. entre autres S. BROOKS THISTLETHWAITE, *"You May Enjoy the Spoil of Your Enemies": Rape as Biblical Metaphor for War*, in *Semeia* 61 (1993) 59-75; N. GRAETZ, *Dinah the Daughter*, in A. BRENNER (éd.), *A Feminist Companion to Genesis* (FCB, 2), Sheffield, Academic Press, 1993, pp. 305-317; L.R. KASS, *Regarding Daughters and Sisters. The Rape of Dinah*, in *Commentary* 93 (1992) 29-38; A.A. KEEFE, *Rapes of Women / Wars of Men*, in *Semeia* 61 (1993) 79-97; M. STERNBERG, *The Poetics of Biblical Narrative: Ideological Literature and Drama of Reading* (Indiana Literary Biblical Series), Bloomington, Indiana University Press, 1985; ID., *Biblical Poetics and Sexual Politics: From Reading to Counter-Reading*, in *JBL* 111 (1992) 463-488.

Cependant, une lecture féministe devrait plutôt s'interroger sur la négation des désirs de la femme que véhicule un récit où des frères tuent l'amant de leur soeur[25]. Le concept de «viol» est totalement étranger à ces deux versets, où aucun autre élément ne suggère l'idée de contrainte. C'est plutôt d'une relation illégitime qu'il est question. Ainsi, la suite du texte traite des négociations de mariage entre Jacob et ses fils d'une part, Sichem et Hamor d'autre part. On y trouve le thème de la dot, ainsi que celui du mariage entre membres de deux communautés différentes, qui suppose le rituel de la circoncision. Les Sichémites se soumettent de bon gré aux exigences de Jacob et de ses fils. Au verset 24, l'affaire semble dès lors aboutir à un *happy end*. La légitimité de la relation sexuelle entre Sichem et Dina est en quelque sorte rétablie. La fille de Jacob est en mesure d'épouser un circoncis.

Le verset 25 a alors l'effet d'un coup de théâtre, puisque deux fils de Jacob s'opposent radicalement au résultat négocié, et par là-même au consensus familial. Or, cette fin (vv. 25-26) reste «ouverte»: en effet, la réaction violente de Siméon et Lévi, et le bouleversement de l'ordre familial qu'elle provoque, appellent forcément une réponse. Celle-ci arrive logiquement en Gn 49,5-7. Les deux fils qui ont cherché à prendre la place de leur père dans la direction politique du clan vont être déchus et dispersés en Israël (Gn 49,7b).

On peut encore se demander si la couche de base du récit que nous venons de dégager (Gn 34,1-4.6-7a.8-13a.14-22.24-26; 49,5-7) témoigne également d'une histoire littéraire en plusieurs étapes. Ceci semble difficile à établir avec certitude.

La distinction entre une couche «Sichem» et une couche «Hamor» pose problème. Ses défenseurs considèrent généralement que la strate «Hamor» intègre le thème de la généralisation des inter-mariages[26]. Cependant, même si l'on contourne la difficulté de l'interdépendance des deux trames narratives par un modèle considérant la strate «Hamor» comme un retravail de la couche «Sichem», on comprend mal comment pourrait fonctionner le texte «Sichem» sans le thème du *conubium* général, car il n'y aurait alors plus aucune justification narrative à la circoncision de *tous* les hommes de la ville[27]. En outre, la présence de deux

---

25. On a d'ailleurs souvent relevé qu'après le v. 3 Dina n'est plus que l'enjeu d'un conflit d'hommes; cf. entre autres D.N. FEWELL et D.M. GUNN, *Tipping the Balance: Sternberg's Reader and the Rape of Dinah*, in *JBL* 110 (1991) 193-211. On peut encore ajouter que les exégètes anciens, tel celui du *Testament de Lévi*, n'ont pas compris l'épisode comme un viol.

26. Les principaux éléments de cette couche seraient les versets 8-10.15-17.20-23. Elle comprendrait aussi diverses fractions de versets, en particulier ceux qui comportent le nom d'Hamor.

27. Il suffirait que Sichem seul soit circoncis. Sinon, il faut supposer que la circoncision de tous les Sichémites avait pour but implicite d'ouvrir la possibilité d'une générali-

protagonistes chez les Sichémites ne peut guère constituer un critère de distinction pertinent. La présence du père et du fils – dont les noms sont déjà présents en 33,19 – paraît «logique» dans un contexte matrimonial. En outre, ce qui aux yeux du lecteur occidental moderne peut apparaître comme des discours redondants reflète probablement la réalité des négociations de mariage dans l'Orient ancien. Il faut tenir compte par ailleurs du fait que Kevers a bien montré l'unité structurelle de l'ensemble formé par les vv. 1-24[28].

Reste la question de l'ancrage primitif de Siméon et Lévi dans le récit. L'argumentation développée par Lehming repose principalement sur l'incompatibilité présumée entre l'omniprésence des «fils de Jacob» et l'apparition soudaine de Siméon et Lévi au verset 25[29]. Or, si l'on considère que 49,5-7 constitue la finale primitive du récit, cette incompatibilité devient sans fondement. En effet, le texte des sentences tribales de Jacob joue également sur la notion de «fils de Jacob» qui se rassemblent (49,2), mais dont une partie, précisément Siméon et Lévi, va être exclue (49,7).

À la suite de notre analyse littéraire, nous proposons de considérer l'insertion de Gn 34,1-26* dans le cycle de Jacob comme l'oeuvre d'un seul auteur et d'attribuer à ce même auteur Gn 49,5-7, qui constitue la suite logique de Gn 34,1-26*.

Contexte idéologique des deux versions

La question de l'environnement idéologique des deux versions doit être brièvement abordée. La seconde version, qui réhabilite Siméon et Lévi, peut être identifiée sans difficulté comme une correction datant de l'époque d'Esdras-Néhémie: contrairement à des pratiques courantes, on cherche alors à interdire le mariage avec des personnes issues du peuple

---

sation des inter-mariages (BLUM, *Die Komposition der Vätergeschichte* [n. 8], p. 215, semble implicitement admettre ce point puisqu'il doute de l'attribution des vv. 15-17 à la couche «Hamor»). Si l'on admet au contraire que la version «Sichem» ne comportait que la circoncision du jeune homme, il faut imaginer que sa finale ne mentionnait pas le massacre de toute la ville mais la mort du seul Sichem, ou même qu'elle ne faisait état d'aucun meurtre.

28. Cf. KEVERS, *Étude littéraire* (n. 4), pp. 63-72.

29. À ce propos, on relèvera que LEHMING, *Zur Überlieferungsgeschichte* (n. 7), admet d'une part que la tradition primitive glorifiait le massacre et d'autre part que la traîtrise de Siméon et Lévi n'a pas pu être étendue à tous les frères. Or l'argumentation que nous avons développée plus haut tend à montrer le contraire: il est bien plus probable que la lecture positive du massacre résulte du fait que la tradition qui l'interprétait négativement avait cessé d'être acceptable à une époque ultérieure. En outre, la possibilité d'un élargissement de l'acte de massacre à tous les fils de Jacob nous semble aussi parfaitement plausible comme volonté de le justifier et d'en rendre tous les frères solidairement responsables.

du pays, qui vivent en Judée sans appartenir à la communauté «orthodoxe» descendant des exilés. Si l'on en juge par le récit de Gn 34, ces gens sont des circoncis, dont le texte tourne en dérision la circoncision.

La première version de l'histoire pose davantage de problèmes. Le milieu producteur est probablement favorable aux mariages avec les gens du pays, mais il y met certaines conditions, en particulier celle de la circoncision. Cette première version peut fort bien refléter la théologie du groupe majoritaire – qui l'était encore à l'époque d'Esdras-Néhémie (voir la présentation de la réforme par le récit de Esd 9-10) – la théologie de la communauté judéenne postexilique pour qui les inter-mariages constituaient une réalité tout à fait naturelle.

Il faut dès lors se demander pourquoi cette première version du récit critique Lévi. Si l'on rejette les thèses qui veulent expliquer ce texte par l'existence d'une très vieille tradition historique, remontant à l'époque supposée où la tribu de Lévi n'était pas encore liée au culte[30], cette critique de Lévi trouve son meilleur parallèle dans des textes postexiliques, en particulier en Ez 44,10-16. Une polémique très vive contre les lévites – considérés comme les prêtres des anciens sanctuaires idolâtres d'Israël – y est développée. Ils sont fortement rabaissés par des milieux issus de la caste sacerdotale, sadocite dans le cas d'Ez 44,10-16. Une problématique similaire se retrouve aussi dans plusieurs textes attribués à P[31]. On signalera par ailleurs une polémique inverse, elle aussi très violente, en Ex 32,26-29 où, après l'épisode de la fabrication du veau d'or, les lévites vont massacrer leurs frères sur ordre de Moïse, alors que le prêtre Aaron avait laissé construire l'idole. L'intransigeance de Lévi est ici louée, alors qu'elle est critiquée en Gn 34.

On peut donc penser que Gn 34* et 49,5-7 remonte à une époque où les lévites étaient d'une certaine manière en concurrence avec le sacerdoce. Peut-être avaient-ils des prérogatives liées à la circoncision, et une

---

30. Bien que le texte de Gn 34 ne mentionne pas expressément le caractère religieux du groupe lévite, il ne permet pas non plus de l'exclure. La thèse d'une tribu séculaire de Lévi a été contestée de manière convaincante par DE GEUS, *The Tribes of Israel* (n. 2), pp. 97-108; GOTTWALD, *The Tribes of Yahweh* (n. 11), p. 373; GUNNEWEG, *Leviten und Priester* (n. 11), en particulier pp. 78-81; B. HALPERN, *The Emergence of Israel in Canaan* (SBL.MS, 29), Chico, Scholars Press, 1983, pp. 26-27; NIELSEN, *Shechem* (n. 6), pp. 259-283; elle est aujourd'hui généralement rejetée. Pour un résumé de ces problématiques, voir D. KELLERMANN, לֵוִי *lewî* לְוִיִּם *lᵉwîjim*, in *ThWAT*, vol. IV, 1984, cc. 499-521. 506-508; H. SEEBASS, *Levi/Leviten*, in *Theologische Realenzyklopädie*, vol. XXI, 1991, pp. 36-40, spéc. 38-39. De plus, comme cette tradition a été insérée tardivement dans le texte biblique il semble de toute façon peu probable qu'elle soit très ancienne.

31. La proximité de Yhwh est très durement refusée aux lévites en Nb 4,15.19-20; 16,3.8; 18,1-7.

réputation d'intransigeance? Cependant, étant donné la rareté des traces laissées par les polémiques anti-lévites, il est difficile de préciser davantage le contexte de la première version de Gn 34.

Conclusions

Nous avons constaté que la narration de Genèse 34 est interprétée de deux manières radicalement opposées. Le texte de base considère les inter-mariages avec le peuple du pays comme naturels; l'attitude intransigeante de Siméon et de Lévi passe dès lors pour absurde. La relecture tend au contraire à justifier cette attitude. Les deux interprétations du récit sont en quelque sorte en opposition l'une avec l'autre. Certes, littérairement parlant, l'attitude tolérante vis-à-vis des mariages mixtes est première, mais on perçoit déjà que la question des inter-mariages pose problème. 34,1-26*; 49,5-7 stigmatise même de manière assez vive les thèses des groupes opposés aux mariages mixtes. La relecture favorable à l'intransigeance de Siméon et de Lévi vient dès lors s'inscrire naturellement comme la réponse des milieux concernés.

La narration – ou plutôt les interprétations qui en sont faites – est souvent le terrain d'affrontements idéologiques. La narration biblique ne fait pas exception à la règle. Dans l'épisode de «l'enlèvement de Dina», le conflit d'interprétation n'apparaît qu'après une analyse diachronique du texte. Ailleurs, il peut en aller autrement: les interprétations différentes sont données côte à côte, comme pour l'épisode de l'enlèvement de la femme du patriarche (Gn 12, 20 et 26), pour les 4 évangiles, ou pour l'exemple puisé chez Tintin.

Dans l'épisode de Dina, les partisans de la justification des actes de Siméon et Lévi ont eu littérairement le dernier mot. D'une certaine manière, le processus de canonisation a même donné à cette lecture de l'événement un statut d'interprétation reçue. C'est ainsi que, pour résumer le récit de Gn 34, on parle du «viol de Dina» ou de «l'enlèvement de Dina», mais que personne ne l'intitule «le mariage détruit de Dina».

Savoir si celui qui parle le dernier a forcément raison est une tout autre question, qui mériterait une reprise herméneutique détaillée.

RÉSUMÉ

L'analyse de Genèse 34, liée à celle de Genèse 49,5-7, permet de distinguer deux interprétations opposées de l'histoire de l'enlèvement de Dina et du massacre des Sichémites. La première version du récit envisage une régularisation de la relation illégitime entre Sichem et Dina et condamne l'intransigeance de Siméon et Lévi; elle émane d'un milieu favorable aux mariages avec les gens du pays et critique face aux prétentions de la tribu de Lévi. La seconde version réhabilite la violence perpétrée par les deux fils de Jacob; elle est à situer à l'époque d'Esdras-Néhémie, dans un milieu qui cherche à interdire les mariages mixtes.

ABSTRACT

Any analysis of Genesis 34 needs to be placed alongside that of Genesis 49,5-7. When that is done, it is possible to distinguish two opposite interpretations of the story of the rape of Dinah and the massacre of the Shechemites. The first version of the story envisages a normalization or regularization of the illegitimate relations between Shechem and Dinah and condemns the intransigence of Simeon and Levi. This version of events emanates from a circle which favoured marriages with Gentiles and which criticised the pretensions of the tribe of Levi. The second version condones the violence perpetrated by the two sons of Jacob; it is to be set in the era of Ezra-Nehemiah, in a milieu which sought to prohibit mixed marriages.

Université de Genève
Faculté Autonome de
   Théologie Protestante
CH-1211 Genève 4

Jean-Daniel MACCHI

2

LA NARRATION, UNE SUBVERSION
L'HISTOIRE DE JOSEPH (Gn 37–50*)
ET LES ROMANS DE LA DIASPORA

«No piece of prose elsewhere in the Bible can equal the literary standard attained by the Joseph story of Genesis 37-50»[1]. C'est ainsi que l'égyptologue Donald Redford a récemment caractérisé l'histoire de Joseph, reprenant un jugement largement partagé par des exégètes vétérotestamentaires de tous bords. Est-ce cette qualité littéraire qui explique la reprise de l'histoire de Joseph par des romanciers comme Thomas Mann (*Joseph et ses frères*[2]) ou tout récemment par le compositeur Andrew Lloyd Webber (*Joseph and the amazing technicolor dreamcoat*)? De fait, nous avons affaire à une histoire bien ficelée, aux rebondissements divers et utilisant des motifs folkloriques attestés dans des civilisations diverses. Pourtant, ces seuls éléments ne suffisent pas à expliquer le statut et la fonction des aventures de Joseph, qui ont été canonisées comme charnière entre l'époque des Patriarches et celle du peuple d'Israël en Égypte. Dans la suite nous essayerons de poser quelques jalons qui nous permettront de mieux situer les particularités de Joseph. Pour ce faire, nous devons d'abord définir notre corpus et notre méthode de travail.

Synchronie et diachronie

L'exégèse historico-critique avait, à l'époque du paradigme wellhausenien, une position paradoxale en ce qui concerne l'interprétation de Gn 37ss. Un Hermann Gunkel ou un Gerhard von Rad soulignaient l'unité de style et de composition de l'histoire de Joseph, tout en y découvrant la fusion de deux documents originellement autonomes[3]. Ces

---

1. D.B. REDFORD, *Egypt, Canaan, and Israel in Ancient Times*, Princeton, Princeton University Press, 1992, p. 422.
2. Cf. à ce propos R. TOMES, *Thomas Mann's «Joseph and his Brothers»*, in *Expository Times* 89 (1977) 72-75.
3. H. GUNKEL, *Genesis übersetzt und erklärt*, Göttingen, Vandenhoeck & Ruprecht, 1902²; G. von RAD, *Josephsgeschichte und ältere Chokma*, in J.A. EMERTON et al. (éds.), *Congress Volume Copenhagen 1953* (VT.S, 1), Leiden, Brill, 1953, pp. 120-127; plus récemment, L. SCHMIDT, *Literarische Studien zur Josefsgeschichte* (BZAW, 167), Berlin/New York, de Gruyter, 1986; H.J. BOECKER, *Überlegungen zur Josephsgeschichte*, in

documents furent attribués au «Yahwiste» et à l'«Elohiste», ce qui diluait toutes les particularités du roman de Joseph, car J et E étaient censés comporter toute la trame narrative du Pentateuque. Malgré la présence de nombreux doublets concernant les acteurs (Jacob//Israël; Ruben//Judah) et les actions (deux rêves de Joseph, deux rêves de Pharaon, deux voyages des frères), la *Quellenscheidung* ne s'avéra pas une méthode pertinente pour l'analyse du cycle de Joseph[4]. Il n'est donc pas étonnant que de nombreuses méthodes synchroniques aient été appliquées à l'histoire de Joseph. Ainsi Hugh White, se basant notamment sur les travaux de G. Genette et de L. Dolezel, a proposé une interprétation narratologique de Gn 37-50[5]. White souligne les points suivants: contrairement à Abraham, Isaac et Jacob, l'auteur présente Joseph comme un protagoniste qui «has no direct dialogue with the divine at all» (p. 237)[6] et établit Joseph «in a role which he is to play consistently as the solitary hermeneut who exists between alienated realms of discourse and social positions» (p. 240). Malgré des analyses souvent très fines, on reste un peu sur sa faim. D'ailleurs White propose finalement une interprétation assez traditionnelle de Gn 37ss, pas très éloignée du commentaire (historico-critique) de Claus Westermann[7].

Une lecture dumézilienne de Joseph a été récemment proposée par Jean Lambert, pour qui Joseph est un représentant typique de la «troisième fonction» de Dumézil, à savoir celle de la fécondité ou de l'économique[8]. Lambert souligne comment, à chaque étape de l'histoire, Joseph (dont le nom est construit à partir d'une racine signifiant l'excédent) stocke et diffère l'échange; ce faisant il n'est rien d'autre que le substitut d'Elohim, puisqu'il rappelle dans tous les moments-clés de l'histoire que c'est Dieu qui agit à sa place (cf. Gn 40,8; 41,16; 45,7-8 etc…). Par cette stratégie de la substitution (ce que fait Joseph, c'est Elohim qui le fait), le roman raconte, selon Lambert, «ce qui est conceptualisé dans les cultures sémitiques, les fonctions du monothéisme de

---

J. HAUSMANN et H.-J. ZOBEL (éds.), *Alttestamentlicher Glaube und biblische Theologie. Festschrift für H.D. Preuss zum 65. Geburtstag,* Stuttgart et al., Kohlhammer, 1992, pp. 35-45.

4. Cf. déjà en 1968 R.N. WHYBRAY, *The Joseph Story and Pentateuchal Criticism,* in *VT* 18 (1968) 522-528.

5. H.C. WHITE, *Narrative and Discourse in the Book of Genesis,* Cambridge et al., University Press, 1991.

6. Pour l'importance des dialogues dans l'histoire de Joseph, cf. également R.E. LONGACRE, *Joseph: A Story of Divine Providence. A Text-Theoretical and Textlinguistic Analysis of Genesis 37 and 39-48,* Winona Lake, Eisenbrauns, 1989, pp. 139ss.

7. C. WESTERMANN, *Genesis. 3. Teilband Genesis 37-50* (BK I/3), Neukirchen-Vluyn, Neukirchener Verlag, 1982.

8. J. LAMBERT, *Le Dieu distribué. Une anthologie comparée des monothéismes* (Patrimoines), Paris, Cerf, 1995.

troisième fonction»⁹. Nous n'avons ni le temps, ni les compétences pour dialoguer en détail avec cette approche anthropologique du cycle de Joseph. La lecture de Lambert ouvre cependant des pistes pour comprendre la fonction du narratif dans l'histoire de Joseph. Si l'histoire de Joseph narre un monothéisme qui se caractérise par la troisième fonction de Dumézil (richesse économique, paix), et si cette histoire met en scène un Joseph grâce à qui tout un peuple arrive à vivre dans l'abondance, nous devons nous poser la question du contexte socio-historique d'une telle stratégie narrative.

Pour avancer dans notre enquête, il nous faut clarifier deux questions préalables: celle de l'autonomie de l'histoire de Joseph et celle de son unité littéraire. Si l'on conteste l'autonomie originelle de l'histoire de Joseph¹⁰ (en y décelant par exemple les sources «J» et «E»), elle fonctionne surtout comme une charnière, voire comme un prologue au séjour du peuple d'Israël en Égypte par lequel s'ouvre le livre de l'Exode. Or, il semble assez évident que le cycle de Joseph a d'abord été conçu comme une nouvelle ou un roman indépendant¹¹. Dans les sommaires historiques qui résument la trame narrative du Pentateuque et des livres historiques, l'histoire de Joseph n'apparaît presque jamais (cf. ci-dessous). La majorité des chercheurs s'accordent à reconnaître dans l'histoire de Joseph un style et une théologie qui contrastent fortement tant avec le cycle des Patriarches qu'avec l'épopée de l'exode. Rappelons seulement que l'histoire de Joseph ne contient aucune théophanie directe et que les grands thèmes de l'alliance et de l'élection y sont totalement absents. Il s'ensuit que l'histoire de Joseph a d'abord été conçue comme une œuvre indépendante¹².

L'unité littéraire de cette œuvre a été magistralement démontrée par Donner, Redford et d'autres¹³. Cela ne signifie nullement que tous les

---

9. *Ibid.*, pp. 50-61, spéc. pp. 60-61.

10. Pour M. NOTH, l'histoire de Joseph a été composée dans le seul but de créer un lien entre le thème des Patriarches et le thème de l'Exode; cf. *A History of Pentateuchal Traditions*, Englewood Cliffs, N.J., Prentice-Hall, 1972, pp. 208-213.

11. Nous gardons délibérément un certain flou quant au genre littéraire de Gn 37ss. Les deux définitions courantes de roman ou de nouvelle s'y appliquent assez bien. Selon le *Petit Robert*, le roman est une «œuvre d'imagination en prose, assez longue, qui présente et fait vivre dans un milieu des personnages donnés comme réels, nous fait connaître leur psychologie, leur destin, leurs aventures». La nouvelle est définie comme un «récit généralement bref, de construction dramatique, et présentant des personnages peu nombreux». Tout dépend de ce que l'on appelle «long» et «bref».

12. Cf. en dernier lieu J. VAN SETERS, *Prologue to History. The Yahwist as Historian in Genesis*, Zürich, Theologischer Verlag, 1992, pp. 311-318.

13. Cf. H. DONNER, *Die literarische Gestalt der alttestamentlichen Josephsgeschichte* (Sitzungsberichte der Heidelberger Akademie der Wissenschaften, Philologisch-historische Klasse, Abh. 2), Heidelberg, 1976; D.B. REDFORD, *A Study of the Biblical Story of*

textes compris entre Gn 37 et Gn 50 aient fait partie de la première version de l'histoire. En sont certainement à exclure: Gn 38; 48; 49[14]. Parmi les autres textes ajoutés au roman de Joseph lors de son intégration dans la Torah figurent notamment 46,1-5; 47,13-26; 50,22-25[15]. Parmi les textes sacerdotaux n'ayant pas de lien originel avec l'histoire de Joseph figurent notamment 37,1-2; 47,6-7.27-28; 49,29-33; 50,12-13[16]. Il n'y a aucune raison d'exclure Gn 39 sous prétexte que c'est seulement dans ce chapitre qu'apparaît le nom de Yhwh[17]. L'histoire de Joseph chez Mme Potiphar est narrativement nécessaire pour préparer la deuxième descente de Joseph (après la citerne, la prison) et pour présenter Joseph comme un modèle de loyauté face à son employeur égyptien[18]. L'histoire originelle de Joseph comporte alors grosso modo: 37*; 39-45*; 46,28-33; 47*; 50,1-11.14-21.26. A l'intérieur de cet ensemble, les nombreux «doublets» n'indiquent pas une combinaison de

Joseph (Genesis 37-50) (SVT, 20), Leiden, Brill, 1970; I. WILLI-PLEIN, *Historiographische Aspekte der alttestamentlichen Josephsgeschichte*, in *Henoch* 1 (1979) 305-331. Cf. également les différents travaux de G.W. COATS, *Redactional Unity in Genesis 37-50*, in *JBL* 93 (1974) 15-21; *The Joseph Story and Ancient Wisdom*, in *CBQ* 35 (1973) 285-297; *From Canaan to Egypt. Structural and Theological Context for the Joseph Story* (CBQ Monograph Series, 4), Washington, D.C., The Catholic Biblical Association of America, 1976, pour qui l'histoire originelle se termine en Gn 45 avec la scène de la réconciliation.

14. L'histoire de Juda et de Tamar en Gn 38 interrompt le récit entre Gn 37 et Gn 39. Joseph n'y est pas mentionné et le contexte socio-culturel est différent de celui de l'histoire de Joseph. Selon B.J. DIEBNER, ce texte a été inséré à cet endroit parce qu'il y est question d'un mariage d'un fils de Jacob avec une étrangère, pour légitimer en quelque sorte le mariage égyptien de Joseph (cf. *Le roman de Joseph, ou Israël en Égypte. Un midrash post-exilique de la Tora*, in O. ABEL et F. SMYTH (éds.), *Le livre de traverse. De l'exégèse biblique à l'anthropologie* (Patrimoines), Paris, Cerf, 1992, p. 65). On peut également penser que Gn 38 sert de contraste au récit de séduction en Gn 39 (Juda succombe à la séduction, non pas Joseph). Pour d'autres interprétations, voir A. WILDAVSKY, *Survival Must not be Gained through Sin: The Moral of the Joseph Stories Prefigured through Judah and Tamar*, in *JSOT* 62 (1994) 37-48. Gn 48 et 49 interrompent la scène de la mort de Jacob. Il s'agit certainement de traditions indépendantes qui ont été tardivement (lors de la rédaction finale?) insérées à cet endroit.

15. Gn 46,1-5 et 50,22-25 veulent rattacher l'histoire de Joseph aux traditions du Pentateuque. Ces ajouts sont dus à une des dernières rédactions; cf. REDFORD, *Study* (n. 13), pp. 19-20.25-26. Gn 47,13-26 interrompt le récit de l'installation de la famille de Joseph en Égypte et ne mentionne ni les frères ni Jacob. Il s'agit d'un midrash tardif qui présente Joseph comme l'inventeur du capitalisme; cf. H. SEEBASS, *Geschichtliche Zeit und theonome Tradition in der Joseph-Erzählung*, Gütersloh, G. Mohn, 1978, pp. 58-61.

16. Cf. par ex. E. BLUM, *Die Komposition der Vätergeschichte* (WMANT 57), Neukirchen-Vluyn, Neukirchener Verlag, 1984, pp. 244-257.

17. Cette idée est un grand classique de l'exégèse historico-critique; cf. récemment W. DIETRICH, *Die Josephserzählung als Novelle und Geschichtsschreibung. Zugleich ein Beitrag zur Pentateuchfrage* (Biblisch theologische Studien, 14), Neukirchen-Vluyn, Neukirchener Verlag, 1989, pp. 26-29.

18. Cf. R. ALTER, *The Art of Biblical Narrative*, New York, Basic Books, 1981.

sources, mais ils ont une fonction narratologique («law of scenic duality»[19]). La structure «par paire» est en effet une caractéristique du roman de Joseph. L'histoire commence par deux rêves qui préfigurent les compétences oniromanciennes de Joseph. Il va interpréter les deux rêves de ses co-prisonniers, préalable nécessaire qui lui permet d'être «repéré» pour interpréter les deux rêves du Pharaon. Deux fois Joseph est confronté à une descente et une ascension (du puits vers la maison de Potiphar, de la prison vers la cour du Pharaon). A la double ascension de Joseph correspondent les deux «descentes» des frères vers l'Égypte; deux fois Joseph perd ses vêtements et son statut social (37 et 39)[20], etc.... Il y aussi une certain *plot symmetry* entre le sort de Joseph dans la première partie et celui de Benjamin dans la seconde[21]. Reste la question du doublet Ruben / Juda. La fonction narratologique de cette «concurrence» entre les deux frères n'est pas toujours évidente. De nombreux exégètes ont alors distingué une *Ruben-Schicht* ancienne et une *Juda-Redaktion*[22]. Il est en effet possible que l'insertion de Juda ait coïncidé avec l'insertion du roman de Joseph dans son contexte actuel[23]; Van Seters par exemple envisage la possibilité qu'à certains endroits le nom de Juda ait été substitué à celui de Ruben[24], dans le cadre d'une relecture «judéenne» et «orthodoxe». Nous pouvons cependant laisser la question ouverte car elle n'a pas d'enjeux majeurs pour l'interprétation que nous allons proposer.

---

19. Cf. J.L. SKA, *«Our Fathers Have Told Us». Introduction to the Analysis of Hebrew Narratives* (Subsidia Biblica, 13), Roma, Pontificio Istituto Biblico, 1990, p. 35. Pour l'importance de la construction par deux dans l'histoire de Joseph, voir notamment D. REDFORD, *Study* (n. 13), pp. 66ss.

20. Pour le rôle important des vêtements dans Gn 37ss, cf. A. DA SILVA, *La symbolique des rêves et des vêtements dans l'histoire de Joseph et de ses frères* (Héritage et projet, 52), Ville St-Laurent, Fides, 1994; V.H. MATTHEWS, *The Anthropology of Clothing in the Joseph Narrative*, in *JSOT* 65 (1995) 25-36.

21. En 43,33-34, Benjamin devient le préféré de Joseph qui, lui aussi, avait été le préféré de son père; comme pour Joseph, le narrateur va ensuite isoler Benjamin de ses frères, qui devient de plus en plus le double de Joseph; cf. J. LAMBERT, *Dieu distribué* (n. 8), p. 51.

22. Cf. D. REDFORD, *Study* (n. 13), pp. 182ss; DIETRICH, *Josephserzählung* (n. 17), pp. 22-27; N. KEBEKUS, *Die Joseferzählung. Literarkritische und redaktionsgeschichtliche Untersuchungen zu Genesis 37-50* (Internationale Hochschulschriften), Münster/New York, Waxmann, 1990, spéc. le résumé, pp. 344-345. La thèse inverse (le récit originel faisait intervenir Juda) est défendue par H.-C. SCHMITT, *Die nichtpriesterliche Josephsgeschichte. Ein Beitrag zur neuesten Pentateuchkritik* (BZAW, 154), Berlin, New York, 1980; ID., *Die Hintergründe der «neuesten Pentateuchkritik» und der literarische Befund der Josefsgeschichte*, in *ZAW* 97 (1985) 162-179.

23. Pour KEBEKUS, *Joseferzählung* (n. 22), p. 339, la *Juda-Schicht* est identique à la rédaction finale du Pentateuque.

24. VAN SETERS, *Prologue* (n. 12), p. 317.

Datation et contexte sociologique

Selon G. von Rad, l'histoire de Joseph remonte à l'époque salomonienne et reflète les idéaux moraux et religieux du milieu des sages de la cour. La narration serait alors mise au service de l'éducation: il s'agirait, selon von Rad, de montrer aux apprentis-fonctionnaires qu'un jeune homme doué à la fois d'intelligence, de sens moral et de confiance en Dieu est capable de survivre dans toutes sortes de situations dangereuses et qu'il peut même s'élever aux responsabilités les plus importantes[25]. W. Dietrich voit dans l'histoire de Joseph une sorte d'allégorie historique écrite dans le royaume du Nord après la scission de 926, dans le but de légitimer la royauté de Jéroboam = Joseph[26]. Kebekus, lui, situe à l'époque d'Ezékias sa *Ruben-Grundschicht*, qui se caractérise par la reprise des traditions du Nord. Le fait que Joseph ne devienne pas roi mais seulement vizir présuppose, selon Kebekus, les événements de 722[27].

Toutes ces datations préexiliques me paraissent difficilement défendables[28]. Elles ne peuvent guère être étayées par des arguments littéraires et philologiques. Contre Dietrich, on ne peut guère lire Joseph comme une allégorie pour le (premier) roi d'Israël. Les textes préexiliques (surtout prophétiques) qui mentionnent Joseph comme ancêtre éponyme du royaume du Nord le font toujours dans un contexte de jugement (cf. par ex. Am 6,6; Abd 18). Ce n'est qu'après l'exil que «Joseph», désignant la Samarie ou même «tout Israël», commence à avoir une signification positive (cf. par ex. Ez 47,13; Za 10,6)[29].

À cela s'ajoute la quasi absence d'une référence à l'histoire de Joseph en dehors de Gn 37-50. Les nombreux sommaires historiques[30] qui parcourent toute la Bible hébraïque expliquent le séjour d'Israël en Égypte sans passer par Joseph. D'autres textes constatent tout simplement la présence des pères en Égypte (Dt 6,2ss; Ez 20,5ss; Os 11,1ss; Ps 78,12ss; 106,6ss; 136,10ss). D'autres encore parlent de la descente de

---

25. VON RAD, *Josephsgeschichte* (n. 3).
26. DIETRICH, *Josephserzählung* (n. 17), pp. 58-66.
27. KEBEKUS, *Joseferzählung* (n. 22), pp. 250-257.
28. Nous n'allons pas nous étendre sur le caractère hautement fantasmagorique des prétendues «lumières salomoniennes». Pour une présentation plus réaliste de l'époque salomonienne, voir D.W. JAMIESON-DRAKE, *Scribes and Schools in Monarchic Judah, A Socio-Archeological Approach* (JSOTS, 109), Sheffield, Almond Press, 1991.
29. Cf. T. RÖMER, *Le cycle de Joseph: Sources, corpus, unité*, in *Foi et Vie* LXXXVI/3 (1987) 3-15; = *Joseph approché. Source du cycle, corpus, unité*, in O. ABEL et F. SMYTH (éds.), *Le livre de traverse. De l'exégèse biblique à l'anthropologie* (Patrimoines), Paris, Cerf, 1992, p. 13.
30. Cf. à ce propos T. RÖMER, *Historiographie et mythes d'origines dans l'Ancien Testament*, in M. DÉTIENNE (éd.), *Transcrire les mythologies. Tradition, écriture, historicité*, Paris, Albin Michel, 1994, pp. 142-148.

Jacob ou des pères en Égypte (Dt 10,22; 26,5; Jos 24,4; 1S 12,8), non pas de celle de Joseph. Un seul de ces sommaires mentionne l'histoire de Joseph. Il s'agit du Ps 105 (v. 18-23), un psaume qui selon l'avis quasi unanime des chercheurs présuppose le Pentateuque dans sa forme finale[31]. Pour la construction de la chronologie officielle du Pentateuque, l'histoire de Joseph n'est donc pas indispensable. Cela est confirmé par le fait que les textes sacerdotaux entre Gn 37 et Ex 1 font le lien entre les Patriarches et l'Égypte apparemment sans référence à l'histoire de Joseph[32].

Le dossier vétérotestamentaire plaide donc plutôt en faveur d'une datation tardive[33]. Cette datation peut être corroborée du côté égyptologique. Selon Redford, les noms et les allusions aux coutumes égyptiennes qui apparaissent dans le roman de Joseph reflètent presque tous la situation de la période saïte[34]. Nous nous contenterons de deux exemples. Le fait que les frères de Joseph puissent être suspectés d'espionnage (42,9) fait seulement sens au moment où l'Égypte peut se sentir menacée par une puissance étrangère contrôlant la Palestine; c'est la situation politique de l'époque perse (et aussi hellénistique). Le terme de «surveillant» en 41,34 (*peqidim*) est omniprésent dans les textes administratifs égyptiens de l'époque perse.

Par conséquent, les meilleurs date et contexte sociologique pour situer l'histoire de Joseph semblent être la communauté juive en Égypte à

---

31. Cf. H.J. KRAUS, *Psalmen* (Biblischer Kommentar Altes Testament, 15), Neukirchen-Vluyn, Neukirchener Verlag, p. 719; G.J. BROOKE, *Psalms 105 and 106 at Qumran*, in *Revue de Qumran* 54 (1989) 267-292.

32. Cf. déjà L. RUPPERT, *Die Josephserzählungen der Genesis. Ein Beitrag zur Theologie der Pentateuchquellen* (StANT, 11), München, 1965, pp. 232-233; T. RÖMER, *Cycle* (n. 29), pp. 8-9; KEBEKUS, *Joseferzählung* (n. 22), p. 292. Le texte P[g] peut être reconstruit comme suit: «Jacob habita au pays où son père avait émigré, le pays de Canaan (37,1). Les fils d'Israël prirent leur cheptel... Jacob se rendit en Égypte avec tous ses descendants ... il fit venir avec lui toute sa descendance en Égypte (46,8-26 = liste secondaire?). Israël habita au pays d'Égypte en terre de Goshen, les Israélites y devinrent propriétaires, ils y furent féconds et très prolifiques. Jacob vécut 17 ans au pays d'Égypte, et la durée de vie de Jacob fut de 147 ans (47,27-28); il donna l'ordre [à ses fils] et leur dit: «Je vais être réuni à mon peuple. Ensevelissez-moi auprès de mes pères ... dans la caverne du champ de Makpéla ...» Quand Jacob eut achevé de donner ses ordres à ses fils ... il expira et fut réuni aux siens (49,29-33). Les fils d'Israël agirent à son égard selon ses ordres. Ils le transportèrent au pays de Canaan et l'enterrèrent dans la caverne du champ de Makpéla (50,12-13). Et voici les noms des fils d'Israël venus en Égypte... (Ex 1,1-5a)». Les mentions de Joseph en Ex 1,5b.6.8 peuvent être attribuées au dernier rédacteur; cf. I. WILI-PLEIN, *Ort und literarische Funktion der Geburtsgeschichte des Mose*, in *VT* 41 (1991) 110-118.

33. Notons encore que D. REDFORD, *Study* (n. 13), pp. 26ss, recense une soixantaine de termes hébraïques qui ne sont attestés que dans la littérature tardive. Même si tous ces exemples ne sont pas toujours convaincants, sa liste constitue néanmoins un argument supplémentaire pour notre propos.

34. REDFORD, *Study* (n. 13), pp. 182ss; ID., *Egypt* (n. 1), pp. 424-427.

l'époque perse[35]. Dès lors, le genre littéraire «nouvelle de la Diaspora» s'impose[36]. Certains motifs narratifs du roman de Joseph sont d'ailleurs présents dans d'autres écrits juifs émanant de la diaspora. C'est le cas pour le motif du jeune subordonné qui réussit à interpréter des énigmes (rêves) que les autorités en place sont incapables de résoudre. Les parallèles entre Gn 41 et Dn 2 (cf. également Dn 5) sautent aux yeux[37]. Dans les deux cas, un jeune juif est d'abord fait prisonnier par suite des intrigues de ses ennemis; il est ensuite convoqué devant le roi étranger dont il interprète les rêves; enfin, il bénéficie d'une ascension sociale. Une variante de ce thème est le *plot pattern* de la «wrongful incarceration and final rehabilitation of the wiseman»[38], qui est présent dans les aventures de Joseph, de Mardochée[39], de Tobie, et en Égypte dans les aventures de Onkh-Sheshonq et Hy-Hor. Ce motif se retrouve également dans l'histoire d'Ahiqar. Est-ce alors seulement un hasard si le manuscrit le plus ancien du sage Ahiqar, en araméen, provient de la communauté juive d'Éléphantine?

JOSEPH ET LA SUBVERSION DU JUDAÏSME ORTHODOXE

Les textes d'Éléphantine[40] nous montrent dans quelle mesure les communautés juives installées en Haute-Égypte, probablement depuis l'époque assyrienne, devaient, à l'époque perse, être éloignées de l'idéal de l'orthodoxie naissante en Mésopotamie et à Jérusalem. Malheureusement, nous n'avons que très peu d'informations sur l'extension et l'orga-

---

35. A. CATASTINI, *Le Testimonziane di Manetone e la «Storia di Giuseppe» (Genesi 37-50)*, in *Henoch* 17 (1995) 279-300.

36. Pour une datation postexilique de l'histoire de Joseph, cf. A. MEINHOLD, *Die Gattung der Josephsgeschichte und des Estherbuches: Diasporanovelle I*, in *ZAW* 87 (1975) 306-324; ID., *Diasporanovelle II*, in *ZAW* 88 (1976) 72-93; cf. également R. GNUSE, *The Jewish Dream Interpreter in a Foreign Court: The Recurring Use of a Theme in Jewish Literature*, in *Journal for the Study of Pseudepigrapha* 7 (1990) 29-53, p. 30; J.A. SOGGIN, *Notes on the Joseph Story*, in A.G. AULD (éd.), *Understanding Poets and Prophets. Essays in Honour of George Wishart Anderson* (JSOTS, 152), Sheffield, JSOT Press, 1993, pp. 336-349; A. CATASTINI, *Storia di Giuseppe (Genesi 37-50)*, Venezia, Marsilio, 1994, pp. 52-58; REDFORD, *Study* (n.13), parle de manière plus vague du VIIe-VIe siècle.

37. S. NIDITCH et R. DORAN, *The Success Story of the Wise Courtier: A Formal Approach*, in *JBL* 96 (1977) 185-189; R. GNUSE, *Dream Interpreter* (n. 35); G.G. LABONTÉ, *Genèse 41 et Daniel 2: question d'origine*, in A.S. VAN DER WOUDE (éd.), *The Book of Daniel in the Light of New Findings* (BETL, 106), Leuven, University Press – Peeters, 1993, pp. 271-284.

38. D. REDFORD, *Egypt* (n. 1), p. 428.

39. Pour une comparaison détaillée entre Est et Gn 37ss, cf. A. MEINHOLD, «Gattung» (n. 36).

40. Cf. P. GRELOT, *Documents araméens d'Égypte* (LAPO), Paris, Cerf, 1972.

nisation de la diaspora juive dans le Nord de l'Égypte[41]. Mais à en juger par l'importance énorme que prendra le judaïsme égyptien à l'époque hellénistique et par ses tendances à l'autonomie par rapport aux autorités de Jérusalem (et de Babylone), on peut supposer que cet «autre» judaïsme avait besoin d'affirmer son identité aussi au niveau littéraire. S'il est vrai que l'élaboration de la Bible hébraïque resta globalement entre les mains du judaïsme issu de la Golah babylonienne, le judaïsme égyptien a réussi malgré tout à y trouver une place. Par ruse ou subversion, il fit entendre ses conceptions théologiques au moyen de diverses narrations. L'histoire de Joseph constitue sans doute l'exemple le plus frappant de cette stratégie. Joseph[42] incarne la réussite exemplaire d'un Juif en Égypte et fournit ainsi un modèle aux destinataires du récit. Retraçons brièvement le roman sous cet aspect subversif.

Dès le début du roman, on retrouve une réplique à la Golah babylonienne; en effet, Gn 37 montre bien que, contrairement à la présentation prophético-dtr (cf. Jr 43-44), l'exil en Égypte a lui aussi commencé par être imposé à celui qui va en profiter. Cependant, il n'a pas été imposé par un roi étranger, mais par les frères de Joseph eux-mêmes. Et tandis que les frères cachent leur responsabilité par des comportements douteux (ils mentent à leur père), Joseph, dans son pays d'accueil, réussit un parcours éthiquement correct, appliquant les maximes de Pr 7,6-27, dans sa rencontre avec Mme Potiphar en Gn 39.

La rencontre entre Joseph et Pharaon met en évidence, contre la théologie dtr de l'élection et de l'exclusivisme, un Dieu universel auquel tous les hommes peuvent avoir accès: Joseph et le Pharaon s'entendent sans difficulté sur la question de Dieu. Du reste, Dieu n'est appelé Yhwh qu'en Gn 39; partout ailleurs, il porte le nom générique d'Elohim.

L'ascension finale de Joseph se termine par un événement qui a beaucoup choqué le judaïsme orthodoxe. En 41,50-52, le héros devient le gendre d'un prêtre égyptien[43]. Joseph pratique ainsi les mariages mixtes

---

41. Cf. à ce propos E. BRESCIANI, *La sixième satrapie. L'Égypte perse et ses sémites*, in O. ABEL et F. SMYTH (éds.), *Le livre de traverse. De l'exégèse biblique à l'anthropologie* (Patrimoines), Paris, Cerf, 1992, pp. 87-99; A. DE PURY et T. RÖMER, *Terres d'exil et terres d'accueil. Quelques réflexions sur le judaïsme postexilique face à la Perse et à l'Égypte*, in *Transeuphratène* 9 (1995) 25-34.

42. Pourquoi l'auteur a-t-il choisi le nom de Joseph pour son héros? Une première réponse pragmatique consiste à dire qu'en utilisant le motif littéraire de l'ascension du jeune/petit contre toute attente, il devait choisir parmi les fils cadets de Jacob. On peut encore spéculer sur la possibilité d'une évocation des origines «nordistes» de la colonie d'Éléphantine.

43. Il faut certainement aussi voir un clin d'œil dans le fait que notre auteur donne au beau-père de Joseph le même nom, «Potiphera», qu'à l'ancien employeur, dont Joseph a dû repousser la femme pour éviter une union illicite. D. REDFORD, *Egypt* (n. 1), p. 424: «*Potiphar* and its variant are modeled on a very common name, ..., meaning «He-

contre lesquels Esdras et Néhémie (Esd 9; Ne 10) luttent avec ferveur (cf. également Dt 7, 1-6). Selon Gn 41, deux des tribus d'Israël descendent d'une égyptienne et sont donc, d'après la loi, des *mamzérîm*, des bâtards. Dans les généalogies chronistes (1 Chr 7,29), une telle vision n'apparaît pas. D'ailleurs, 1 Chr 7 présente Ephraïm et Manassé comme habitant le pays de Canaan. Rien n'est dit d'une naissance ou d'un séjour en Égypte[44]. Cet épisode a très vite fait réagir les milieux plus orthodoxes qui, en produisant le roman «Joseph et Aseneth» insistent fortement sur la conversion d'Aseneth[45].

Le roman de Joseph prône donc la cohabitation et l'intégration en recourant à l'ironie. Ainsi, dans le seul passage où une séparation entre juifs et non-juifs est rapportée, l'initiative en est attribuée aux Égyptiens: «les Égyptiens mangeaient à part, ... car les Égyptiens n'ont pas le droit de manger avec les Hébreux: ce serait pour eux une abomination[46]» (Gn 43,23). Le ton ironique de ce passage montre bien que nous sommes en présence d'une pointe contre la *kashrout* du judaïsme orthodoxe[47].

Contre l'Exode officiel de l'orthodoxie babylono-jérusalémite, le roman de Joseph met en place un Exode à l'envers. Le père et les frères sont finalement obligés de se déplacer vers l'Égypte, car c'est de la périphérie que vient le salut pour le centre. Le judaïsme «libéral» qui s'exprime en Gn 37ss ne veut pourtant pas rompre sa relation avec la mère-patrie; il reste souhaitable que les ossements de ceux de l'extérieur soient ramenés en Palestine pour y être ensevelis (Gn 50,14). En insistant sur la providence divine – qui fournit en quelque sorte le clef de toute l'intrigue – la finale du roman (50,20) se plaît à rappeler que c'est grâce à l'exil du frère innocent que les frères coupables ont été sauvés. C'est grâce à la réussite économique de l'exilé, qui profite d'ailleurs aussi au pays d'accueil, qu'Israël peut (re)devenir un peuple nombreux et prospère.

Malgré ses positions «anticonformistes», le récit de Joseph a été canonisé. Cela s'explique par la volonté de rassemblement qui caractérise

---

Whom-God-N-gives» ... very common from the Kushite 25th Dynasty to Greco-Roman times».

44. Le fait est peut-être lié à l'idéologie autochtone de 1 et 2 Chr, qui présentent Israël comme ayant vécu depuis toujours et sans interruption dans son pays; cf. à ce sujet S. Japhet, *L'historiographie postexilique: pourquoi et comment?*, in A. de Pury, T. Römer et J.-D. Macchi (éds.), *Israël construit son histoire*, Genève, Labor et Fides, 1996, pp. 123-152.

45. Cf. la contribution de G. J. Brooke dans ce volume.

46. L'expression «abomination pour Yhwh» se trouve dans de nombreux textes du Deutéronome.

47. Cf. Römer, *Cycle* (n. 29); J.A. Soggin, *Notes* (n. 35), pp. 340-341. On notera que Flavius Josèphe omet cet épisode dans les *Antiquités*.

le judaïsme. Au moment où l'identité juive va se fonder dans le livre, il importe que tous les courants puissent se retrouver dans le même livre[48]. Une fois insérée entre les Patriarches et l'Exode, l'histoire de Joseph change certes de fonction. Devenue partie intégrante des récits patriarcaux, la descente de Joseph en Égypte forme en quelque sorte l'«Ancien Testament»[49] du Pentateuque, prologue nécessaire mais subordonné à l'«évangile» de la libération de l'esclavage égyptien. Néanmoins, pour celui ou celle qui le lit attentivement, le récit de Joseph n'a rien perdu de sa force subversive.

Joseph et les autres

Via le roman de Joseph, un autre judaïsme se fait entendre. C'est la voix d'une diaspora qui ne ressent pas un besoin urgent de revenir en *eretz yisraël* pour vivre sa judéité. Et cette diaspora dit sa manière d'être juive en narrant des histoires de héros exemplaires: Joseph, Daniel (Dn 1-6*), Esther et Mardochée, Tobie. Tous ces récits peuvent être caractérisés comme des «romans de la diaspora». Ils n'émanent pas tous du même milieu producteur, les différences chronologiques et idéologiques entre eux étant trop grandes. En ce qui concerne le roman de Joseph, nous avons insisté sur la fonction subversive de la narration.

Dans la Bible hébraïque, cette voix subversive est également présente dans des récits beaucoup plus brefs, des *short stories*, voire des anecdotes. Prenons l'exemple de la grande épopée nationale relatant l'histoire du peuple hébreu depuis la sortie d'Égypte jusqu'à la fin de la royauté (Ex – 2 R). Cette fresque historique correspond peut-être à la deuxième édition de «l'historiographie deutéronomiste». Pour l'école dtr, l'identité du peuple de Yhwh ne peut se maintenir que par une théologie ségrégationniste; une telle stratégie se comprend dans le contexte de l'exil ou de l'époque perse. Or, ce n'est certainement pas un hasard si ce grand ensemble historiographique a été encadré par deux petits récits qui défendent une autre théologie.

En Ex 1, les versets 15-21 constituent une insertion dans la trame narrative originelle. Ils relatent l'histoire des sages-femmes égyptiennes qui, par la ruse, déjouent les projets meurtriers du roi. Leur motivation est expliquée à deux reprises par la «crainte d'Elohim» (1,17 et 1,21; c'est d'ailleurs la première fois que le mot «Dieu» apparaît dans le livre de l'Exode). C'est donc l'intervention des femmes étrangères qui permet

---

48. Cf. Diebner, *Roman* (n. 14), pp. 64-68
49. Cf. R.W.L. Moberly, *The Old Testament of the Old Testament* (Overtures to Biblical Theology), Philadelphia, Fortress, 1992.

la survie du peuple d'Israël. Ces femmes «païennes», nous dit-on, craignent Dieu. La préoccupation de montrer que la crainte de Dieu existe chez les non-juifs se retrouve également en Gn 20 et dans le livre de Jonas, textes qui émanent sans doute du milieu de la diaspora[50]. L'insertion d'Ex 1,15ss veut ainsi éviter tout triomphalisme dans la lecture du récit fondateur du peuple de Yhwh. Israël a besoin des autres s'il veut survivre.

La fin du livre des Rois fait apparaître une stratégie littéraire comparable. Depuis M. Noth, la finale de 2 R 25 relatant la réhabilitation du roi Yoyaqin (25,27-30) a intrigué les exégètes. A mon avis, il ne s'agit pas d'une simple notice historiographique qu'il faudrait exploiter pour dater l'œuvre dtr[51]. En effet, la conclusion originelle de l'édition exilique de l'historiographie dtr (2 R 25,26)[52] a été augmentée de cette nouvelle finale. Et celle-ci propose une relecture de toute l'historiographie dtr en faveur de la diaspora.

Les parallèles entre 2 R 25,27-30 et les romans de la diaspora (Joseph, Esther, Dn 1-6*) sont patents. Ces récits partagent d'abord le thème de la «sortie de prison»[53]. L'expression *nasa' ro'sh* (2 R 25,27) constitue un leitmotiv en Gn 40. Tous ces récits retracent le parcours d'un exilé juif qui devient «deuxième du royaume». Est 10,3: «Mardochée le Juif était le deuxième du royaume après Xerxès»; Dan 2,48: «le roi éleva Daniel ... et le fit le surintendant de tous les sages du royaume»; Gn 41,40 (Pharaon à Joseph): «C'est toi qui seras mon majordome. Tout le peuple se soumettra à tes ordres»; 2 Rois 25,28: «Il établit son trône au-dessus du trône des rois qui étaient avec lui à Babel». Enfin, l'accession du héros au nouveau statut est symbolisé par un changement de vêtements. Est 6,10-11: «Alors le roi dit à Haman: «Vite! Prends le vêtement et le cheval comme tu l'as dit et fais ainsi pour Mardochée, le Juif ...». Haman prit le vêtement ... il revêtit Mardochée ...»; Dan 5,29: «Belshassar ordonna de revêtir Daniel de la pourpre»; Gn 41,42: «Il le revêtit d'habits de lin fin»; 2 R 25,29: «Il lui fit quitter ses vêtements de prisonnier».

Ainsi, 2 Rois 25,27-30 partage l'idéologie des romans de la diaspora, puisqu'il transforme l'exil en diaspora. Le pays d'exil devient le pays d'accueil où l'on peut vivre aisément.

50. Cf. E. BLUM, *Die Komposition der Vätergeschichte* (WMANT, 57), Neukirchen-Vluyn, Neukirchener Verlag, 1984, pp. 415-416.
51. M. NOTH et ses disciples avaient utilisé cette finale pour dater l'édition exilique de l'historiographie deutéronomiste entre 560-540.
52. Cf. R.E. FRIEDMAN, *The Exile and Biblical Narrative: The Formation of the Deuteronomistic and Priestly Works* (HSM, 22), Chico, CA, Scholars Press, 1981, pp. 35-36.
53. Pour Joseph et Daniel, c'est le cas à plusieurs reprises; Mardochée ne se trouve pas corporellement en prison, mais il est promis à la pendaison.

À l'intérieur de la Bible hébraïque, on trouve donc une tension qui caractérise le judaïsme jusqu'à nos jours. La «théologie officielle», selon laquelle tout juif doit faire son *aliyah* vers l'*eretz yisraël*, côtoie des théologies qui s'expriment par la narration et qui ne contestent pas ouvertement l'idéologie canonique dominante. Elles lui instillent néanmoins une dose de subversion et rappellent ainsi à tout lecteur de la Bible la nécessité d'un décloisonnement géographique et dogmatique.

RÉSUMÉ

Après examen des résultats traditionnels de l'exégèse de Genèse 37-50*, l'auteur montre comment le "Roman de Joseph" a inscrit, par ruse et ironie, les voix d'un judaïsme anticonformiste et libéral dans le canon vétérotestamentaire. Ce Roman sert en effet non seulement de fonction identitaire à la Gola égyptienne, à qui il donne un père fondateur, mais il s'oppose aussi à l'orthodoxie du judaïsme hiérosolymite (et babylonien), face à laquelle il propose un contre-Exode, ou un *Exode à l'envers*.

ABSTRACT

After an examination of the traditional results of the exegesis of Genesis 37-50, the author shows how the Joseph Story has brought into the Old Testament canon, by deceit and irony, the voice of a non-conformist and liberal Judaism. The Joseph cycle serves in effect not only to provide an identity for those exiled in Egypt for whom it provides a founding father, but it also opposes the orthodoxies of Jerusalemite (and Babylonian) Judaism, against which it proposes a neat reversal of the Exodus pattern in which Israel is depicted as finding its salvation by journeying to rather than escaping from Egypt.

Université de Lausanne Thomas RÖMER
Faculté de théologie
BFSH-2
CH-1015 Dorigny

3

LAW, WISDOM, AND NARRATIVE

I. Introduction

I have argued in earlier papers for a concept of "wisdom-laws" at the beginning of the Israelite legal tradition: a concept of laws based in orally transmitted, sometimes "arbitrary" rules which can be used for immediate, rough-and-ready dispute resolution, without the need to involve third parties or formal institutions[1]. I have also argued that, in approaching such laws, we must abandon the concept of "literal meaning" to which we are habituated, and adopt instead a "narrative approach", in which the meaning of rules is to be identified with the typical social situations they evoke – rather than with all the possible situations which may be subsumed under the words of the rule, as literally understood[2].

In this paper, I ask how this might relate to the Law and Wisdom debate. There is no *necessary* connection, in that the model which underlies my "wisdom-laws" claim is based primarily on interdisciplinary resources. Nevertheless, there are affinities between wisdom and this early stage of Israelite legal history sufficient at least to raise the question. We

---

1. See my *Practical Wisdom and Literary Artifice in the Covenant Code*, in B.S. JACKSON and S.M. PASSAMANECK (eds.), *The Jerusalem 1990 Conference Volume* (JLAS, 6), Atlanta, Scholars Press, 1992, pp. 67-78; *Code and Custom*, in R. KEVELSON (ed.), *Critic of Institutions Vol. I: Codes and Customs*, New York, Peter Lang, 1994, pp. 124-127; *"Law" and "Justice" in the Bible*, in *JJS* 44 (1998) 220-222; on the original biblical conception of the judicial role, as in 2 Chron 19,5-11, Deut 16,18-20; Exod 18,19-22; Deut 1,19-17, see further my *Ideas of Law and Legal Administration*, in R.E. CLEMENTS (ed.), *The World of Ancient Israel: Sociological, Anthropological and Political Perspectives*, Cambridge, Cambridge University Press, 1989, pp. 187f.; *Legalism and Spirituality: Historical, Philosophical and Semiotic Notes on Legislators, Adjudicators, and Subjects* in *Religion and Law, Biblical-Judaic and Islamic Perspectives*, E.B. FIRMAGE, B.G. WEISS and J.W. WELCH (eds.), Winona Lake, Eisenbrauns, 1990, pp. 244-249; *Modelling Biblical Law: The Covenant Code*, in *Chicago-Kent Law Review* 70:4 (1995) 1818-1823.

2. *An Aye for an I?: The Semiotics of Lex Talionis in the Bible*, in W. PENCAK and J.R. LINDGREN (eds.), *New Approaches to Semiotics and the Human Sciences: Essays in Honor of Roberta Kevelson*, New York and Bern, Peter Lang, 1997, pp. 135-138; *Significato letterale. Semantica e narrativa nel diritto biblico e nella teoria contemporanea del diritto*, in *Ragion Pratica* 12 (1999) 153-177; *The Original 'Oral Law'*, in G.J. BROOKE (ed.), *Jewish Ways of Reading the Bible*, Oxford, Oxford University Press, 2000 (= JSS Supp 11), forthcoming.

find a strong expression of the wisdom value of keeping disputes out of the courts in Prov 25,7-10; indeed dispute avoidance more generally is a prominent theme in Proverbs, as reflected in the frequent admonitions against general contentiousness[3], the stress on internalisation of wisdom[4] and the value placed upon "reproof"[5]. Moreover, a not insignificant collection of wisdom themes and terminology may be identified in the Covenant Code. Within the *Mishpatim*[6] (often viewed as an originally separate, early section[7]) we find the identification of quarrels as the source of physical contention[8] and, conversely, the legitimacy of physical correction in domestic discipline[9]; the stereotype of the nocturnal thief[10]; and a section of regulations concerning disputes arising in agricultural contexts which are reflected also in the imagery of Proverbs: falling into a pit[11]; clearing land for the next crop[12]; the goring ox[13]; shepherding[14].

3. Prov 3,30; 17,1; 20,3; 26,21 (*riv*); 10,12; 13,10; 15,18; 17,14; 26,20-21; 28,25 (*madon*).
4. Prov 2,10; 3,3; 4,4; 4,21; 7,3.
5. Prov 1,23.25.30; 10,17; 12,1; 13,18; 15,10.31-32; 25,10; 27,5; 28,23.
6. Indeed, the very term *mishpat* is not infrequent in Proverbs, applied not only to inspired decisions of a king (Prov 16,10) but also to "the thoughts of the righteous" (Prov 12,5), and those who "seek the Lord" (Prov 28,5), to whom such divine understanding is also vouchsafed. Cf. the inspiration promised to the judges appointed by Jehoshaphat, *ve'imakhem bidvar mishpat*, 2 Chron 19,6.
7. E.g. A. ALT, *The Origins of Israelite Law*, in *Essays on Old Testament History and Religion*, Sheffield, JSOT Press, 1989, p. 88; B.S. CHILDS, *Exodus. A Commentary*, London, SCM Press, 1974, pp. 455-58; H.J. BOECKER, *Law and the Administration of Justice in the Old Testament and Ancient East*, London, SPCK, 1980, p. 138; C. van HOUTEN, *The Alien in Israelite Law*, Sheffield, Sheffield Academic Press, 1991, pp. 44f.; B.M. LEVINSON, *The Case For Revision and Interpolation within the Biblical Legal Corpora*, in B.M. LEVINSON (ed.), *Theory and Method in Biblical and Cuneiform Law*, Sheffield, Sheffield Academic Press, 1994, p. 40. *Contra*, J.M. SPRINKLE, *The Book of the Covenant – A Literary Approach*, Sheffield, JSOT Press, 1994, p. 204; J. VAN SETERS, *Cultic Laws in the Covenant Code (Exodus 20,22-23,33) and their Relationship to Deuteronomy and the Holiness Code*, in M. VERVENNE (ed.), *Studies in the Book of Exodus*, Leuven, Leuven University Press/Peeters, 1996, p. 321.
8. Exod 21,18f. and 21,22ff.; quarrelling is a frequent theme of Proverbs. On *riv* and *madon*, see sources cited n. 3, *supra*.
9. Exod 21,20f., cf. the use of the *shevet* in Prov 10,13; 13,24; 22,15; 23,13-14; 29,15, though the recipient here is normally the son, to whom much of Proverbs is addressed (1,8.15; 2,1; 3,1.11.21; 4,1 (plural); 4,10.20; 5,1; 6,1.21; 7,1; 23,15.19; 27,11), rather than the *eved* or *amah* of Exod 21,20f.
10. Exod 22,1-2, MT, cf. Job 24,14.16, discussed in JACKSON, *An Aye for an I?* (n. 2), p. 136; *Significato letterale* (n. 2), pp. 157-159; *The Original 'Oral Law'* (n. 2), forthcoming.
11. Exod 21,33-34, cf. Prov 26,27, and see also the metaphor of the pit as a grave: Prov 1,12.
12. Exod 22,4-5 (MT); on which see JACKSON, *A Note on Exodus 22:4 (MT)*, in *JJS* 27 (1976) 138-141; cf. Prov 24,31.
13. Exod 21,28-32.35-36, cf. the emphasis on the strength of the ox in Prov 14,4 and its potential slaughter in 7,22.
14. Exod 22,9-12 (MT), cf. Prov 27,23. See also Prov 12,10.

And in the "second half" of the Covenant Code, equal ranking and protection is afforded to God and the political authorities[15]; altruism towards one's enemy is enjoined in respect of straying and overburdened animals[16], as is concern for the "neighbour"[17] and the poor[18].

Such a preliminary statement will rightly prompt many to raise the definitional questions which have increasingly troubled those who study the place of "wisdom" within the Hebrew Bible. Indeed, for "Law and Wisdom" such questions arise in relation to "law" as well as "wisdom". The very conception of "wisdom-laws" serves in part to problematise the common assumption that relatively modern, western models may be used when discussing biblical law[19]. As for wisdom, three types of criteria are available[20]: criteria of form[21] (including terminology[22]),

---

15. Exod 22,27 (MT), "You shall not revile God, nor curse a ruler of your people", cf. Prov 24,21, "My son, fear the Lord and the king, and do not disobey either of them". See also A. PHILLIPS, *Ancient Israel's Criminal Law*, Oxford, Blackwell, 1970, pp. 42f., 160, identifying the *nasi* in Exod 22,27 with the king.

16. Exod 23,4-5; cf. Prov 26:21, "If your enemy is hungry, give him bread to eat; and if he is thirsty, give him water to drink".

17. Exod 21,35; 22,6.8.9.10.13.25; cf. Prov. 27,10.

18. Exod 22,25; 23,3.6.11; cf. Prov 13,8; 14,31; 21,13; 22,7.16.22; 28,8; Job 24,9; 29,12.16; 31,16.19; Eccles 5,8. Lohfink argues that the poor laws in the Covenant Code "take-up well-known themes of traditional Ancient Near Eastern education and royal ideology, to be just and good to the poor in daily life, in business and at court": N. LOHFINK, *Poverty in the Laws of the Ancient Near East and of the Bible*, in *TS* 52 (1991) 40; see also J.L. CRENSHAW, *Urgent Advice and Probing Questions. Collected Writings on Old Testament Wisdom*, Macon GA, Mercer University Press, 1995, pp. 417-420. But this begs the question (addressed below) whether the wisdom orientation of the Covenant Code derives from oral or literary sources. There are also reflections of the special obligation of the king in Prov 29,14; 31,9, but royal ideology is not to be imputed to most of the book's references to the poor (above).

19. See JACKSON, *Modelling Biblical Law* (n. 1), pp. 1745-49, 1760-71.

20. CRENSHAW, *Urgent Advice* (n. 18), p. 46, distinguishes between wisdom literature, wisdom tradition (a content criterion?) and wisdom thinking (a cognitive criterion?).

21. Thus, C.R. FONTAINE, *Traditional Sayings in the Old Testament*, Sheffield, The Almond Press, 1982, p. 169, rightly distinguishes between direct literary influence on the one hand and "affinities with the general values and goals of the sages" on the other.

22. In *The Intellectual Tradition in the Old Testament* (BZAW, 135), Berlin, de Gruyter, 1974, ch. 4, R.N. WHYBRAY considered the influence of the "intellectual tradition" of the wisdom literature on other parts of Old Testament literature, opting for the presence of the terminology of "wise" (*hakham*) as his definitional criterion of wisdom. At pp. 113-116, he is critical of the approach of Gerstenberger, as not having dealt adequately with the fact that in the laws the theme of the *hakham* is totally ignored. In my view, Whybray placed too much emphasis on this single criterion, particularly since the term *hakham* is an attribute of a person, while *hokhmah* is an explicit (later) characterisation of the possible source of laws; neither term is likely to figure within the content of the laws themselves. Indeed, the terminological criterion of Whybray can itself lead to a form of wisdom reductionism. Does every general endorsement of wisdom, or association of it with *Torah*, as in Ps 119, indicate "wisdom" influence? Or is the endorsement of "wisdom" a central feature of the general culture?

criteria of theme/content[23] and what might be termed pragmatic (in the linguistic sense) criteria: the purposes and behaviour patterns of the "users" of wisdom (most commonly conceived in scribal[24] or didactic[25] terms). More important, for present purposes, is the identification of the setting and concomitants of the kind of oral "wisdom-laws" for which I am arguing, and the relationship between the transformation from the oral to the written in the two spheres conventionally referred to as "law" and "wisdom". After inspecting these substantive issues, I shall revisit the question of definition.

Biblical scholarship has tended to associate law with wisdom in its written, literary form, following the lead of Jeremiah (8,8):

> How can you say, 'We are wise,
> and the law of the LORD is with us'?
> But, behold, the false pen of the scribes
> has made it into a lie.

This, it is commonly argued, is directed specifically against the wisdom associations of Deuteronomy[26]. Moreover, Blenkinsopp argues for increasing *convergence* between law and wisdom. He highlights the following expressions of the injunction against judicial bribery[27].

Prov 17,23: A wicked man accepts a bribe from the bosom to pervert the ways of justice.
Exod 23,8:   And you shall take no bribe, for a bribe blinds the officials, and subverts the cause of the righteous.
Deut 16,19: And you shall not take a bribe, for a bribe blinds the eyes of the wise and subverts the cause of the righteous.

Blenkinsopp stresses the fact that the version in Deuteronomy replaces the *pikhim* ("officials") of Exodus with *hakhamim* ("the wise"). Certainly, it does[28], but it is interesting that (a) the closest literary relationship here is between Exod 23 and Deut 16, and (b) both Exod 23 and Deut 16 might be regarded as "more proverbial than proverbs", at

---

23. As exemplified in the last paragraph.
24. E.g., M. WEINFELD, *Deuteronomy and the Deuteronomic School*, Oxford, Clarendon Press, 1972, pp. 158-164.
25. Thus, J. BLENKINSOPP, *Sage Priest Prophet. Religious and Intellectual Leadership in Ancient Israel*, Louiseville, Ke.: John Knox Press, 1995, pp. 39, 81f., stresses the moral teaching function of the priesthood.
26. WEINFELD, *Deuteronomy* (n. 24), p. 158; BLENKINSOPP, *Sage Priest Prophet* (n. 25), p. 40.
27. *Sage Priest Prophet* (n. 25), p. 36.
28. Whybray (n. 22) would have approved of the use of this criterion.

least in their use of a striking metaphor (blindness) to convey their message.

Perhaps the most extreme version of the view that association of law with wisdom in the Hebrew Bible is to be located at the literary, rather than the oral stage, has been provided recently by Fitzpatrick-McKinley, who takes what I would regard as an entirely diffusionist view: the biblical codes originate purely as imitations of the comparable documents in the ancient Near Eastern scribal tradition[29]. In my view, a movement from orality to literacy is traceable independently in both Law and Wisdom. In both, that movement reflects increasing professionalisation. It is reasonable to start with the assumption that both oral law and oral wisdom are "popular", while written law and literary wisdom are not popular, but rather the preserve of an intelligentsia or bureaucratic cadre. In this paper, I shall explore whether we can find an association between law and wisdom at the oral, popular stage. To do so, I shall argue, we have to commence by making the definitional problem appear even worse before it can get better – by bringing narrative into the equation. We also have to pay proper attention not only to the semantics but also to the pragmatics of speech: not just what is said, but how it is used in speech behaviour.

II. ORALITY IN WISDOM

Within the Book of Proverbs, we encounter an overwhelming stress on *oral* instruction: wisdom has a (public) "voice"[30] and "calls"[31] its addressees, who (are supposed to) "listen"[32]; the "ear" is the channel of wisdom[33] and specifically of *torah*[34]; *mitsvot* are also oral, parental instructions[35]. Virtually isolated is the reference to writing which occurs early in the "Second Collection": "Have I not written for you thirty sayings of admonition and knowledge"[36]. Often, we may note, it is disciplined oral instruction, the instrument of discipline being the same *shevet*[37] that the master uses on his *eved* or *amah,* with fatal effect, in

---

29. A. FITZPATRICK-MCKINLEY, *The Transformation of Torah from Scribal Advice to Law,* Sheffield, Sheffield Academic Press, 1999. See my forthcoming review in *JSS.*
30. Prov 1,24; 8,1.
31. *kara:* Prov 8,1.4.
32. *shama:* Prov 1,5.33; 4,10; 7,24; 22,17.
33. Prov 2,2; 4,20; 5,1.
34. Prov 28,9.
35. Prov 2,1; 3,1.
36. Prov 22,20, which A. Cohen, *Proverbs,* Hindhead, Soncino Press, 1945, pp. 149f., compares with Eccles 12,10.12.
37. See n. 9, *supra.*

Exod 21:20. Large sections of the Book consist in individual proverbs strung together in a literary series. Are we to suppose that this is the form in which the instruction provided by Proverbs was orally conveyed – by repeating, perhaps learning by heart, such sequences of aphorisms? I venture to suggest that one could hardly think of anything more boring and pedagogically counter-productive. A preferable view, in terms of educational theory and its underlying cognitive and linguistic assumptions, is that of Fontaine, who looks to the narratives for evidence of what she calls "proverb performance"[38]. Recall the story of the woman of Tekoa, sent by Joab to David to provide a parable designed to prompt the return of Absalom. Her plea to David is as follows (2 Sam 14,5-7, *RSV*):

> Alas, I am a widow; my husband is dead. And your handmaid had two sons, and they quarrelled with one another[39] in the field; there was no one to part them, and one struck the other and killed him. And now the whole family has risen against your handmaid, and they say, 'Give up the man who struck his brother, that we may kill him for the life of his brother whom he slew'; and so they would destroy the heir also. Thus they would quench my coal which is left, and leave to my husband neither name nor remnant upon the face of the earth.

What *locus standi* does the woman have and what resources does she use? She is introduced into the narrative with the statement: "And Jo'ab sent to Tekoa, and fetched from there a wise woman" (2 Sam 14,2). However, it is the woman's status as a widow, not her status as a wise woman which explains recourse to the king (though it is her standing as a "wise woman" that prompted Joab to employ her): there is a strong tradition, both in the ancient Near East and the Bible, which stresses the particular responsibility of the king towards various classes of powerless

---

38. *Traditional Sayings* (n. 21), pp. VII-VIII, defining "proverb performance" as "the way in which a saying is selected from a given stock of proverbs, applied to a given context and the "rules" by which it is interpreted by its hearers". So viewed, the proverb appears as "a vital, traditional wisdom which is operant in society at a variety of levels and not simply in the elitist bureaucracies of the court sages and scribes. The functional goal of such traditional wisdom is the restoration of order in society (according to that society's construal of "order") through the use of verbal behaviors rather than physically destructive ones." Cf. C.V. CAMP, *The Wise Women of 2 Samuel: A Role Model for Women in Early Israel*, in *CBQ* 43 (1981) 18. Fontaine's analysis of Judg 8,2; 21; 1 Sam 16,7; 24,14, and 1 Kings 20,11, reveals the proverb as a biblical model for conflict resolution "by means of negotiation rather than aggression" (*Traditional Sayings*, p. VIII).

39. *veyinatsu sheneyhem*, cf. the terminology of Exod 21,22. L.L. LYKE, *King David with the Wise Woman of Tekoa*, Sheffield, Sheffield Academic Press, 1997, p. 89, points out, however, that the closest analogy to the parable, in terms of vocabulary if not theme, is Deut 25,11: "When men struggle (*yinatsu*) together, a man and his brother, and the wife of one approaches to save (*lehatsil*) her husband from (*miyad*) the one who would strike him (*makeyhu*)…"

persons, including widows[40]. There has been dispute as to whether the woman "acts" to a script provided by Joab, or displays independent wisdom[41]. It is difficult, however, to imagine that Joab could have "scripted" the woman's responses in the entire dialogue (four conversational turns) that ensues, even if her first and last speech were pre-rehearsed:

David: "Go to your house, and I will give orders concerning you." (v. 8)

Woman: "On me be the guilt, my lord the king, and on my father's house; let the king and his throne be guiltless." (v. 9)

David: "If any one says anything to you, bring him to me, and he shall never touch you again." (v. 10)

Woman: Pray let the king invoke the LORD your God, that the avenger of blood slay no more, and my son be not destroyed." (v. 11)

David: "As the LORD lives, not one hair of your son shall fall to the ground." (v. 11)

Woman: "Pray let your handmaid speak a word to my lord the king." (v. 12).

David: "Speak." (v. 12).

Woman: "Why then have you planned such a thing against the people of God? For in giving this decision the king convicts himself, inasmuch as the king does not bring his banished one home again. We must all die, we are like water spilt on the ground, which cannot be gathered up again; but God will not take away the life of him who devises means not to keep his banished one an outcast. Now I have come to say this to my lord the king because the people have

---

40. See, e.g., F.C. FENSHAM, *Widow, Orphan and the Poor in Ancient Near Eastern Legal and Wisdom Literature*, in *JNES* 21 (1962) 129-139. Cf., in this context, A. ROFÉ, *The History of the Cities of Refuge in Biblical Law*, in S. JAPHET (ed.), *Studies in Bible* (Scripta Hierosolymitana, 31), Jerusalem, Magnes Press, 1986, p. 219.

41. For R.N. WHYBRAY, *The Succession Narrative: A Study of II Samuel 9-20, 1 Kings 1 and 2*, London, SCM Press, 1968, p. 59, Joab has told her precisely what to say (including, presumably, the use of the metaphor of quenching her coal); indeed, "Joab instructed the woman with respect to the entire content of her conversation with the king and not only the initial speech or the general strategy." Thus the story is one of Joab's wisdom rather than that of the woman. Cf. G.G. NICOL, *The Wisdom of Joab and the Wise Woman of Tekoa*, in *ST* 36 (1982) 97. *Contra*, J. HOFTIJZER, *David and the Tekoite Woman*, in *VT* 20 (1970) 444 n. 1, who stresses the woman's diplomatic skill in persuading David to give the wished for ruling and at the same time confronting him with its consequences for his own situation, without provoking any fit of temper either against Joab or herself. Cf. A. BRENNER, *The Israelite Woman*, Sheffield, JSOT Press, 1985, p. 35; CAMP (n. 38), p. 14f. n. 1. See also Lyke (n. 39), pp. 182f., 191.

made me afraid; and your handmaid thought, 'I will speak to the king; it may be that the king will perform the request of his servant. For the king will hear, and deliver his servant from the hand of the man who would destroy me and my son together from the heritage of God.' And your handmaid thought, 'The word of my lord the king will set me at rest'; for my lord the king is like the angel of God to discern good and evil. The LORD your God be with you!" (vv. 13-17)

What is it that qualifies the woman's performance as "wise"? She uses two striking metaphors, which may well have been "proverbial" (whatever that means: again, let us defer the question of definition): in her first speech: "thus they would quench my coal which is left"[42]; in her last: "We must all die, we are like water spilt on the ground, which cannot be gathered up again." But beyond that, she has to keep the conversation with David going, despite the king's clear initial reluctance to intervene. Brenner comments on the combination of rhetorical and psychological skill she deploys in manipulating David to achieve her (Joab's) end[43]. Fontaine comments that we must assume that the local "wise women" of 2 Samuel 14 (Tekoa) and 20 (Abel) were esteemed and considered "wise" for their adroitness in the use of traditional language to deal with conflict-ridden situations[44]. Some have suggested a "professional" status for such women[45]; indeed, Fontaine, has herself cited a Middle Kingdom Stele of the Chamberlain Intef, which includes the lines: "I am a speaker in the hall of justice, Skilled in speech in anx-

---

42. 2 Sam 14,7, cf. Prov 25,21-22; JACKSON, *Modelling Biblical Law* (n. 1), pp. 1764f.; ID., *Justice and Righteousness in the Bible: Rule of Law or Royal Paternalism?*, in *Zeitschrift für Altorientalische und Biblische Rechtsgeschichte* IV (1998) 249f. F.W. GOLKA, *The Leopard's Spots. Biblical and African Wisdom in Proverbs*, Edinburgh, T.&T. Clark, 1993, p. 76, comments, in comparing the use of proverbs by the Anang of southeastern Nigeria, that such proverbs "are not used to quote judicial precedent, but rather they have a function of supporting one's own case and of undermining that of one's opponent."

43. *The Israelite Woman* (n. 41), p. 35: "This 'wise' woman can be commissioned to manipulate a person to act the way she wants him to. She achieves that by enlisting the person's cooperation instead of arousing his anger or animosity. She can be counted on for sensing undercurrents of emotions and opinions, and for utilizing them. She can adapt easily to changes in the atmosphere, and redirects these changes according to her purpose through improvization." On the use of the juridical parable as psychological manipulation, see also CAMP (n. 38), p. 21.

44. *Traditional Sayings* (n. 21), p. 142.

45. W. MCKANE, *Prophets and Wise Men*, London, SCM Press, 1965, p. 59; S. WEEKS, *Early Israelite Wisdom*, Oxford, Clarendon Press, 1994, pp. 70f.; CRENSHAW, *Urgent Advice* (n. 18), p. 591.

ious situations", as "perhaps the most complete statement of how greatly the art of "good speech" was valued – and the practical uses to which such an art was put"[46]. I do not think we need enter into the question – or indeed the definition – of "professionalism" in this context. It suffices to conclude that the Tekoite was employed by Joab on this occasion for her rhetorical skill, which included the deployment of traditional sayings, and she put them to effective use.

The cases of proverb performance discussed by Fontaine are set very often in conflictual (narrative) situations, which are resolved by speech-based forms of dispute resolution. A story like that of the woman of Tekoa provides us with arguments of two distinct kinds: first, it may be taken to provide evidence of a rhetorical practice, the actual use of proverbs in dispute resolution; secondly, the very telling of the story may have had a didactic function: the blood feud ought not to be pursued mechanistically, in a way such as will extinguish an entire family line. Indeed, a proverb may often function not as the beginning of an argument but rather as its distillation, sometimes even as a rhetorical flourish. When we turn to a literary production like the Book of Proverbs we encounter an attempt – views may differ as to how successful – to replace the presupposed social/narrative life settings of use of many individual proverbs with a set of interdiscursivities: relationships between the end products of this process of distillation.

III. Orality in Law

The search for the oral origins of Israelite law has been conducted largely through form-critical arguments, particularly the form-critical analysis of Albrecht Alt. He distinguished between the (to him, Israelite) apodictic forms and the (to him, non-indigenous) casuistic, associating the former with the Israelite cult and the latter with an administration of justice which reflected the practices of the Canaanite environment[47]. Neither the Israelite/Canaanite distinction nor the cultic *Sitz* of the apodictic law are widely followed today[48]. But the basic method, of seeking the settings in life of the speech patterns whose traces survive in the literary sources, remains a useful starting point for the investigation of the pre-history of Israelite law.

---

46. *Traditional Sayings* (n. 21), pp. 142f. She compares Prov 1,2-6 (*sed quaere*).
47. ALT, *Origins* (n. 7), esp. pp. 93-103, 125-132.
48. See, e.g., F. CRÜSEMANN, *The Torah. Theology and Social History of Old Testament Law*, Edinburgh, T.&T. Clark, 1996, p. 11.

As for the apodictic law, Alt (controversially) saw it as having three versions[49]. For each one of them, it is possible to locate the *Sitz im Leben* in the domestic setting. Thus, we find in Proverbs the use of the *participial* form in precisely the same context – domestic relations – as we find it used in the participial section of the *Mishpatim*. In the latter, two of the four participial provisions are offences against parents:

Exod 21,15: וּמַכֵּה אָבִיו וְאִמּוֹ מוֹת יוּמָת

Exod 21,17: וּמְקַלֵּל אָבִיו וְאִמּוֹ מוֹת יוּמָת

with which we may compare:

Prov 20.20: מְקַלֵּל אָבִיו וְאִמּוֹ יִדְעַךְ נֵרוֹ בְּאִישׁוֹן [בֶּאֱשׁוּן] חֹשֶׁךְ

Prov 28,24: גּוֹזֵל אָבִיו וְאִמּוֹ וְאֹמֵר אֵין־פָּשַׁע חָבֵר הוּא לְאִישׁ מַשְׁחִית

It is hardly difficult to reconstruct the setting which explains these parallels in both form and content. Within the constant theme of domestic instruction in Proverbs[50] (one in which the role of mother[51] as well as father is stressed) we frequently encounter references to physical correction[52]. Indeed, the very term *musar* is sometimes used with that connotation[53]. Some children will react against that correction, either verbally (cursing[54]) or physically[55].

49. ALT, *Origins* (n. 7), pp. 109-123. The classification of the participial form, in particular, has proved controversial. Alt associated the caesura between subject and predicate with "the metre of a five-beat Hebrew verse" (p. 109). In favour of such an apodictic classification, see, e.g., BOECKER (n. 7), pp. 194-201 (reviewing earlier German scholarship); L. SCHWIENHORST-SCHÖNBERGER, *Das Bundesbuch (Ex 20,22-23,33). Studien zu seiner Entstehung und Theologie* (BZAW, 188), Berlin, de Gruyter, 1990, pp. 213ff. C. HOUTMAN, *Das Bundesbuch. Ein Kommentar,* Leiden, E.J. Brill, 1997, p. 14, regards them, essentially, as casuistic in form but apodictic in force. In favour of a casuistic classification, see G. WENHAM, *Legal Forms in the Book of the Covenant,* in *Tyndale Bulletin* 22 (1971) 97, 102; M. WEINFELD, *The Origin of the Apodictic Law. An Overlooked Source,* in *VT* 23 (1973) 63; D. PATRICK, *Old Testament Law,* London, SCM Press, 1985, pp. 156f., who, while seemingly approving Alt's view that all three types of apodictic law "would engender a different sort of transaction with an audience than would those carefully calibrated conditional statements Alt termed 'casuistic', and therefore must belong to a different oral setting," sees similarities between the participial and casuistic forms: "… like casuistic law, these laws are impersonal and judicial, whereas apodictic commandments are personal and moral (nonjuridical)" (at 72). Cf. SPRINKLE (n. 2), p. 74: "essentially casuistic".

50. E.g. Prov 4,4.11 and sources in n. 9.

51. Prov 1,8; 6,20: *torat imekhah,* and the role of the mother in Prov 29,15 (which seems to imply that the mother also has a role in physical correction), 30,11.17; 31,1-2.26.

52. E.g. Prov 13,24 and further sources cited n. 9, *supra*.

53. Prov 13,24; 22,15; 23,13.

54. Prov 20,20 (above); cf. 30,11.17.

55. For parallels to Exod 21,15 from the ancient Near East as well as the Bible, see FITZPATRICK-MCKINLEY (n. 29), pp. 120f.

The form *lo* or *al* + a verb in the 2nd person, as in the Decalogue and frequently elsewhere, may be regarded as the "classical" version of the apodictic form. It is, of course, a natural way of expressing a *prohibition*, and as such is found in the domestic setting, as in Gen 28,6, where Isaac prohibits Jacob from taking a Canaanite wife in the words:

וַיְצַו עָלָיו לֵאמֹר לֹא־תִקַּח אִשָּׁה מִבְּנוֹת כְּנָעַן׃

The form is also found in Proverbs (3,30), in the context of dispute avoidance:

אַל־תָּרוֹב [תָּרִיב] עִם־אָדָם חִנָּם אִם־לֹא גְמָלְךָ רָעָה׃
Do not contend with a man for no reason,
when he has done you no harm.

Alt's third form was that of *curses*: *arur*. Here too, we do not have to search far in the biblical narratives for a domestic setting: not only cursing in reaction to domestic discipline[56], but also the use by both Isaac and Jacob of deathbed blessings and curses in regulating the future of the clan[57].

As for the casuistic form, it is much more difficult to find an oral life setting with which to associate it. Blenkinsopp nevertheless suggests the following relationship to wisdom thinking:

> Case law is also comparable to the kind of aphorism found in Proverbs, in the sense that both draw on social experience to link act with consequence, the former in the legal sphere, the latter in that of moral behavior in general. Common to both case or common law and aphorisms, therefore, is the association of specific behaviors with certain consequences, based on the accumulated experience of the social group[58].

---

56. *Supra* n. 54.
57. See esp. Gen 27,12 (Isaac), where Jacob fears that if the ruse is discovered he will receive a curse rather than a blessing. In the event, that is, in effect, what Esau receives (Gen 27,39-40), though described in the language of blessing – what we might term a "mixed blessing". Cf. Jacob's blessing of Reuben in Gen 49,3-4. There may well be a connection here with the wisdom theme of the relationship between good conduct and the motivation that you "live", as explored very recently by S. BURKES, *Wisdom and Law: Choosing Life in Ben Sira and Baruch*, in *JSJ* 30/3 (1999) pp. 253ff.
58. *Sage Priest Prophet* (n. 25), p. 38. Cf. his *Wisdom and Law in the Old Testament*, Oxford, Oxford University Press, 1995², p. 92, where the casuistic form is described as "really a case of group experience applied to the solution of specific problems. In this respect it is analogous to those proverbial sayings... in which, as experience teaches, certain consequences are seen to flow from certain behaviours. In such a society, then, law may be described as a specialization of tribal wisdom." See also R.N. WHYBRAY, *The Book of Proverbs: A Survey of Modern Study*, Leiden, Brill, 1995, pp. 29-32, and his account (at 26) of the 1960 article of J.-P. AUDET, *Origines comparées de la double tradition de la loi et de la sagesse dans le Proche-Orient ancien*, in *Akten des 25*

However, the casuistic form is not prominent in Proverbs, and where we find it, it is in a 2nd person (thus more directly didactic) version: e.g. Prov 3,24

אִם־תִּשְׁכַּב לֹא־תִפְחָד וְשָׁכַבְתָּ וְעָרְבָה שְׁנָתֶךָ:
If you sit down, you will not be afraid;
when you lie down, your sleep will be sweet.

Moreover, we have a number of narratives (mostly regarding disputes arising during the Israelites' wanderings in the desert) regarding disputes, their resolution and the resultant statement of rules for the future: the casuistic form does *not* appear in the narratives of dispute resolution as the regular formula of either decision/judgment or rule for the future (though it is found sometimes in the latter context). Thus

(a) Even in the first case of the daughters of Zelophehad, where the rules applicable for the future are expressed as a paragraph of casuistic laws[59], the narrative itself distinguishes that form from the speech act of decision-making in the case itself: Num 27,7:

כֵּן בְּנוֹת צְלָפְחָד דֹּבְרֹת נָתֹן תִּתֵּן לָהֶם אֲחֻזַּת נַחֲלָה בְּתוֹךְ אֲחֵי אֲבִיהֶם

and the authority of the casuistic paragraph derives not from the decision *per se* but rather from God's command to Moses to proclaim it[60]. Without such proclamation, no precedent would have been set for the future[61].

Internationalen Orientalistenkongresses, Moscow, 1962, I, pp. 352-57 (to which I have not had direct access): "He saw the origins of Israel's wisdom literature not in generalized "popular" proverbs but, more precisely, in a pre-literary and even pre-urban oral instruction promulgated in a tribal society and with the authority of patriarchal fathers or tribal heads, based on the accumulated experience of the past and having something of the force of law: in fact, he maintained that wisdom and law had a common origin as regulators of the *mores* of society. The later reduction of the proverbs to written form did not change their essential character."

59. Though not precisely in the form of the *mishpatim:* the first (Num 27,8) commences with *ish ki,* commonly found in the priestly source, followed by three *ve'im* clauses.

60. CRÜSEMANN, *Torah* (n. 48), p. 84, has plausibly suggested that these narratives are designed to provide authority to propound new, divinely-authorised rules, which are *not* claimed to have been given on Sinai.

61. Cf. B.S. JACKSON, *Some Semiotic Questions for Biblical Law*, in A.M. FUSS (ed.), *The Oxford Conference Volume* (Jewish Law Association Studies 3), Atlanta, Scholars Press, 1987, pp. 6-9. An argument to similar effect has been advanced by R. KNIERIM, *The Problem of Ancient Israel's Prescriptive Legal Traditions*, in D. PATRICK (ed.), *Thinking Biblical Law* (Semeia 45), Atlanta, Scholars Press, 1989, pp. 16f., against Liedke's account of the casuistic laws. The latter, Knierim argues, fails conceptually to distinguish between a case decision and the use of prescriptive language in formulating a binding (legislative) rule for the future. "In these formulations, Liedke actually misses the point in his own awareness of the differences between a judgment and a law. It is the question as

(b) In the second case involving the daughters, where the tribal leaders seek successfully to prevent the land inherited by the daughters from being alienated from the tribe[62], the same speech form is used in relation to the decision itself: Num 36,5: *ken mateh benei yosef dovrim,* but the rules for the future are here stated in an apodictic form (Num 36,7-9).

(c) In the case of the blasphemer, the decision is stated as a direct command (Lev 24,14: *hotsi et hamekalel...*) while the rules for the future, again introduced by a direct command from God to Moses to proclaim them, follow in an elaborate literary mix of short casuistic (*ish ki,* vv. 15, 17, 19) and participial (vv. 16, 18, 21) provisions and other apodictic forms (vv. 16, 20, 22)[63].

(d) The case of the passover defaulters does not state the decision separately, but the rules for the future are again a mix of casuistic forms (*ish ish ki... ish asher*) and apodictic (Num 9,10-13).

(e) David's adjudication regarding the booty after the defeat of the Amalekites at Ziklag (I Sam 30,23-25) commences with a decision using a similar speech form to those in the desert narratives (*lo ta'asu ken...,* v. 23), and the rule stated to have been adopted as *hok umishpat* to the present day (v. 25) is stated apodictically (if not proverbially): *kehelek hayored bamilhamah ukehelek hayoshev al hakelim yahdav yahaloku,* v. 24[64].

Indeed, the most influential theory which associates the casuistic form with judicial decision-making in individual cases is *not* based on Alt's kind of form critical argument, seeking the underlying *speech* patterns: rather it is what we might call a primitive *literary* theory, that of the derivation of the casuistic form from (written) "trial transcripts". In surviving ancient Near Eastern trial transcripts, we find a statement of the circumstances followed by a statement of the verdict. Liedke argued that by excising the names of the parties and other purely circumstantial detail, the two statements could be combined so as to generate, respec-

---

to what constitutes a law as law once it is transformed from the formulation of a decision into a prescriptive statement. Liedke does not explain why such transformations happened, who made them, how the persons who made them functioned, and what the function of these new formulations was meant to be."

62. On the relationship between the two cases, and the narrative function of their separation in the text, see D.R. ULRICH, *The Framing Function of the Narratives about Zelophehad's Daughters,* in *JETS* 41 (1998) 529-538.

63. See further JACKSON, "Talion and Purity: Some Glosses on Mary Douglas", in J.F.A. SAWYER (ed.), *Reading Leviticus, A Conversation with Mary Douglas,* Sheffield: Sheffield Academic Press, 1996, pp. 119-21.

64. See further on this narrative, JACKSON, *Modelling Biblical Law* (n. 1), pp. 1774f. n. 89.

tively, the protasis and apodosis of the casuistic form[65], a view which has been followed by both Otto[66] and Crüsemann[67].

Such arguments, we may note, assume the existence of written trial records in ancient Israel, no evidence of which has yet been found[68]. But even if they existed in the form we know from the ancient Near East, there is no necessity in identifying them as the source of the form: the clauses follow a natural narrative sequence[69]. The "trial transcript" theory does highlight, however, an apparent paradox in dealing with the *Mishpatim*. On the one hand, they are widely regarded as the earliest of the biblical legal collections; they do, as argued above, have notable thematic and some terminological links with individual proverbs; and in terms of content they are compatible with an early, pre-institutional stage of legal development[70]. On the other hand, they seem to have the closest literary connection with the codes of the Ancient Near East. This would appear to suggest that the oral tradition which preceded the scribal formulation of these laws itself had elements in common with the

---

65. G. LIEDKE, *Gestalt und Bezeichnung alttestamentlicher Rechtssätze: Eine formgeschichtlich terminologische Studie* (WMANT, 39), Neukirchen-Vluyn, Neukirchener Verlag, 1971, pp. 39ff., esp. 54-56. For such trial records, see more recently those from Nippur, discussed by C. LOCHER, *Die Ehre einer Frau in Israel*, Freiburg (Schweiz), Universitätsverlag, 1986, pp. 93-109. As BOECKER (n. 7), p. 153, puts it: "For the account of a suit to become a casuistic legal principle, it had to undergo a radical process of abstraction. Names and above all circumstances and details were excised. The only thing finally remaining was the case and its verdict raised by its conditional formulation to the level of universal validity", citing E. GERSTENBERGER, *Wesen und Herkunft des "apodiktischen Rechts"* (WMANT, 20), Neukirchen-Vluyn, Neukirchener Verlag, 1965, p. 24 n. 2, and quoting Liedke (pp. 55f.): "the development of the casuistic principle began... as the attempt to preserve and hand on, in written or oral form, a judicial sentence." Note the indeterminacy here regarding the form of transmission. J. GOODY, *The Interface Between the Written and the Oral*, Cambridge, Cambridge University Press, 1987, p. 74, sees the process as associated specifically with literacy: "... the stripping away of the individual and the casual, as well as the process of selection this involves, is part of the process of recording a court case or any other set of events. Moreover the very fact of writing them down means that one can make, record, and hence *compare* repeated observations in a precise away."

66. E. OTTO, *Town and Rural Countryside in Ancient Israelite Law: Reception and Redaction in Cuneiform and Israelite Law*, in *JSOT* 57 (1993) 4, 18, 22.

67. CRÜSEMANN, *Torah* (n. 48), p. 160.

68. We do, by contrast, have reflections of orally delivered verdicts: *tsadik ata* (Prov 24,24; cf. BOECKER (n. 7), p. 38); even perhaps *naki* in Exod 21,18.

69. For the theoretical foundations of this claim, see B.S. JACKSON, *Making Sense in Law*, Liverpool, Deborah Charles Publications, 1995, pp. 144-48, 203-205, 218f., 228-234. On the use of the casuistic form in other legal cultures, see B.S. JACKSON, *Evolution and Foreign Influence in Ancient Law*, in *American Journal of Comparative Law* 16 (1968) 381 and n. 48; S. Segert, *Form and Function of Ancient Israelite, Greek and Roman Legal Sentences*, in H.A. Hoffner (ed.), *Orient and Occident, Essays presented to C.H. Gordon*, Neukirchen-Vluyn, Neukirchener Verlag, 1973, pp. 164f.

70. See n. 1, *supra*.

orally transmitted custom of the region.

The conclusion of this review of the form critical argument is thus that whereas the very forms (as well as some of the content) of the apodictic laws can be associated with domestic speech forms, we cannot say the same of the casuistic form, even though there are other reasons to believe that the themes of the casuistic laws would have been of domestic concern.

IV. WISDOM, LAW, AND NARRATIVE

If the themes of the casuistic laws would have been of domestic concern, how might that concern have been expressed? Not, I suggested earlier, by rote learning of proverbs in the abstract. They need to be put in a narrative context. That narrative context may be either ordinary social experience, or the narratives that provide the cultural context of that social experience, or, indeed, the interaction of the two[71] (the relationship between ordinary social experience and TV drama – even "soaps" – is the modern counterpart). Story telling, and even our knowledge of stereotypical social situations, with their narrative structures[72], are accompanied always by what may variously be described as modalities, attitudes, affect. They are "moral tales" in that they prompt social evaluation (often through the very language in which they are told), even though such evaluation is not made explicit. Indeed, it may be all the more powerful just because it is not made explicit. Let me illustrate my argument with two examples of wisdom or wisdom-associated sources where the evaluation is, in fact, a critical one.

My first is Prov 24,29:

אַל־תֹּאמַר כַּאֲשֶׁר עָשָׂה־לִי כֵּן אֶעֱשֶׂה־לּוֹ אָשִׁיב לָאִישׁ כְּפָעֳלוֹ׃
Do not say, "I will do to him as he has done to me;
I will pay the man back for what he has done."

We might well be tempted to interpret this against our assumptions regarding everyday social interaction. But the language in which it is expressed – the formula *ka'asher* + *asah l'* – is the very language in which the talionic principle is expressed not only in two biblical laws[73]

---

71. For a classic exposition of this theme, see D. DAUBE, *The Exodus Pattern in the Bible*, London, Faber & Faber, 1963.
72. I here use the term in a more technical, semiotic sense. See my *Making Sense in Law* (n. 69), pp. 141-163.
73. Deut 19,19, *va'asitem lo ka'asher zamam la'asot le'ahiv*; Lev 24,19, *ka'asher asah, ken ye'aseh lo*.

but also two biblical narratives[74]. In Judg 1,6-7 the Canaanite king "Adoni-Bezek" responds to his mutilatory punishment with the words: "Seventy kings with their thumbs and their great toes cut off used to pick up scraps under my table; as I have done, so God has requited me" (כַּאֲשֶׁר עָשִׂיתִי כֵּן שִׁלַּם־לִי אֱלֹהִים)[75]. More significant, in that it is not accompanied by a justification in terms of divine punishment, is Samson's invocation of the principle (to the consternation of some modern commentators). Recall the structure of events: Samson's father-in-law had given his wife to his companion (Judg 14,20), after Samson had gone back to his own father's house (14,19), thus seemingly deserting/divorcing her[76]. Samson takes revenge through the blazing foxes (15,4-6), a purely property-oriented response[77]. The Philistines clearly recognise that this act is in response to the loss of his bride (15,6). They then burn the bride and her father (15,6). Samson swears further revenge for this: "'If this is what you do, I swear I will be avenged upon you, and after that I will quit'. And he smote them hip and thigh with great slaughter" (15,7-8). The Philistines then attack Lehi, claiming that they want to take Samson prisoner and "to do to him as he did to us" (15,10): לַעֲשׂוֹת לוֹ כַּאֲשֶׁר עָשָׂה לָנוּ. The Judaites send 3000 men to Samson, and ask him to explain his actions[78]. Samson does so by using the same *ka'asher* formula which the Philistines had used in justifying their own actions: "And he said to them, 'As they did to me, so have I done to them'", כַּאֲשֶׁר עָשׂוּ לִי כֵּן עָשִׂיתִי לָהֶם (15,11). The reference, in context, is surely to

---

74. The talionic idea is, of course, a common theme in biblical narrative (e.g. the deceiver deceived (Jacob), the kidnapped as kidnapper (Joseph). The brothers who put Joseph into a *bor* (Gen 37, 22.28.29) are themselves threatened by him (Gen 42,16, though ultimately only Shimon suffers this fate: Gen 42,18.24) with imprisonment; the Egyptian dungeon where Joseph was himself imprisoned is itself described as a *bor* (Gen 41,14). On the story of Judah and Tamar, P.J. NEL, *The Talion Principle in Old Testament Narratives*, in *JNSL* 20 (1994) 23, observes: "In terms of the talion principle her deed was justified, because Judah had deprived her of having an offspring."

75. See also B.S. JACKSON, *Essays in Jewish and Comparative Legal History*, Leiden, E.J. Brill, 1975, pp. 83f., 102f. D. PIATTELLI, *Zedaqà: Pursuit of Justice and the Instrument of 'Ius Talionis'*, in *Israel Law Review* 29 (1995) 68, regards this as one of the first cases which "transferred to divine justice a punishment of already human application."

76. As her father later claims: "I really thought that you utterly hated her; so I gave her to your companion", Judg 14,2.

77. Which some see as based on the metaphor which Samson had himself used when he found out that his wife had revealed the riddle to her people: "If you had not plowed with my heifer, you would not have found out my riddle": Judg 14,18.

78. Their purpose at first appears to be ambivalent. Is it to warn and protect him, as the numbers involved might suggest, or is it to seek an explanation from him and, failing an adequate response, to hand him over, as their comments to him might suggest: "Do you not know that the Philistines are rulers over us? What then is this that you have done to us?": 15,11.

Samson's "great slaughter" in response (explicitly: "If this is what you do ...", 15,7) to the killing of his wife and father-in-law[79], rather than to his destruction of their fields by the foxes[80]. Clearly, that explanation does not satisfy the Judaites – or, if it does, they fear that it will not satisfy the Philistines – and they carry out their mission to take Samson prisoner and hand him over to the Philistines (Judg 15,12-13). What apparently made Samson's justification problematic was its quantitative rather than its qualitative disproportion – a characteristic of those expression of talion where we find this *ka'asher* formula rather than the alternative *tahat* formula. It may well be such unacceptable connotations of this use of the *ka'asher* formula in narrative sources that our proverb is seeking to target.

My second example is the law of primogeniture in Deut 21,15-17:

> If a man has two wives, the one loved and the other disliked, and they have borne him children, both the loved and the disliked, and if the first-born son is hers that is disliked, then on the day when he assigns his possessions as an inheritance to his sons, he may not treat the son of the loved as the first-born in preference to the son of the disliked, who is the first-born, but he shall acknowledge the first-born, the son of the disliked, by giving him a double portion of all that he has, for he is the first issue of his strength; the right of the first-born is his.

The law of primogeniture is not phrased, as we might have expected, in general terms: the first born shall have a double portion. Rather, it is formulated in terms of a contest between the sons of different wives, where the oldest son happens to be the son of the wife in disfavour. On one reading, all the law is saying is: do not discriminate against that son for that reason. Moreover, nowhere else in the Hebrew Bible do we hear of a "double portion" – except in the narrative of the succession to Jacob, where the two sons of Joseph take his place, thus effectively giving his line just such a double portion. That Joseph, the son of the favoured Rachel, is given the birthright in preference to Reuben, the (oldest) son, who happens to be the son of Leah (the unfavoured wife), is indeed stated explicitly in 1 Chron 5,1:

> The sons of Reuben the first-born of Israel (for he was the first-born; but because he polluted his father's couch, his birthright was given to the sons of Joseph the son of Israel, so that he is not enrolled in the genealogy according to the birthright ...

---

79. Cf. NEL (n. 74), p. 26.
80. Or, if it is that as well, the latter is in response to the deprivation of his bride – and her "fruits": Cf. NEL (n. 74), p. 26, citing H. GESE, *Die altere Simsonüberlieferung (Richter c. 14-15)*, in his *Alttestamentliche Studien*, Tubingen, J.C.B. Mohr, 1990, pp. 57f.

Carmichael has very plausibly argued that the Deuteronomic law has the patriarchal narrative in mind[81]; indeed, that it was probably composed as a criticism of Jacob's behaviour[82]. And the Deuteronomic laws are widely viewed as the closest to the wisdom literature. It is difficult to imagine what else might have prompted the formulation of the primogeniture law in this way. And even if it does have an independent, customary origin, the law, thus written, could hardly be read – or listened to – by anyone familiar with the patriarchal narratives without evoking such associations.

Can we transpose this relationship – between the law and the narrative – from the literary setting where Carmichael locates it (courtly scribes pondering and reacting to the tradition[83]: no doubt our own civil servants wished they had the time for such pursuits!) to a domestic setting of oral instruction? To me, that makes a lot more sense. Just as the teller (or the audience) of the Samson story might react: "Well, wasn't that going a bit over the top?", so too the behaviour of Jacob to his sons might well have prompted disquiet (at least, amongst a non-Ephraimite audience).

This is not to endorse this modified version of Carmichael's thesis as a general account of the relationship between law and narrative in the Hebrew Bible, as Carmichael has increasingly done. Neither laws nor proverbs necessarily have a single origin or relationship to narrative. In some cases, it may indeed have been a narrative that prompted the evaluation (positive or negative) expressed in a law or proverb. In others, the law or proverb may originate in domestic instruction informed by purely social (rather than cultural) knowledge[84]. And in yet others, social and cultural knowledge may interact in ways that make it difficult

---

81. C.M. CARMICHAEL, *The Laws of Deuteronomy*, Ithaca, Cornell University Press, 1974, pp. 61f.; ID., *Women, Law, and the Genesis Traditions,* Edinburgh, Edinburgh University Press, 1979, ch. 3; ID., *Law and Narrative in the Bible*, Ithaca, Cornell University Press, 1985, pp. 142-145.

82. The story of Reuben's "anticipation" of his inheritance with Bilhah, referred to both in 1 Chron 5,1 and Gen 49,4, might well be viewed as a later reaction to this criticism.

83. See, most recently, C.M. CARMICHAEL, *The Origins of Biblical Law: The Decalogues and the Book of the Covenant*, Ithaca, Cornell University Press, 1992, pp. 15-21.

84. E.g. the judicial bribery theme (*supra*, p. 34f.). Yet even here there are narrative sources which could be connected, but are not necessarily even evoked. L.H. SCHIFFMAN, *The Prohibition of Judicial Corruption in the Dead Sea Scrolls, Philo, Josephus and Talmudic Law*, in J. Magnes and S. Gitin (eds.), *Hesed ve'Emet. Studies in Honor of Ernest S. Frerichs*, Atlanta, Scholars Press, 1998, pp. 156f., refers to the practice of the sons of Samuel reported in 1 Sam 8,1-3, as well as Isa 1,23; 5,23; 33,15; Ezekiel 22,12; Micah 3,11; 7,3; cf. Psalms 15,5; 26,9-10. On the other hand, he notes, Prov 17,8 and 21,14 simply indicate that bribes are given with the expectation of their influencing ruling parties.

to decide questions of priority. An example of this last is Prov 28,24, already noted above for its parallelism in form and content with the participial Exod 21,15,17:

גּוֹזֵל אָבִיו וְאִמּוֹ וְאֹמֵר אֵין־פָּשַׁע חָבֵר הוּא לְאִישׁ מַשְׁחִית׃

He who robs his father or his mother and says, "That is no transgression"
is the companion of a man who destroys.

Robbery from – or, more likely, economic oppression of – parents may indeed have been a social problem on which the proverb comments (though in fact we hear more of sale by parents of children into debt-slavery). But it is striking that the terminology of *pesha* is used in two narratives of *domestic* disputes: Laban's accusation that Jacob or a member of his family had stolen his household gods (Gen 31,36), and the kidnapping of Benjamin (Gen 50,17). Did the proverb originate as a critical comment on Rachel's behaviour? If not, might it still not have evoked that narrative, or been used to comment on the narrative, in the context of domestic instruction?

V. Towards a Pragmatics of Wisdom, Law, and Narrative

Can we reconstruct with any precision the pragmatic setting in which such critical discussion of the narrative tradition might have taken place? Blenkinsopp stresses the role of the *paterfamilias*, presiding over the informal education of a "cluster of households" (an extended family) as well as possessing disciplinary powers[85]. Blenkinsopp does not himself tie narrative into this informal educational practice. For myself, I find it difficult to exclude. If narrative is not, after all, a source of instruction, why does it occupy so prominent a role at the beginning of the *Torah*? The patriarch, on this account, may have a dual role: an instructional role through telling and commenting upon traditional stories, and an adjudicatory role, arising from the incidents of daily domestic life. He may thus serve as a source (or mediation) of both "wisdom" and "law". Both "wisdom" and "law", on this account, have a different form from that which they are given by our written texts. Both are closer to narrative, and in both we may discern the presence of a "critical" as well as a "traditional" attitude.

85. *Sage Priest Prophet* (n. 25), p. 26. More controversially, he identifies the patriarch with the *zaken*, though the term is rarely found in the singular with clear reference to such a domestic role. Indeed, Conrad in *TWOT*, s.v. *zaqen* (IV.12), goes so far as to claim that the term always refers to officials. I am grateful to Roger Tomes for raising this issue when this paper was presented to the Ehrhardt seminar in Manchester.

A possible objection to this type of theory has been voiced by Crenshaw[86]. Noting "the rich diversity of ancient sapiential speech", he challenges those who identify wisdom and law as a common phenomenon to explain the sharp divergencies: "in a few instances where identical prohibitions exist in law and wisdom, the differences of expression stand out. Why would fathers choose such distinct language if both law and wisdom derive from family paraenesis?" The answer may reside in differences in the form of discourse to which the speaker is responding: the (hypothetical) moral problems presented by the tradition on the one hand, the immediate problems presented by the behaviour of his own family on the other.

I return finally to the definitional issue. My suggestion is that we can locate a common domestic setting in which oral instruction is given for both disciplinary and educational purposes. Later, both of these instructional roles were professionalised (judges, "the wise"), as these forms of instruction became literate. Just as we have a differentiation (notwithstanding some overlapping roles) in the personnel involved, so too – and indeed perhaps as a very reflection of that differentiation – we also have the emergence of separate literary genres of law and wisdom. Such a differentiation, I maintain, is far less clear, at the domestic, oral level: there, we may indeed speak of "wisdom-laws".

ABSTRACT

The auhor has elsewhere proposed a concept of "wisdom-laws", laws based in orally transmitted, sometimes arbitrary rules which can be used for immediate, rough-and-ready dispute resolution, without the need to involve third parties or formal institutions. The meaning of such rules is to be identified with the typical social situations they evoke. This paper considers the relationship of this idea to the Law and Wisdom debate. It is suggested that it is possible to locate a common domestic setting in which oral instruction, most probably in a narrative form, is given for both disciplinary and educational purposes. Later these informal instructional roles were institutionalized (judges, "the wise") as these forms of instruction became written down.

RÉSUMÉ

Dans une étude précédente, l'auteur a introduit le terme "wisdom-laws" pour désigner des lois fondées sur des règles transmises oralement, parfois arbitraires,

---

86. CRENSHAW, *Urgent Advice* (n. 18), pp. 419, 425.

qui peuvent être utilisées pour résoudre une querelle de manière directe et rapide, sans qu'il soit nécessaire de faire intervenir des tiers ou des institutions formelles. La signification de telles règles doit être identifiée avec les situations sociales typiques qu'elles évoquent. La présente étude vise à mettre en rapport cette idée avec le débat sur Loi et Sagesse. Elle cherche à montrer qu'il est possible de définir un milieu domestique commun, dans lequel une instruction orale, revêtant très probablement une forme narrative, est donnée dans un but à la fois disciplinaire et éducatif. Par la suite, ces rôles instructionnels informels ont été institutionnalisés (les juges, "les sages"), au fur et à mesure que ces formes d'instruction ont été mises par écrit.

Centre for Jewish Studies   Bernard S. JACKSON
Department of Religions and Theology
University of Manchester
Manchester M13 9PL

4

"COME AND SEE MY ZEAL FOR THE LORD"
READING THE JEHU STORY

From at least the time of Wellhausen[1] it has been generally recognised that the story of Jehu's revolt in 2 Kings 9-10 has been subject to editing. Some of the passages regarded as editorial are summaries or provide background material:

> 9,14-15a: parenthesis announcing the conspiracy and describing the situation when the revolt began (sometimes taken as a misplaced introduction to the story[2])
> 9,(28-)29: announcement of the accession of Ahaziah of Judah, whose death has just been related
> 10,28-31: summary verdicts on Jehu's revolt and subsequent reign.

Other passages regarded as secondary however are those which supply the motivation for the revolt, and in particular:

> 9,7-10a: the unnamed "son of the prophets" charges Jehu to execute divine vengeance on the house of Ahab for Jezebel's persecution of prophets and worshippers of Yahweh. It is thought that, since the young man has been instructed by Elisha to anoint Jehu and then open the door and flee, the story would hardly make him pause to explain, especially as he uses language which has previously been used in prophetic denunciations of Jeroboam (1 Kings 14,10-11) and Baasha (1 Kings 16,4)
> 9,36-37: makes Jehu recall a prediction of the fate of Jezebel, attributed to Elijah, in part reproducing the language of 1 Kings 21,23 and 2 Kings 9,10
> 10,10: makes Jehu claim that the fate of the house of Ahab is the fulfilment of prophecy by Elijah
> 10,17: the narrator himself claims that the destruction of the house of Ahab is the fulfilment of Elijah's prophecies.

Readings of the story have tended to discount these passages and interpret a reconstructed pre-existing source or sources[3] used by the (Deuteronomistic) editor or editors. Gunkel[4], for example, thought that, stripped of the passages mentioned, the narrative recovered its original life and showed Jehu as a *Realpolitiker*, using religion for his own pur-

---

1. J. WELLHAUSEN, *Die Composition des Hexateuchs und der historischen Bücher des Alten Testaments*, Berlin, Reimer, 1889, p. 288.
2. H. GUNKEL, *Die Revolution des Jehu*, in *Deutsche Rundschau* 40 (1913), 289-308, p. 290.
3. H.-D. HOFFMANN, *Reform und Reformen* (AThANT 66), Zürich, Theologischer Verlag, 1980, p. 98.
4. GUNKEL, *Revolution*, pp. 294, 295, 306.

poses, much as Napoleon did. Lloyd Barré[5] would in addition eliminate Jehu's reminder of earlier prophecy in his conversation with his aide Bidkar (9,25-26), the meeting with Jehonadab (10,15-16) and the account of the destruction of the Baal temple (10,25b-27). The result is to remove any religious motivation for the revolt and to highlight Jehu's violence in contrast with the much more restrained restoration of the Davidic line in Judah related in 2 Kings 11. Yoshikazu Minokami[6] even more drastically eliminates all reference to retribution and the fulfilment of prophecy and regards 10,18-27, the destruction of the Baal cult, as an aetiological legend appended to the account of how Jehu became king. Alexander Rofé[7] regards the narrative as consisting of stories assembled by a number of writers drawing on varied traditions. He believes that the attribution of the revolt to Elisha's initiative and that of the fulfilled prophecies to Elijah were made at a late stage, and that 10,1-10 and 17-28 relate historical events anecdotally. Martin Mulzer[8], after a close syntactical study of the text, concludes that the interest in the fulfilment of prophecy and the theme of vengeance for Naboth's murder are secondary, but still thinks that the story presents Jehu as acting for Yahweh and against Baal and not merely in his own interests.

Study of the Jehu story as narrative is thus faced with a problem. Should the need to recognise secondary material and identify an original story be accepted? If so, whose reconstruction should be followed? Or should an attempt be made to justify the alleged secondary material as integral to the narrative in its present form? Should we assume that Elisha's instructions included the terms of the commission as the young man delivered them, but that the fact is passed over in silence to avoid unnecessary repetition[9]? Undoubtedly biblical narrative often does forego repetition[10], but it is more natural to omit or abbreviate on the second occasion rather than on the first. That is what happens when Jehu reports what was said to his fellow officers: "Thus and so (כָּזֹאת וְכָזֹאת) he spoke to me" (9,12; and cf. e.g. Gen 24,30; Exod 6,9; 19,7.25; 24,3; Num 14,39; 22,7; Judg 16,18; 1 Sam 3,18; 8,10). Or should we assume

---

5. L.M. BARRÉ, *The Rhetoric of Political Persuasion: the Narrative Artistry and Political Intentions of 2 Kings 9-11* (CBQ Monograph Series 20), Washington, Catholic Biblical Association, 1988.

6. Y. MINOKAMI, *Die Revolution des Jehu* (Göttinger Theologische Arbeiten 38), Göttingen, Vandenhoeck & Ruprecht, 1989.

7. A. ROFÉ, *The Prophetical Stories*, Jerusalem, Magnes, 1988, pp. 79-86.

8. M. MULZER, *Jehu schlägt Joram. Text-, literar- und strukturkritische Untersuchung zu 2 Kön. 8,25- 10,36* (Arbeiten zu Text und Sprache im AT 37), St Ottilien, EOS, 1992.

9. I.W. PROVAN, *1 and 2 Kings* (New International Biblical Commentary), Carlisle, Paternoster, 1995, p. 212.

10. M. STERNBERG, *The Poetics of Biblical Narrative*, Bloomington, Indiana University Press, 1987, p. 383.

that the young man is being presented as a character with a certain independence of mind, ready to improve on his instructions[11]?

Where the message delivered differs from the one the messenger received, it is usually made clear that this is so, either by giving both versions of the message (2 Kings 8,10.14) or by stating that the messenger lied (1 Kings 13,18) or withheld the whole truth (1 Sam 10,16). It is difficult to agree that suggestions like these are genuine insights into the biblical narrative, when the evidence for editorial expansion is so strong. They are all too reminiscent of the way difficulties in the biblical text were explained in pre-critical days and are explained now when the case for different sources is being resisted.

It seems to me that there is a way out of the dilemma. It is possible to recognise the presence of secondary material without having to discount it in a reading of the narrative. If we recognise the secondary material as itself a *reading* of the narrative, we may find that it helps us to read the same narrative ourselves with greater insight. It has been an unspoken assumption of at least two of the studies I have mentioned (those of Barré and Minokami) that the secondary material represents a *misreading* of the story, which needs to be cleared out of the way before it can be read properly. However, since nowadays we are much more cautious about calling any reading a misreading, the ancient reading has as much right to be heard as any modern (or postmodern) one.

This reading of the story is embodied above all in the passage which has been almost universally regarded as secondary, 9,7-10a. Its prominent position almost at the beginning of the narrative indicates its importance. It tells us what Yahweh intends Jehu to do:

> You shall strike down the house of your master Ahab, so that I may avenge on Jezebel the blood of my servants the prophets, and the blood of the servants of Yahweh.

But its appearance here also tells us something about the narrative as narrative. Why was it necessary to put these words into the mouth of the young prophet? Why couldn't the story simply speak for itself? It seems to me that there are three reasons.

I

The first is that *the story is part of a larger story*. It is possible of course that the story of Jehu's revolt was once told and heard, or written

---

11. J. ELLUL, *The Politics of God and the Politics of Man*, trans. G.W. BROMILEY, Grand Rapids, Michigan, Eerdmans, 1972, p. 98; F.O. GARCIA-TRETO, *The Fall of the House: a Carnivalesque Reading of 2 Kings 9 and 10*, in *JSOT* 46 (1990), 47-65, p. 55.

and read, quite independently of other stories in the Bible. But that was no longer possible once it was incorporated in the books of Kings. Readers now come to it after reading the previous history and they will expect it to bear some relation to that previous history. The story has been explicitly anticipated in the passage where Elijah complains that

> the Israelites have forsaken your covenant, thrown down your altars, and killed your prophets with the sword (1 Kings 19,10.14),

and is given the following commission:

> Go, return on your way to the wilderness of Damascus; when you arrive, you shall anoint Hazael as king over Aram. Also you shall anoint Jehu son of Nimshi as king over Israel; and you shall anoint Elisha son of Shaphat of Abel-meholah as prophet in your place (1 Kings 19,15-17).

This commission was not fulfilled to the letter, but it would be difficult to forget it as subsequent events are related. Although there is no mention of an anointing, Elisha does succeed Elijah as prophet (2 Kings 2,1-18); although neither Elijah nor Elisha anoints Hazael, the latter does precipitate Hazael's usurpation of the throne in Damascus (2 Kings 8,1-15); although Elijah did not anoint Jehu, and Jehu is now said to be the grandson rather than the son of Nimshi, we are bound to conclude that the third element in the commission is being fulfilled, when Jehu is anointed at the instigation of Elisha.

The same context gave notice that these changes would be accompanied by violence:

> Whoever escapes from the sword of Hazael, Jehu shall kill; and whoever escapes from the sword of Jehu, Elisha shall kill (1 Kings 19,17).

Again, this prediction is not fulfilled to the letter. We do not hear of any slaughter by Elisha, but in the chapter immediately preceding the account of Jehu's revolt Hazael commits a violent act (2 Kings 8,15) and Elisha weeps at the prospect of his ruthless warfare against Israel:

> You will set their fortresses on fire, you will kill their young men with the sword, dash in pieces their little ones, and rip up their pregnant women (2 Kings 8,12).

Joram, the king of Israel, has been wounded but not killed in battle against Hazael (2 Kings 8,29). In a sense then he may be said to have "escaped the sword of Hazael". This in itself virtually predestines him to be the victim of Jehu.

So far we have seen how Jehu's revolt is prepared for as the working out of Yahweh's response to Elijah's complaint about the apostasy of Israel and the persecution of the prophets and worshippers of Yahweh.

But there is other unfinished business to be attended to as well. In the story of Naboth's vineyard, Elijah is sent to tell Ahab:

> In the place where dogs licked up the blood of Naboth, dogs will also lick up your blood (1 Kings 21,19).

Once again, this is not fulfilled to the letter. Ahab is fatally wounded in battle, and the dogs licked up his blood when they washed out his chariot, but in Samaria, not in Jezreel (1 Kings 22,38).

In the account of Naboth's vineyard there is also a more comprehensive condemnation of Ahab:

> You have sold yourself to do evil in the sight of Yahweh.... You have provoked me to anger and have caused Israel to sin (1 Kings 21,20.22);

and there is correspondingly an announcement of a more comprehensive punishment:

> I will bring disaster on you; I will consume you, and will cut off from Ahab every male, bond or free, in Israel (1 Kings 21,21).

There is also an announcement of the fate of Jezebel:

> The dogs shall eat Jezebel within the bounds of Jezreel (1 Kings 21,23).

However, because Ahab fasted and put on sackcloth, a stay of execution was granted:

> Because he has humbled himself before me, I will not bring the disaster in his days; but in his son's days I will bring the disaster on his house (1 Kings 21,29).

But now the sentence is repeated by the young man sent to anoint Jehu: both the general sentence on the house of Ahab and the specific sentence on Jezebel (2 Kings 9,8.10). The time for them to be carried out has arrived.

There is one further anticipation of the prophet's charge to notice. The announcement of the fate of the house of Ahab is here as in 1 Kings 21,21-22 compared with that of the house of Jeroboam the son of Nebat and that of the house of Baasha the son of Ahijah, earlier kings of Israel whose downfall was predicted by prophets in similar terms (1 Kings 14,10-11; 16,3-4) and interpreted as the fulfilment of prophecy (1 Kings 15,29; 16,12). Therefore, if we want to know what to expect of Jehu, we are told to recall what Baasha did to the house of Jeroboam and what Zimri did to the house of Baasha. This is how Yahweh deals with those who have "provoked him to anger" (1 Kings 14,9; 15,30; 16,2.13; 21,22), "thrust him behind their back" (1 Kings 14,9) and "caused Israel to sin" (1 Kings 14,16; 15,30; 16,2.13; 21,22). He "raises up for himself a king over Israel", not necessarily a reformer, but certainly an avenger, who "cuts off the house of Jeroboam" (1 Kings 14,14) or "deals with the house of Ahab in accordance with all that was in Yahweh's heart" (2 Kings 10,30).

The larger story to which the Jehu narrative belongs is thus a story of Yahweh's judgment on successive dynasties in Israel. It is admittedly not an entirely straightforward story of Yahweh's anger being satisfied. On the one hand there will be statements to the effect that Yahweh had compassion on his people and spared them (2 Kings 13,4-5; 14,26-27); on the other there are indications from early on that the purges were only partial and temporary cures, and that Yahweh will have finally to give Israel up and root them up out of the land (1 Kings 14,15-16; cf. 2 Kings 17,7-18.21-23). But that does not detract from the fact that the Deuteronomistic historian[12] counsels us to read the story of Jehu's revolt as an episode in Yahweh's response to the apostasy of Israel and its monarchs.

II

The second reason for beginning the story of Jehu's revolt with this commission in the name of Yahweh is that *there were already features in the story which made such an interpretation plausible*. The interpretation is not just a Deuteronomistic invention[13]. Indeed, the story of Jehu could have been responsible for the whole idea of retribution by revolt. For, although the overthrow of the house of Jeroboam and the house of Baasha are interpreted as the fulfilment of Yahweh's sentence upon them, in neither case is it said that the usurpers, Baasha and Zimri, received a commission to execute that sentence. It is true that Yahweh is said to have "exalted [Baasha] out of the dust" and made him נָגִיד over his people Israel (1 Kings 16,2), but he is not praised for overthrowing the house of Jeroboam: rather, it is part of the indictment against him:

> The word of Yahweh came by the prophet Jehu son of Hanani against Baasha and his house, both because of all the evil that he did..., in being like the house of Jeroboam, and also because he destroyed it (1 Kings 16,7).

Zimri's actions are described simply as "conspiracy", קֶשֶׁר (1 Kings 16,16.20). It is therefore inconceivable that Jehu's revolt and subsequent

---

12. W. DIETRICH, *Prophetie und Geschichte: eine redaktionsgeschichtliche Untersuchung zum deuteronomischen Geschichtswerk* (FRLANT 108), p. 172, identifies these threats and notices of fulfilment as the work of a particular Deuteronomistic editor (DtrP).

13. As HOFFMANN, *Reform und Reformen* (n. 3), pp. 102-104, believes.

purges should be represented as instigated by Yahweh on analogy with these previous revolts. But it is not inconceivable that the previous revolts, unpromising though they were, were interpreted as divine judgments on analogy with Jehu's revolt. What features in the Jehu story would have suggested the Deuteronomistic interpretation?

First we have the anointing of Jehu by Elisha's messenger. Whether or not he spoke all the words attributed to him, the anointing in the name of Yahweh – "Thus says Yahweh: I anoint you king over Israel" (2 Kings 9,3; cf. 9,6) – while Jehoram was still king, strongly suggests that Jehu is the chosen instrument of judgment on the house of Ahab. Benzinger suggested[14] that 9,1-13 was a prophetic story grafted on to a purely secular Jehu narrative, which told the story of the rebellion without any mention of support from the prophets. 9,14-15 was the seam which joined the two. This has not generally found favour, on the ground that a prophetic story would not allow a character to describe a prophet as a "madman" (מְשֻׁגָּע; 9,11)[15]. We may add that, even if the story of Jehu's revolt could be told without the story of the prophetic anointing, it is difficult to think of the latter story having no sequel.

Again the idea that Jehu was motivated by personal ambition would be difficult to substantiate from the text. He seems to be taken completely by surprise; he is reluctant to tell his fellow officers what has happened. Matters are taken out of his hands when they spread their cloaks on the steps and blow the שׁוֹפָר and proclaim him king (9,13). Only at that point does Jehu begin to take the initiative. Contrast the behaviour of Hazael in the previous chapter, who takes matters entirely into his own hands and murders Benhadad without any prophetic commission and without any encouragement from his peers (8,15).

Then we have the lookout's identification of Jehu by his driving:

> It looks like the driving of Jehu son of Nimshi; for he drives like a maniac (בְּשִׁגָּעוֹן ; 9,20).

Of course, to make narrative sense this must be a description of how Jehu usually drove. But since the young prophet has already been described by the officers as "this madman" (הַמְשֻׁגָּע הַזֶּה; 9,11), there may also be a suggestion that Jehu had caught the contagion of prophetic inspiration.

Next we have the exchange between Jehoram and Jehu.

---

14. I. BENZINGER, *Die Bücher der Könige* (KHC), Leipzig, Mohr (Siebeck), 1899, p. 149; J. GRAY, *I & II Kings* (OTL), London, SCM, 1963, p. 484; E. WÜRTHWEIN, *Die Bücher der Könige: 1. Kön. 17-2. Kön. 25* (ATD 11/2), Göttingen, Vandenhoeck & Ruprecht, 1984, pp. 328-30;

15. R. KITTEL, *Die Bücher der Könige* (HKAT, I/5), Göttingen, Vandenhoeck & Ruprecht, 1900, p. 227.

> When Joram saw Jehu, he said, "Is it peace, Jehu?" He answered, 'What peace can there be, so long as the many whoredoms and sorceries of your mother continue?' (9,22)

It is unlikely that this is a literal accusation of sexual immorality and dabbling in the occult; much more probable that the allusion is to foreign religious practices which Jezebel had introduced into Israel. This again would indicate a religious motivation for the revolt.

What are we to make of Jehu's instructions to his aide Bidkar after Jehoram has been shot?

> Lift him out and throw him on the plot of ground belonging to Naboth the Jezreelite; for remember, when you and I rode side by side behind his father Ahab how Yahweh uttered this oracle against him: "For the blood of Naboth and for the blood of his children that I saw yesterday, says Yahweh, I swear I will repay you on this very plot of ground." Now therefore lift him out and throw him on the plot of ground, in accordance with the word of Yahweh (9,25-26).

Some scholars consider this no part of the original story, on the grounds that 9,27 is the direct continuation of 9,24 – Ahaziah fled, not after he had heard Jehu speaking, but when he saw the attack on Jehoram; that the word for "oracle" (מַשָּׂא) is met elsewhere only in late prophetic texts; that the formula נְאֻם־י׳, "says Yahweh", never occurs in early narrative and is a secondary feature in prophetic usage; and that the verb translated "repay", שִׁלֵּם, occurs with Yahweh as subject only in late contexts[16]. On the other hand, the terms in question are not characteristically Deuteronomistic and there is no conclusive evidence that they could not have been used in early narrative. It has also been pointed out that the passage is no mere echo of 1 Kings 21[17]: it refers to Naboth's "field" (שָׂדֶה) rather than his vineyard, and it is outside Jezreel, not beside the palace; there is no mention here of Elijah or of dogs licking up Ahab's blood (cf. 1 Kings 21,17-19), and no mention there of others overhearing the prophet's announcement of doom or of Naboth's children being involved in his fate. Vengeance is to be executed on Naboth's property rather than on the spot where he was killed[18]. It has therefore been suggested that an early prophetic oracle has been inserted here[19], or that the verses are an original part of the narrative[20]. There

---

16. E. WÜRTHWEIN, *1. Kön. 17-2. Kön. 25*, pp. 332-333; MINOKAMI, *Revolution* (n. 6), pp. 37-39.

17. BENZINGER, *Könige*, pp. 149, 151.

18. O. H. STECK, *Überlieferung und Zeitgeschichte in den Elia-Erzählungen* (WMANT 26), Neukirchen-Vluyn, Neukirchener Verlag, 1968, p. 44 n. 2; DIETRICH, *Prophetie und Geschichte* (n. 12), pp. 50-51.

19. H. SCHMITT, *Elisa: traditionsgeschichtliche Untersuchungen zur vorklassischen nordisraelitischen Prophetie*, Gütersloh, Mohn, 1972, pp. 25-27.

20. ROFÉ, *Prophetical Stories* (n. 7), pp. 84-85.

does not seem to be any compelling case for removing the incident from the narrative. And if it is original to the story, it clearly supports the claim that Jehu was consciously acting from religious motives.

Jehu recalls prophecy again after the death of Jezebel, after he has been told how little there is left of her.

> This is the word of Yahweh, which he spoke by his servant Elijah the Tishbite, "In the territory of Jezreel the dogs shall eat the flesh of Jezebel; the corpse of Jezebel shall be like dung on the field in the territory of Jezreel, so that no one can say, This is Jezebel" (9,36-37).

While there is no earlier equivalent of verse 37, in verse 36 there is verbal reminiscence of 1 Kings 21,23 and the prophecy is attributed to Elijah. There is a greater likelihood that this passage is secondary than there was in 9,25-26[21]. But if the interpretation of 9,22 is correct, the motivation for the assassination of Jezebel already given is a religious one.

10,10 must also be regarded as suspect[22], because instead of alluding to a specific prophecy it implies the existence of a body of prophecy attributed to Elijah relating to the downfall of the house of Ahab:

> Know then that there shall fall to the earth nothing of the word of Yahweh, which Yahweh spoke concerning the house of Ahab; for Yahweh has done what he said through his servant Elijah.

It is doubtful whether anyone but the compiler of the history would be aware of the interrelations between 1 Kings 19,15-17; 21,17-19; and 22,38.

The same verdict may be passed on 10,17[23], in which the narrator echoes as comment what he has already put into the mouth of Jehu. The meeting with Jehonadab which precedes it (10,15-16) is however a different matter. There is no Deuteronomistic language here, and no appeal to prophecy. Jehu simply invites Jehonadab to "Come with me, and see my zeal for Yahweh". Once again, there seems to be no compelling reason for removing this graphically told incident from the story. If original to it, this is the clearest indication yet that Jehu is represented as acting from religious motives. It refers primarily to what is yet to happen – the massacre of the worshippers of Baal and the destruction of his temple – but there is no reason to suppose that a different motivation for what has already happened is implied.

The oracle reported in 10,30 clearly presupposes that Jehu did not, like Baasha and Zimri, carry out Yahweh's vengeance involuntarily, act-

---

21. BENZINGER, *Könige* (n. 14), p. 152; GUNKEL, *Revolution* (n. 2), p. 301; DIETRICH, *Prophetie und Geschichte* (n. 12), pp. 37, 60.
22. GUNKEL, *Revolution*, p. 303; DIETRICH, *Prophetie und Geschichte*, pp. 24-25.
23. DIETRICH, *Prophetie und Geschichte*, pp. 61-62.

ing from quite different motives, but that he consciously cooperated with what he believed was Yahweh's will.

> Yahweh said to Jehu, "Because you have done well in carrying out what I consider right, and in accordance with all that was in my heart have dealt with the house of Ahab, your sons of the fourth generation shall sit on the throne of Israel."

We are told no more in detail about the reign of Jehu, which lasted 28 years (10,36). This could well mean that even in his own eyes, once he had wiped out the house of Ahab and eliminated the worship of Baal from Israel, the work for which he had been anointed had been done. Jehu is presented as a religious zealot, even fanatic, and maybe that is what he was.

III

There could however be a third reason for stressing the divine commission at the beginning of the story. If the religious motivation had been crystal clear in the story as originally told, there would have been no need to emphasise it by inserting the commission. But while there were features in the story which made this plausible, *there were also features in the story which cast doubt upon it*. Hence the need to set the reader thinking along the right lines.

The Deuteronomistic historian himself had reservations about Jehu's zeal for Yahweh. These reservations frame the oracle which praised Jehu for carrying out Yahweh's sentence on the house of Ahab[24].

> Jehu did not turn aside from the sins of Jeroboam son of Nebat, which he caused Israel to commit – the golden calves which were in Bethel and in Dan... Jehu was not careful to follow the law of Yahweh the God of Israel with all his heart; he did not turn from the sins of Jeroboam, which he caused Israel to commit (10,29.31).

These reservations concern what Jehu failed to do, and do not pass adverse judgment on what Jehu actually did. If the historian had qualms about the actions he has related, he has not expressed them. Nevertheless it is likely that he felt the need to anticipate misgivings which the reader might have while reading the story. It is possible that verdicts such as that expressed in Hosea 1,4 – "I will punish the house of Jehu for the

---

24. DIETRICH, *Prophetie und Geschichte*, p. 34, attributes these comments (apart from the sentence "Jehu was not careful to follow the law of Yahweh the God of Israel with all his heart", which he assigns to DtrN, the reviser who concentrated on the kings' attitude to the law) to the original Deuteronomistic compiler of Kings (DtrG).

blood of Jezreel" – needed to be contested, and that the settled conviction of 2 Chronicles 22,7-10, that Yahweh had anointed Jehu to destroy the house of Ahab and to execute judgment upon it, did not yet hold the field.

In the first place it is admitted that Jehu conspired (קָשַׁר) against Jehoram (9,14). Jehoram himself interprets Jehu's action as treason (מִרְמָה; 9,23), and Jezebel reminds him that Jehoram was his master (9,31). Jehu himself later admits that he conspired against his master and killed him (10,9). His motives may have been different from those of Zimri, but that is the comparison which immediately springs to Jezebel's mind. The reader who comes across this narrative as part of an even larger story than that in Kings may wonder why Jehu did not wait for God's good time. David was anointed in Saul's lifetime and yet made no move to claim the throne until after Saul's death. Why was Jehu not afraid to lift his hand against Yahweh's anointed (1 Sam 24,6.10; 26,9.11.23; 2 Sam 1,14)?

Again, the murder of Ahaziah (9,27-28) and later of his relatives (10,12-14) seems to be entirely gratuitous and no part of his commission. To take the forty-two princes alive and then kill them is particularly cold-blooded. Even Chronicles, which says that "it was ordained by God that the downfall of Ahaziah should come about through his going to visit Joram" (2 Chron 22,7), stops short of saying that Jehu had a commission to kill Ahaziah and the Judaean princes.

When Jehu arrives at Jezreel and demands that Jezebel should be thrown down from her window, he does not appeal to his divine commission but only to his own bid for the throne. He does not say, "Who is on Yahweh's side?" but "Who is on my side?" (9,32). When later the authorities in Samaria capitulate and say, "We are your servants; we will do anything you say. We will not make anyone king; do whatever you think right" he accepts their pragmatic view of his actions: "If you are on my side, and if you are ready to obey me..." (10,6).

The treatment of Jezebel is unnecessarily savage, as Jehu himself half acknowledges, when he says:

> See to that cursed woman and bury her; for she is a king's daughter (9,34).

The statement that "he went in and ate and drank" (9,34) immediately after her brutal murder is also intended to present Jehu as extremely callous[25].

---

25. S. BAR-AFRAT, *Narrative Art in the Bible* (JSOTSup 70), Sheffield, Almond, 1989, p. 79.

The letters to the authorities in Samaria (10,1-6) do not appeal to a divine commission. The first is a straight challenge to them to put up a rival candidate for the throne and fight. The second is possibly ambiguous: "take the heads of your master's sons" could mean "bring the most important of them" rather than literally "bring their heads". Letters often have a threatening aspect in the Bible: when the king of Israel receives a letter from the king of Aram his immediate reaction is, "Just look and see how he is trying to pick a quarrel with me" (2 Kings 5,7), and Hezekiah found the letter from the king of Assyria equally unwelcome (2 Kings 19,14 || Isa.37,14). To the reader of the larger story Jehu's second letter will have particularly unpleasant echoes of the letter David wrote to Joab ordering the liquidation of Uriah (2 Sam 11,14-15) and the letters Jezebel wrote in Ahab's name to the authorities in Jezreel telling them to bring a trumped up charge against Naboth. His denial of responsibility for the massacre (10,9) is disingenuous to say the least.

When Jehu announces his design to offer a great public sacrifice to Baal, the Deuteronomistic historian is at pains to point out that this was merely a strategic move to wipe out Baal worship; he didn't really mean to do anything of the kind (10,19). The reader however may have different misgivings. Is such duplicity permissible? Does the end justify the means? Why didn't Jehu first give the worshippers of Baal the chance to change their minds, as Elijah did (1 Kings 18,21)? How could he be certain that among the worshippers of Baal on this occasion there were not some who had previously been "limping with two different opinions" and had committed themselves out of fear of Jehu? Zeal for Yahweh Jehu certainly had, but the way that zeal was expressed gave rise to serious questions. Even the Deuteronomist does not include the wholesale massacre of Baal worshippers either in the commission Jehu receives or in the praise he is accorded in the summing up of the narrative.

IV

The way the story of Jehu is read has important theological and ethical implications. When it was read as an authoritative witness to God's purposes and the way he achieves them, it could be used to justify atrocities committed in the name of religion[26]. In the 16th century both Catholics and Protestants appealed to it. After the massacre of a Huguenot congregation at Vassy in 1562 Catholic preachers appealed to the

---

26. F.W. FARRAR, *Second Book of Kings* (Expositor's Bible), London, Hodder & Stoughton, 1894, p. 133.

example of Jehu, who killed two kings and 112 princes and left Jezebel to be eaten by dogs[27]. It could be the warrant for radical reformation by political means: Thomas Müntzer, in his *Sermon before the princes* of 1524, appealed to the rulers of Saxony to acquire the same zeal for reformation as Jehu showed[28]; and in Reformation England Jehu's zeal in destroying Baal worship was an important precedent for the rooting out of the Roman Catholic allegiance[29]. Zwingli cited the case of Jehu among others to argue that the authorities, who were commissioned by God to kill, could do so with a clear conscience[30]. But the story might equally well sanction the removal of a tyrant by force. Luther was cautious: he believed that God might decree that a people should rise against their ruler, though he hesitated to say that it would be right for the people to do so[31]. John Knox held that the story of Jehu proved that "subjects were commanded to execute judgments upon their king and prince"[32]. James VI and I of Scotland and England, understandably, believed that it was dangerous to treat such an exceptional case as a precedent[33]. But in the mid 17th century Jehu's removal of Jehoram was appealed to in defence of the overthrow and execution of Charles I[34].

Most Christians were prepared to accept the premise that God punished wickedness and used human instruments to do so. Not all however were happy about the encouragement the Jehu story gave to religious fanaticism. In England, after the Restoration, the fear of extreme sectarianism and civil disruption became far greater than the fear of being ruled by ungodly princes, and Jehu became the type of the religious fanatic, a figure for mockery and contempt[35]. Others were troubled about

---

27. H. MARTIN, *Histoire de France depuis les temps les plus reculés jusqu'en 1789*, 4th edition, Paris, 1870, IX, p. 114.

28. G.H. WILLIAMS and A.M. MERGAL (eds.), *Spiritual and Anabaptist Writers* (LCC 25), London, SCM, 1957, p. 64.

29. L.B. KENNELLY, *"Had Zimri peace, who slew his master?"* : *The Role of Jehu (2 Kgs 9-10) in 17th Century Religious and Political Literature*, in William P. SHAW (ed.), *Praise Disjoined: Changing Patterns of Salvation in 17th Century English Literature* (Seventeenth Century Studies 2), New York, Peter Lang, 1991, pp. 37-49.

30. ZWINGLI, *De vera et falsa religione*, 1525, in F. BLANKE (ed.), *Zwingli, der Theologe 2*, Zürich, Zwingli-Verlag, 1963, p. 241.

31. LUTHER, *Whether soldiers, too, can be saved*, in Robert C. SCHULTZ (ed.), *The Christian in Society III*, *Luther's Works*, American edition, 46, Philadelphia, Fortress, 1967, p. 104.

32. KNOX, *On Rebellion*, ed. Roger A. MASON (Cambridge Texts on the History of Political Thought), Cambridge, 1994, p. 198.

33. *The True Lawe of Free Monarchies* (1598), in *Minor Prose Works of King James VI & I*, ed. J. Craigie (Scottish Text Society, 4th series/14), Edinburgh, 1982, p. 68.

34. KENNELLY, *"Had Zimri peace"* (n. 29), pp. 38-39.

35. KENNELLY, *"Had Zimri peace"*, pp. 45-49; ID., *Swift's Yahoo and King Jehu: Genesis of an Allusion*, in *English Language Notes* 26 (1988-89) 37-45.

conceding that the end justified the means. Symon Patrick, the 18th century commentator, accepted that Jehu was "God's instrument to punish the house of Ahab", but drew the line at his duplicity towards the worshippers of Baal: "His zeal for the Lord exceeded its bounds; for he ought not to have taken any indirect course to fulfil his will... God doth not stand in need of any man's sin, to compass his ends"[36]. Adam Clarke, early in the 19th century, said: "The cutting off of Ahab's family was decreed by the divine justice; the *means* by which it was done, or at least the *manner* of doing, were not entirely of this appointing"[37]. At the end of the 19th century F.W. Farrar still believed that "divine justice" made use of "human executioners", but in answer to the question, "And did God approve all this detestable mixture of zealous enthusiasm with lying deceit and the insatiate thirst of blood?", he said: "If right be right, and wrong be wrong, the answer must be... an uncompromising 'No!'"[38]. He was able to put the acceptance of such brutality down to "the wild spirit of the times" and believed that "the nation was on the eve of purer teaching", appealing to Amos' condemnation of the cruelty of the rulers of Edom and Moab (Amos 1,11; 2,1). In spite of that, however, Israel's conviction that the barbarities of war were to be interpreted as divine judgment did not quickly die out.

The 20th century has both contributed its own fanaticisms and atrocities and raised further questions about the assumptions which lie behind the narrative. How did the worshippers of Baal understand their faith? Were its practices so degrading that they deserved to be described as "whoredoms and sorceries"? Isn't the right attitude towards religions other than one's own tolerance and even respect?

The late 20th century has had its own answers to these questions. Before we acknowledge the Jehu narrative and the wider context of the Deuteronomistic history as scripture with an absolute claim we should recognise that it is driven by ideology. It represents the interests of particular groups within Israel. The same events, related by others, would be seen in a very different light. And so the religious standpoint of the story is relativised, and very different motivations are sought. Or the story is valued simply as one of the best examples of Hebrew narrative, to be analysed and admired.

I hope I have been able to show that the story of Jehu's revolt raised ethical and theological questions from the beginning, and that we should

---

36. S. PATRICK, *A Commentary upon the Historical Books of the Old Testament*, London, 1756[6], II, on 2 Kings 10,10.18.

37. A. CLARKE, *Holy Bible with Commentary and Critical Notes*, New edition, ed. T. SMITH, London, 1844, II, on 2 Kings 10,34.

38. FARRAR, *Second Book of Kings* (n. 26), p. 138.

not attempt to by-pass them. It is to the credit of the Deuteronomists that they have told the story in such a way that, while making their own convictions clear, they have not disguised the brutality, duplicity and fanaticism of Jehu's actions, thus providing us with the material on which to base very different conclusions.

ABSTRACT

Attempts to distinguish an original Jehu story from secondary material have been succeeded by attempts to read the narrative as an integrated whole. Neither have proved entirely satisfactory. It is suggested here that the secondary material (especially 2 Kings 9,7-10a) is an ancient *reading* of the story, relating it to the larger story of Israel's apostasy and Yahweh's response to it. The programmatic material was needed because, while there were features in the story which made it plausible to see Jehu as the instrument of Yahweh's vengeance, there were also features, such as his cruelty and duplicity, which cast doubt upon it. The ambiguities in the story have been amply reflected in later interpretation.

RÉSUMÉ

La recherche a d'abord tenté d'opérer une distinction dans 2 Rois 9-10 entre une histoire primitive de Jéhu et des matériaux secondaires; elle a essayé ensuite d'interpréter le récit comme un tout homogène. Ces deux approches n'ont abouti ni l'une ni l'autre à des résultats entièrement satisfaisants. La présente étude propose de voir dans le matériel secondaire (en particulier dans 2 Rois 9,7-10a) une *lecture* ancienne qui vise à mettre l'histoire de Jéhu en rapport avec l'histoire plus vaste de l'apostasie d'Israël et de la réponse de Yahvé à cette apostasie. L'adjonction de ce matériel programmatique a été rendu nécessaire par le fait que, même si l'histoire contenait déjà des éléments qui permettaient de voir en Jéhu un instrument de la vengeance de Yahvé, elle présentait aussi des traits, comme la cruauté et la duplicité de Jéhu, qui rendaient problématique une telle interprétation. Les ambiguïtés qui caractérisent l'histoire de Jéhu sont largement reflétées par la suite dans l'histoire de l'interprétation.

Department of Religions and Theology   Roger TOMES
University of Manchester
Manchester M13 9PL

5

NARRATIVE PATTERNS FOR THE COMMUNICATION
OF COMMISSIONED SPEECH IN THE PROPHETS
A THREE-SCENE MODEL

I. INTRODUCTION

While the majority of literary forms in the prophets are directly related to prophetic speech, the prophets also contain a variety of narrative forms[1]. These include discourse forms related to narrative[2] and extended narratives some of which are drawn from or related to other biblical books[3]. Generally, however, narrative in the prophetic books is not lengthy or continuous; rather it is fragmentary, episodic and focuses on a small number of actions or on speech. The latter has been characterised as "false narrative" in which the theological interest of the reported speech supersedes the importance of the narrative elements[4]. However,

---

1. Cf. e.g. O. EISSFELDT, *The Old Testament: An Introduction*, Oxford, Blackwell, 1965, pp. 48-56, ET from *Einleitung in das Alte Testament*, Tübingen, Mohr (Siebeck), 1964³, trans. by P.R. ACKROYD, pp. 63-75; G. FOHRER, *Introduction to the Old Testament*, London, SPCK, 1968, pp. 88-89, 99, 361, 365, 398-399, trans. from E. SELLIN and G. FOHRER, *Einleitung in das Altes Testament*, Heidelberg, Quelle und Meyer, 1965¹⁰, by D. GREEN; O. KAISER, *Introduction to the Old Testament: A Presentation of its Results and Problems*, Oxford, Blackwell, 1975, pp. 296-297, trans. from second German edition, Gütersloh, Mohn, ²1970 by J. STURDY; J.A. SOGGIN, *Introduction to the Old Testament* (OTL), London, SCM, 1976, pp. 216-217, trans. from *Introduzione all'Antico Testamento*, Brescia, Paideia, ²1974 by J. BOWDEN and R.J. COGGINS; J. LINDBLOM, *Prophecy in Ancient Israel*, Philadelphia, Fortress, 1962, pp. 220-221. It has not been possible to take account of alternations between prose and poetry as a narrative medium (cf. comments by R. ALTER, *The Art of Biblical Poetry*, New York, Basic Books, 1985, pp. 137-140 and F.I. ANDERSEN and D.N. FREEDMAN, *Amos: A New Translation with Introduction and Commentary* (AB, 24), Garden City, NY, Doubleday, 1980, pp. 144-149, 391-392). This awaits further work.
2. David M. GUNN and Danna Nolan FEWELL, *Narrative in the Hebrew Bible* (Oxford Bible Series), Oxford, OUP, 1993, p. 4.
3. Cf. Isa 36-39 (2 Kings 18,13 - 21,19 cf. also 2 Chron 32,1-31); Jer 39,1-10.40,7 - 41,3.3b-34 (2 Kings 25).
4. Cf. esp. N. LOHFINK, *Die Landverheissung als Eid: Eine Studie zu Gn 15* (SBS, 28), Stuttgart, Katholisches Bibelwerk, 1967, p. 33 who writes of Gen 15: "Erst recht der Höhepunkt in V.12.17 ist durch unnatürliche Häufung und auffallenden Parallelismus der syntaktischen Mittel zu künstlich gestaltet. Es kann noch offen bleiben, ob Gn 15 ein Einzelstück ist oder als „konstruierte Erzählung" im Sinne Richters in einem größeren

the observation of G.W. Coats that "... in OT narratives, dialogue carries as much of the weight of the depiction ... as description"[5] indicates the importance of speech in Hebrew narrative. The casting of prophetic speech into a narrative framework is literarily significant and these small narrative elements are often highly nuanced, repaying closer study.

This paper focuses on narratives dealing with the communication of commissioned speech in the prophetic books. I shall review an attempt to analyse the narrative patterns for such stories in the narrative books of the Hebrew Bible, before proposing a more general model based on the insights of structural linguistics and comparative anthropological studies of prophecy. I shall then offer readings of some prophetic narratives.

There are two issues we must resolve before moving on. First, what is meant by "commissioned speech"? While prophetic speech is to be generally understood as having been commissioned by Yahweh[6], we will deal only with speeches with some indication of specific commissioning. Indications may be found in the speech itself, the introduction to the speech, or in a formulaic or narrative framework. The most common indications of commissioning are the messenger formula and *Wortempfangsformel*. For the purposes of this paper, however, the stereotyped nature of such formulas does not allow us to infer the specific commissioning of every message associated with them.

Second, what might we accept as "narrative"? In this study one hundred and thirty-nine cases of commissioned speech communication have been examined of which only forty-three[7] can be regarded as "narration" of some sort, including vision reports and interpreted actions. Prophetic speech is represented in a variety of forms and settings most of which have no contextual reference to situation, commissioning or delivery. Even where the *Wortempfangsformel* is elaborated to provide indications of context it is usually too brief and stereotypic to be regarded

---

Erzählungszusammenhang steht". Cf. also C. WESTERMANN, *Genesis 12-36: A Commentary*, London, SPCK, 1986, pp. 214-215; ET from *Genesis 12-36* (BK, 2), Neukirchen-Vluyn, Neukirchener, 1981, trans. by J.J. SCULLION.

5. George W. COATS, *Genesis with an Introduction to Narrative Literature* (The Forms of Old Testament Literature, 1), Grand Rapids, Eerdmans, 1983, p. 4.

6. Cf. Claus WESTERMANN, *Basic Forms of Prophetic Speech*, London, Lutterworth, 1967, pp. 11-12 (English only); OT from *Grundformen prophetischer Rede*, Munich, Kaiser, ²1964, trans. by Hugh Claydon WHITE.

7. The forty-three cases are tabulated in Figure 3, *infra*.

as a narrative fragment[8]. In another group of texts the descriptive element is minimal and can hardly be regarded as narrative[9]. Finally, a group of forty-three texts portray the communication of commissioned speech in the context of narrative, either as part of a narrative or combined with short narrative fragments. The current paper deals with texts from this group.

II. Communicating Commissioned Speech in Hebrew Narrative and Prophecy

A.M. Vater[10] has studied narrative patterns in stories of commissioned speech in the narrative books of the Hebrew Bible, focusing on the commissioning and delivery of messengers' speeches. Vater's analysis is based upon a two-scene model: first, a commissioning scene in which the message is commissioned; second, a delivery scene in which the message is delivered and any reaction noted. Vater isolates eight basic patterns together with a number of variations. Vater's descriptions of her basic patterns, in four groups, are shown in Figure 1 *infra*. Vater notes four "narrative loci" in which these patterns occur – introduction, climax, conclusion and the whole narrative. However, she also notes that commissioned speech patterns serve to delay or quicken the pace of narrative, indicating that her four narrative loci do not give a complete picture of their use. Vater suggests four levels on which her patterns may be significant, although she does not always distinguish clearly between them[11]. These are the levels of simple story, redaction, tradition (where the words are important in themselves) and of the final narrator. Vater sees her study as an attempt "to energize the image of the final author ... to discover how the narration of messages and oracles can tell a story in its own right"[12].

8. The *Wortempfangsformel* is used to indicate commissioning in approximately 50 cases, including 11 of the 43 cases identified above which have richer narrative elements in the other scenes.
9. Such "minimal narration" is normally of the order "A said to B" or "Then A said...".
10. Ann M. VATER, *The Communication of Messages and Oracles as a Narrative Medium in the Old Testament* (Ph.D. diss., Yale), Ann Arbor, UMI, 1976; ID., *Narrative Patterns for the Story of Commissioned Communication in the Old Testament*, in *JBL* 99 (1980) 365-382.
11. See, for example, her description of the function of pattern II on the four levels (*The Communication of Messages and Oracles*, p. 54).
12. *The Communication of Messages and Oracles*, p. 3.

Figure 1: A.M. Vater's synopsis of patterns for narrating incidents of communication in Old Testament narrative books		
A. Double Scene Patterns		
I	C(M) + D(M)	The message is narrated twice, once in the situation of its commissioning, and again in the situation of its delivery. This pattern occurs in three variations:
Ia	C(M) + D(M)	The messages are identical,
Ib	C(M) + D(M1)	one message is a slight modification of the other,
Ic	C(M1) = D(M2)	two different wordings of the same message.
B. Commissioning Scene Patterns		
II	C(M) + Dd	The message is narrated in the situation of its commissioning and a brief notice of its delivery is added.
III	C(M) + ~~D~~	The message is narrated in the situation of its commissioning and no mention is made of its delivery.
C. Delivery Scene Patterns		
IV	Cd + D(M)	The message is narrated in the situation of its delivery, which is preceded by a brief notice that a message or messenger was sent.
V	~~C~~ + D(M)	The message is narrated in the situation of its delivery, with no notice of its commissioning prior to delivery.
D. Citation of Message Patterns		
VI	Cd + M + ~~D~~	A brief notice of a message being sent is followed by the message, narrated neither in the commissioning nor the delivery situation, but cited with no mention of its delivery.
VII	~~C~~ + M + ~~D~~	The message is simply narrated as a reply to another message, without a commissioning or a delivery situation.
VIII	Cd + M + Dd	A brief notice of a message being sent is followed by the message, narrated neither in the commissioning nor the delivery situation, but followed with a brief notice.

Where "M" = "message"; "C" = "commissioning scene"; "D" = "delivery scene". "Cd" indicates that the commissioning is noted and "Dd" that the delivery is noted. The strike-through indicates that the deleted element is not present. Cf. A.M. VATER, *The Communication of Messages and Oracles* (n. 10), pp. 40-60; ID., *Narrative Patterns* (n. 10), p. 367. The table in Vater's paper has substantial typographical errors which I have corrected from her dissertation.

Vater expresses the hope that her results will pave the way for a similar analysis of the prophetic literature, the dynamics of which are more complex and the patterns more fluid than in the narrative books. However, it is difficult to apply Vater's analysis to the prophets without reformulating it significantly. The main problem is the two-scene model she adopts. Vater's interest is primarily in uni-directional communication (from commissioning agent to messenger to audience) and this appears to result almost inevitably in a two-scene model that suppresses the element of audience response in the biblical text. Her analysis of Moses' call, for example, plays down Moses' response to his commission. In other analyses she records response to the delivery of a speech, such as "reaction" or "performance of the action desired by the message-sender", as a subsidiary element of the delivery scene.

While this may be acceptable in the narrative books it is not adequate for analysing the prophets where reaction to the prophetic word is important[13]. In some texts the message is repeated for a "third" time usually in the form of an accusation by one or more of the audience[14]. In others the message is not repeated but the narrative focuses upon reaction to the message[15]. Vater's two-scene model does not cope adequately with such texts.

Vater's model might be improved simply by positing a third "Reaction Scene" in which the primary focus is on audience reaction to the delivery or proclamation of a message and, in particular, where all or part of a summary of the message is repeated. This pragmatic solution, however, obscures a basic theoretical deficiency in Vater's approach which undervalues audience response to messages. Such a deficiency is pronounced in relation to Hebrew prophecy, especially in Jer.

---

13. In Jer see, for example, 26,1-19.24 esp. 26,7f.; 42,1-43,7 esp. 43,1-3; 32,1-5; 38,1-6.

14. Cf., e.g., Jer 26,7-9; 27,9-11.14-15.16-22; 29,27-28; 32,4-5; (42,19); 43,1-4; Ezek 20,49; 44,24-25; Amos 7,10-11.15-17. In some instances an earlier message sent is quoted or summarised to emphasize its urgency e.g. Zech 1,4-5 or authority (cf. Jer 35,1-19). There are numerous examples where a saying is quoted and (critical) comments made, and these are especially common in Ezek (cf. 11,2-12; 12,(8-16).21-25.26-28; 18,2-18.19-24.25-32; 20,32; 26,2; 27,3; 28,2.9; 29,9b; 33,10.17.20.24; 35,10; 36,2.20; 37,11; 38,11; some references to speech are more general, e.g. 13,1-7.8-16.17; 25,3), though not uncommon in Jer.

15. Cf., e.g. Jer 18; 19,1 - 20,6; 28; 29; 36; 44; Jonah 3-4; Isa 36; 37.

T.W. Overholt[16] among others[17], has studied Hebrew prophecy from an anthropological perspective. In particular, Overholt[18] has made a strong case for including the reaction of the prophet's society to both the prophet and his message in our understanding of prophecy. Overholt has devised a model of the "prophetic process" involving the three poles of God, prophet and "society" or audience. These are related by direct contact between God and the prophet and between the prophet and his audience, and also by a system of "feedback" or reaction between the prophet and God and between society and the prophet (cf. Figure 2). In Overholt's model the feedback mechanisms may lead to further direct communication that supplements or modifies the original communication[19] and there is also a mechanism of "confirmation" between God and society[20]. These developments of Overholt's model are not directly

16. Thomas W. OVERHOLT, *The Ghost Dance of 1890 and the Nature of the Prophetic Process*, in *Ethnohistory* 21 (1974), 37-63; ID., *Jeremiah and the Nature of the Prophetic Process*, in Arthur L. MERRILL and Thomas W. OVERHOLT (eds.), *Scripture in History and Theology: Essays in Honor of J. Coert Rylaarsdam* (PTMS, 17), Pittsburgh, Pickwick, 1977, pp. 129-150; ID., *Prophecy: The Problem of Cross-Cultural Comparison*, in *Semeia* 21 (1981) 55-78, ID., *Model, Meaning and Necessity*, in *Semeia* 21 (1981) 129-132; ID., *The End of Prophecy: No Players Without a Program*, in *JSOT* 42 (1988) 103-115.

17. Cf. e.g. R.C. CULLEY and T.W. OVERHOLT (eds.), *Anthropological Perspectives on Old Testament Prophecy*, *Semeia* 21; Martin J. BUSS, *Understanding Communication*, in M.J. BUSS, (ed.), *Encounter with the Text: Form and History in the Hebrew Bible* (Semeia Supplements), Philadelphia and Missoula, Fortress and Scholars, 1979, pp. 3-44; ID., *The Social Psychology of Prophecy*, in J.A. EMERTON (ed.), *Prophecy: Essays Presented to Georg Fohrer* (BZAW, 150), Berlin, de Gruyter, 1980, pp. 1-11; ID., *An Anthropological Perspective Upon Prophetic Call Narratives*, in *Semeia* 21 (1981) 9-30; ID., *On Social and Individual Aspects of Prophecy*, in *Semeia* 21 (1981) 121-123; B.O. LONG, *Recent Field Studies in Oral Literature and their Bearing on Old Testament Criticism*, in *VT* 26 (1976) 187-198; ID., *Recent Field Studies in Oral Literature and the Question of Sitz im Leben*, in *Semeia* 5 (1976) 35-49; ID., *Prophetic Authority as Social Reality*, in G.W. COATS and B.O. LONG (eds.), *Canon and Authority: Essays in Old Testament Religion and Theology*, Philadelphia, Fortress, 1977, pp. 3-20; ID., *Social Dimensions of Prophetic Conflict*, in *Semeia* 21 (1981) 31-53; David L. PETERSEN, *The Roles of Israel's Prophets* (JSOT Sup. 17), Sheffield, JSOT, 1981; Robert R. WILSON, *Prophecy and Society in Ancient Israel: The Present State of the Inquiry*, in *SBL 1977 Seminar Papers*, pp. 341-358; ID., *Prophecy and Society in Ancient Israel*, Philadelphia, Fortress, 1980; also Kenelm O.L. BURRIDGE, *Reflections on Prophecy and Prophetic Groups*, in *Semeia* 21 (1981) 99-102; Norman K. GOTTWALD, *Problems and Promises in the Comparative Analysis of Religious Phenomena*, in *Semeia* 21 (1981) 103-112; Ioan M. LEWIS, *Prophets and their Publics*, in *Semeia* 21 (1981) 113-117.

18. OVERHOLT, *The Ghost Dance of 1890*; *Jeremiah and the Nature of the Prophetic Process*; *Prophecy: The Problem of Cross-Cultural Comparison*; *The End of Prophecy*, pp. 110-112.

19. Biblical examples might include Moses' role in the development of the law and some call narratives. The encounters between Jeremiah and Hananiah (Jer 28) might require analysis of "feedback" and confirmation/disconfirmation or development of an initial message (cf. Jer 27,2-7.11.16-22).

20. The elders' use of a quotation from Micah in Jer 26,17-19 may qualify as "confirmation", but see further *infra*.

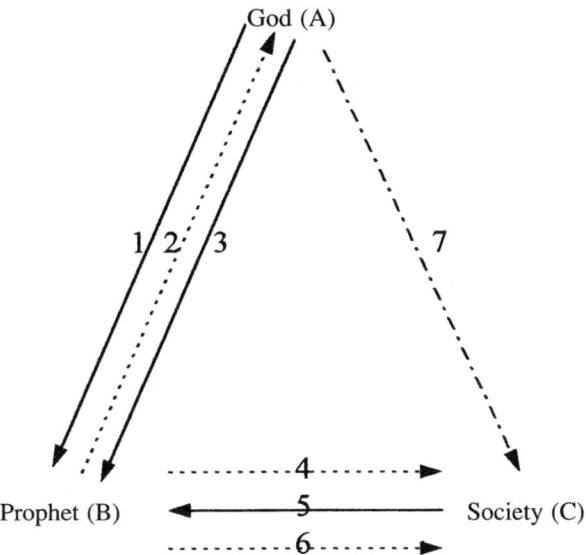

Figure 2: T.W. Overholt's representation of his model of the "prophetic process"

Overholt has produced a number of versions of the above diagram. The version above is taken from T.W. Overholt, *The End of Prophecy* (n. 16), p. 111 and I have identified each of the "poles" A, B, and C.

Each arrow represents communication between the three poles of God (A), Prophet (B) and Society or Audience (C). Each of the arrows represents a different stage in the process: 1. revelation from the god to the prophet; 2. "feedback" from the prophet to the god; 3. further communication from the god; 4. proclamation by the prophet to the audience; 5. "feedback" from the audience to the prophet; 6. additional proclamation from the prophet to the audience; 7. "confirmation" about the prophet or the message from the god to the audience. Elements may be repeated many times. The best summary of Overholt's position is in his article *The End of Prophecy*, pp. 110-112 (cf. n. 21).

relevant to our current discussion of basic narrative patterns, although they are of importance for a small number of texts. For our purposes the important point to note, and it is the major point stressed by Overholt, is that audience reaction is a constitutive element of prophecy: indeed, Overholt claims that social recognition of prophecy is *the* constitutive element[21].

Overholt's conclusion is by no means surprising, since the most basic understanding of Hebrew prophetic speech is that it is uttered to provoke or elicit a response among its hearers[22]. Robert Alter[23] has drawn attention to the "powerfully vocative character" of Hebrew prophetic poetry as "represented speech". Prophetic oracles of judgment, for example, are usually addressed to an audience with the aim of rebuking and altering behaviour. In Roman Jakobson's terms the *conative* function of verbal communications is of a high order both in Hebrew prophetic speech and texts. The *conative* focuses on the response of the audience addressed by the message[24]. Many texts in the Judaeo-Christian tradition

21. The best summary of OVERHOLT's position is found in his 1988 article *The End of Prophecy* (n. 16), esp. pp. 110-112. "This model seeks to represent the social dynamics of prophetic activity as a set of interactions among a god (A), a prophet (B), and the prophet's audience (C). These interactions occur along three axes: the god's revelation to the prophet (1,3) and the prophet's response (2), the prophet's speech to the audience (4,6) and its response (5), and direct manifestations from the god to the prophet's audience (7). Any component of this set can occur many times ... Since revelation (1) is in essence a private matter not normally (or ever fully) observable by persons other than those who are its recipients, its presence can be *claimed* even in its absence. Furthermore, its presence may be *attributed* even in the absence of such a claim ... Elements 2 and 3 are not structurally necessary for an act of prophecy; element 1 is the critical component on this axis. On the prophet-audience axis element 4, the statement of the message from the god to the prophet, is theoretically necessary, and its absence would be easily noticed. But there can be mitigating factors. The audience, for example, can *understand as prophecy* that which was not intended to be such ... leaving the primary A-B-C-B sequence intact. On this axis 4 is primary, so the absence of 6 (additional proclamation) is not a reliable signal that there is no prophecy. Element 7 is basically an enhancer of prophetic activity and is not necessarily present. Element 5, feedback from the audience to the prophet turns out to be the key. Though the speaker may claim to have received a revelation from the god and to be a prophet by virtue of proclaiming it, the failure of the audience to acknowledge, in effect to authorise this activity means that the A-B-C-B chain is truncated, losing its final stage." This view must be qualified to the extent that different audiences within a single society may respond differently to a given prophet or utterance, some rejecting, others accepting the message and the authority of the prophet. Social divisions over Hebrew prophecy are seen clearly in texts dealing with prophetic conflict, especially in Jer (cf. esp. Jer 26).

22. Cf. Claus WESTERMANN, *Basic Forms of Prophetic Speech* (n. 6), *passim*, esp. p. 11 (English only); also, G. FOHRER, *Introduction* (n. 1), pp. 349-358; O. KAISER, *Introduction* (n. 1), pp. 294-295; N.K. GOTTWALD, *A Light to the Nations*, New York, Harper and Row, 1959, p. 275.

23. Robert ALTER, *The Art of Biblical Poetry*, New York, Basic Books, 1985, pp. 139-140.

24. Roman JAKOBSON, *Closing Statement: Linguistics and Poetics*, in Thomas A. SEBOEK (ed.), *Style in Language*, Cambridge, MA, MIT, 1960, pp. 350-377, describes six

are highly *conative*, seeking to elicit response of some sort, including *Torah*. However, this function of calling; inviting; demanding response is especially characteristic of Hebrew prophecy and leads to the particular theological interest in response to prophets and their message shown in the texts I have analysed below. More generally, the *conative* function of language is often of a high order in other forms of message communication[25]. A general model of commissioned message communication would therefore seem to demand the inclusion of a third "reaction" scene to adequately describe narrative patterns for the communication of commissioned messages. Such a third scene would seem to be particularly appropriate when dealing with Hebrew prophecy.

Although I do not have the space here to comment further, my revision of Vater's analysis suggests that her work on Hebrew narrative should be reconsidered[26]. The fact that Vater was able to complete her analysis without reference to a third scene suggests that it may be unnecessary in some contexts. In general, a third scene should be available in order to satisfy theoretical requirements. In practice, of the forty-three prophetic narratives identified, thirty instantiate a reaction scene.

The modification I propose to Vater's scheme of analysis is as follows[27]:

aspects of verbal communication, each associated with a function of language: 1) Jakobson locates the expressive or emotive function of language with the addresser; 2) the context is involved in communication through language's referential or denotative function; 3) the message for its own sake Jakobson understands as language's poetic function; 4) Jakobson analyses the contact between addresser and addressee as the phatic function of language which describes modes and forms of communication such as ritualised forms of address and specific literary forms; 5) the metalingual function of language is to check that both addresser and addressee share the same semantic code so that mutual understanding is a possibility; 6) the addressee is the focus of language's conative function which is to call, order, persuade, etc.

25. On the *conative* function of didactic texts cf. Glendon E. BRYCE, *The Structural Analysis of Didactic Texts*, in Gary A. TUTTLE (ed.), *Biblical and Near Eastern Texts: Essays in Honor of William Sanford LaSor*, Grand Rapids, Eerdmans, 1978, pp. 107-121.

26. The element of response in Isa 36-39 (which parallels 2 Kings 18,13-21,19) is significant (cf. 36,11-12.14-16a.18.21-22; 37,1-4.14-20.21; 38,2-3.4) and would seem to indicate some inadequacy in Vater's analysis.

27. I have considered how best to include "confirmation" in Overholt's prophetic process in my analysis, and also texts in which a prophecy is "fulfilled". At this point in my study I do not think it necessary to include a fourth "fulfilment" scene for the following reasons: (1) instances are rare in prophetic narrative – I have found seven examples (Isa 37,36-38; 38,8b-9; Jer 28,17; 32,8; 40,2-3; Ezek (11,13a,b?); 24,18b; 33,21-22 with 24,25-27); (2) "fulfilment" scenes and citations are not always contiguous with the speech or scene in which the prediction is recorded: this complicates analysis and a resolution to this problem must await further study; (3) Overholt's categories of "feedback" and "confirmation" can be accommodated in the reaction scenes I propose as a series of responses and, in cases where the messenger questions the sender, they may be accommodated as part of the commissioning scene. See below on call narratives.

Commissioning Scene: in which a messenger is commissioned to deliver a message. In its fullest form the scene might involve dialogue between the sender and messenger as, for example, in several of the call narratives (e.g. Exod 3; 5,22-6,13; 1 Sam 2,2-18; Isa 6,1-13; Jer 1,4-19). The message to be communicated may be given in full or summarised; the scene may be reduced to a note of the commissioning or simply implied by the messenger formula or the *Wortempfangsformel*[28].

Delivery Scene: in which the messenger delivers the commissioned message to the receptor audience. The message is sometimes given in full and may or may not be identical to that in the commissioning scene (if one is reported). The scene is often reduced, however, to a short notice of the message's delivery, or it is implied or it is omitted entirely (which is usually the case in the prophets).

Reaction Scene: in which reaction to the messenger or the message is reported. Especially important are examples where the message is repeated, summarised or referred to by the audience (usually as an accusation against the messenger or as a question). Often, no response is reported: however, there are more reaction scenes than delivery scenes. The presence of a reaction scene implies the delivery of a message even when it is not narrated. However, this paper focuses on the way particular scenes are narrated and represented.

III. SOME REACTION-SCENE PATTERNS

Once we allow for a third scene several new patterns emerge which I shall term "reaction scene patterns". Three scene patterns become possible, the number of possible two-scene patterns is increased and single scene narratives that focus on reaction to a message may be accommodated. The forty-three cases I have identified are tabulated in Figure 3 according to the pattern with which they conform.

The variety of reaction scene patterns theoretically possible is large once the way in which the message is reported is taken into account. As with Vater's patterns, in each scene the message might be reported, varied, summarised, noted or passed over. In fact, only a few patterns are instantiated in prophetic narrative, although some are complex and some

---

28. The formal nature of the messenger formula may not allow this inference to be drawn. This paper does not rely upon the messenger formula alone to identify a commissioning scene, although its presence in a delivery scene or reaction scene may imply commissioning. Similar considerations apply to the *Wortempfangsformel* although there are instances where this formula is elaborated significantly.

> **Figure 3: Patterns for the Communication of Commissioned Speech in the Hebrew Prophets**
>
> One-Scene Patterns
>
> | | |
> |---|---|
> | Commissioning only | Jer 3,6-14; 51,59-64b; Ezek 3,22-27; 20,1-44; 40,1-48,35; Zech 7,1-8,23 |
> | Delivery only | Jer 40,1-6 |
> | Reaction only | Jer 32,4-5; Amos 7,10-17; Mal 3,16-18 (uncertain case) |
>
> Two-Scene Patterns
>
> | | |
> |---|---|
> | Commissioning/ Delivery | Jer 25,15-38; 34,1-7; Zech 1,7-6,15; Isa 20,1-6; Jer 13,1-11; Hos 1,2-3,5 |
> | Commissioning/ Reaction | Jer 18,1-23; 37,3-10.16-21; 44,1-30; Ezek 1,1-3,15 |
> | Delivery/Reaction | Isa 38,1-22; Jer 28,1-10; 28,11-17; 38,1-13 |
>
> Three-Scene Patterns
>
> Isa 7,1-24; 8,1-4; 36,1-37,38; Jer 19,1-20,6; 21,1-14; 26,1-24; 29,1-32; 32,6-33,26; 35,1-19; 36,1-32; 38,14-28; 42,1-43,13; Ezek 12,1-20; 24,15-24; 37,1-14; Jonah 1,1-4,11; Hag 1,1-15; Zech 11,4-17

involve a series of reactions. In some cases it is not easy to tell whether we are dealing with a one, two or three scene pattern since, as Vater noted, patterns for communicating commissioned messages in the prophets are often complex. In the analyses that follow I shall deal with a variety of one, two and three scene reaction scene patterns with the aim of indicating both simple and complex narrative patterns.

One-Scene Reaction Patterns

Jer 32,4-5; Amos 7,10-17; Mal 3,16-18 (uncertain).

The clearest example of a reaction scene pattern with one scene is Jer 32,1-5. Here, Zedekiah's response to Jeremiah's preaching is recorded with an account of the prophet's message. Zedekiah is portrayed as quoting offensive aspects of Jeremiah's preaching:

> For Zedekiah king of Judah had imprisoned him, saying, "Why do you prophesy and say, 'Thus says Yahweh: Behold, I am giving this city into the hand of the king of Babylon and he shall take it ...

The tone is accusatory. The placing of Jeremiah's words on the lips of Zedekiah implies a delivery scene and the messenger formula may imply a specific commissioning scene. However, only the "reaction scene" is present and it is clear that the focus lies on the message and Zedekiah's response to it rather than on its commissioning and delivery.

A more complex single scene pattern is found in Amos 7,10-17. This is an extended reaction scene with two parts that portray different aspects of Amaziah's response to Amos' preaching[29]. In the first, Amaziah reports Amos' rebellious words to Jeroboam (7,10-11). Amaziah's quotation (or summary) of Amos' preaching implies a delivery scene in which Amos has spoken his message publicly. We note again that the quotation of the message in a reaction scene is accusatory. In the second part of the reaction scene, Amaziah confronts Amos directly (7,12-17) and Amos defends his right to prophesy on the grounds of Yahweh's commissiong. The reaction scene thus implies both Amos' commission to speak and his delivery of Yahweh's message although neither are explicitly narrated.

The reference to Jeroboam's death by the sword in Amaziah's report of Amos' preaching in 7,11 almost certainly refers back to Yahweh's warning in the preceding vision report (7,9c) that he will fight against Jeroboam's dynasty[30]. Amos 7,10-17 is undoubtedly linked with 7,9[31] and the redactional cohesion of Amos 7,7-17 is therefore to be maintained. However, Amos 7,7-9 contains no elements suggesting either commissioning or proclamation[32]. Consequently, despite the redactional

29. On the two scenes, cf. H.W. WOLFF, *Joel and Amos: A Commentary on the Books of the Prophets Joel and Amos* (Hermeneia), Philadelphia, Fortress, 1977, p. 308; ET from *Dodekapropheten 2: Joel und Amos* (BK XIV/2), Neukirchen-Vluyn, Neukirchener, ²1975, trans. by W. JANZEN, S.D. MCBRIDE and C.A. MEUNCHOW.

30. Such a warning might well be understood as a direct threat against the reigning monarch and in the context of Israelite prophecy and its relation to the monarchy (prophets were often involved in and motivated revolt and dynastic changes cf. e.g. 1 Kings 11,29-39; 19,15; 2 Kings 8,7; 9,1 and the comments of J.L. MAYS, *Amos: A Commentary* (OTL), London, SCM, 1969, p. 135; C.R. NEWCOMBE, *The Prophetic Attitude to Hebrew Kingship* (PhD. diss., Vanderbilt), Ann Arbor, UMI, 1966, ch. 4 *passim*; and H.W. WOLFF, *Joel and Amos*, pp. 309, 316) it would have been a highly charged political statement.

31. H.W. WOLFF, *Joel and Amos*, pp. 295, 302 argues that 7,9 was added to the original form of the third vision report (7,8-9) with the specific aim of introducing 7,10-17 and in order to point up the significance of the third vision report. A.G. AULD, *Amos* (OT Guides), Sheffield, JSOT Press for SOTS, 1986, pp. 20, 28 urges that 7,10-17 was inserted into the cycle of vision reports in which 7,9 was already present. S.M. PAUL, *Amos: A Commentary on the Book Amos* (Hermeneia), Minneapolis, Fortress, 1991, p. 238 notes (*inter alia*) the catch-word connection between 7,9 and 10 as the reason for the insertion of 7,10-17.

32. H.W. WOLFF, *Joel and Amos*, pp. 302-304, believes the visions were determinative of Amos' message, forming part of his experience of calling. However, the vision reports do not constitute a call narrative and contain no commission to speak. Wolff suggests that the visions were reported to Amos' Judahite disciples after his Israelite ministry in order to explain his certainty about Israel's end rather than to defend his right

links between Amos 7,7-9 and 7,10-17 their connections can not be sustained on the level of narrative with which we are here concerned and we must regard Amos 7,10-17 as a separate *narrative* unit.

However, the matter is not quite so easily resolved. J.L. Mays[33] notes that Amaziah mentions only the content and place of delivery of the message and shows no concern for the origin of the message. Similarly, Amaziah has no regard for Amos as a messenger of Yahweh despite calling him a seer (חזה). Amos' replies that he has been commissioned by Yahweh to deliver his message to Israel and recalls his prophetic call "... in order to stress that it is really Yahweh (v. 15), rather than Amos (v. 14), whom Amaziah has denounced and rejected"[34]. The narrative, therefore, unlike the vision reports, refers to both Amos' commission and his delivery of Yahweh's message. The redactor uses these characteristics of the narrative to reflect back upon the vision reports, Yahweh's commission to speak and Amos' obedience to that commission[35]. Consequently we are led back to consider the vision reports in terms of commission and delivery, although for our purposes we have gone far enough in describing this complex "one scene" reaction pattern. While the narrative of the conflict between Amos and Amaziah stands as a single scene reaction pattern, its close links with the preceding vision report might suggest that it can be thought of as a two-scene pattern[36].

Two-Scene Reaction Patterns

Commissioning/reaction — Jer 18,1-23; 37,3-10.16-21; 44,1-30; Ezek 1,1-3,15.

Delivery/reaction — Isa 38,1-22; Jer 28,1-10; 28,11-17; 38,1-13.

There are two types of two-scene reaction patterns; commissioning/reaction and delivery/reaction. Both are present in the prophets and examples of both are examined below.

Jer 38,1-6 is a simple two-scene reaction pattern of the delivery/reaction type. 38,1-3 forms the delivery scene in which four princes hear Jer-

to speak by referring to his call. This does not preclude such a defence, nor the public proclamation of similar reports. However, it is difficult to determine whether the vision reports as recorded in Amos were uttered publicly or in some other form. A narrative connection between Amos 7,7-9 and 7,10-17 would seem to require public proclamation (7,11).

33. J.L. MAYS, *Amos*, pp. 135-136.
34. H.W. WOLFF, *Joel and Amos*, pp. 308, 312, 316.
35. Cf. also H.W. WOLFF, *Joel and Amos*, p. 308 on the narrator's faithfulness to Amos' commission.
36. Cf. my comment in note 1, *supra*, on the need to develop an approach to changes between prose and poetry.

emiah preaching to the people of Jerusalem. The initial focus of the delivery scene lies not on Jeremiah and his message but on the princes who "heard the words that Jeremiah was saying to all the people". This is an important indication that this short narrative will focus on Jeremiah's audience and its response to his speech. Jeremiah's message is recorded in vv. 2-3 using the stereotyped language of Yahweh's "giving" common in the Jeremiah prose[37].

38,4-6 forms the reaction scene in which the princes approach the king and appeal for Jeremiah's death because of the effect on the troops and other people of "these words" (38,4). Although Jeremiah's message is not quoted it is referred to and, again, in an accusatory manner. 38,5-6 records the king's response to the princes' accusation and the punishment they then inflict on Jeremiah. From the opening of the pericope it is clear that it will focus on the prince's response to Jeremiah's preaching rather than the message itself.

Jer 37,3-10 is a two scene reaction pattern of the commissioning/reaction type. The commissioning scene (37,3-5) is of a type found in a number of prophetic books in which a prophet is asked to pray to or enquire of Yahweh[38]. These commissioning scenes may constitute a special case since the commission to speak comes not from the sender of the message but from a potential audience seeking a message. Often in such scenes the request to the prophet is delivered by messengers but in this case the messenger's own commissioning by Zedekiah is portrayed (37,3). The remaining verses set the scene for Jeremiah's arrest and imprisonment in 38,11ff. The messengers' delivery of Zedekiah's request is passed over and we move directly to the reaction scene in 37,6-10. Jeremiah's response is to give Zedekiah's messengers a message to take back to the king.

In Jer 37,16-21 a similar request is made by Zedekiah to Jeremiah but without intermediaries. In this case the request for a word from Yahweh evokes Jeremiah's immediate and terse response using the stereotyped language of Yahweh's "giving". This is followed by further responses from Jeremiah questioning his imprisonment and quoting in accusation the words of "your prophets", together with a plea not to be sent back to the house of Jonathan the secretary for fear of his life. The king's response is to move Jeremiah to another place of detention and ensure that he is fed. In this instance of commissioning/reaction the reaction scene

---

37. Cf. John APPLEGATE, *The Fate of Zedekiah: Redactional Debate in the Book of Jeremiah*, in *VT* 58 (1998) 137-160, esp. pp. 143-145.

38. Other examples include Isa 37,1-7; Jer 21,1-2; 37,16-17; 38,14-16; 42,1-6; Ezek 20,1 (cf. also Ezek 8,1; 14,1); Zech 7,2-3. In Isa 37,8-35 Hezekiah prays to Yahweh and receives a response through Isaiah.

is composed of a series of responses both to the commissioning request and the circumstances described in the commissioning scene.

Three-Scene Reaction Patterns

Isa 7,1-24;8,1-4; 36,1-37,38; Jer 19,1-20,6; 21,1-14; 26,1-24; 29,1-32; 32,6-33,26;35,1-19; 36,1-32; 38,14-28; 42,1-43,13; Ezek 12,1-20; 24,15-24; 37,1-14; Jonah 1,1-4,11; Hag 1,1-15; Zech 11,4-17.

Three-scene patterns show the greatest variety. A simple three-scene pattern is found in Jer 42,1-43,7 which narrates the flight of the Judahite remnant from the land to Egypt following the murder of Gedeliah. The commissioning scene is set out slightly unusually in 42,1-7 where the Judahites remaining in the land ask Jeremiah for Yahweh's guidance and promise to obey whatever he says. The narrative thus highlights the response of the audience (which has requested the message) from the outset. The scene closes as Yahweh's word comes to Jeremiah and moves into the delivery scene as Jeremiah sends for those who had sent him to Yahweh (42,7). The delivery scene continues with a lengthy speech that warns the remnant not to flee to Egypt. The speech also anticipates the audience's response to Yahweh's command (42,8-22) and seeks to persuade the remnant to remain in the land. The reaction scene opens immediately with an accusation against Jeremiah (43,1-3). A summary of Jeremiah's speech is given as part of the accusation, repeating some of the words of 42,19. The narrative then notes that the people and their leaders did not obey Yahweh's will (43,4) before describing the flight of the remnant into Egypt.

Throughout the narrative the response of the remnant is highlighted: in the commissioning scene they promise to do as Yahweh says, in the delivery scene Jeremiah sets out their options and seeks to persuade them to obey Yahweh (which would be unnecessary if they were as committed to Yahweh's will as they say they are) and in the reaction scene they choose to go their own way. I note again that Jeremiah's words are quoted in the reaction scene as part of an accusation against him.

In the following two examples simple three-scene patterns have been built into more complex narratives. In Jonah 3-4 the reaction scene is extended by adding Jonah's own response to Yahweh's commission, his message and the Ninevites' response. It is also used to make further theological points. The extended reaction scene is formed by a series of reaction scenes that bring the book to its climax. In the commissioning scene (3,1-2) Yahweh commissions Jonah again to preach to the Ninevites (cf. 1,2). In the delivery scene (3,3-4) Jonah preaches and his message is briefly recorded. The reaction scene begins in 3,5 as the Ninevites respond to Jonah's preaching by repenting. In 3,6-9 the king of Nineveh responds by repenting and ordering his people to fast and pray that Yahweh may relent. In 3,10 Yahweh responds by relenting and in 4,1-5 Jonah responds by getting angry. Yahweh then seeks to persuade Jonah that his actions are justified in 4,6-11.

In the initial reactions a new relationship is established between God and the Ninevites and this is arguably the climax of the narrative. Jonah's speech is represented as being commissioned with the aim of eliciting repentance from the Ninevites (4,2), and this is confirmed when the threat it contains is not carried out once the Ninevites repent. This emphasises the importance of audience reaction when dealing with prophetic speech (or the *portrayal* of prophetic speech — Jonah is not, after all, entirely typical of Hebrew prophecy[39]). The narrative focuses on the response of the Ninevites and to subsume this into the delivery scene would distort the story at a fundamental level, and make a nonsense of any further analysis of functions in the narrative. In this case, a sequence of reactions is developed and this creates a clever narrative climax to the book.

In Ezek 37 two simple three-scene patterns are combined with a third commissioning to form a complex narrative in the form of a vivid vision report (37,1) concerning the valley of bones. The third commissioned message in 37,11-14 complicates the analysis since it indicates that the vision has the purpose of preparing Ezekiel to communicate another message concerning Yahweh's intentions towards his people and raises the issue of whether the entire pericope should be seen as a single (though complex) commissioning scene. Ezek 37,1-3 introduces the commissioning scene that follows and in 37,4 Yahweh commissions Ezekiel to prophesy to the bones and the message is recorded. The short delivery scene (37,7a) notes that Ezekiel delivered the message as he was told and the reaction scene (37,7b-8) notes that the bones responded. In the second commissioning scene (37,9) Yahweh again commissions Ezekiel to prophesy and the message is recorded. The associated delivery scene (37,10a) notes that Ezekiel again delivered the message as he was told and the reaction scene (37,10b,c) again notes the response. In this case two parallel sequences of commissioning scene with message, note of delivery and note of response prepare Ezekiel for

---

39. Cf. e.g. Robert B. COOTE, *Amos Among the Prophets: Composition and Theology*, Philadelphia, Fortress, 1981, pp. 129-134 for Jonah as midrash on Amos and some of the book's incongruities.

the message Yahweh then commissions him to communicate to his people (Ezek 37,12, reduced commissioning scene with message).

For the final example I have chosen a narrative from Jer that illustrates some of the subtlety of narrative use of the patterns for the communication of commissioned speech.

Jer 26 is generally accepted as being closely related to the so-called "temple sermon" of ch. 7. Jer 26 opens by noting the historical setting of the coming of Yahweh's word to Jeremiah (26,1). The messenger formula precedes Yahweh's commission to Jeremiah; he is told where to go and to speak to those to whom Yahweh commands (26,2). This command is followed by what in Jer is a rare statement of Yahweh's intention in commissiong Jeremiah:

> It may be they will listen, and every one turn from his evil way, that I may repent of the evil which I intend to do to them because of their evil doings (26,3)

In 26,4-6 the commissioning scene closes with Yahweh's statement of the message Jeremiah is to proclaim in the form of protasis with apodosis.

Jer 26,7 is the delivery scene. As in Jer 38,1-6 the scene is reported in the passive and might be better termed a reception scene.

> The priests and the prophets and all the people heard Jeremiah speaking these words in the house of Yahweh (26,7)

Jer 26,8b then opens the extensive reaction scene: Jeremiah is seized, threatened with death for blasphemy[40], and accused or questioned about this preaching. Again part of the message commissioned by Yahweh is repeated by Jeremiah's accusers.

The reaction scene continues with the arrival of the royal princes (שׂרי). Their intervention leads to some form of judicial proceeding before them (26,10) and possibly the people (26,11). Jeremiah is accused of blasphemy by the priests and prophets who call for the death penalty. He then speaks in his own defence, emphasising that he has spoken only because Yahweh commissioned him to speak (26,12-15 cf. *supra* on Amos 7,12-17). Jeremiah is then acquitted by the princes and people (26,16) supported by the appeal to prophetic tradition by some of the elders (26,17-19). There follows an excursus on the fate of Uriah-ben-Shemaiah whose prophecy was similar to Jeremiah's (26,20b) but who

---

40. Cf. Lev 24,10-16. So M. KESSLER, *A Prophetic Biography: A Form Critical Study of Jeremiah 26-29,32-45* (Ph.D. diss. Brandeis), Ann Arbor, UMI, 1965, pp. 94-114; also E.W. NICHOLSON, *Preaching to the Exiles: A Study of the Prose Tradition in the Book of Jeremiah*, Oxford, Blackwell - New York, Schocken, 1970, pp. 52-55.

was hounded and eventually extradited from Egypt for summary execution by King Jehoiakim[41]. The chapter closes by noting that only through the intervention of Ahikam-ben-Shaphan was Jeremiah saved from a similar fate at the hands of the people (26,24)[42].

Jer 26 is concerned primarily with response to Jeremiah and Yahweh's word[43] not only in the extensive reaction scene but throughout. First, the commissioning scene, although it contains a report of the message commissioned, is shortened and highly nuanced[44]. We have already noted that the statement of Yahweh's intention in commissioning Jeremiah to speak (26,3) is unusual in Jer. By noting Yahweh's motivation for commissioning Jeremiah the orientation of the narrative towards the response of Jeremiah's audience is established from the beginning, even before the message itself is noted. Second, the delivery scene is portrayed passively — more as a reception scene, focusing attention upon the prophet's audience. The emphasis here is not upon Jeremiah's delivery of the message so much as his audience's *hearing* it. Third, following E.W. Nicholson[45] and C. Rietzschel[46] we note that the literary unit does not end at 26,16 with Jeremiah's acquittal, but that there are two further related sections focussing on response to the prophetic word before the unit closes with the comment upon Ahikam's intervention. In the first of these two sections (26,17-19) some of the elders cite Micah's words a century before as a precedent in received prophetic tradition for

---

41. One wonders at the wisdom of a political fugitive from Jehoiakim, who was installed by the Pharoah, fleeing to Egypt!

42. E.W. Nicholson, *Preaching to the Exiles*, p. 5, together with C. Rietzschel, *Das Problem der Urrolle: Ein Beitrag zur Redaktionsgeschichte des Jeremiabuches*, Gütersloh, Gütersloher Verlag, 1966, p. 98, suggests that the acquittal of 26,16 is the point at which Jeremiah's life is sagefuarded and that the elders' speech in defence of the prophet would have preceded this. However, 26,24 suggests that Ahikam still had to intervene to save Jeremiah. 26,24 *perhaps* suggests that the people would have lynched Jeremiah had Ahikam not saved him, despite the acquittal, further emphasising their rejection of Jeremiah and Yahweh's word to them. It may be that Jeremiah was acquitted on the strength of his own defence but that the people would not accept the judicial verdict. The elders may then have intervened to save Jeremiah and finally Ahikam. This would preserve the narrative order of ch. 26, but it is difficult to construct historical events from literary texts. Cf. also note 47.

43. Against M. Kessler, *A Prophetic Biography*, pp. 99-114; Id., *Jeremiah 26-45 Reconsidered*, in *JNES* 27 (1968) 81-88, p. 83, who views the ch. as Jeremiah's vindication as a true prophet before Judah's highest court. However, this view cannot be sustained; cf. esp. the discussion of E.W. Nicholson, *Preaching to the Exiles*, pp. 52-55. My comments in this section are indebted to Nicholson, although many of the observations presented are independent.

44. Cf. Jer 26,4-6 with the so-called temple sermon in Jer 7,1-8,3, of which ch. 26 is a recapitulation.

45. E.W. Nicholson, *Preaching to the Exiles*, pp. 53-55.

46. C. Rietzschel, *Das Problem der Urrolle*, p. 98.

prophecy against Jerusalem (26,18; cf. Micah 3,12). But this is not the whole of the elders' argument: the crux is that Micah's threats moved Hezekiah and his people to repentance rather than violence. Hence the people of Hezekiah's time averted Yahweh's punishment. The elders draw a direct contrast between the response of repentance drawn from Hezekiah's people and the violent reaction of Jehoiakim's people. There is also an implicit contrast drawn between the responses of Hezekiah and Jehoiakim, although the latter has yet to be mentioned. In the second section (26,20-23) this implicit contrast is made explicit by the account of Uriah's fate at the hands of Jehoiakim.

Finally, we should note through a comparison with Jer 7,1-8,3 that the narrator has skilfully chosen two perspectives on the communication of a commissioned speech. In the so-called Temple Sermon the narrator emphasises Yahweh's authority, Jeremiah's obedience and the (rather extensive) content of the message. In Jer 26 most of this is suppressed[47] to concentrate upon reaction to and rejection of Yahweh's word. The point is simply to state that the narrator's perspective is chosen, and chosen carefully.

IV. Conclusion

My analysis of reaction scene patterns leads to the following conclusions for our argument overall. First, a three-scne scene model for the communication of commissioned speech is an improvement on Vater's two-scene model practically as well as theoretically. I have demonstrated that response to prophets and their preaching is significant in prophetic narratives. The careful shaping of narratives to focus on responses to prophetic speech argues against Vater's subsuming of reaction to the delivery of a message into the delivery scene.

Second, I have noted in several cases that elements of the commissioned message are repeated in response to the message's delivery. Further, repetition of the messenger's speech by the audience is usually a form of accusation and indicates a negative response to the message delivered.

Third, reaction scenes are not generally instantiated in narratives dealing with the communication of commissioned speech, but are present for some literary and theological purpose. The absence of a reaction scene in many narratives does not invalidate our more general three-scene

---

47. Cf. E.W. Nicholson, *Preaching to the Exiles*, pp. 53-55 on the non-biographical nature of Jer 26.

model for the communication of commissioned speech, but serves to underline the point that their inclusions is significant.

ABSTRACT

The paper argues that the adoption of a three scene model (commissioning, delivery and reaction scenes) is both theoretically required and practically useful in studying narrative patterns for the communication of commissioned speech in the prophets. A two scene model (commissioning and delivery scenes) used in a study of Hebrew narrative books is shown to be inadequate by under-valuing response to Yahweh's prophets and their message. Readings of several "reaction scene patterns" (Jer 26; 32,4-5; 38,1-6; 37,3-10.16-21; 42,1-43,7; Jonah 3-4; Ezek 37; Amos 7,10-17) indicate the importance of reactions in which the audience repeats the prophet's message in accusation.

RÉSUMÉ

Cette étude a pour objet les schèmes narratifs utilisés dans les livres prophétiques pour rapporter la communication du discours dont le prophète est chargé. Elle cherche à montrer que le recours à un modèle comportant trois scènes (commission, exécution de la commission, réaction) est à la fois nécessaire en théorie et utile en pratique. Un modèle ne comportant que deux scènes (la commission et son exécution), qui a été utilisé dans une étude des livres narratifs en hébreu, s'avère inadéquat parce qu'il sous-estime la signification de la réponse suscitée par les prophètes de Yahvé et leur message. La lecture de plusieurs "schèmes de scène de réaction" (Jr 26; 32,4-5; 38,1-6; 37,3-10.16-21; 42,1-43,7; Jon 3-4; Ez 37; Am 7,10-17) montre l'importance de certaines réactions, où l'on voit l'auditoire répéter le message du prophète sous forme d'accusation.

Broughton Rectory
237 Great Clowes Street
Salford M7 2DZ

John APPLEGATE

THE NEW TESTAMENT

6

JESUS WALKING ON THE SEA
THE SIGNIFICANCE OF MATTHEW 14,22-33
FOR THE NARRATIVE DEVELOPMENT OF THE GOSPEL

The elevation to prominence of text-centred approaches to the New Testament in recent years has called into question much of the confidence previously invested in the results of historical criticism. For the student brought up on a diet of Source, Form and Redaction Criticism the encounter with methods such as Narrative Criticism, and the opportunity of teaching them to others, raises many fundamental questions. It is in such a context that this paper appears. Having already completed some substantial unpublished research exploring the sea-walking story from a historical-critical perspective, I now turn to see what may be gained from the application of a narrative methodology.

Despite Rudolf Bultmann's confident assertion that "there must have been stories of walking on the water in Hellenism"[1], virtually nothing can be found which offers any real parallel to the stories of Jesus doing so, which we find recorded by the evangelists Mark, Matthew and John. The historical endeavour to uncover such material was directed at helping the modern reader to understand the significance and function of this strange tale in the way that the original author intended the ancient hearer to do so within the Gospel. The search for relevant materials outside the Jewish and Christian scriptures has proved relatively fruitless.

What little there is may be summarised briefly. Virgil, in the *Aeneid*, describes the ability of the Greek god of the sea to subdue the elements and even to "skim the liquid plains"[2], but since Poseidon does so from the comfort of a chariot, without setting foot on the waves, it hardly bears comparison! Then again, Homer speaks of the ability of Hermes, the messenger of Zeus, to speed "over the wave like a bird, the cormorant, which in the quest for fish... wets its thick plummage in the brine"[3], but only with the help of his magic sandals. This bears no relation to the pictures painted of Jesus by the Gospel writers.

---

1. R. BULTMANN, *The History of the Synoptic Tradition*, Oxford, Blackwell, 1963, p. 236.
2. VIRGIL, *The Aeneid*, trans. J. DRYDEN, New York, Collier & Son, 1909, pp. 80-81.
3. HOMER, *The Odyssey*, trans. A.T. MURRAY, (LCL), London, William Heinemann Ltd, 1919, book V, 51-53.

Dio Chrysostom recalls the power of Xerxes not only to cross the sea himself by chariot, but also to make his men walk across with dry feet[4]! A little investigation, however, uncovers a more rational assessment, from the account of Herodotus, indicating that this hyperbole refers to the incident in which Xerxes made a pontoon bridge out of boats across the Bosphorus over which he marched his army from Asia Minor into Europe[5].

The magical papyri also produce little to help us in understanding the nature or function of this tale. Reitzenstein[6], Dieterich[7] and Bultmann[8] all note short texts which make reference to the ability of both gods and demons to traverse the sea, but these range from solidifying it and then walking across, through hovering above it, to flying over it. None shows the kind of parallel which would illuminate the task of the reader of the Gospel accounts.

Another source of interest has been a story from Buddhist literature, which has been examined by Stehly[9]. It tells of a Buddhist disciple who, finding no boat to transport him across a river, walks over while in a meditative trance inspired by the Buddha. While Stehly may be correct in seeing this story as existing prior to the writing of the Gospel, his positive assessment of the similarities to the Matthean account fails to account for the massive differences[10]. Even if we allow that stories of water-walking from the Indian subcontinent may have indirectly influenced the hellenistic allusions, this is a long way removed from helping our understanding of the function of the Evangelists' accounts.

The attempt to provide extra-canonical historical parallels for this story as a means of understanding its presence and function in the Gospel tradition yields little of significance for us, other than, perhaps, the general inference that the ability to walk on water is something hinted at

---

4. *Dio Chrysostom I*, trans. J.W. COHOON (LCL), London, William Heinemann Ltd, 1949, par. iii, 30-31.

5. *Herodotus V-VII*, trans. A.D. GODLEY (LCL), London, William Heinemann Ltd, 1963, VII, 33-37.

6. R. REITZENSTEIN, *Hellenistische Wundererzählungen*, Stuttgart, Teubner, ²1963, p. 125.

7. A. DIETERICH, *Abraxas. Studien zur Religionsgeschichte des späteren Altertums*, Leipzig, Teubner, 1891, p. 190, lines 13-14.

8. BULTMANN, *History of Synoptic Tradition*, pp. 236-237.

9. R. STEHLY, *Bouddhisme et Nouveau Testament. À propos du miracle de Pierre sur l'eau*, in *RHPR* 57 (1977) 433-437. Cf. R. GARBE, *Indien und das Christentum*, Tübingen, 1914, pp. 56-57; W.N. BROWN, *The Indian and Christian Miracle of Walking on the Water*, London, 1928.

10. See the critique of J.P. HEIL, *Jesus Walking on the Sea. Meaning and Gospel Function of Matt 14:22-33; Mark 6,45-52 and John 6:15b-21* (AnBib 87), Rome, Biblical Institute Press, 1981, pp. 64-65.

only in relation to divine figures or their entranced followers. Since the Matthean account already acknowledges this in some measure by the acclamation of verse 33, this leaves little reward for much historical hard searching. In adopting a narrative approach to Matthew's version, the most highly developed of the three, we shall see if new light may be thrown on its literary and theological function within the grand narrative of the Gospel.

Structurally speaking, the sea-walking tale stands near the centre of Matthew's story. In doing so it occupies, with the surrounding micro-narratives, a crucial place in the development of the macro-narrative. Like all centres, it has the potential to act as a pivot for the material which lies before and that which is yet to come. In this respect it occupies a different place from its partners in the Markan and Johannine accounts, in both of which it appears at an earlier point in the macro-narrative.

Its *immediate* context is the section which runs from 13,53 through to 16,20. The literary marker at 13,53 – καὶ ἐγένετο ὅτε ἐτέλεσεν ὁ Ἰησοῦς – is commonly used in Matthew's story to enable the implied reader to hear the movement of the scene from teaching to story-telling[11]. Another special literary marker is found at 16,21 – ἀπὸ τότε ἤρξατο ὁ Ἰησοῦς – and this helps delineate the *wider* context, since a parallel is found at 4,17. The implied author anticipates that the reader will hear the ministry of Jesus in two clear blocks under specific rubrics. The first of these runs from 4,17-16,20 and concerns the 'preaching of the kingdom of heaven, which is at hand'. The second block, beginning in 16,21, indicates the focus of the coming material on the suffering, death and ultimate resurrection of the one immediately previously confessed as the Christ, the Son of God.

In order to see more clearly the function of the sea-walking story within the Gospel as a whole it is first necessary to offer a brief outline of the text itself. Since by its very nature the narrative approach to the Gospels demands that we allow space for meaning to emerge from the ebb and flow of the macro-narrative, our immediate attention to this micro-narrative will take the form of description and identification of themes. We shall then turn to see what light the interaction of the micro- and macro-narrative sheds one on the other.

The story opens with the deliberate[12] separation of Jesus from the disciples through the command to enter the boat. This already raises some

---

11. Cf. Mt 7,28; 11,1; 19,1; 26,1.
12. The use of the rare word ἀναγκάζω here indicates the "compelling" nature of the separation. Cf. W. GRUNDMANN, ἀναγκάζω, in *TDNT*, I, p. 345.

tension for the reader, who knows that in the only previous sea story, where the disciples were also left in charge, danger has threatened to overwhelm them (Mt 8,18-27). The indication that they should "go on ahead" (προάγειν) suggests that Jesus will follow, but his means and timing are left unclear.

Jesus, now separated from the occupants of the boat, dismisses the crowd – a fact which the narrator rather pedantically refers to twice. This probably serves to underline "the private character of the epiphany about to take place between Jesus and his disciples"[13]. Using a typical intertextual echo of the Jewish scriptures[14], the narrator reports Jesus' ascent into the mountain, from whence, following prayer, his coming will take place. Although the reader has already heard much about prayer (5,44; 6,5-15), this is the first occasion on which Jesus himself actually prays. Schweizer suggests that this is "to show where the source of Jesus' authority is to be found"[15].

Given the importance of temporal markers for the development of narrative, it is striking to find in verse 23 an apparently superfluous reference to the fall of night. In verse 15 the reader has previously been informed, using the identical phrase, that evening has come. Indeed, the boat has set off with this in mind. The reemphasis thus serves to highlight the development of two temporally parallel scenes and to continue building the tension of separation, loneliness and foreboding. Echoes of the prior night-storm story are apparent to the reader here.

The boat is by now well out into the lake, battling against the elements in a scene strongly reminiscent of that earlier sea story. It also evokes the Psalmist, whose picture of distressed sailors crying on Yahweh's power over the elements is easily noted by the informed narratee (Ps 107,23-30). The distress of Matthew's boat and its occupants calls for action.

About three in the morning, Jesus comes to the boat, walking on the water. The many direct quotations and implicit echoes from the Torah, the Psalms and the prophets in the macro-narrative, indicate that the implied reader knows "the scriptures"[16]. An allusion may be heard here to the hour before dawn, when Yahweh comes to the rescue of Israel[17], raising the expectation of the reader.

13. HEIL, *Jesus Walking on the Sea* (n. 10), p. 32.
14. The phrase ἀνέβη εἰς τὸ ὄρος is precisely that used in the LXX version of Exod 19,3, where Moses goes up to receive the Law at Sinai. The ascent of the mountain also echoes several other appearances within the Gospel itself: 4,8; 5,1; 15,29; 17,1; 24,16; 26,30; 28,16.
15. E. SCHWEIZER, *The Gospel According to Mark*, London, SPCK, 1970, p. 142.
16. Given that the work is written in Greek, it must be the LXX which is assumed here.

The approach of Jesus at first seems to add to the problems of the occupants of the boat rather than relieving them. They mistake him for a "ghost" and cry out in terror. In a previous epiphany narrative, the unbelieving Herod's fear (2,3) was described in exactly the same way (ταράσσειν), so the reader is now anxious to know the end result of Jesus' miraculous appearance[18]. The story appears to be coming to a climax with the self-identification of Jesus and words of reassurance, again with echoes of Yahweh's mode of speech[19]. A surprise awaits the reader, however, as the story does not reach its resolution at this point.

Perhaps the reader *should* expect a conversation to follow here, since the narrator has already frequently placed such dialogues at the centre of miracle stories[20]. The nature of the request, however, remains startling. Peter asks Jesus to empower him also to walk on water, *if* it really is Jesus. The element of doubt in Peter's request maintains the tension of the unfolding drama, which still seeks a resolution to the plight of the boat and its occupants. It is notable that the narrator changes the language slightly at this point, with the request to come on the "waters" (ἐπὶ τὰ ὕδατα) rather than on the sea (ἐπὶ τῆς θαλάσσης). Again, the implied reader's knowledge of the scriptures leaves open an echo of the Psalmist's plight, as the "waters" come up to his neck (Ps 69,1). This will become all the more poignant as the story progresses. For the meantime, Peter responds to the command of Jesus – "Come" – disembarks[21] from the boat, walks on the water and reaches Jesus[22]. In the parable of faith, Peter's first steps lead on to triumph.

17. For example, see Isa 17,14. There are other notable references to divine presence at this hour in the Exodus tradition, for example, in Exod 14,24; 34,2,4, the latter being a *theophany* story. Cf. J. GNILKA, *Das Evangelium nach Markus* (EKK II,1), Neukirchen, Neukirchener Verlag, 1978, pp. 268-269.

18. Such fear will strike again in the post-resurrection stories of Mt 28.

19. The ἐγώ εἰμι formula is common in the LXX, but see most importantly at Exod 3,14, and Isa 43,1-13 where it is found in close conjunction with the command μὴ φοβεῖσθε.

20. Cf. Mt 8,5-13; 8,23-27; 8,28-34; 9,18-26; 9,27-31. Cf. H.-J. HELD, *Matthew as Interpreter of the Miracle Stories*, in G. BORNKAMM, G. BARTH, H.-J. HELD, *Tradition and Interpretation in Matthew*, London, SCM, 1963, pp. 233-237.

21. Καταβαίνω is a rather strange choice of word here, where one would expect ἐκβαίνω. The same applies to the use of ἀναβαίνω in verse 32, not least since Matthew uses the regular word ἐμβαίνω on all other occasions. The terms καταβαίνω and ἀναβαίνω more usually carry overtones of eschatological revelation in Matthew.

22. It is important to decide on the nature of the aorist ἦλθεν here. If it is ingressive (cf. R.V.G. TASKER, *The Gospel According to Matthew: An Introduction and Commentary*, Grand Rapids, Eerdmans, 1961, p. 145) then the point of contrast in the parable of faith is lost – Peter in no way succeeds. If it is taken as a simple past tense, then Peter initially succeeds in his attempt, before later doubting and sinking. The point of the narrative seems to be the latter. Only an effort to protect the historicity of the account (*not a* concern of the narrative critic) would necessitate an ingressive understanding.

The triumph is short-lived as the storm, earlier a threat and hindrance to the boat, now re-enters the frame as a main player. Peter takes his eyes off Jesus and sees the overwhelming forces of nature at work around him. He loses his faith and immediately begins to sink: the reader, like Peter, fears the worst. Now there is nowhere else to turn than to the one whom he has clearly doubted. The cry is an echo of the previous storm story: κύριε, σῶσον, as is the response: rescue, followed by the rebuke, ὀλιγόπιστος, a catchword link for the reader. Almost casually, then, as Jesus and Peter climb into the boat, the narrator notes that the storm subsides, binding the two sea stories yet more closely together.

The account now finally reaches its climax as the occupants of the boat fall down and worship Jesus, declaring him to be the Son of God. Whether or not this number includes Peter is left unclear, though the later development of the narrative may help us suggest an answer. The reason for their confession is also unstated, but it might initially be assumed to be a response to the demonstration of power over the elements. That the prior sea-story did not evoke such devotion from the occupants of the boat does, however, leave the question open to further clarification from the macro-narrative context.

It is to that context, and the setting of this micro-narrative therein, that we now turn. The *main* themes which emerge from the sea-walking story may be summarised in order of appearance as follows:

a. the tension arising from the separation of Jesus from the boat's occupants;
b. the authority of Jesus over the elements;
c. the ambivalent nature of discipleship: doubt and faith as equal partners;
d. the saving power of Jesus in the face of failure and distress;
e. the identity and nature of Jesus as Son of God.

That these themes are part of an ongoing narrative development may be seen from an examination of the relationship to certain other micro-narratives which appear at key points of the Gospel. The choice of these is limited within the confines of this present paper and the discussion does not take account of their mutual interdependence, being restricted to their relationship to the *sea-walking* story. This may be represented diagrammatically, thus[23]:

---

23. Section B may be divided into two large sections under the rubrics noted above (4,17; 16,21). Given the limited space of this study I have chosen two micro-narratives from the first part. In the second part it would easily be possible to show similar relationships between, for example, the Transfiguration (17,1-13) and the Entry into Jerusalem (21,1-11).

Section A 1,1-4,16	Section B 4,17-25,46			Section C 26,1-28:20
4,1-11 Temptation Story	8,23(18)-27 Storm Stilling	14,22-33 Sea-Walking	16,13-20 Caesarea Philippi	28,16-20 Commissioning

The Temptation Story (Mt 4,1-11)

Following upon the baptism of Jesus (3,13-17), in which his Sonship has been declared by the "heavenly voice", the Temptation narrative connects both linguistically and theologically through the use of the title Son of God. For the implied reader this story becomes a stepping-stone to the forthcoming public ministry of Jesus, in which the character and consistency of this intimate connection with God will be put to the test. The first two temptations function as a clarification of the nature of Jesus' Sonship. As Schweizer puts it: "the temptation is for Jesus to misconstrue divine sonship as the power to do miracles"[24]. The third temptation concerns the understanding of "kingdom", an important precursor to the declaration of 4,17, that in this Jesus the kingdom has come near. Jesus' rejection of the taunt to prove himself through miraculous intervention and of a territorial understanding of kingdom leave the reader with the expectation of an unfolding ministry which reinforces these ideals. Filson anticipates this when he comments: "throughout his ministry he refused to use his power for his own benefit"[25].

With this is mind we turn again to the declaration of Jesus as Son of God by the occupants of the boat in 14,33. For the alert reader, this confession, the first such by any of the followers of Jesus, needs to be tested in the light of the defining dialogues of the temptation narrative. Has Jesus succumbed to the testing which he previously resisted, to prove himself in miraculous self-disclosure? Other echoes will need to be heard before this can be answered with any degree of security, but the implied reader is called upon to question such an easy response in the light of 4,1-11. The emphasis of the sea-walking story upon the rescue of both Peter and, less prominently, the whole boatload through stilling the wind and waves must be taken together with the defining nature of the temptation narrative. When seen in this way it points to the miraculous action

---

24. E. SCHWEIZER, *The Good News According to Matthew*, trans. D.E. GREEN, London, SPCK, 1975, p. 62.
25. F.V. FILSON, *The Gospel According to St Matthew*, London, A&C Black, 1960, p. 70. Filson's interest is entirely historical rather than literary at this point.

of Jesus as a response to the distress of the boat's occupants and thus in line with other miraculous interventions of Jesus on behalf of distressed humanity.

The Storm-Stilling (Mt 8,18-27)

This becomes yet clearer in the light of the relationship between the two sea stories, on which we have already briefly remarked. The similarities between these micro-narratives are so numerous that it is helpful to gain an overview through placing them alongside one another in tabular form:

	Storm-Stilling (8,18-27)	*Sea-Walking* (14,22-33)
Disciples separated from crowd (& Jesus)	8,18	14,22
Storm threatens to engulf *the boat*	8,24	14,24
Storm does not seem to trouble Jesus	8,24 – he is sleeping	14,25 – he walks through it
Fear noted	8,26	14,26-27
Cry for help, using the title 'Lord'	8,25 – κύριε, σῶσον	14,30 – κύριε, σῶσον
Rescue linked to word of rebuke	8,26 – ὀλιγόπιστοι	14,31 – ὀλιγόπιστε
Closing communal response	8,27 – what kind of man is this?	14,33 – truly you are the Son of God

When we observe these literary parallels several notable intertextual echoes seem to be evoked for the implied reader. The specific separation of the disciples from the crowd in both instances indicates the stress upon *discipleship* as a theme. This is also reinforced in the storm-stilling narrative by the narrator's deliberate introduction of two short sayings about discipleship into the early part of the story (8,19-22). It is only those who are really prepared to follow who actually disembark on the fateful journey[26]. The reader approaches the sea-walking story already knowing the outcome of the previous storm incident and its implications for discipleship. Peter's actions, in 14,28-31, thus stand under this

---

26. The fateful nature of the entire journey of discipleship will be clarified further in the opening of the next major section, 16,21-26.

shadow and illustrate for the reader both the consequences of high faith (reaching Jesus) and of little faith (needing to be rescued).

Jesus' action is miraculous in both instances, but given the context of concern for the meaning of discipleship, his motivation becomes clearer. Far from being a mere theophanic display of power over nature, both stories become examples of what the temptation narratives have foreshadowed: namely, the power of Jesus to exercise authority as Son of God in the interests of struggling humanity, rather than for self-glorification.

The emphasis on the *boat* rather than the group of disciples, appears to invite the reader to be a part of these stories. They are not merely for those disciples who belong in the narrative with Jesus, but for all who belong to such living narratives in isolated, storm-tossed boats, literal or metaphorical. This has its implications also in the designation of the boat's occupants, and Peter, as people of "little faith". On three of the five occasions when the disciples play an active role in miracle stories in the macro-narrative, they are addressed as ὀλιγόπιστοι[27]. The implied reader recognises the failure of discipleship and the need for Jesus' outstretched arm to calm and to save.

The obvious echoing within these two stories offers us an important insight into the narrative development of Matthew's christology. The reader has been left with an unanswered question at the end of the storm-stilling. Far from confessing Jesus as Son of God, the occupants of the boat ponder "what kind of man" this is. Although the Gaderene demoniacs will ironically point the way in the following micro-narrative (8,29), the followers of Jesus need more persuasion. As the reader approaches the sea-walking with the storm-stilling in mind, an answer suddenly offers itself. The "kind of man" who enters the boat, stilling the waves for a second time, is none other than the Son of God, who comes in power *to rescue and save those in distress*. The two stories thus echo each other as question and answer.

This also helps to push along the narrator's disclosure of the nature of Jesus' revelation of God, from baptismal voice, through temptation and miraculous intervention to confession. The many intertextual references to the Jewish scriptures which both these stories evoke also point the scripturally literate implied reader to the one whom Jesus represents. The Gentile centurion at the foot of the cross will later echo and confirm all these developments in the identical declaration of the suffering, dying Jesus as Son of God (27,54).

27. Cf. HELD, *Matthew as Interpreter* (n. 20), pp. 181-206.

Caesarea Philippi (Mt 16,13-20)

The narrative relationship of the sea-walking to the incident at Caesarea Philippi provides the reader with further clarification of the meaning of the title Son of God. Clearly the two are linked by the prominent role of Peter in both and by the use of the title for the second time. In fact, the reader encounters not one, but *three* titles for Jesus in the space of a few verses (Son of Man, 16,13; Messiah, 16,16.20; Son of [the living] God, 16,16), the close conjunction allowing each to clarify the others[28]. What emerges from this is that the title Son of God is, in fact, the defining one for the reader's proper understanding of who Jesus really is. The two titles, Messiah and Son of God, initially come as clarification of who Son of Man is, but the command to secrecy is applied only to the first of these, Messiah (16,20). Given the baptismal voice, the temptation clarification, the voice of the demoniacs and the earlier confession in 14,33, the reader knows that a command to silence on Jesus' identity as Son of God would be highly inconsistent. What Jesus rejects here is the implied reader's potential misunderstanding of the Jewish messianic title as a true definition of Son of God. Instead this stands under the influence of its previous usage in the macro-narrative.

An interesting narrative reversal takes place in the conjunction of these two stories, which is easiest illustrated diagrammatically:

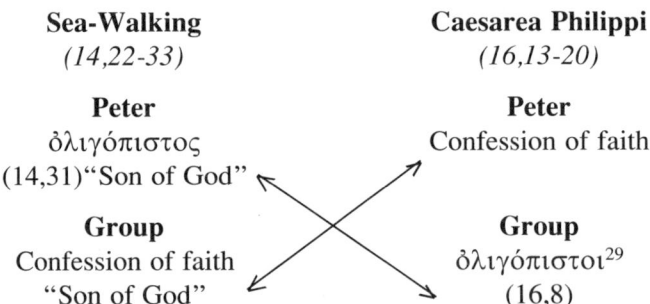

This reversal of roles between the two actors in these scenes illustrates again for the reader what Peter himself has demonstrated in 14,28-31, the constant ambiguity of discipleship. On the one hand there are moments of abject failure, doubt and misunderstanding, while on the other there can be moments of the highest success, faith and insight. That the

---

28. SCHWEIZER, *Matthew* (n. 24), p. 340 notes this exegetical relationship, as, more fully, does J.P. MEIER, *The Vision of Matthew. Christ, Church and Morality in the First Gospel*, New York, Paulist Press, 1979, p. 109.

reader should see this as a pattern common to *all* disciples is attested by the character reversal between the two moments of doubt and faith.

This reversal of role may also help the reader to attempt an answer to the question left open before as to whether Peter is included amongst those "in the boat" who confess Jesus as Son of God in 14,33. On the model shown here, it is at least possible to suggest that the role reversal indicates that 16,16 is the point at which *Peter* has the opportunity to illustrate such "high faith", while the rest of the disciple group demonstrates "little faith". This would then parallel his "little faith" in 14,31 and the rest of the group's "high faith" (14,33).

The narrator is keen to move the understanding of Jesus as Son of God on a little further in this incident and does so by the addition of the word "living" in 16,16 (τοῦ ζῶντος). This is a title full of intertextual echo of the Jewish scriptures, where the implied reader's knowledge of the LXX makes an immediate connection with the image of Yahweh as the giver of life[30]. This helps to clarify further the nature of the person whom the group, and now Peter, have confessed as Son of God in response to the saving intervention through the sea-walking. No confusion may now arise for the reader, who sees in Jesus the saving and liberating presence of the living God. That this one is also Son of Man (who suffers and dies and comes again in glory – 16,21-28) maintains the consistency of christological development from its inception (or *con*ception – 1,18-25), through the public ministry to this point.

The Commissioning (Mt 28,16-20)

If the sea-walking stands as a pivot near the centre of the macro-narrative, it is hardly surprising that it should be heard in echo once again as the reader reaches the conclusion of the book. Since "settings often participate in the drama of the narrative... [and] contribute to the meaning of the narrative for the implied reader"[31], it is notable that we again find a "mountain-top" experience to lie at the centre of this concluding piece of narration. An immediate link is established not only with the rich intertextual echoes of the Jewish scriptures, but also with

29. Although this verse does not belong in the Caesarea Philippi incident directly its relationship to the misunderstanding of the group is rehearsed again in 16,14. Peter is singled out as the one with the correct understanding in 16,17-19.

30. For examples of direct reference to Yahweh in this way see, Isa 37,17; Dan 6,20.26; Hos 1,10. The creation imagery of Yahweh as the giver of life is overwhelmingly part of Jewish tradition.

31. E.S. MALBON, *Narrative Criticism: How Does the Story Mean?* in J.C. ANDERSON and S.D. MOORE (eds.), *Mark and Method. New Approaches in Biblical Studies*, Philadelphia, Fortress Press, 1992, p. 31.

the frequent episodes in which the ascent of the mountain has played a role. Amongst these, of course, is the sea-walking story.

Since these mountain-top words bring the narrative to an end, their primary literary function is to look back, rather than forwards as all the previous micro-narratives have done[32]. There are three particular allusions which connect with the sea-walking: [1] the element of continuing ambivalence between doubt and faith (28,17); [2] the question of the nature of Jesus' authority (28,18); [3] the tension between the absence and presence of Jesus (20,20).

We have seen in both the sea-walking and the Caesarea Philippi incident how the implied reader recognises the wavering nature of faith and doubt. This has been seen as a common experience of all disciples. Once again the mountain top encounter proves this to be the case. While some, like the group in the boat, fall down in worship (προσκυνέω – 14,33; 28,17), others are still left doubting (διστάζω – 14,31; 28,17). That *all* are addressed by the risen Jesus is indicative of the acceptance which accords to disciples, despite their little, or wavering faith. The final words affirm that doubt may be overcome where and when the commission of the risen Lord is heard and followed, a point earlier illustrated by Peter's coming to Jesus on the water in 14,29.

This raises the question of the nature of Jesus' authority both to act and to command. That his authority has been exercised with a view to the relief and salvation of people in their distress has been amply demonstrated in the miracle stories, among which the sea-walking has been seen as definitive. The reader is finally reminded of this *earthly* authority, and pointed to the *cosmic* dimension which accompanies it with the addition of the word "heaven" (οὐρανός – 28,18). The reader hears in this, and the following words, that the authority of Jesus is not merely part of a future realm, but is already present. And it is in that authority that the disciple, in trepidation or high faith, goes forth into the mission of the risen Jesus, now known as the Christ, the Son of God.

The closing words of the narrative – ἐγὼ μεθ' ὑμῶν εἰμι – also point back to our sea-walking story. Much more than that, they form an *inclusio* with the opening chapter, where the theme of God's immanence in Jesus was announced (1,23). The reader has seen from the beginning the indicators pointing to what the final words confirm. The epiphanic nature of God's presence is clearly symbolised at the heart of the macro-narrative by the coming of Jesus at the most impossible and distant moment, walking on the sea. Heil sums this up when he says:

32. That is not to deny the possibility that the reader still looks "forward", entering a narrative "dialogue" beyond the written text.

Just as the power of Jesus to overcome the obstacles separating him from his disciples so that he could be with them in the sea-walking epiphany exemplified that he represents Immanuel, "God with us" (1,23), so also the sea-walking power of Jesus substantiates the promise of his last words to his disciples in 28,20[33].

The narrative relationship between the announcement of the birth of Jesus as the epiphany of God, the symbolic enactment of that presence in the sea-walking, and the final words of promise, forms a crucial framework for the Gospel. All that lies within invites the reader to ponder the significance of this for their own journey of discipleship.

The sea-walking thus finds its place as a pivotal micro-narrative in the grand scheme of Matthew's story. Just as the historical approach to understanding the story as a possible parallel to other ancient stories of the type proved largely unsatisfying, so too the attempt to view it as an historical event misses its point entirely. By catching a glimpse of its literary and theological role in the developing narrative we begin to come closer to understanding its overall significance. The constant ebb and flow of meaning, and the persistent re-echoing of the themes of the macro-narrative draws the reader ever more into the story. The narrator aims to convince the implied reader of the ambiguity of discipleship, the authority of Jesus and the continuing presence of the God whose mission Jesus has begun and entrusted to the disciple until the end of the age. These are constant themes of both micro- and macro-narrative, and the ones to which we ourselves as readers and companions in the narrative are drawn anew.

ABSTRACT

The historical-critical method has largely concentrated on either the search for parallels in ancient literature or redactional elements as a key to understanding the presence and function of this story in Matthew's Gospel. Given the often meagre results of such investigation, a narrative approach is adopted here to see if new light may be thrown on its literary and theological function within the grand narrative of the Gospel. By highlighting the story's literary relationship to other micro-narrative elements, we see the pivotal role which Matthew 14,22-33 plays in the development of some crucial themes in Matthew's Gospel. Amongst these themes are the identity and nature of Jesus as Son of God; the ambiguity of discipleship and the saving power of Jesus in the face of failure and distress; the authority of Jesus and the continuing presence with the disciple

---

33. HEIL, *Jesus Walking on the Sea* (n. 10), p. 117.

of the God whose mission Jesus has begun. The Sea-Walking story thus appears as an integral, indispensable element in the emergence of Matthew's literary and theological framework, both building upon earlier accounts (the Temptation; the Storm-Stilling), and opening the way for later theological developments (Caesarea Philippi; the Great Commission). Its persistent intertextual echoes also reflect Matthew's wider attempt to draw the reader into the scope of Israel's salvation history, now centred in Jesus

RÉSUMÉ

La méthode historico-critique, à la recherche d'une clé permettant de comprendre la présence et la fonction de l'histoire de la marche de Jésus sur les eaux dans l'Évangile de Matthieu, s'est concentrée soit sur la quête de parallèles dans la littérature ancienne, soit sur l'identification d'éléments rédactionnels. Étant donné les résultats assez maigres d'une telle d'étude, l'auteur adopte ici une approche narrative, susceptible de jeter un éclairage nouveau sur la fonction littéraire et théologique de l'épisode au sein du macro-récit de l'Évangile. L'étude met en lumière la relation littéraire qu'entretient Matthieu 14,22-23 avec des éléments d'autres micro-récits; elle montre ainsi que l'histoire de la marche sur les eaux a un rôle de pivot dans le développement de certains thèmes essentiels de l'Évangile de Matthieu. Parmi ces thèmes on relève entre autres ceux-ci: l'identité et la nature de Jésus en tant que Fils de Dieu; l'ambiguïté du statut du disciple et le pouvoir salvateur de Jésus face à l'échec et à la détresse; l'autorité de Jésus et la présence ininterrompue avec le disciple de ce Dieu dont Jésus a inauguré la mission. L'histoire de Jésus marchant sur les eaux se révèle ainsi être un élément constitutif et indispensable dans la mise en place de la structure littéraire et théologique de l'évangile de Matthieu; d'un côté, elle prend appui sur des récits antérieurs (la Tentation; la Tempête apaisée); de l'autre elle ouvre la voie à des développements théologiques ultérieurs (la Confession à Césarée de Philippe; l'Envoi en mission). Les échos intertextuels ainsi créés reflètent également une visée plus large de Matthieu, qui cherche à faire entrer le lecteur dans le champ de l'histoire du salut d'Israël, désormais centrée sur Jésus.

73 Inverleith Row J. Martin C. Scott
Edinburgh EH3 5LT

7

MARKAN INTERCALATION IN CULTURAL CONTEXT

There have been a number of monographs and articles of late discussing "intercalation" in Mark's writing. He repeatedly "sandwiches" one narrative that would seem able to stand on its own within another that would seem entirely coherent without it, "cutting" sharply from the one to the other and back again: a^1-b-a^2. Yet, independent as they seem, each, inner and outer, would seem to illuminate the other. Attention has tended to focus on examples where the inner story (b) includes a character or characters who do not appear in the "framing" episode (a); but other instances are suggested, for instance, where the "inner" (b) is a monologue, discourse material. The history of research, from Ernst von Dobschütz onwards is summarised by others (and I have not pursued it myself). I am largely persuaded by Tom Shepherd, *The Narrative Function of Markan Intercalation*, but accept some critical comments from Geert Van Oyen[1].

Where earlier commentators have discerned simply (but still significantly) a device to engage and maintain interest, more recent ones find it used to emphasise important theological themes: for instance, faith, witness, judgment, apostasy[2].

Most of the authors I have read seem content to restrict their discussion of the narrative function and force of this phenomenon to its appearance in Mark. James R. Edwards does call attention to instances of "flashback" in Homer which "interrupt" a narrative; but only Mk 6,14-29, the death of the Baptist, seems at all analogous. In 2 Maccabees, 8,30-33 seem to disrupt the main sequence of the battle with Nicanor, 8,23-36; but Edwards cannot discern there any of the sorts of interconnection that most now perceive in the Markan examples. He has more confidence in proposing the discourse material of Hos 2 within the nar-

---

1. T. SHEPHERD, *The Narrative Function of Markan Intercalation*, in NTS 41 (1995) 522-540; G. VAN OYEN, *Intercalation and Irony in the Gospel of Mark*, in F. VAN SEGBROECK et alii (eds.), *The Four Gospels 1992. Festschrift Frans Neirynck* (BETL, 100), Leuven, University Press-Peeters, 1992, pp. 949-974.

2. J.R. EDWARDS, *Markan Sandwiches. The Significance of Interpolations in Markan Narratives*, in NT 31 (1989) 193-216, p. 216; as noted with apparent agreement by VAN OYEN, *Intercalation*, p. 962; cf. T. SHEPHERD, *Narrative Function*, p. 540, "secrecy and revelation, life and death, cleansing and cursing, poverty and riches, suffering and resurrection."

rative of chapters 1 and 3; or Nathan's dialogue with David, within 2 Sam 11,1-12,25. However, he then points out that here, too, there is an important difference, the inner matter is in each case an intentional comment on the flanking narrative, whereas in Mark this is true only of 4,1-20 (which others, of course, often exclude from their lists); and himself concludes, "We are thus left to examine Mark's material on its own"[3]. My main concern in what follows is to see whether analogies to this procedure of Mark's may be found elsewhere in the available literature of Mediterranean late antiquity.

Of course, it is not impossible that Mark may have been very innovative; but at least it would seem obvious that we should look further for possible precedents. If recent commentators are right that this is a frequent and significant device in Mark's construction of his narrative, but one for which there is no indication that his lector is expected to provide any explanation (there is no "let the reader understand" inserted at these points), then it would seem likely that Mark expected the hearers to be equiped to cope.

Other studies over the past fifteen years or so, often picking up much older ones, would at least tend to encourage such a search. Strong arguments have been advanced against concluding that Mark (and the other gospels) were in any strong sense *sui generis*; we may note in particular Richard Burridge's *What are the Gospels?*[4]. Vernon Robbins has argued cogently that Mark will have learned his "three-step progressions" "where he learned to compose in Greek"; and suggests various analogies from Greco-Roman literature for Mark's portrayal of Jesus with disciples[5]. In his study of the abrupt ending of Mark, J. L. Magness has adduced relevant comparisons from Homer, Vergil, Xenophon and Philostratus[6]. Mark's composition is significantly formed by the Jewish Scriptures, for sure, but by other influences and expectations besides.

---

3. J.R. EDWARDS, *Markan Sandwiches*, p. 203; as noted with apparent agreement by G. VAN OYEN, *Intercalation*, p. 961, n. 58.

4. R.A. BURRIDGE, *What are the Gospels?* (SNTSMS, 70) Cambridge, University Press, 1992, building on while criticising C.H. TALBERT, *What is a Gospel? The Genre of the Canonical Gospels*, London, SPCK, 1978; P.L. SHULER, *A Genre for the Gospels: The Biographical Character of Matthew*, Philadelphia, Fortress Press, 1982.

5. V.K. ROBBINS, *Summons and Outline in Mark: The Three-Step Progression*, in *NT* 23 (1981) 97-114; and *Jesus the Teacher. A Socio-Historical Interpretation of Mark*, Philadelphia, Fortress Press, 1984; cf. his careful consideration of the abusive mockery of a prisoner in the wider Mediterranean world, *The Reversed Contextualisation of Psalm 22 in the Markan Crucifixion*, in F. VAN SEGBROECK, *The Four Gospels* (n. 1), pp. 1161-1182; cf. also, F. NEIRYNCK, *Duality in Mark. Contributions to the Study of the Markan Redaction* (BETL, 31), Leuven, University Press-Peeters, 1972.

6. J.L. MAGNESS, *Sense and Absence. Structure and Suspension in the End of Mark's Gospel*, Atlanta, Scholars Press, 1986.

We need now to define a little more clearly that for which we are seeking analogies. Although a main character or characters (in this case, mostly, Jesus) may act in both stories, there are always characters who (or items which – the fig-tree in ch. 11) appear only in the middle; 14,53-72 (with Peter's Denial) has no protagonists common to both narratives[7]; nor has 6,7-32 (with the death of the Baptist). Although mostly the inner tale fits within the time of the outer one (and makes and fills a gap there), the two may well in one instance be contemporaneous (14,53-72, again)[8]. The two events are located in different even if nearby places. Similar or else very clearly contrasting actions are performed (including ideas enunciated) by contrasting or similar protagonists in each, so that each tale seems to interpret the other, with the resonances drawing our attention to the themes at issue as well as engaging our interest, as indeed the interruption does itself. There is then a dramatic irony evoked, for the author and the hearer obviously understand more than the protagonists can, unable as the latter are to share in comparing and contrasting the stories which both link and separate them.

We need then to tabulate and label those common features that are widely discerned in the Markan intercalations.

(A) Some distinct or entirely distinct character(s) [item(s)] in the middle sequence (b).

(B) A distinct even if neighbouring locality for the middle sequence (b).

(C) An a^1-b-a^2 time sequence (even a^1-b^1-a^2-b^2, as at Mk 11,11-25) *or* contemporaneity (but not "a" complete before "b" starts).

(D) There are similarities and contrasts in characters and actions.

(F) We may well discern a dramatic irony – as hearers we know more than do the actors. Nonetheless, even should we find that some or all of these motifs so described and labelled occur in other narratives, we might well want to make yet more detailed comparisons, and might still find Mark distinctive, even if perhaps not quite as unprecedented in his intercalations as recent studies of the device may lead us to conclude.

We are, however, presented with a somewhat unpromising start. However effective some of today's readers find this aspect of Mark's

---

7. Agreeing with VAN OYEN, *Intercalation*, p. 967, against SHEPHERD in his earlier dissertation, *The Definition and Function of Markan Intercalation as Illustrated in a Narrative Analysis of Six Passages*, Andrews University, 1991, pp. 327-328; but see SHEPHERD's response, *Narrative Function*, pp. 527-28.

8. Again agreeing with VAN OYEN, as in n. 7, above.

story-telling, it is well known that Matthew and Luke seem to have been much less impressed. In only one instance from the most frequent list of six do both find Mark's sandwich worth preserving, at Mk 5,21-23 (Jairus' daughter and the woman with a haemorrhage)[9]. In two cases neither follow Mark (Mk 3,20-35, Jesus' family and "Beelzebul"; 11,11-25, the Fig-tree and the Temple). Luke takes one more which Matthew refuses (from Mk 6,7-30), and Matthew two more which Luke refuses. Perhaps their sense for narrative logic and hearers' expectations indicate that Mark was indeed innovating – and not all that acceptably?

We might certainly draw just such a negative conclusion from surveying Josephus' re-telling of the Jewish Scriptures. We have seen from James Edwards that there are not in the Scriptures many intercalations of the sort analysed above for Josephus to deal with; but, as I have myself illustrated elsewhere, Josephus is in fact noticeably concerned to "improve" the flow of his narrative, either by removing all sorts of items that might seem to interrupt it, or else by re-ordering them. The people do not return to the Jordan for commemorative stones, they bring them with them; the booty taken from Jericho is described along with Achan's theft and what he took all in one sequence; and so forth[10]. Where possible each event or sequence of events is narrated from start to finish and left there. The "order" Josephus claims is thematic, one theme at a time, one narrative sequence at a time. And I certainly cannot recall any instance where Josephus himself interrupts a given sequence with a distinct but thematically related incident.

Lucian, in the next century, would seem to indicate much the same attitude to avoidable interruptions, digressions, in an historical narrative, however vivid and interesting in themselves. In a battle the narrator will describe initial deployments and plans in turn and completely; only when battle is joined will he switch attention between the two sides, and then only when the turn of events demand it. Thematic order and clarity seem to be the over-riding aim. "Let the clarity of the writing be limpid, achieved, as I have said, both by the diction and by the inter-connecting of events (τῇ συμπεριπλοκῇ τῶν πραγμάτων). The historian will make everything distinct and complete, and when he has finished the first topic he will introduce the second, fastened to it and linked with it

---

9. Assuming Matthew and Luke both used Mark (a common conclusion for which I have myself offered supporting arguments). Those not so convinced can re-phrase, perhaps to read, "Matthew and Luke only once (or twice) join in offering Mark a ready-made intercalation, and in all use the device only half as often."

10. F.G. DOWNING, *Redaction Criticism: Josephus' Antiquities and the Synoptic Gospels (I)*, in *JSNT* 8 (1980) 46-64, pp. 50 and 56-57; citing here Josephus *Ant.* 5,1-33.

like a chain, to avoid breaks and a multiplicity of disjointed narratives"[11].

I do not claim to have read widely among the historians for this paper. However, a brief skim through Dionysius and through Thucydides afforded no obvious counter-examples. What we seem to find is strings of individually coherent events arranged in sequences; we may well switch from one sequence to another as we follow different protagonists in turn. But there is nothing here at all like the intercalation discerned in Mark, the cutting from within one apparently self-contained account to another as complete in itself and back again, yet so that each resonates with the other.

Although Mark was clearly not writing history in Lucian's sense of the term, Richard Burridge has cogently described and analysed a wide range of analogies between Mark (and the other Gospels) on the one hand, and contemporary *Lives* on the other. Important for the present discussion is the observation that apart from often very brief chronological notes, *Lives* seem to be made up of anecdotes (with or without utterances), usually arranged topically. As is often pointed out, there is little or no sense of development of character to trace. Instead, character is revealed by individual sayings and incidents[12]. So here the logic of events, an ascribed explanatory chain of cause and effect, is not important, and one thing just seems to happen after another, albeit illuminatingly, as in Mark. We might then expect to find a similar freedom in writers of *Lives* to intercalate one narrative meaningfully into another. However, Burridge does not include any such phenomenon in his list of possible characteristics of the genre; and a search through ten of Plutarch's *Lives* was not very rewarding.

Between Theseus deciding to take the perilous land route to Athens and the dissuasions of Pitthaeus comes a brief account of Herakles dealing with similar threats; but this is really only an explanatory aside, similar to others before and later, and itself prepares for Theseus' ambition to repeat Herakles' achievements. We may compare a second comparison with Herakles a few chapters later[13]. If we contrast Plutarch's *Romulus* with Dionysius' story, then the single combat with Akron (taken from Livy?) might seem to interrupt the account of the Sabines as a whole marshalling their forces; but the episode may better be read as

---

11. LUCIAN of Samosata, *How to Write History*, 28 and 49-50, and 55 (cited from LCL with slight emendation).
12. R.A. BURRIDGE, *What are the Gospels?* (n. 4), p. 121, citing ARISTOTLE, *Rhetoric* I ix 33 1367b; but cf. also PLUTARCH, *Alexander* 1,2.
13. PLUTARCH, *Theseus* 6,4-6 and 11,1-12,1.

the first of three campaigns, each more dangerous than the last. It does not "interrupt" a specific incident[14]. In an account of the feuds in Athens with which Solon had to deal Plutarch includes a note of a visit from Epimenides of Phaestus; but he is following as his cue the themes of "pollution" and cleansing arising from the massacre of Kylon and his followers, and that sequence ends before Epimenides arrives. It is really just another thematic aside involving a different character. Perhaps the incident of his friends' insider-dealing within the account of Solon's ultimately succesful cancellation of debts might at first sight seem a slightly stronger example; yet it clearly presupposes the start of the main account, which Markan intercalations do not[15].

Much more to the point is the exchange with Aesop in the middle of the narrative of Croesus' encounter with Solon. Solon has refused to be dazzled by Crocsus' opulence, and has warned that none can be adjudged happy until their life is complete.

> When he had said this, Solon departed, leaving Croesus vexed, but none the wiser for it. Now it so happened that Aesop, the writer of fables, was in Sardis, having been summoned there by Croesus, and receiving much honour at his hands. He was distressed that Solon met with no kindly treatment, and said to him by way of advice, "O Solon, our converse with kings should be either as rare or as pleasing as is possible." "No, indeed!" said Solon, "but either as rare or as beneficial as possible." At this time, then, Croesus held Solon in a contempt like this, but afterwards, when he encountered Cyrus... [he acknowledged the truth of what Solon had said, invoked Solon by name; and this occasioned his release from death by fire...][16].

We here at last do have (A) a distinct character (Aesop); (B) a different place but nearby location (Solon has left Croesus before he meets Aesop); (C), an a^1-b-a^2 time-sequence; (D) a contrast (the worldly-wise Aesop honoured by Croesus admires the still wiser Solon whom Croesus fails at the time to honour; and perhaps there is (E) irony (we know, or will discover, that Croesus comes to acknowledge Solon and find his unflattering wisdom as beneficial as Solon had insisted in his counter to Aesop's conformist prudence).

Not quite so striking is an episode in the *Publicola*: the "miraculous" delivery of Tarquin's terracotta chariot to Rome from Veii interrupts the tale of the consecration of the temple for which it was originally intended, and has no link with the completion of the temple's dedication

---

14. PLUTARCH, *Romulus* 16-17 and LIVY 1,10 with DIONYSIUS of Halicarnassus' *Roman Antiquities* 2,32-34.
15. PLUTARCH, *Solon* 12,1-13.1; 15,3-16,3.
16. PLUTARCH, *Solon* 28,1 within 27-28.

by Horatius in the place of Publicola. It is difficult, though, to discern any ironic (or other) comment on the main story, the consecration as such[17]. Also, into his account of the mixed reception accorded Cicero when exiled by Clodius Plutarch inserts a note of an earthquake and the response of local soothsayers; but the theme of exile remains continuous throughout[18].

A secondary source, Chares, presents Plutarch with a tale of yet another brave solo exploit of Alexander against Arab foes, and this is recounted in the midst of the siege of Tyre, with no other link but the implicit relative proximity of the sets of adversaries. So we have again (A) some distinct characters (the Arabs, and Lysimachus, the elderly tutor protected); (B) a distinct geographical situation; (C) an a^1-b-a^2 time sequence. We should perhaps also note something of a contrast (D) (as elsewhere in this *Life*) between Alexander the powerful leader for whom others fight, and Alexander the audacious individual at risk in the midst of the fray. Just possibly there is also an intended irony (E) in the comparison between the calculating general and the impetuous young man, yet if so it is very understated; much more obvious is Plutarch's unqualified admiration for Alexander's all-round greatness[19].

As announced at the outset, the results of this investigation of ten of Plutarch's *Lives*[20] are not very encouraging. A scholarly writer such as Plutarch is obviously able to create occasional intercalations here of a sort that share some features with those in Mark; but just as clearly they are far fewer proportionately. In both the interruptions may well seem designed to enhance the hearers' interest as well as emphasise a point; but whereas in Mark suspense is created by the break in the flow of the outer tale, in Plutarch at best a rather lengthy sequence may in this way be marginally enlivened. It is worth looking a little further, a little wider, for possible analogies for Mark's practice, both in kind and in frequency.

One further possibility is the theatre, and especially comedy. Unfortunately we seem not to have preserved for us any examples of what would have been certainly available for Mark and his contemporaries, any extended account of popular mimes in particular. It seems that the surviving (Latin) plays of Plautus and Terence, derived extensively from the Greek works of Menander, were only read, not performed, in the

---

17. PLUTARCH, *Publicola* 13-14.
18. PLUTARCH, *Cicero* 32,4.
19. PLUTARCH, *Alexander* 24,10-14 within 24,1-25,3; cf. the apologia for Alexander as self-disciplined, *Alexander* 23, and even more, *de alexandri magni fortuna aut virtute*.
20. In addition to those cited in the text, *Lycurgus, Numa, Demosthenes* and *Caesar*.

first century CE. However, it is worth noting the extent to which dramatic (and comic) effects are produced by these two playwrights precisely by interrupting one sequence of events with another, so that the outcome of the first remains for the time being unsure – and the "intervening" actions of fresh, or remaining and fresh actors, suggest further possibilities to the audience. We are told that the long and narrow Roman stage with two or three house-fronts, and perhaps an intervening alley-way readily allowed for such changes of focus[21]. In Plautus' *The Two Bacchides*, for instance, a young man finds a girl who is sought by a friend of his, but is persuaded by her sister to pretend to court her so as to protect her from an unwanted suitor in whose power she is; but before this can happen, the young man's tutor and the slave of the girl's more welcome suitor see parts of the action and of course misinterpret it, while yet other encounters complicate their responses[22]. Such complications become even more convoluted in some of the plays of Terence. The Markan intercalations are certainly "dramatic" in a theatrical sense; it must remain possible, but no more, that the conventions of the contemporary stage could have had some influence on Mark's way of telling his stories.

Yet another genre worth considering, and one perhaps having rather more in common with Mark, is the kind of story telling with which Lucian entertained his audiences. In his *True Story* Lucian certainly strings amazing episodes together rather as Mark seems to, with no causal link between one and the next[23]. Yet quite otherwise than in Mark, there appear to be no structural devices either, no anticipations of later events, nor any allusions to those that have gone before; and neither do we seem to find here anything like Mark's "sandwiches".

However, the main narrative of *Lucius or the Ass* (quite likely an abbreviation of a longer tale by Lucian himself) and the body of the often very similar tale from Lucius Apuleius, *The Golden Ass,* do both comprise what amounts to a series of "interruptions" of a sort, frustrations of the quest for the roses that will turn the disgraceful ass into a proper human being. Apuleius' version also contains three quite unrelated tales introduced by other protagonists (Aristomenes, Thelyphron, the brigands' cook); another (of Thrasyllus) is told as a self-contained narrative

---

21. G.E. DUCKWORTH (ed.), *The Complete Roman Drama,* I & II, New York, 1942, pp. xxv-xxvi, xxix.

22. PLAUTUS, *The Two Bacchides*, trans. E. H. SUGDEN, in G.E. DUCKWORTH, *Roman Drama,* I, pp. 158-221.

23. Cf. the brief note on the novels and Mark in K. BERGER, *Formgeschichte des Neuen Testaments*, Heidelberg, Quelle und Meyer, 1984, p. 369: "Reihung von Szenen und Episoden, kaum komplexe und gleichzeitige Handlungen (in den Evv nur in der Passionsgeschichte). Die kurzen Szenen werden oft durch das Mittel der Reise aneinandergereiht."

by a fresh narrator, though with a link to the ass's fortunes at the end; and yet a fifth (the murderous step-mother) is told by the ass, but has no bearing on his lot. Though none of these "intercalations" are at all like Mark's in detail (they do not cut from one otherwise self-contained account of an incident to a second and then cut back again), it still seems quite clear that interrupting a main narrative with lesser and often quite independent ones is a device readily available to story tellers in late antiquity.

In his *The Carousal,* however, Lucian does include just one "intercalation" which more closely resembles our Markan ones. "Lucinus" introduces us to a rowdy Cynic gate-crasher called Alcidamus, and tells us that the climax of the tale will involve a drinking bowl the host has ordered to try to pacify the nuisance. Always postponing the climax, Lucian proceeds to tell of disputes among other guests as tension mounts, but also inserts a quite self-contained story from a further guest, a physician, who has just escaped from a crazed patient. So here we have (A) one distinct character (the patient), as well as the physician who only reappears very much later; (B) a house elsewhere in the same town; (C) the encounter had taken place at the time at which the other guests were arriving (contemporaneity); and (D-E) the violence the physician had escaped ironically both echoes a fight he's just missed and anticipates the fracas with which the dialogue ends, as well as contrasting with the apparent peace of the supper when the delayed guest arrived. Yet even so, the physician and his tale come at the end of one incident and before the next, without splitting any[24].

The closest analogies that I can discern both to the frequency, the kind and the effect of the Markan intercalations are to be found in the Hellenistic romances. There are still very significant differences; but the similarities seem worth considering.

The romances have two main actors who are newly wed or about to wed or very likely to wed, only to be separated as they journey through the east Mediterranean world, suffering various perils before finally being reunited. Mark, obviously, has only the one main character, and there is no amorous interest discernible.

Attention is engaged and maintained in the romances, and their themes of devotion and loyalty, misfortune and suffering are emphasised by cutting between the two main protagonists, but also from them to subordinate characters and back again. It is this cutting between incom-

---

24. LUCIAN, *The Carousal,* 20.

plete scenes that seems to me to afford the closest analogy in effect to the Markan intercalations[25].

So, early in Chariton's *Chaereas and Callirhoe*, we cut from Callirhoe's tomb to the piratical Theron who has been watching the costly preparations, and then back to Callirhoe coming out of her coma, back again to Theron who is all the while approaching, and yet again to Callirhoe hearing the robbers breaking in[26]. This illustrates something of the rapidity of the cross-cutting (compare Mk 11,11-25). Had he wanted to, Chariton could have offered a much simpler narrative: we could have stayed with the comatose girl until a tomb robber arrived (compare, in fact, Callirhoe's own account, 2.5[27]). The analogy is still only partial, though, for these incidents in the novel are interrelated in the narrative, rather than independent but resonating, as in Mark.

We then spend quite a long time with Callirhoe illegally sold to be a slave, cutting to and fro between her installed in a country house and Dionysius its owner, until the ceremony of her wedding to him, when we cut abruptly over to Chaereas, and a series of events contemporary with the foregoing but which have no bearing on the wedding as such at all. We leave Chaereas himself now enslaved and in bonds, and return abruptly to Callirhoe, who dreams of him in chains. But while their circumstances display similarities and contrasts (we cut ironically from Callirhoe holding a requiem for Chaereas to Chaereas about to be crucified), and are linked through third parties, and through dreams and through reports received (true and false), they run in parallel with no direct connections, even – or especially – when they are geographically close. (There is one exception, when the two do encounter each other at the Persian court; but they meet only to be separated yet again.) Both series has its own (fictional) causal logic, but each narrative interrupts the other sequence with distinct characters and events engaged in variations on common themes. The scale is much larger than Mark's; many of the formal characteristics are similar[28].

---

25. The commentators I have read do not seem to find this feature particularly remarkable. G. ANDERSON, in his *Ancient Fiction. The Novel in the Graeco-Roman World*, London, Croom Helm, 1984, p. 123, notes "Achilles and Longus both have plots in which hero and heroine move from crisis to crisis, with one not usually solved before the next can begin;" cf. p. 125, "a 'Jack and Jill' plot"; but he seems to argue as though this intertwining were only incidental, p. 31.

26. CHARITON, *Chaereas and Callirhoe* 1,6-9, first century CE/BCE; trans. B.P. REARDON, in ID., *Collected Ancient Greek Novels*, Berkeley, University of California Press, 1989, pp. 17-128.

27. And that in XENOPHON's *Ephesian Tale* 3.8.

28. We may note again, in passing, that the incognito of the protagonists, and recognition scenes, as in Mark, are also important motifs.

Xenophon of Ephesus' *An Ephesian Tale* is constructed in a very similar way, though more lurid[29]. "Meanwhile" is probably as frequent as is "immediately" in Mark; the cutting from one strand to another is very frequent. "Meanwhile (A) Habrocomes' tutor..." drowns nearby (B) while trying to rejoin his kidnapped charge: a quite separate incident sandwiched (C: a^1-b-a^2) within the account of Corymbus' relationship with the young man, but affording a comparison and a contrast between tutorly and erotic attachment (D). From 2,9 we mostly switch in turn between the plight of Habrocomes and his young bride, Anthia; we leave him in prison to find Anthia given in spite to a goatherd who in fact respects her, and then back to her husband in gaol. As soon as Anthia is captured by Hippothous we cut back to Habrocomes going to seach for her and then immediately return to Anthia in fresh peril from her new captors. She is rescued, only to face a forced marriage; "meanwhile" Habrocomes meets up with Hippothous, before we return to the wedding. Anthia, like Callirhoe, is entombed in a coma and then also captured by pirates; between their decision to sell her and her actual sale Habrocomes hears the story of her death and the grave-robbers. Later, leaving Anthia thrown to the dogs we find Habrocomes meeting Aegialeus, a kindly fishermen, and we hear the latter's life-story in brief; it has no link with either strand of the main story, apart from affording a further reminder of marital devotion; but only then do we see Anthia emerge from her peril. (We also cut from time to time to the fate of the faithful slaves of the couple who return at the end to help reunite them in prosperity.)

The cuts to and fro are not quite as frequent in Achilles Tatius' novel *Leucippe and Clitophon*, as it is narrated by Kleitophon himself, the male of the pair; but interruptions still occur, as he gathers from others (or simply "knows") what is or has been happening elsewhere, and to Leukippe in particular[30]. The episode of Charikles, boy-lover of Kleitophon's cousin and confidant, Kleinias, affords an opportunity for an early disquisition on erotic arousal, homosexual and heterosexual; but the account of Charikles' death as Kleinias' lesson in love continues, "suddenly" intrudes, (1.12) without any direct effect on the action that follows: Kleitophon goes straight from the funeral to practice what he has been told. The incident may well, however, be meant to presage the perils that will beset the young lovers. We switch from a delay to an ar-

---

29. XENOPHON OF EPHESUS, *An Ephesian Tale*, 2nd century CE(?); trans. G. ANDERSON, in B.P. REARDON, *Greek Novels*, pp. 125-169.
30. ACHILLES TATIUS, *Leucippe and Clitophon*, "third quarter of the second century" CE; trans. J.J. WINKLER, in B.P. REARDON, *Greek Novels*, pp. 170-284.

ranged wedding with the wrong woman, step-sister Kalligone, to Kallisthenes' prior plot to kidnap her, and back to the resumed nuptials; and then comes the kidnapping itself. Kleitophon's campaign of seduction is simply prolonged by some interplay between a compliant servant, Satyros, and a suspicious domestic, Gnat. The lovers flee; the happy start of their sea-voyage is divided from the storm that follows by a meeting with a stranger, Menelaos, who occasions a second monologue on homosexual and heterosexual love. The lovers' recovery after shipwreck is interrupted by a lengthy description of a temple mural of Andromeda. They are parted, then re-united: but this is interrupted by a flash-back to events involving Satyros and Menelaos, and the reported arrival of a Phoenix. Achilles Tatius also intrudes into his narrative other descriptive passages, *"ekphraseis"*, though these do set the mood[31] (pictures, gardens, the origins of wine, a dress, a dye-stuff, water stories, philosophical psychology, and the like). By book six it is time for a parting that Kleitophon assumes is final, and then finds is not, and from this point we cut constantly between him and Leukippe, with as frequent "meanwhiles" as in Xenophon (without being told till 8.15 how the author knows what is happening to Leukippe in his absence)[32].

(It is perhaps also worth noting our further evidence for early Christian awareness of the Romance genre, in *Paul and Thecla,* in the Clementine *Recognitions*, and in other apocryphal Acts.)

Some of our New Testament commentators have insisted that intercalation in Mark is more than a device to engage and hold interest, it also focusses our attention on important themes, while the element of irony enhances our involvement. Can we discern any similar intention or effect in the other writings we have here briefly surveyed? Certainly themes of constancy in captivity and suffering, of loyalty and betrayal, and such like, are common among them, and are emphasised by the cutting to and fro between the characters. But further, many of the romances make explicit reference to a hidden divine providence, and each story encourages the hope that things will come out well in the end for those who display constancy and loyalty. More than that, the ironies in the narratives encourage the hearer to seek for and perceive meaning – and even purpose – in what the characters can only experience as coincidence. Life is not, perhaps, just one damn thing after another, for the novelists any more than for Mark. Simply that.

---

31. T. HÄGG, *The Novel in Antiquity* (ET) Oxford, Blackwell, 1983, p. 48.
32. LONGUS' *Daphnis and Chloe*, second century CE (simpler, with two main characters), and HELIODORUS' probably much later *An Ethiopian Story* (much more complex) both maintain this system of breaking an account involving one character with (part of) a tale of another.

As was insisted at the outset of this discussion of the romances, there is still no close analogy with Mark. In the entire survey we have noted only a few "intercalations" that include the first four features we discerned, and even fewer with all five. We have to allow still that Mark's predilection for this device may have been idiosyncratic, although the device as such is clearly not his invention.

But furthermore, it seems to me, at least, that we need to allow for the possibility that Mark had learned the narrative value of cutting from the midst of one scene to another and back from the contemporary stage, perhaps, but more from the widespread popular story-telling of which the romances are simply our few remaining survivals. What may have been original would be Mark's practice of deploying such cutting quite frequently in a *Life* of one individual, imposing it on a number of the items of the (oral) traditions he shared; and very effectively.

ABSTRACT

Mark frequently "sandwiches" one self-contained narrative within another, involving some distinct character(s) and locality, overlapping time-sequence, similarities and contrasts; and perhaps dramatic irony. Most discussions concentrate on the perceived narrative function (creating interest, emphasizing a theme). There seems to have been little attention to any such device among Mark's near contemporaries. Perhaps he is even unique? In fact few parallels are to be found among the histories and lives, and only very few more in the older theatrical comedies. The most promising comparisons are afforded by the romances. Here it would appear that tension is maintained by such intercalation, themes (such as constancy, loyalty and betrayal) are emphasized; but also that a divine providence is shown to underlie the apparent chances and coincidences. It is perhaps here that we find the context for what remains in its elaboration and frequency nonetheless a quite distinctive feature of Mark's narrative.

RÉSUMÉ

A plusieurs reprises Marc utilise un procédé d'intercalation: il place "en sandwich" à l'intérieur d'un premier récit un second récit; cette construction implique des personnages et des lieux différents, des séquences temporelles qui se chevauchent, des ressemblances et des contrastes, voire même une ironie dramatique. La plupart des études se sont concentrées sur l'effet narratif du procédé (il vise à éveiller l'intérêt, il sert à mettre l'accent sur un thème), mais elles se sont peu intéressées à l'existence de ce type de procédé dans la littérature contemporaine. Est-ce à dire que Marc est un cas unique? En fait, on ne trouve que très peu de parallèles dans les *historiae* et les *vitae*; les points de comparaison sont un peu plus nombreux dans les comédies antiques. Mais ce sont les romans qui fournissent les parallèles les plus riches. Dans les romans, il semble bien que le recours au procédé de l'intercalation serve à entretenir la tension dramatique, à mettre en évidence certains thèmes (la constance, la loyauté, la trahison), mais aussi à faire ressortir l'action cachée de la providence dans des événements qui semblent être le produit du hasard ou d'une coïncidence. Peut-être les romans fournissent-ils un contexte permettant de situer ce procédé de l'intercalation – procédé qui reste néanmoins une caractéristique distinctive du récit de Marc, par l'usage fréquent et élaboré qu'il en fait.

33 Westhoughton RoadF. Gerald DOWNING
Adlington
Chorley
Lancs PR7 4EU

8

LES SÉJOURS DE JÉSUS
À BÉTHANIE AU-DELÀ DU JOURDAIN
SELON LE CHRONOTOPE DE L'ÉVANGILE DE JEAN

I. Préliminaire

Depuis l'ouvrage pionnier d'Alan Culpepper, *Anatomy of the Fourth Gospel*, l'évangile de Jean (= Jn) a fait l'objet d'une série d'études de type narratif, qui se donnent pour tâche de déceler l'intrigue et ses éléments constitutifs (personnages, espace, temps, narrateur, lecteur, commentaire implicite)[1]. Dans la présente étude, nous voulons montrer l'importance de la topographie dans le récit johannique; cet aspect est souvent oublié ou minimisé par les lectures narratives au profit du temps[2],

---

1. R.A. Culpepper, *Anatomy of the Fourth Gospel. A Study in Literary Design*, Philadelphia, Fortress, 1983; J.-L. Staley, *The Print's First Kiss. A Rhetorical Investigation of the Implied Reader in the Fourth Gospel* (SBLDS, 82), Atlanta, Scholar Press, 1988; F.F. Segovia, *The Journey(s) of the Word of God: A Reading of the Plot of the Fourth Gospel*, in *Semeia* 53 (1991) 23-54; M.W.G. Stibbe, *John as Storyteller. Narrative Criticism and the Fourth Gospel*, Cambridge, Cambridge University Press, 1992; Id. (éd.), *The Gospel of John as Literature. An Anthology of Twentieth-Century Perspectives* (NTTS, 17), Leiden, Brill, 1993; D. Marguerat, *L'évangile de Jean et son lecteur*, in *Le temps de la lecture. Exégèse biblique et sémiotique. Hommages pour J. Delorme* (LD, 155), Paris, Cerf, 1993, pp. 305-324; J. Zumstein, *L'apprentissage de la foi. À la découverte de l'évangile de Jean et de ses lecteurs*, Poliez-le-Grand, Moulin, 1993; *L'évangile de Jean. Une lecture narratologique*, Lausanne, Animation biblique œcuménique romande, [1993]; F.J. Moloney, *Belief in the Word. Reading the Fourth Gospel: John 1-4*, Minneapolis, Fortress, 1993; V. Manucci, *Giovanni il Vangelo narrante. Introduzione all'arte narrativa del quarto Vangelo*, Bologna, Dehoniane, 1993.

2. À en croire L.M. O'Toole, il s'agit d'une tendance générale en narratologie: «A curious feature of modern literary scholarship is the almost universal neglect of setting in the study of narrative prose. Narrative structure, plot, point of view and character are the subjects of elaborate theorizing, close analysis and comparison, and comprehensive literary history, but setting often gets no more than a passing reference. This may be partly a reaction against the priority accorded by the nineteenth century to descriptive writing in criticism, against the cult of nature in poetry and prose, and the ease with which the 'pathetic fallacy' was both exploited by writers and noticed by critics» (*Structure, Style and Interpretation in the Russian Short Story*, New Haven - London, Yale Univesity Press, 1982, p. 180). Dans ce contexte, les travaux de E. Struthers Malbon sur la géographie constituent plutôt d'heureuses exceptions: *Mythic Structure and Meaning in Mark: Elements of a Lévi-Straussian Analysis*, in *Semeia* 16 (1979) 97-129; *Narrative Space and Mythic Meaning in Mark*, San Francisco, Harper & Row, 1986.

alors que les études diachroniques y ont toujours accordé une attention soutenue[3].

Cependant, il ne s'agit pas ici de négliger l'axe temporel, comme Mikhail Bakhtine le montre dans son concept littéraire de *chronotope*:

> Nous appellerons *chronotope*, ce qui se traduit, littéralement, par <temps-espace>: la corrélation essentielle des rapports spatio-temporels, telle qu'elle a été assimilée par la littérature [...] Dans le chronotope de l'art littéraire a lieu la fusion des indices spatiaux et temporels en un tout intelligible et concret. Ici le temps se condense, devient compact, visible pour l'art, tandis que l'espace s'intensifie, s'engouffre dans le mouvement du temps, du sujet, de l'Histoire. Les indices du temps se découvrent dans l'espace, celui-ci est perçu et mesuré d'après le temps [...] En tant que catégorie de la forme et du contenu, le chronotope établit aussi (pour une grande part) l'image de l'homme en littérature, image toujours essentiellement spatio-temporelle [...] Le chronotope, principale matérialisation du temps dans l'espace, apparaît comme le centre de la concrétisation figurative, comme l'incarnation du roman tout entier. Tous les éléments abstraits du roman – généralisations philosophiques et sociales, idées, analyse des causes et des effets, et ainsi de suite – gravitent autour du chronotope et, par son intermédiaire, prennent chair et sang et participent au caractère imagé de l'art littéraire[4].

Bakhtine a analysé les traits principaux du roman grec pour illustrer sa théorie et a abouti à la conclusion suivante:

> Le chronotope des aventures se caractérise précisément, par *le lien technique abstrait entre l'espace et le temps, par la réversibilité des moments de la série temporelle, et par leur possibilité de changer de place dans l'espace*. Dans ce chronotope, l'initiative et le pouvoir ne relèvent que du hasard. Aussi, le degré de *détermination et de concrétisation* de ce monde-là ne peut être qu'extrêmement limité. Car enfin, toute concrétisation, qu'elle

---

3. K. KUNDSIN, *Topologische Überlieferungsstoffe in Johannes-Evangelium* (FRLANT, 22), Göttingen, Vandenhoeck & Ruprecht, 1925; R.H. LIGHTFOOT, *Locality and Doctrine in the Gospels*, New York, Harpers, 1937; D. MOLLAT, *Remarques sur le vocabulaire spatial du quatrième évangile* et R.D. POTTER, *Topography and Archaeology in the Fourth Gospel*, in *Studia evangelica* (Texte und Untersuchungen, 73), Berlin, Akademie Verlag, 1959, pp. 321-328 et pp. 329-337; O. MERLIER, *Itinéraires de Jésus et chronologie dans le quatrième évangile* (Connaissance de la Grèce, 11), Paris, Presses universitaires de France, 1961; J. WILLEMSE, *La patrie de Jésus selon Saint Jean iv. 44*, in *NTS* 11 (1964-65) 349-364; W.A. MEEKS, *Galilee and Judea in the Fourth Gospel*, in *JBL* 85 (1966) 159-169; R.T. FORTNA, *Theological Use of Locale in the Fourth Gospel*, in *AThRSup* 3 (1974) 58-95; ID., *The Fourth Gospel and Its Predecessor. From Narrative Source to Present Gospel*, Edinburgh, T & T Clark, 1989, pp. 294-314; J.M. BASSLER, *The Galileans: A Neglected Factor in Johannine Community Research*, in *CBQ* 43 (1981) 243-257; S. FREYNE, *Locality and Doctrine. Mark and John Revisited*, in *The Four Gospels 1992. Festschrift F. Neirynck* (BETL, 100), Leuven, University Press – Peeters, 1992, vol. 3, pp. 1889-1900.

4. M. BAKHTINE, *Esthétique et théorie du roman*, Paris, Gallimard, 1978, pp. 237-238, 390.

soit géographique, économique, socio-politique, quotidienne, paralyserait la liberté et la facilité des aventures, et imposerait des limites au pouvoir absolu du hasard [...] Le temps des aventures du roman grec ne laisse pas de traces ni dans le monde ni sur les êtres. Aucune modification d'ordre externe ou interne ne résulte de toutes ces péripéties. L'équilibre initial, rompu par le hasard, est rétabli vers la fin du roman [...] Le marteau des événements ne broie ni ne forge rien: il ne fait qu'éprouver la solidité du produit fabriqué. Et ce produit supporte l'épreuve. C'est le sens littéraire et idéologique du roman grec[5].

Nous allons voir en quoi Jn ressemble à cette description et s'en distingue dans le cadre de la séquence des séjours de Jésus au-delà du Jourdain (Jn 1,28-10,40). Mais avant d'entreprendre notre lecture narrative de Jn, nous tenons à souligner que nous utilisons généralement le système narratologique de Gérard Genette[6] et ne retenons de la théorie bakhtinienne que l'imbrication narrative du temps et de l'espace suggérée par la notion de *chronotope*.

II. Jésus à Béthanie au-delà du Jourdain

Note géographique. Nos passages parlent de *Béthanie au-delà du Jourdain* (Jn 1,28: ἐν Βηθανίᾳ πέραν τοῦ Ἰορδάνου), ou seulement d'*au-delà du Jourdain* (3,26; 10,40: πέραν τοῦ Ἰορδάνου). À la place de Béthanie en 1,28, on trouve – dans certains manuscrits – Béthabara (C² K Ψ* 083 etc.) ou Betharaba (ℵ² sy^hmg), mais la plupart des critiques maintiennent Béthanie comme la leçon la plus difficile, donc la plus probable. La difficulté commence avec l'identification du lieu en question. Parmi les solutions les plus probables, signalons celle de Dockx qui pointe vers un village au sud de Bethsaïde[7], celle de Murphy-O'Connor

---

5. *Ibidem*, p. 251 et 257. L'abstraction s'accomode bien des détails descriptifs, car «toute description dans les romans grecs est comme *isolée, exceptionnelle, unique*. Nulle part n'y est évoqué le pays tout entier avec ses particularités, les traits qui le distinguent ou le rapprochent d'autres pays. On y trouve la description de tel édifice, sans aucun lien avec son environnement, des phénomènes de la nature isolés, tels des animaux bizarres» (p. 253).
6. G. Genette, *Nouveau discours du récit*, Paris, Seuil, 1983; J.L. Ska, *'Our Fathers Have Told Us'. Introduction to the Analysis of Hebrew Narratives* (Subsidia biblica, 13), Roma, Pontificio Istituto Biblico, 1990; D. Marguerat, *Entrer dans le monde du récit*, in *Bulletin d'information biblique* 42 (1994) 8-12. Voir aussi S. Chatman, *La rhétorique de la fiction*, in *Mesure* 3 (1990) 129-146.
7. «Cet endroit, au-delà du Jourdain, ne peut se trouver entre le Jourdain et Bethsaïde, car ce village est situé tout près de l'endroit où le Jourdain se jette dans le lac [de Gennésaret]. Il doit être situé au sud de Bethsaïde, en sorte que, Jésus, voulant se rendre de là en Galilée, doit passer par Bethsaïde où il rencontre Philippe (Jn 1,43)»; S. Dockx, *Chronologies néo-testamentaires et vie de l'église primitive*, Leuven, Peeters, 1984, p. 18.

qui cherche un endroit au sud-ouest de la Pérée dans la vallée du Jourdain[8], et enfin celle de Riesner qui plaide pour la Batanée au nord de la Transjordanie[9]. Il est difficile d'en décider; mais une région plus près de Jérusalem, en Pérée, serait plus réaliste pour le récit johannique: puisque la patrie de Jésus est la Judée, et non la Galilée, selon Jn (4,44)[10], il peut atteindre facilement le milieu du Baptiste (1,29), de même que peut le faire l'ambassade des Juifs de Jérusalem (1,19). Ce choix narrativement motivé ne préjuge pas de l'historicité ou non de cette indication géographique. Par la suite, nous nous intéresserons seulement à la trame narrative de Jn.

Une lecture attentive du quatrième évangile montre que les déplacements des personnages du récit d'un village à l'autre, ou d'une région à l'autre, prennent une place considérable dans l'intrigue et déterminent le parcours des héros. En effet, les changements de place de Jésus, par exemple, ont lieu non seulement en fonction du développement de l'action (cf. Jn 2,1.12.13; 3,22; 4,3-5.43; 5,1; 6,1; 11,18-20; 12,1.12), mais aussi en raison d'un désir précis (cf. Jn 1,43: «Le lendemain, Jésus voulut [ἠθέλησεν] sortir en Galilée»; 7,1: «Après cela, Jésus parcourait la Galilée, car il ne voulait pas [οὐ γὰρ ἤθελεν] séjourner en Judée, parce que les Juifs cherchaient à le faire mourir») ou d'une tactique cachée (cf. 7,10: Jésus «monta aussi lui-même [à Jérusalem], non publiquement, mais comme en secret [ὡς ἐν κρυπτῷ]»; 11,54: «Jésus ne circula plus ouvertement [οὐκέτι παρρησίᾳ] parmi les Juifs; mais il se retira dans la contrée voisine du désert, dans une ville appelée Éphraïm«). En outre, chacun de ces déplacements est caractérisé par la qualité de l'accueil réservé à Jésus par les habitants, de sorte qu'on peut établir une typologie des régions dans la narration johannique[11]. (1) La Samarie (Jn

8. «Mark's information that the place was wilderness (1,4), accessible to Jerusalemites and close to the Jordan (1,5) narrows 'beyond the Jordan' to the south-west corner of Peraea in the Jordan valley. It is within this framework that the identification of 'Bethany beyond the Jordan' (Jn 1,28) has to be discussed»; J. MURPHY-O'CONNOR, *John the Baptist and Jesus: History and Hypotheses*, in *NTS* 36 (1990) 359-374 (citation p. 359, n. 3).

9. «"Beyond the Jordan" (*peran tou Iordanou*) does not have to carry the political sense of the Perea of Herod Antipas by any means, but simply denotes the land E(ast) of the Jordan, and sometimes the more northerly Transjordan (especially so in Matt 4:15) [...] John, according to John 10,40, "first" (*to prôton*) began to baptize in the Batanea, that is in the northernmost area of the Holy Land»; R. RIESNER, *Bethany Beyond the Jordan*, in *Anchor Bible Dictionary* 1 (1992) 703-705, p. 704.

10. J. WILLEMSE, *La patrie de Jésus* (n. 3), pp. 349-364 et W.A. MEEKS, *Galilee and Judea* (n. 3), pp. 163-166.

11. Cette typologie reflète un *schéma* rédactionnel bien précis (cf. K.L. SCHMIDT, *Der Rahmen der Geschichte Jesu*, Berlin, Trowitzsch & Sohn, 1919, pp. 1-17); pour l'analyse narrative, elle dévoile le *point de vue spatio-temporel du narrateur*: «In bestimmten Fällen kann der Standpunkt des Erzählers mit mehr oder minder großer Exaktheit im

4,4-42) et la Transjordanie (Jn 1,28; 3,26; 10,40) représentent l'adhésion de la foi et le témoignage sur la personne de Jésus. (2) La Galilée (Jn 1,43; 2,1.11; 4,3.43-54; 6,1; 7,1) est un endroit de foi et de suivance de Jésus, malgré les marques d'incomplétude (cf. 6,26). (3) La Judée, patrie de Jésus (Jn 4,44) et fief des Ἰουδαῖοι[12] (très probablement, les Judéens; cf. Jn 1,19; 2,13; 5,1; 7,1.11.25; 10,22-24; 11,7-8; 11,55), incarne l'incrédulité et l'hostilité envers Jésus[13]. Ces considérations générales, que nous n'avons pas à développer dans cette étude, vont nous aider à situer les séquences où il est question de la Béthanie transjordanienne.

Dans le cadre du quatrième évangile, les indications **géographiques** «Béthanie au-delà du Jourdain» (1,28-29 et 10,39-40) ont une fonction **temporelle** fondamentale: elles délimitent la mission publique de Jésus[14]. Nous avons donc ici une unité narrative où la dimension *chronotopique* est plus visible et plus significative qu'ailleurs.

> *Ces choses se passèrent à Béthanie au-delà du Jourdain, où Jean baptisait. Le lendemain, il vit Jésus venant à lui, et il dit: "Voici, l'Agneau de Dieu qui ôte le péché du monde"* (Jn 1,28-29).

La mention du nom de lieu, Béthanie, vient **après** le récit des événements qui s'y sont déroulés, pour montrer au lecteur l'importance primordiale du témoignage rendu à Jésus par le Baptiste. En effet, le prologue a annoncé d'avance (proleptiquement, dirait Genette) le rôle exact que Jean aura à jouer dans la narration: il «est venu [ἦλθεν] témoigner [εἰς μαρτυρίαν], afin qu'il rende témoignage à la lumière, afin que tous

---

Raum oder in der Zeit fixiert werden, das heißt: der Leser kann den durch die Raum-Zeit-Koordinaten festgelegten Ort erraten, von dem aus das Erzählen erfolgt […] In einer anderen Terminologie könnte man in diesem Zusammenhang auch von der Raum- oder Zeit-*Perspektive* im Aufbau der Erzählung sprechen, wobei die Analogie zur perspektivischen [Bild-]Konstruktion freilich mehr als eine bloße Metapher ist» (B.A. USPENSKIJ, *Poetik der Komposition. Struktur des künstlerischen Textes und Typologie der Kompositionsform*, Frankfurt am Main, Suhrkamp, 1975, p. 69).

12. Comparer R.T. FORTNA, *Theological Use of Locale* (n. 3), pp. 66-81; J. ASHTON, *The Identity and Function of the Ἰουδαῖοι in the Fourth Gospel*, in *NT* 27 (1985) 40-75; P. GRELOT, *Les Juifs dans l'évangile selon Jean. Enquête historique et réflexion théologique* (CRB, 34), Paris, Gabalda, 1995, pp. 25-47.

13. «Baptist Transjordan, then, is a place of faith, and like Samaria stands in contrast to Judea […] Galilean belief is not depicted as normative. It is always simply contrasted with Judean unbelief. We are to look favorably on Galilee, then, but no matter how faithful the Galileans they are finally only a foil to the Judeans»; R.T. FORTNA, *The Fourth Gospel and Its Predecessor* (n. 3), p. 308 et p. 310.

14. «After the baptism, Jesus will enter the Promised Land and stay there until his people reject him, when once more he will retreat beyond the Jordan. Bethany beyond Jordan frames the public ministry of Jesus»; R.E. BROWN, *The Gospel and Epistles of John. A Concise Commentary*, Collegeville, The Liturgical Press, 1988, p. 25.

croient par lui[15]» (Jn 1,7). Ce verbe ἦλθεν ne concerne pas seulement l'envoi de Jean dans le monde, mais surtout son *advenue dans le récit* qui le confine précisément à l'acte de témoigner, selon le début de la narration proprement dite: «Jean lui rend témoignage [μαρτυρεῖ] et s'écrie [κέκραγεν λέγων]...» (Jn 1, 15)[16]. C'est le témoignage du Baptiste qui intéresse en premier lieu le narrateur (1,15-27): nous avons le premier «cri confessant» de Jean au v. 15, suivi immédiatement d'un commentaire du narrateur (1,16-18); puis vient le dialogue entre les Juifs de Jérusalem et Jean (1,20-28), qui ne débouche pas sur la foi des interlocuteurs, mais se clôt par une affirmation (infructueuse?[17]) du témoin. Ce sont là les choses (ταῦτα) dont parle le v. 28. Mais Béthanie n'est pas uniquement un lieu de *témoignage oral*, mais aussi un endroit particulier où des *actes symboliques* sont posés, où Jean baptisait (ἦν βαπτίζων). C'est la troisième fois que le baptême est évoqué dans Jn: «Pourquoi baptises-tu, si tu n'es pas le Christ, ni Élie, ni le prophète?» (1,25); «Moi, je baptise d'eau...» (1,26). Ce contexte suggère deux choses au lecteur: d'une part, le baptême n'est pas un geste banal que tout le monde pourrait accomplir, mais un acte lié à l'exercice d'une autorité spécifique (messianique ou prophétique); d'autre part, le baptême de Jean se limite à l'usage de l'eau comme symbole et s'effectue *en attente d'accomplissement* (cf. «Celui qui vient après moi»). Pourtant, Jean ne se réclame d'aucune des figures messianiques ou prophétiques nommées par les envoyés juifs, mais s'impose simplement à l'ouïe des entendants *comme la voix criant dans le désert*. Celle-ci est promise par Ésaïe et, contrairement aux titres, elle ne se discute pas, mais s'écoute. Cette revendication du privilège de la *voix* est tout à fait conforme à la nature de la mission du Baptiste: la μαρτυρία. Ainsi, le baptême réalisé par Jean a suscité la curiosité des Juifs et les a renvoyés à Celui qui vient (1,26b) et qui – comme la suite du récit le dira – baptise d'Esprit Saint (1,33).

15. Par la proposition ἵνα πάντες πιστεύσωσιν δι' αὐτοῦ (Jn 1,7), le narrateur exprime l'analogie de son propre projet avec la vocation du Baptiste (voir Jn 20,31: ἵνα πιστεύητε ὅτι Ἰησοῦς ἐστιν ὁ Χριστὸς ὁ υἱὸς Θεοῦ). Cette coïncidence entre l'intention avouée *du texte* et une trajectoire *dans le texte* confirme l'envergure narrative du personnage «Jean».
16. Si on fait commencer le récit au v. 19, on obtient le même résultat: «Voici le témoignage [μαρτυρία] de Jean...».
17. «Welchen Eindruck diese runde und klare Antwort auf die Boten oder auf ihre Auftraggeber gemacht hat, hören wir nicht. Die Boten werden überhaupt nicht mehr erwähnt: dem Verfasser ist nur wichtig, daß seine Leser diese klare Antwort hören und beherzigen»; W. HEITMÜLLER, *Das Johannes-Evangelium*, in *Die Schriften des Neuen Testaments neu übersetzt und für die Gegenwart erklärt*, Göttingen, Vandenhoeck & Ruprecht, 1918³, pp. 9-184 (citation p. 50). Ainsi, le message de Jean qui était inefficace auprès des Juifs continue à se faire entendre auprès du lecteur pour le conduire à la foi. Pour cette raison, les Juifs ne peuvent pas être une figure d'identification pour le lecteur.

Les événements à Béthanie ne s'arrêtent pas là, car ils ont un prolongement, un lendemain (cf. τῇ ἐπαύριον 1,29) qui les fait rebondir. En effet, la prophétie de Jean (ὁ ὀπίσω μου ἐρχόμενος 1,15.27) se concrétise par la venue de Jésus vers lui (τὸν Ἰησοῦν ἐρχόμενον). Ce verset marque l'entrée en scène de Jésus comme personnage du récit, car jusque-là il n'était qu'un thème de discours. Son nom n'a été mentionné que furtivement dans le commentaire théologique du narrateur en 1,17b (*Jésus*-Christ); en revanche, ses qualités ont été maintes fois soulignées et développées depuis le début de l'évangile (Verbe, vie, lumière, Fils unique, Christ). Le narrateur ne dit pas explicitement le but de la «visite» de Jésus, mais il en raconte les conséquences: (1) les démonstratifs (ἴδε ... οὗτός ἐστιν 1,29.30) désignent le visage jusque-là nébuleux de Celui qui doit venir après Jean; (2) celui-ci poursuit son témoignage (1,32a.34a) en qualifiant Jésus par de nouveaux titres (1,29: «agneau de Dieu qui enlève le péché du monde»; 1,34: «Fils de Dieu»), en précisant la nature de son baptême d'eau (1,31c.33b) et en avouant sa propre ignorance (1,31a.33a: κἀγὼ οὐκ ᾔδειν αὐτόν).

Il est intéressant de constater dans cette rencontre entre Jésus et Jean à Béthanie que Jean n'a pas d'énonciataire intradiégétique; il parle *de* Jésus et non pas *à* lui, ni à personne d'autre. En fait, c'est au lecteur que s'adresse le discours de Jean: seul le lecteur peut se rendre compte du passage chez Jean de l'ignorance (1,31a.33a) à la confession de foi (1,29b.34b) par le biais de la vision (βλέπει 1,29a; τεθέαμαι 1,32b; ἑώρακα 1,34a). En effet, tout ce processus demeure hors d'atteinte pour un personnage intradiégétique, à cause de la focalisation interne opérée par le narrateur. Le temps verbal utilisé au v. 34 corrobore ce point: le parfait (ἑώρακα καὶ μεμαρτύρηκα) suggère que le temps du lecteur est impliqué par cet épisode[18]. La réaction au témoignage du Baptiste se fait donc dans le présent de la lecture.

Le surlendemain (τῇ ἐπαύριον πάλιν), Jean réitère à deux de ses disciples la même confession de foi (1,36b: «Voici l'Agneau de Dieu») et

---

18. «Eine ähnliche Verwendung des Präsens ist charakteristisch für die gewöhnliche Erzählung im Alltag. Man denke an eine so typische Wendung (und zwar innerhalb einer Erzählung über Vergangenes, wo deshalb das Präteritum vorherrscht) wie diese: "... da *sagt* er plötzlich zu mir..." Sehr häufig wird das Präsens auch auf dem Höhepunkt einer Erzählung verwendet (Typus: "Ich trat ein und sehe..."). Dieses Verfahren dient eindeutig dazu, *den Hörer mitten in die Erzählhandlung hinein zu versetzen, ihn auf denselben Platz zu stellen, auf dem der Held der Erzählung steht*»; B.A. USPENSKIJ, *Poetik der Komposition* (n. 11), pp. 85-86 (c'est nous qui soulignons). Voir déjà chez W. HEITMÜLLER: «Das Zeugnis des Johannes, in der Vergangenheit abgelegt, reicht, das ist der Sinn des griechischen Ausdrucks V. 34, bis in die Gegenwart hinein, vgl. V. 15. Die Leser sollen es hören, Gläubige wie Nichtgläubige. Es ist ein schlechthin einwandfreies Zeugnis» (*Das Johannes-Evangelium* [n. 17], p. 51).

ceux-ci se mettent à suivre Jésus (1,37b.38b). Ici, on est en présence d'un témoignage efficace (parole suscitant la foi et la suivance, cf. 1,7) et d'une foi exemplaire (écouter et suivre l'indication du témoin, cf. 1,12). On peut dire que les deux disciples ont parfaitement saisi la portée du credo *Voici l'Agneau de Dieu*, qui renvoie à l'agneau pascal[19], source de pardon et de délivrance (cf. l'accomplissement de Ex 12,46b en Jn 19,36). Nous entendons au v. 38 la première parole de Jésus: «Que cherchez-vous?» (premier usage de ζητέω). Cette parole s'avère être une prolepse de sa dernière question à Marie Madeleine près du tombeau vide: «Qui cherches-tu?» (20,15: dernier usage du même verbe). Cela fait de l'évangile une histoire de recherches, réussies ou ratées, en cours ou à venir[20]. Ainsi, Béthanie devient lieu d'apprentissage de la foi et lieu de recrutement des premiers disciples.

Concernant le temps, l'épisode inaugural de Béthanie fait démarrer le mouvement temporel du récit: (1) le témoignage de Jean est situé – sur l'axe temporel – par rapport à l'envoi d'une délégation juive (1,19: ὅτε ἀπέστειλαν πρὸς αὐτὸν οἱ Ἰουδαῖοι) et à la venue de Jésus (1,29: τῇ ἐπαύριον βλέπει τὸν Ἰησοῦν ἐρχόμενον πρὸς αὐτόν); (2) la succession des jours (1,29.35.43: τῇ ἐπαύριον) renforce, avec la description des actions, la signification symbolique de l'espace. Dans ce sens, Béthanie se comprend comme le *début* du témoignage du Baptiste et le *commencement* de la suivance de Jésus. En dehors de ce flux temporel, Béthanie serait un lieu vide, un lieu du non événement.

> *Il s'éleva de la part des disciples de Jean une dispute avec un Juif touchant la purification. Ils vinrent trouver Jean, et lui dirent: "Rabbi, celui qui était avec toi au-delà du Jourdain, et à qui tu as rendu témoignage, voici, il baptise, et tous vont à lui"* (Jn 3,25-26).

D'après le récit johannique, Jésus n'a plus séjourné à Béthanie jusqu'au chap. 10. Cependant, dans l'exclamation des disciples de Jean, Jésus est qualifié *topographiquement*, comme pour dire que son identité personnelle reste fondamentalement liée au témoignage du Baptiste, au moins pour l'entourage immédiat de ce dernier: «Rabbi, *celui qui était avec toi au-delà du Jourdain, et à qui tu as rendu témoignage,* voici, il baptise, et tous vont à lui» (Jn 3,26). Cette analepse renvoie, par-delà la scène de Béthanie, à la situation de départ du prologue, où la manifesta-

---

19. À côté de la connaissance scripturaire, W. HEITMÜLLER pense aussi à la compétence liturgique du lecteur: «Die Leser dachten bei dem Wort an die Hymnen ihrer Versammlungen: "Würdig ist das Lamm, das geschlachtete, zu nehmen Macht und Reichtum, Weisheit und Kraft, Ehre, Preis und Segen" (Offb. 5,12). Ja, so kannten sie ihn, als den Leidenden und Gekreuzigten» (*Das Johannes-Evangelium* [n. 17], p. 51).

20. Le verbe ζητέω apparaît 34 fois dans Jn.

tion historique du Logos est liée de manière inséparable à l'envoi de Jean comme témoin (1,6-8). Le lecteur entend certes la modestie de Jean à l'égard de Jésus (3,27-31), mais il se rend aussi compte de la *dépendance symbolique* de Jésus à l'égard de son humble précurseur (cf. «celui qui était *avec toi* au-delà du Jourdain»).

Cependant, le narrateur se démarque de l'affirmation des disciples du Baptiste, car si ces derniers avaient vraiment compris le *témoignage* de leur maître et la *scène* de Béthanie, ils auraient suivi Jésus comme les premiers disciples l'ont fait en 1,37. Cette incompréhension va pousser Jean à donner son dernier témoignage sur le Christ (3,28-30). Ainsi, les mots employés par les disciples de Jean résonnent comme une *ironie*[21] chez le lecteur qui, lui, a déjà saisi depuis le prologue le rôle exact de Jean et la dignité messianique de Jésus.

Ici, Béthanie est un fait *lointain* devenu opaque et incompréhensible, une tradition du *passé* colportée par des locuteurs qui en ignorent le sens. Le déplacement géographique (cf. 3,23) et la distance temporelle (cf. l'imparfait ἦν en 3,26) engendrent dans le milieu baptiste le doute à propos de Jésus. Une telle situation historique, qui est précisément celle du lecteur, ne devrait pourtant pas conduire inévitablement à l'incrédulité, car la μαρτυρία de Jean se répercute dans le présent (cf. le parfait μεμαρτύρηκας en 3,26; 5,33) et pourrait éclairer momentanément le lecteur (cf. 5,35).

Jésus s'en alla de nouveau au-delà du Jourdain, dans le lieu où Jean avait d'abord baptisé. Et il y demeura. Beaucoup de gens vinrent à lui, et ils disaient: "Jean n'a fait aucun signe [σημεῖον]; *mais tout ce que Jean a dit de cet homme était vrai". Et, dans ce lieu-là, plusieurs crurent en lui* (Jn 10,40-42).

Vu le caractère fondateur du premier séjour à Béthanie, il est significatif que Jésus s'y rende de nouveau (10,40: πάλιν). Ce retour signale l'aboutissement du geste initial de 1,28-29 (Jean vit Jésus venir vers lui à Béthanie), il confirme que Jésus trouve un *chez-soi* en ce lieu (cf. ποῦ μένεις en 1,38-39 // ἔμεινεν ἐκεῖ en 10,40c) et il annonce l'accomplissement de la μαρτυρία de Jean à propos de Jésus. L'inclusion ainsi for-

---

21. Retenons la définition donnée par B. USPENSKIJ: «Eine Inkongruenz der Standpunkte auf den Ebenen der Phraseologie und der Ideologie liegt z. B. dann vor, wenn in der phraseologischen Sicht einer bestimmten Figur erzählt wird, während gleichzeitig die Wertung dieser Person aus ganz anderer Sicht als spezielle Kompositionsaufgabe gilt. Dadurch nämlich tritt diese Person auf der Ebene der Phraseologie als Träger des Autoren-Standpunkts, auf der Ebene der Ideologie jedoch als Objekt der Autorenwahrnehmung auf (als Gegenstand der Wertung durch den Autor) [...] Andrerseits gilt gerade dieses Verfahren als eines der typischsten Ausdrucksmittel der *Ironie*» (*Poetik der Komposition* [n. 11], pp. 118-119).

mée par 1,28 et 10,40[22] devient le cadre interprétatif de ce qui s'est passés entre les deux moments. Tous les signes réalisés (cf. σημεῖον en 2,11.18.23; 3,2; 4,48.54; 6,2.14.26.30; 7,31; 9,16) et les enseignements donnés (surtout 3,10-21; 5,19-47; 6,26-59; 8,12-59; 10,1-39) sont des oeuvres de l'Agneau de Dieu annoncé par le Baptiste. Les croyants de la Transjordanie sanctionnent positivement le témoignage de Jean (cf. 10,41b: πάντα ... ἀληθῆ ἦν) en adhérant à Jésus – à l'instar des premiers disciples (1,37) –, alors que les Juifs cherchent à mettre la main sur lui (10,39: πιάσαι) selon la ligne de conduite des inquisiteurs juifs (1,19). La permanence de ces attitudes prouve clairement que les événements de Béthanie sont considérés comme *paradigmatiques* par le narrateur.

Le dernier séjour de Jésus à Béthanie au-delà du Jourdain précède immédiatement la résurrection de Lazare, un σημεῖον (11,47) qui enclenchera définitivement le processus conduisant à son arrestation et à sa mise à mort. D'ailleurs, c'est à Béthanie en Transjordanie que Jésus va entendre parler de la mort de son ami, mais il prolonge encore son séjour de deux jours (11,6: ἔμεινεν δύο ἡμέρας). Le rythme détendu et tranquille de son μένειν au-delà du Jourdain ne doit pas être bousculé par l'urgence de la maladie de Lazare: Jésus *prend son temps* et demeure en ce lieu presque aussi longtemps que lors de son premier séjour.

Il s'agit, dans cet épisode final, de renforcer l'identité de Jésus en *faisant mémoire* des déclarations du Baptiste à son sujet. L'absence de celui-ci est d'ailleurs suppléée par la *reprise*, l'*appropriation* de son témoignage par les πολλοί: «Tout ce que Jean a dit de cet homme était vrai» (10,41b). Ainsi, avant de passer au sacrifice (11,50), «l'Agneau de Dieu» fait halte dans le lieu où son sort a été annoncé de façon symbolique. Le lecteur est associé lui aussi à cet acte d'anamnèse, car il doit revenir au témoignage antérieur de Jean pour pouvoir évaluer la véridicité du v. 41.

Quand on prend en compte l'ensemble formé par le premier et le dernier séjour à Béthanie, on constate qu'ils ont un caractère *positif*, conforme au projet évangélique (20,31): d'une part, l'adhésion des premiers disciples, de l'autre, la foi de la multitude. De cette façon, le ministère

---

22. «Jesu öffentliche Wirksamkeit hat ihr Ende erreicht; der Ring schließt sich (V. 40): Jesus begibt sich an den Ort zurück, von dem er seinen Ausgang nahm, in die Gegend östlich von Jordan, zur Taufstätte des Täufers» (R. BULTMANN, *Das Evangelium des Johannes* [KEK, 2], Göttingen, Vandenhoeck & Ruprecht, 1964, pp. 299-300); «The departure of Jesus from Jerusalem to the territory east of Jordan was doubtless prompted by the virulent opposition of the Jewish leaders. In going to the place where John the Baptist first baptized and bore his decisive witness to Jesus (i.e. Bethany, see 1:28-34), the wheel has come full circle» (G.R. BEASLEY-MURRAY, *John* [WBC, 36], Waco, Word Books, 1987, p. 178).

terrestre de Jésus peut être conçu comme une réussite, malgré l'incrédulité des Juifs et la crucifixion en Judée. Le narrateur a donc élevé les passages de Jésus à Béthanie à un tel niveau qu'ils sont devenus le *cadre temporel* des activités publiques du Christ, et qu'à ce titre ils représentent le *point de vue fondamental* du narrateur.

III. CHRONOTOPE, FOI ET CHRISTOLOGIE

1. Poursuivant notre réflexion à partir de la remarque déjà citée de Bakhtine sur le roman grec, il est utile de vérifier si les séjours à Béthanie ont «laissé des traces» sur Jésus, ou si «aucune modification n'en résulte». En 1,28-42, Jésus a reçu de la bouche du Baptiste deux titres (Agneau de Dieu, Fils de Dieu) qui vont le marquer tout au long du récit: l'appellation *Agneau de Dieu* le conduira jusqu'à la mort en vue de l'accomplissement de l'Écriture (19,36), et le titre *Fils de Dieu* l'impliquera dans des disputes mortelles avec les Juifs (10,24-39). En outre, l'adhésion des premiers disciples qui l'ont suivi à Béthanie fait de lui *ipso facto* un «leader de groupe»; elle complique sensiblement la compréhension de son ministère (cf. les nuances entre 3,22 et 4,1-2) et détermine l'avenir de son mouvement (cf. les discours d'adieux de Jn 13-17). En 3,26, nous trouvons une indication significative: le nom propre *Jésus* est remplacé par une circonlocution liée à un séjour (initiatique?) en un lieu donné: *Celui qui était avec toi au-delà du Jourdain*. Cela signifie que, dans la conscience d'un groupe de gens au moins, l'image sociale de Jésus reste ancrée dans son passage à Béthanie. En 10,40-42, le nouveau séjour à Béthanie conforte Jésus dans son identité, révélée par Jean, et le prépare à affronter l'engrenage de la mort violente. Il est donc clair que les voyages au-delà du Jourdain ont laissé des traces indélébiles sur Jésus.

2. Le récit des séjours à Béthanie ne concerne pas seulement Jésus, mais engage aussi la foi, qui se trouve d'ailleurs au centre de la préoccupation du narrateur (Jn 20,31). En 1,24-39, les disciples attestent, par leur marche à la suite de Jésus, la vérité de la μαρτυρία de Jean. Ils changent de camp pour mieux répondre à l'exigence de la confession de foi. Ainsi, le premier séjour à Béthanie est un moment de décision et de suivance. En 3,26, le doute s'installe parmi certains disciples de Jean à propos de l'envergure réelle de *Celui qui était avec lui au-delà du Jourdain*; ainsi, après un certain laps de temps, la mémoire de Béthanie devient moins précise et exige un témoignage renouvelé de la part du Baptiste. Néanmoins, les disciples de Jean constatent bel et bien l'efficacité de Jésus auprès des autres: «Voici, il baptise, et tous vont à lui». En

10,40-42, les πολλοί prennent la relève de Jean en cautionnant son message et en croyant en Jésus. Ce relais entre Jean et les πολλοί prouve que, pour le narrateur, le Baptiste est une figure d'identification du croyant. De cette façon, Béthanie devient aussi le lieu de la *tradition* et de l'*histoire* de la foi.

3. Nous voici à la fin de notre parcours narratif. Il en ressort que Jésus est un personnage «*topophorique*»; il porte les marques de son passage dans des lieux privilégiés comme Béthanie au-delà du Jourdain et il en assume le destin. Il devient un «Christ local»: il voyage certes beaucoup, mais son identité est attachée à certaines mémoires locales. À vrai dire, cela a déjà été programmé par notre narrateur, quand il parle de la «Parole faite chair, qui a planté sa tente parmi nous» (Jn 1,14). Une fois dans le récit, cette *tente-là* a été montée quelque part au-delà du Jourdain, et les premiers disciples l'ont trouvée (cf. Jn 1,38-39). Ainsi, pour paraphraser Bakhtine, nous dirions que le chronotope de l'évangile de Jean établit l'image de Jésus dans le récit, une image toujours essentiellement spatio-temporelle.

RÉSUMÉ

L'étude met en évidence l'importance d'une dimension négligée dans les lectures narratives de l'évangile de Jean: la topographie. Elle se concentre sur les passages mentionnant un séjour de Jésus à "Béthanie au-delà du Jourdain" (Jean 1,28-29; 3,25-26; 10,40-42). Empruntant à M. Bakhtine le concept de "chronotope" (corrélation essentielle entre indices spatiaux et indices temporels), l'auteur montre que les mentions de Béthanie ont une fonction temporelle fondamentale, délimitant l'époque de la mission publique de Jésus et signalant les traces qu'ont laissées sur lui les séjours au-delà du Jourdain.

ABSTRACT

The study focuses on an importamt and neglected dimension of the narrative reading of the Gospel of John: its topography. The study concentrates on the passages which mention a stay by Jesus at "Bethany beyond the Jordan" (John 1,28-29; 3,25-26; 10,40-42). Borrowing the concept of "chronotope" (the essential correlation between spatial and temporal indices) from M. Bakhtine, the author shows that the mentions of Bethany have a basic temporal function, delimiting the period of the public mission of Jesus and indicating what was important about Jesus' stays beyond the Jordan.

Faculté de théologie Andrianjatovo RAKOTOHARINTSIFA
Antananarivo
Madagascar

9

PILATE IN JOHN 18–19
A NARRATIVE-CRITICAL APPROACH

A widely held interpretation of John's account of the trial of Jesus before Pilate would see John's presentation of the figure of Pilate as at worst neutral, and with perhaps more than a tinge of sympathy. As is well known, "the Jews" in John's story are portrayed in almost entirely negative terms; and this negative portrait comes to its terrible climax in the cry of the Jews at the end of the trial in 19,15 "we have no king but Caesar". On the other hand, it is often claimed that Pilate is presented much more positively. He is a man who wants to be fair, to be neutral, who doesn't want to get involved, who would gladly have acquitted Jesus: convinced of Jesus' innocence he tries to release him but in the end succumbs to the machinations of the Jews[1]. Some indeed have gone further and tried to argue that Pilate represents the state itself which has to decide between the world and truth[2]. This is probably too abstract (and those who have advocated this have probably been heavily influenced by their own situation of living in the era of the Nazi regime)[3]. Nevertheless, Pilate is still for many the would-be neutral observer for whom John has far more sympathies than he does for the Jews. Thus Brown writes: "Pilate is typical ... of the many honest, well-disposed men who would try to adopt a middle position in a struggle that is total"[4]. Whilst

---

1. Some have seen this as part of a more widespread political apologetic, seeking to shift responsibility for the death of Jesus away from the Roman authorities and on to the Jews (cf. Matt 27,24f.; Lk 23). Thus Barnabas LINDARS, *The Gospel of John*, London, Oliphants, 1972, p. 536, writes: "Even before Mark's narrative was written the tendency had begun of shifting the blame for the crucifixion away from Pilate and on to the Jews. John's highly dramatic handling of the trial before Pilate shows a definite advance in this direction by comparison with Mark". Cf. too C.H. DODD, *Historical Tradition in the Fourth Gospel*, Cambridge, University Press, 1963, pp. 104-107.
2. See R. BULTMANN, *Das Evangelium des Johannes*, Göttingen, Vandenhoeck & Ruprecht, 1941, pp. 505-509; H. SCHLIER, *Jesus und Pilatus nach dem Johannesevangelium*, in *Die Zeit der Kirche. Exegetische Aufsätze und Vorträge*, Freiburg, Herder, 1956, pp. 56-74; ID, *The State according to the New Testament*, in *The Relevance of the New Testament*, New York, Herder & Herder, 1968, pp. 215-238.
3. Cf. R.E. BROWN, *The Gospel according to John XIII-XXI* (AB, 29A), New York, Doubleday, 1970, p. 864; E. HAENCHEN, *John 2* (Hermeneia Commentary), Philadelphia, Fortress, 1984, p. 182f.
4. BROWN, *John*, p. 864. Cf. the comment of C.K. BARRETT, *The Gospel according to St John*, London, SPCK, 1955, p. 448: "Pilate is represented as not unfriendly to Jesus; he does not wish to put him to death, and he sees that he is the victim of a Jewish plot" (though see n. 5 below). For similar views, cf. J. BLANK, *Die Verhandlung vor Pilatus*

some acknowledge that John's attitude to any attempt to be neutral is ultimately a negative one[5], many would still claim that the main villains of the passion narrative are "the Jews"[6]. Thus Stibbe writes:

> Pilate is not ultimately a character whom the reader of this narrative is supposed to condemn. He may be an example of the impossibility of neutrality, but his dilemma is not so much of his own making as scholars have traditionally asserted. His indecisiveness may be a lamentable feature of his character, but that indecisiveness itself is directly caused by the fact that no one, at any point, answers the perfectly legitimate questions which he asks... We should not, therefore, be too hard on Pilate[7].

By contrast, I suggest that a close reading of John's narrative suggests a rather different interpretation of John's presentation of Pilate[8]. I would suggest that John shows absolutely no sympathy at all for Pilate and that his account shows with devastating clarity the true nature of Pilate as one who is opposed to all that Jesus stands for and all that is of God (in John's eyes).

One should also remember that the trial narrative, with its three "characters" of Jesus, Pilate and the Jews, focuses on all three: Pilate is only one character in a developing scene whose dramatic power and in-

---

Joh 18,28–19,16 im Lichte johanneischer Theologie, in *BZ* 3 (1959) 60-81 (repr. in *Der Jesus des Evangeliums. Entwürfe zur biblischen Christologie*, München, Kösel, 1981, pp. 169-196); A. DAUER, *Die Passionsgeschichte im Johannesevangelium. Eine traditionsgeschichtliche und theologische Untersuchung zu Joh 18,1–19,30* (StANT, 30), München, Kösel, 1972, pp. 308-311; E. HAENCHEN, *Jesus vor Pilatus (Joh 18,28–19,15)*, in *TLZ* 85 (1960) 93-102 (repr. in *Gott und Mensch*, Tübingen, Mohr, 1965, pp. 144-156); ID., *John 2*, pp. 186-7. See the overview in D. RENSBERGER, *Overcoming the World. Politics and Community in the Gospel of John*, London, SPCK, 1988, p. 92; also C. DIEBOLD-SCHEUERMANN, *Jesus vor Pilatus. Eine exegetische Untersuchung zum Verhör Jesu durch Pilatus (Joh 18,28–19,16a)* (SBB, 32), Stuttgart, Katholisches Bibelwerk, 1996, p. 212.

5. Cf. BROWN, *John* (n. 3), p. 864: "Having failed to listen to the truth and decide in its favor, he [Pilate] and all who would imitate him inevitably finish in the service of the world." Cf. too R.A. CULPEPPER, *Anatomy of the Fourth Gospel. A Study in Literary Design*, Philadelphia, Fortress, 1983, p. 143: "Pilate is a study in the impossibility of compromise, the inevitability of decision, and the consequences of each alternative. In the end, although he seems to glimpse the truth, a decision in Jesus' favor proves too costly for him. In this maneuver to force the reader to a decision regarding Jesus, the evangelist exposes the consequences of attempting to avoid a decision." So too BARRETT, in the same comment as cited in the previous note, continues: "Yet sympathy is, in John's mind, a quite inadequate response to Jesus; like Nicodemus (7.50f.), Pilate for all his fair play and open-mindedness is not of the truth; he is of the world."

6. Cf. DIEBOLD-SCHEUERMANN, *Jesus vor Pilatus*, pp. 217-219, for a forceful statement of this view: Pilate simply acts as the tool of the Jews in the story and John's portrayal serves to highlight even more the guilt of the Jews in rejecting Jesus.

7. M.W.G. STIBBE, *John as Storyteller. Narrative Criticism and the Fourth Gospel*, Cambridge, University Press, 1992, pp. 109-110.

8. For similar interpretations of Pilate in John's story, see P.D. DUKE, *Irony in the Fourth Gospel*, Atlanta, John Knox, 1985, pp. 126-137; also RENSBERGER, *Overcoming*, pp. 92-95.

tensity have been well analyzed many times. As already noted, one of the other "characters" in the story is "the Jews", whose final self-condemnation comes in this scene (cf. above on 19,15)[9]. Yet John is surely a writer whose sympathies for "the Jews" cannot have been non-existent. Whatever the social realities of John's own day, and whatever antagonism of hostility there may have been between John's Christian community and the Jewish synagogue[10], John is thoroughly convinced that, however new the situation brought by the Christ event is, salvation is "of the Jews" (4,22) and the Jewish scriptures bear witness to Jesus (cf. 5,46 etc.). John is no Marcion. If then "the Jews" are failing to respond to the Johannine Jesus, there is more than an element of real tragedy in this. The cry of 19,15 has a terrible pathos in John's presentation. Writing about this verse, Culpepper says: "The final rejection of Jesus is simultaneously a denial of their allegiance to God and their theocratic heritage... The implied author does not wink or smile. Is that grim satisfaction or tears in his eyes?"[11] Given John's clear awareness of the Jewish heritage of Jesus and the Christian movement, the latter possibility may be the most plausible. Indeed I would argue that it may be the dominant motif. But what/who in John's narrative drives the Jews to this position? One answer is: Pilate!

We should perhaps also remind ourselves of some general features of John's way of writing. It has become almost standard to speak of John as "two-level drama", meaning that in John's account we see as much, if not more, the situation of John and his community as we do of Jesus and his situation[12]. Yet John is a "two level drama" in another sense: in

9. The negative aspect of John's language about "the Jews" is well known, and the problem of whether, or how far, this betrays an incipient "anti-Semitism" on the part of John has been much discussed. I leave aside here the question of who exactly "the Jews" are in John (cf. U. VON WAHLDE, *The Johannine "Jews": A Critical Survey*, in *NTS* 28 [1982] 33-60; J. ASHTON, *The Identity and Function of the IOYΔAIOI in the Fourth Gospel*, in *NovT* 27 [1985] 40-75). But it seems highly likely that the term is rather more limited in scope than a reference to the whole Jewish people in their entirety. For a sensitive discussion of the question of possible anti-Semitism, see D. CRANSTON, *Anti-Judaism in the Passion Accounts of the Fourth Gospel*, in P. RICHARDSON & D. CRANSTON (eds.), *Anti-Judaism in Early Christianity*, vol. 1, Waterloo, Ontario, W. Laurier University Press, 1986, pp. 201-216.

10. Cf. the well-known theories of J.L. MARTYN, *History and Theology in the Fourth Gospel*, Nashville, Abingdon, 1979, and R. BROWN, *The Community of the Beloved Disciple*, New York, Paulist Press, 1979, who trace a developing history of hostility and separation between the Johannine Christian community and the Jewish synagogue to explain in part the very strong anti-Jewish language in the gospel. See the recent survey in M.C. DE BOER, *Johannine Perspectives on the Death of Jesus*, Kampen, Kok Pharos, 1996, pp. 53-71, for a summary with further discussion of more recent literature.

11. CULPEPPER, *Anatomy* (n. 5), p. 169.

12. Cf. MARTYN, *History*, e.g., p. 37: the Fourth Gospel is "a two-level stage so that each [actor] is actually a pair of actors playing two parts simultaneously". See also DE BOER, *Death*, pp. 53-55.

his literary narrative, John often makes devastating use of the element of irony. Quite how one defines irony is not entirely clear[13]. But most would probably argue that an essential feature of irony is the presence of two levels of meaning, one of which is unknown to characters in the story but of which the reader is aware. In this then irony differs from sarcasm, where again there is a double level of meaning, but everyone is fully aware of the two levels of meaning concerned. Perhaps John's most devastating use of irony is to present his story in such a way that so often characters in the narrative think they are using sarcasm, when in fact by more subtle irony they are expressing a truth of which they are totally unaware. As we shall see, the picture of Pilate is shot through with this kind of irony.

In what follows I consider a few details of the account of the trial of Jesus before Pilate in John (Jn 18,33–19,22). No attempt is made here to offer a comprehensive commentary on this section of the gospel. Moreover, my focus will be entirely on the figure of Pilate in the story. As already noted, Pilate is only one of three main "characters" in John's narrative, and probably not the major focus of attention for John: no doubt for John, it is the figure of Jesus that is the dominant and all-important character in the narrative[14]. Thus the observations which follow relate to what is perhaps something of a subsidiary element in the narrative. Nevertheless, it is clear that John's narrative, both here and throughout the gospel, is a highly complex one, and the characters other than Jesus still have a significant role to play in the story[15].

The narrative starts with the question of Pilate to Jesus in 18,33: "Are you the king of the Jews?" The question comes out of the blue and unprepared. It may be a traditional element in the story (cf. the similar focus in the Pilate trial in Mark's gospel); but for John the focus is throughout on Jesus' kingship[16]. Jesus' reply in v. 34, asking where

13. See the full treatment of DUKE, *Irony* (n. 8), ch. 1 (with a good discussion of the varieties of different ironies that can be developed by a text). Also W.C. BOOTH, *A Rhetoric of Irony*, Chicago, University of Chicago Press, 1974.
14. See HAENCHEN, *John 2* (n. 3), p. 188: "It might appear as though the Jews, who put Pilate under pressure, and Pilate, who resists them, are the real actors in this drama, and that Jesus is only an object, with reference to which the two parties propose to make decision, but in different ways. But it only appears to be so. In truth, the silent prisoner, who speaks only when meeting alone with Pilate, is the fixed point around which everything turns."
15. Cf. CULPEPPER, *Anatomy* (n. 5), passim.
16. The agreement between John and Mark here may of course simply reflect that fact that John knows Mark's account. But whatever we may decide about the question of dependency here, it is still the case that the issue of Jesus' kingship is not just a small, incidental motif within John's story, representing only the vestige from a source. It is one of the main Christological foci of John's whole presentation.

Pilate has got his question from, leads into Pilate's reply in v. 35a "Am I a Jew?" Clearly on the surface, by Pilate in the story, it is intended as a mocking taunt, expecting the answer No[17]. Yet as the story goes on, it will become clear that Pilate's position, by being opposed to Jesus, *is* exactly that of "the Jews"[18]. He *is* by the end a "Jew" in that he fails to acknowledge Jesus. And indeed this may be already hinted at in the form of the question with μήτι. John's usage of μήτι elsewhere suggests that questions of this form are more hesitant, and leave open the possibility that the answer may be Yes (cf. 4,29; 21,5). And indeed this is paralleled elsewhere in the NT[19]. By typical Johannine irony, John's Pilate thus already hints unwittingly at what will come. He thinks that he is not a "Jew", but in reality (i.e. Johannine reality!) he is becoming one.

Jesus now replies with his assertion that his kingship is not of this world (v. 36). Whatever the precise interpretation of the statement by Jesus, it is clear that the kingship concerned is *not* a political threat to Pilate. There should therefore be nothing for Pilate to be concerned about. Yet Pilate refuses apparently to listen. He fails to understand, or perhaps even deliberately misunderstands, Jesus' words (cf. v. 37). He takes Jesus as saying he is a "king" and as such a political threat to himself. Jesus replies evasively with the statement that Pilate says he is a king and goes on to speak of one of his purposes in coming into the world as being to bear witness to the "truth" (v. 37b). This leads to Pilate's dismissive mocking question "What is truth?" (v. 38a)[20]. Clearly for Pilate it has no profound significance. Yet also it makes clear Pilate's total failure to understand anything at all of the realities of the situation (at least in Johannine terms): for while Pilate mockingly dismisses the "truth" as unknowable, illusory or unreal, he is totally unaware that the one standing before him *is* himself the truth (cf. Jn 14,6).

---

17. And it is usually taken as such without question in the commentaries: cf. BARRETT, *John* (n. 4), p. 447 and many others; DIEBOLD-SCHEUERMANN (n. 4), p. 33.

18. See DUKE, *Irony*, p. 129; RENSBERGER, *Overcoming*, p. 93. Also W.A. MEEKS, *"Am I a Jew?" Johannine Christianity and Judaism*, in J. NEUSNER (ed.), *Christianity, Judaism and Other Greco-Roman Cults* (FS Morton Smith), vol. 1, Leiden, Brill, 1975, pp. 163-186, on p. 163: "The absurd question does more than add just a touch of sarcasm to the portrayal of the prefect, for the scenes of the drama are so contrived that the reader is made to see Pilate scurrying back and forth between Jesus within the praetorium and 'the Jews' outside. And despite his protests he is forced step by step to carry out the will of 'the Jews'."

19. Cf., for example, the question of Judas to Jesus in Matt 26,25 μήτι ἐγώ εἰμι; In one way this expects/hopes for the answer No; but the Judas of Matthew's story world, as well as the implied reader of Matthew's gospel, both know full well that the answer is Yes. See also BDF §427 (2).

20. For the range of possible interpretations of the meaning of Pilate's question, see DIEBOLD-SCHEUERMANN, *Jesus vor Pilatus*, p. 265f.

Pilate now declares Jesus innocent (v. 38b), a motif emphatically repeated in 19,4.6. Thus everything that happens from now on is under this rubric. Some have seen here a clear indication that Pilate is being regarded positively: in contrast to the Jews, he is the one who recognises that Jesus is not guilty[21]. However, it seems more likely that exactly the reverse is the case. If Pilate now fails to release Jesus, then he shows himself to be blameworthy, for he has come to this clear decision about Jesus' innocence. Here is no "honest, well disposed" person. Insofar as he fails to release Jesus, he is dishonest, corrupt and evil. And the repetition of the assertion by John's Pilate only serves to drive the message home for the reader.

With v. 39, John starts his account of Pilate's taunting of the Jews. Whatever the origin, or the historicity, of the "custom" involved in releasing a prisoner to the Jews at Passover, the way the possibility here is put to the Jews makes the outcome inevitable. For Pilate knows full well that Jesus' kingship is not accepted by the Jews. Thus to put the choice before the Jews as a question whether they want to have "the king of the Jews" released for them invites only one reply[22]. In v. 40 the reply comes with devastating inevitability as the Jews ask for Barabbas.

Pilate now has Jesus scourged. As Duke points out, "the irony here is macabre"[23]. The scourging elsewhere in the tradition is intended as part of the capital punishment; here however, it appears to be part of Pilate's attempt to "excuse" Jesus from punishment. The nature of scourging in the ancient world makes such a story line bizarre in the extreme. John hereby does not seem to be excusing Pilate in any way. Rather, his narrative is showing all too clearly how Jesus and Pilate are diametrically opposed to each other.

The irony embedded in the mockery scene in 19,1-5 is well known and has been fully analyzed by many others, even if the precise interpretation is disputed and uncertain. (What, for example, is the force of "the man" in v. 5?[24]) Jesus is mocked, with the crown of thorns and the pur-

21. See DIEBOLD-SCHEUERMANN, *Jesus vor Pilatus* (n. 4), p. 217: "Daß Pilatus im Kontrast zu den Juden positiver dargestellt wird, machen die dreimalige Schuldlosigkeiterklärung und der zweimalige Entlassungsversuch ... deutlich."

22. Even STIBBE, *John as Storyteller*, p. 107, who interprets the portrayal of Pilate as generally fairly positive (cf. at n. 7 above), sees the problem in the narrative here: "If Pilate intends the passover amnesty to act as a bridge for the accusers to that they can withdraw from this farce without loss of face, he makes his task singularly difficult by referring to Jesus as 'king of the Jews' (v. 39) – a title which he must have known would not endear him to the accusers. Inevitably, therefore, the Jews opt for Barabbas, and Pilate is consequently trapped into doing the very thing which he has taken the greatest trouble to avoid – punishing Jesus."

23. DUKE, *Irony* (n. 8), p. 132.

24. See the survey in DIEBOLD-SCHEUERMANN, *Jesus vor Pilatus*, pp. 155-161.

ple robe, and yet of course for John the royal clothing is entirely appropriate (cf. 19,14 here as well). The soldiers and others act and speak in mocking jest, but express what is for John a profound truth[25].

The response of the Jews is to clamour again for Jesus' death with the shouting demand that he be crucified (v. 6). This leads to Pilate's reply "*You* take him and crucify him"[26]. Yet for John's Pilate this too is just a mocking jest. John's Pilate knows that the Jews are not allowed to execute anyone, as the Jews have already told him this explicitly in the story earlier in 18,31. (Whatever the historical realities of Jewish powers of execution at this period of history, we are considering primarily John's story world here, and so the historical questions do not arise.) This is then, in John's story world, a taunt, a cruel mockery of the Jews' impotence. There is no note of sympathy for Pilate here from the storyteller. It is a taunting offering of a possibility that Pilate knows is in fact totally impossible.

The Jews then retort that Jesus deserves to die because he has claimed to be "son of God" (a claim that the Johannine Jesus has himself explicitly justified to the Jews on the basis of Jewish scripture itself: cf. 10,34-36). This in turn leads to a reaction of "greater fear" on the part of Pilate (v. 8). Whatever the reason for this "greater fear", Pilate now questions Jesus again and asks: "Where are you from?" (v. 9). In Johannine terms, the question reveals Pilate's true colours, for failure to know where Jesus is from is a sign of not knowing Jesus at all[27]. Pilate's question is thus not that of a genuine seeker after truth, or of an honest but weak man[28]; it is the question of one who is totally of "the world" in failing to see the light and respond to it.

Pilate now tries to claim an authority for himself (v. 10), claiming to have the power of life and death in his own hands[29]. Yet this is immedi-

---

25. DUKE, *Irony* (n. 8), p. 132; RENSBERGER, *Overcoming* (n. 4), p. 94, and many others. A similar kind of irony also pervades the synoptic accounts: cf. e.g. Mk 15,16-20.

26. The personal pronoun is clearly emphasised here.

27. Cf. the debates in chs. 6 and 7 of the gospel, as well as the savage irony of a verse like 7,27 (on which see DUKE, *Irony*, p. 65f.), whereby the audience are made unwittingly to testify to Jesus' credentials, precisely as they deny any knowledge of where he is from.

28. So, for example, DIEBOLD-SCHEUERMANN, *Jesus vor Pilatus* (n. 4), p. 62: Pilate is seeking to get more knowledge about Jesus. Or STIBBE, *John as Storyteller* (n. 7), p. 108: Pilate "timidly" puts this question. There is no suggestion elsewhere in the story that Pilate is timid!

29. Once again STIBBE, *John as Storyteller*, p. 109, seems driven to interpret the figure of Pilate in a way somewhat inimical to his overall theory: "Pilate's fear now reduces him to a desperate remark about his authority to release or condemn Jesus (v. 10), a grandiose claim which hardly rings true when Pilate has already tried, unsuccessfully, to release Jesus."

ately (v. 11) shown to be a sham. Pilate has no real authority, and he does not even realise this. He is living in a world of total illusion, completely blind to the truth.

The moment comes for the final act of judgement in the trial. There is the well-known crux in v. 13 of who it is that John implies actually sits down on the judgement seat: is it Pilate who sits down, or does Pilate make Jesus sit down?[30] The problem is probably ultimately insoluble, and it may even be that the ambiguity is intentional on John's part. But if it is Pilate who sits Jesus down (as I would argue makes excellent Johannine sense), then Pilate is shown to have abrogated all his status, power and authority. He is shown to have nothing and be worth nothing in the eyes of the world as well as of John.

The final exchange of the trial scene between Pilate and the Jews now takes place as Pilate says to them "Behold your king" (v. 14). Again at one level, this is mocking sarcasm by the Pilate of the story, but, by Johannine irony, an expression of a deeper truth which he would clearly be unwilling to accept himself. Yet it is also a savage taunt to the Jews. Pilate knows full well that, just as he cannot accept the claim of Jesus' kingship, neither do the Jews[31]. And it is Pilate who takes the initiative. The scene is then driven inexorably on with the dialogue in v. 15. The Jews initially clamour again for Jesus' death in their demand that he be crucified (v. 15a). Yet Pilate goads them again: "Shall I crucify your king?" (v. 15b). Indeed the Greek of John's story emphasises the word for "king" by placing it at the start of the question: "Is it your *king* that I am to crucify?" This is not the action of an honest, but weak man. This is clearly intended to play on the Jews' sensibilities and to goad them into further response[32]. Whatever the terrible consequences of the Jews' cry in v. 15c ("we have no king but Caesar"), and John makes no attempt to excuse it, it is still the case that the cry is only articulated at the goading instigation of – Pilate! It is thus Pilate in John's story who is as much responsible for the Jews' self condemnation. Further, it is quite clear that the cry of the Jews is not one with which Pilate can possibly disagree. And so, insofar as the cry of v. 15 is a denial of the Godness of God, and hence the ultimate blasphemy, Pilate is no less guilty than the Jews.

---

30. See the discussion in all the commentaries; also the extended note in R. BROWN, *The Death of the Messiah*, New York, Doubleday, 1994, pp. 1388-1393, with full bibliographical details.

31. See LINDARS, *John* (n. 1), p. 571: "There is no mockery of Jesus here: it is rather a taunt to the people, bringing the irony of the whole affair to a point."

32. Cf. LINDARS, *John*, p. 572: "What he [Pilate] has to say next is calculated to enrage them [the Jews] still further."

Finally the part played by Pilate in John's story concludes with the incident of the Jews' coming to him and asking that the wording of the titulus over the cross be changed (19,19-22). As such it seems to function as the ultimate taunt of the Jews. Again it is of course a piece of Johannine irony: the claim that Jesus is the King of the Jews *does* express profound truth for John. But for Pilate, as for the Jews, the words are just a taunt, a mockery, a distortion of the truth: neither Pilate nor the Jews believe that Jesus is the King of the Jews. Pilate has already decreed that Jesus is innocent: he is in his terms *not* a king. Hence Pilate's insistence that "what I have written I have written" is not the action of a stubbornly honest man refusing to compromise his principles. Nor is it easy to regard it as a "rediscovery of composure, stature and dignity" on the part of Pilate[33]. It is the action of a pig-headed and insolent man, bent on driving the final nail in the coffin of the condemnation of the Jews in John's eyes. Nor is it an affirmation of truth by the Pilate of the story, for it is *the charge on which Pilate is condemning Jesus to death*! It cannot be a claim which John's Pilate regards in any way positively.

I suspect that there may be tears in John's eyes at the final state of the Jews. But I suspect that for Pilate there are no tears. Pilate is for John the one who would stay neutral and would be uninvolved (see n. 5 above). But for this, John has no sympathy at all. Yet Pilate is more than just a neutral observer for John: in his opposition to Jesus he is also the arch-opponent of the Jews as well and, as such, the one who drives them to the situation where they deny their heritage and their God. He is the real instigator of the ultimate blasphemy. It is only in his stubbornness and above all in his mocking jest that he becomes the unwitting vehicle for the expression of profound truth about who Jesus is. But, by John's devastating irony, Pilate in the story remains totally unaware of this. It is John's narrative genius that succeeds where Pilate himself totally fails[34].

---

33. So STIBBE, *John as Storyteller*, p. 109.
34. After this essay was completed and submitted to the Editors for publication in this volume, another study of the figure of Pilate in the gospels was published: Helen K. BOND, *Pontius Pilate in History and Interpretation* (SNTSMS, 100) Cambridge, 1998. In her chapter 7 (pp. 163-93), BOND deals with Pilate in John and has independently come to very similar conclusions to those offered here, although offering slightly different arguments in some places.

ABSTRACT

The figure of Pilate in the Fourth Gospel is often held to be presented by John as at worst neutral and with perhaps more than a tinge of sympathy. Unlike "the Jews" who are presented almost uniformly negatively, John's Pilate is regarded by many as a figure who genuinely struggles to be neutral and fair, even if he fails in the end. The analysis given in this essay would suggest a rather different picture of Pilate. A study of John's passion narrative reveals a number of features which, via the use of characteristic Johannine irony, show that Pilate is not being presented with any sympathy at all. His questions to Jesus, his failure to make any account at all of what, in the story world, he should clearly have known and remembered, and his final savage jesting with the Jews, driving them to make their final terrible denial of their God (Jn 18,15) may indicate that Pilate is for John a figure for whom the reader should show no sympathy at all. In his stubbornness and mocking jest he becomes the unwitting vehicle for the expression of who Jesus is by John's devastating use of irony; but he himself remains totally unaware of this. It is John's narrative genius that succeeds where Pilate himself totally fails.

RÉSUMÉ

On considère souvent que l'auteur du quatrième évangile présente le personnage de Pilate de manière neutre – au pire – ou même peut-être avec une touche de sympathie. À la différence des "Juifs" qui sont presque constamment dépeints sous un jour négatif, le Pilate de Jean est, aux yeux de nombreux interprètes, un personnage qui s'efforce sincèrement d'être neutre et impartial, même si finalement il ne parvient pas à l'être. L'analyse menée ici propose un portrait assez différent de Pilate. L'étude du récit johannique de la passion fait apparaître de nombreux traits qui, par le biais de l'ironie caractéristique de Jean, montrent que Pilate n'est aucunement présenté avec sympathie. Ses questions à l'adresse de Jésus, son incapacité à tenir compte, dans le monde du récit, de ce qu'il aurait manifestement dû comprendre et garder en mémoire, la manière cruelle dont il se moque des Juifs, les poussant finalement à un reniement terrible de leur Dieu (Jn 18,15), tous ces éléments suggèrent que Pilate, aux yeux de Jean, est un personnage qui ne doit susciter aucune sympathie chez le lecteur. À travers son entêtement et sa moquerie railleuse, il devient l'instrument involontaire qui exprime l'identité de Jésus, grâce à l'ironie dévastatrice dont use Jean; mais Pilate lui-même demeure totalement inconscient de cet état de fait. La réussite est le fait du génie narratif de Jean, qui parvient à son but là où Pilate a totalement échoué.

Theology Faculty Centre
41 St Giles
Oxford OXI 3LW

Christopher M. TUCKETT

10

THE NARRATIVE FUNCTION OF PILATE IN JOHN

I. The Portrayal of Pilate in John

The depiction of Pilate in the extended drama found in John 18,28-19,22 has been assessed in contrary ways by scholars. On the one hand, some scholars understand John's Pilate to be a "weak" and even sympathetic figure. He is manipulated by the Jewish authorities to deliver Jesus over for crucifixion against his own better judgment. The Jewish authorities, not Pilate, are the villains of the drama. On the other hand, some scholars understand John's Pilate to be a "strong" character. He manipulates, even bullies, the Jews into betraying their identity as God's people when they reject Jesus as their king. Pilate, not the Jews, is the villain of the piece because he forces the Jews into an action against their fundamental beliefs and hopes. Pilate, in this view, is not a sympathetic figure at all; John shows nothing but contempt for him[1].

That John[2] wishes to exonerate Pilate or to depict him as a sympathetic figure is surely unlikely, especially given the brutal treatment of Jesus in 19,1-2 and Pilate's role in the crucifixion itself[3]. But it is also rather unlikely that John would need to *demonstrate* (to the Johannine reader) that Pilate is an evil man who belongs to the realm of darkness, the realm of "this world" (18,36)[4]. That Pilate belongs to "this world"

---

1. See the introduction to the essay by Christopher Tuckett in this volume (*Pilate in John 18-19: A Narrative Critical Approach*) for a survey of the debate and bibliography. Tuckett argues for the latter view, following the lead of P. Duke, *Irony in the Fourth Gospel*, Atlanta, John Knox, 1985, pp. 126-137, and D. Rensberger, *Overcoming the World. Politics and Community in the Gospel of John*, London, SPCK, 1988, pp. 92-95.

2. For convenience, I shall refer to both the Fourth Gospel and its author (or authors) as "John." Quotations follow the NRSV, with occasional modifications.

3. So rightly Tuckett.

4. Here I disagree with the major thrust of Tuckett's essay. For the purposes of this essay, the "Johannine reader" is the reader (or perhaps better, listener) created or implied by the narrative itself. This implied reader or listener (a) is a Greek-speaking Jewish Christian living in the latter decades of the first century CE, (b) is familiar with the basic tradition about Jesus underlying the Fourth Gospel, and (c) shares in the peculiar history and experience of a distinct community (especially excommunication from the synagogue; cf. 9,22; 12,42; 16,2). This portrait of the implied reader may or may not be historical, but I leave that question aside here. For the historical questions, see especially J.L. Martyn, *History and Theology in the Fourth Gospel*, 2nd ed., Nashville, Abingdon, 1979; Id., *A Gentile Mission That Replaced an Earlier Jewish Mission?*, in

is an assumption rather than a matter of demonstration[5]. However, John also depicts the Roman governor as *an extremely reluctant participant* in the drama of Jesus' trial and crucifixion. I note the following points:

1. In the opening scene (18,28-32) of this drama[6], Pilate leaves Jesus behind in the praetorium and goes out to ask "the Jews" (v. 31) why they have brought Jesus to him[7]. They respond that they would not have handed Jesus over to Pilate if he were not a wrongdoer. Thus Jesus is for them *already guilty* of a capital crime, the true nature of which is not disclosed to Pilate until later (19,7: "he made himself Son of God"). Pilate then tells the Jewish authorities to judge Jesus themselves, according to their own Law. They point out to Pilate, however, that they "are not permitted to put anyone to death" (18,31), i.e., without Roman indulgence or approval[8]. John adds a comment to highlight the significance of this claim: "This was to fulfill what Jesus had said when he indicated the kind of death he was to die" (18,32, referring back to 12,32-33)[9]. From this opening scene it is clear to the Johannine reader *(a) that the Johannine Pilate wants no part in Jesus' trial and execution,*

R.A. CULPEPPER & C.C. BLACK (eds.), *Exploring the Gospel of John. In Honor of D. Moody Smith*, Louisville, KY, Westminster John Knox, 1996, pp. 124-144; R.E. BROWN, *The Community of the Beloved Disciple*, New York, Paulist Press, 1979. See also M.C. DE BOER, *Johannine Perspectives on the Death of Jesus* (Contributions to Biblical Exegesis & Theology, 17), Kampen, Kok Pharos, 1996, pp. 43-82; ID., *Narrative Criticism, Historical Criticism, and the Gospel of John*, in *JSNT* 47 (1992) 35-48 (repr. in J. ASHTON [ed.], *The Interpretation of John*, Edinburgh, T & T Clark, 1997, pp. 301-314).

5. This becomes transparent in 19,15 where "the chief priests" declare that they have "no king but Caesar." This astonishing claim would lose all rhetorical impact if the realm of Caesar did not by assumed implication stand opposed to God and to Jesus.

6. TUCKETT (above p. 134) says that the "narrative starts with the question of Pilate to Jesus in 18,33". But the narrative arguably starts in 18,28-32 (a scene without parallel in the Synoptic Gospels) where Pilate has a preliminary and illuminating exchange with "the Jews" *about* Jesus, who *has already been brought* to him (18,28). For the division of the drama in 18:28-19:16a into seven distinct scenes, see R.E. BROWN, *The Gospel According to John XIII-XXI* (AB, 29A), New York, Doubleday, 1970, p. 858: (1) 18,28-32; (2) 18,33-38a; (3) 18,38b-40; (4) 19,1-3; (5) 19,4-8; (6) 19,9-11; (7) 19,12-16a. BROWN bases this analysis on Pilate's movements into and out of the praetorium. It is to be noted, however, that Pilate also plays a prominent role in 19,16b-22 (the crucifixion scene), and reappears in two further scenes (19,31.38).

7. On the distinctive meaning of the term "the Jews" in John's narrative presentation, see below (Section B).

8. Cf. R.E. BROWN, *The Death of the Messiah. From Gethesemane to the Grave. A Commentary on the Passion Narratives in the Four Gospels* (Anchor Bible Reference Library), New York, Doubleday, 1994, I, pp. 363-372, 747-749; see also my *Perspectives*, pp. 68-69.

9. In 12,32 Jesus says: "And I, when I am lifted up from the earth, will draw all people to myself." John comments: "He said this to indicate the kind of death he was to die" (12,33). Cf. 3,14; 8,28; and see my *Johannine Perspectives* (n. 4), pp. 162-168. John 18,32 is a good example of how the intelligibility of the narrative, and especially of such narrative asides, depends upon the assumption of a "Johannine reader" (see n. 4 above).

and (b) that Jesus will nevertheless be crucified on a Roman cross. The Johannine reader immediately wonders how Pilate, despite his evident reluctance to become involved, will hand Jesus over for crucifixion anyway[10].

2. After the initial exchange with "the Jews," Pilate goes back into the praetorium (v. 33) in order to interrogate Jesus. Elements of the ensuing conversation between Jesus and Pilate remain teasingly obscure. Yet, as a result of this opening conversation with Jesus, Pilate goes out to "the Jews" again (v. 38b) in order to declare to them with great emphasis that he finds *"no case"* (οὐδεμίαν αἰτίαν) against Jesus at all[11]. This is the first of three emphatic declarations by Pilate that he can find no grounds to prosecute Jesus (cf. 19,4.6). Pilate backs up the first declaration with an appeal to a custom of releasing a prisoner at Passover and he proposes Jesus as the beneficiary of this custom. The Jews reject this proposal, choosing Barrabas instead (18,39-40). It is once again evident that John wants to portray Pilate as a reluctant participant in the drama, someone who is looking for a way to release Jesus.

3. That such is the case becomes further evident in the following scene (19,1-3). Pilate now has Jesus scourged and the Roman soldiers mock him as the supposed "king of the Jews." In Mark 15,15-20a and Matt 27,26-31a[12], the scourging and mocking of Jesus occur as a prelude to his crucifixion, i.e., when his fate has been finally and irrevocably decided by Pilate. In John, however, the scourging and mocking of Jesus constitute *an attempt by Pilate to release him.* Pilate once again goes out to the assembled Jews and declares with emphasis: "Look, I am bringing him out to you *to let you know that I find no case against him*" (19,4). When Pilate does bring Jesus out (19,5), "the chief priests and the (police) officers" (19,6) shout for Jesus' crucifixion. Pilate responds by asking them to crucify Jesus themselves since he, as he now says *for the third time*, finds "no case" against Jesus (19,6)[13].

---

10. As I will point out later, the Johannine reader assumes that Pilate will hand Jesus over for crucifixion; the only question is how and why he does so. Cf. C. DIEBOLD-SCHEUERMANN, *Jesus vor Pilatus. Eine exegetische Untersuchung zum Verhör Jesu durch Pilatus (Joh 18,28-19,16a)* (SBB, 32), Stuttgart, Katholisches Bibelwerk, 1996, p. 217.

11. TUCKETT maintains (above p. 135) that "Pilate refuses apparently to listen" since he "takes Jesus as saying he is a 'king' and as such a political threat to himself." But this interpretation is unconvincing in view of 18,38b (and what then follows). The Pilate created by John may not understand what Jesus is truly talking about in connection with his kingship ("Am I a Jew?", "What is truth?"), but he is certainly portrayed as understanding that Jesus' kingship is no political threat to him whatsoever.

12. Luke omits the scene.

13. TUCKETT claims (above p. 137) that this is "just a mocking jest" since "John's Pilate knows that the Jews are not allowed to execute anyone, as the Jews have already

4. In 19,12, it is clearly stated that "Pilate was seeking (ἐζήτει) to release" Jesus. The imperfect ἐζήτει implies repetition or persistance. "The Jews" tell Pilate that if he were to release Jesus he would not be a "friend of Caesar" (19,12). In 19,15, "the Jews" again cry out for Jesus' crucifixion. Pilate's attempts to have "the Jews" agree to Jesus' release are thus in vain: they want him to do not the right thing but the Roman thing, i.e., to crucify someone *they* have presented to Pilate as an opponent and rival of Caesar (19,12). Though Pilate is not convinced of this appraisal of Jesus, he finally hands Jesus over to be crucified (19,16a).

In sum, it is evident that John's Pilate is a reluctant participant in the trial and execution of Jesus[14]. It is "the Jews" who in the Johannine presentation force Pilate's hand from beginning to end[15]. They repeatedly point out Jesus' guilt (18,30; 19,7.12), giving Pilate reasons to proceed against Jesus. They repeatedly call for his crucifixion (18,40; 19,6; 19,15), reminding Pilate of his obligations to his superior, the emperor (19,12)[16]. The Jewish authorities, according to John, "handed Jesus over" (παρέδωκαν) to Pilate (18,35; cf. 18,30). In 19,11, Jesus declares that "the one who handed me over"[17] to the Roman governor "has greater sin," i.e., sin greater than Pilate's. Clearly, Pilate is not exonerated, for he also plays his despicable part in the crucifixion of Jesus, but someone else "has greater sin[18]". According to John 19,16a, Pilate finally hands Jesus over (παρέδωκεν) "*to them*" (αὐτοῖς) for crucifixion. John could be referring here to the Roman soldiers who actually do carry out the crucifixion in the following verses, though the immediate

told him this explicitly in the story earlier in 18,31." But a Johannine reader would probably assume that the Jewish authorities could kill someone with the Roman governor's approval and indulgence (cf. BROWN, *Death of the Messiah* [n. 8], pp. 364-368, 719). In John, furthermore, the Johannine reader has been told repeatedly that "the Jews" want to kill Jesus (5,18; 7,1.19.20.25; 8,22.37.40; 11,53). Then there is 8,28 where Jesus says to his Jewish opponents that *they* will "lift him up," i.e., crucify him. It would seem then that John has Pilate here repeat the command for "the Jews" to crucify Jesus themselves (λάβετε, as in v. 31) mainly in order to allow Pilate to make his third declaration that he finds no case against Jesus. This then allows John to depict the Jewish authorities as bearing primary responsibility for Jesus' crucifixion. See below.

14. The Gospel of John is not alone in this. See BROWN, *Death of the Messiah*, p. 728: "all the evangelists create the impression that Pilate's condemnation of Jesus was under public coercion and against the prefect's better judgment".

15. Cf. DIEBOLD-SCHEUERMANN, *Jesus vor Pilatus* (n. 10), pp. 195-198, 217-219.

16. I therefore do not find convincing the claim that John's Pilate has driven "the Jews" to reject Jesus and their heritage.

17. Presumably this a reference back to 18,28 and Caiaphas the high priest.

18. John 19,11 shows, however, that for John Pilate's participation in the drama of Jesus' crucifixion is an anomaly and can only be explained as part of a strange divine plan (cf. 18,32).

antecedent is actually "the chief priests" in 19,15[19]. The ambiguity may be intentional – John thereby implies that "the Jews" are morally accountable for Jesus' death (cf. 8,28). The Johannine reader knows that they have sought to kill Jesus (5,18; etc.), and made a formal decision to do away with him (11,45-57) long before Pilate became involved in the drama (cf. 18,12-27).

The final result of the drama, Jesus' crucifixion on a Roman cross, is no surprise: That Jesus would be crucified was made clear (to the Johannine reader) in 18,31-32 (see point 1 above). Even apart from 18,31-32, however, John and his readers know that Jesus was crucified under Pontius Pilate. This fact was an irremoveable and unchangeable part of the tradition about Jesus' death[20]. The creative contributions of John to the narrative of Jesus' final hours are many, but this is one very disturbing fact John could not (or would not) change, certainly not without losing credibility with his Johannine reader(s). In recounting Jesus' appearance before Pilate, therefore, John cannot have Pilate actually release Jesus. This is an impossible outcome from the outset, given the tradition[21]. With hindsight, John (like the Synoptics) also gives a divine dimension to Jesus' crucifixion: Jesus himself predicted how he would die (18,31-32 with 12,32-33), by being lifted up onto a Roman cross. Furthermore, Pilate has authority over Jesus only with divine indulgence (19,10-11). Jesus is in control of events, not Pilate; he interrogates Pilate, Pilate does not interrogate Jesus (cf. 18,34-35). Pilate's attempts to release Jesus (19,12) in John's narrative are thus doomed to failure on two counts: (1) the tradition can allow no outcome other than Jesus' crucifixion on a Roman cross[22], and (2) this outcome is ultimately in the control of Jesus (and God), not Pilate. The Pilate of John's narrative is a prisoner of the facts mediated by the tradition and of Johannine theological reflection on those facts.

However, Johannine theological reflection upon Jesus' encounter with Pilate has produced a narrative presentation which is much more extensive than the Synoptic counterparts and is also given impressive dra-

---

19. See BROWN, *John* (n. 6), p. 863: "Jesus is handed over to the Jews for crucifixion" (otherwise in *Death of the Messiah* [n. 8], pp. 855-856).

20. The other Gospels testify that this tradition is widespread. Cf. also 1 Tim 6,13; Acts 3,13; 4,27; 23,28; JOSEPHUS, *Ant.* 18.3.3 §§ 63-64. TACITUS, *Annals* 15.44. The tradition is very probably historical. See R.E. BROWN, *The Death of the Messiah*, vol. 1, p. 725: "there is a historical kernel in the Roman trial: Pilate sentenced Jesus to die on the cross on the charge of being 'the King of the Jews'".

21. For John, this tradition contains the hard facts of history.

22. This is clear from the opening scene in 18,28-32. DIEBOLD-SCHEUERMANN makes a similar observation (*Jesus vor Pilatus* [n. 10], p. 217).

matic shape. So our question must be: What is the narrative function of the *extended* and *dramatic* Johannine portrayal of Pilate as an extremely reluctant participant in Jesus' trial and crucifixion[23]? In my view, an answer is to be found in the fact that Jesus is repeatedly characterized in the account as "the king of the Jews." Pilate is John's chosen narrative vehicle for the emphatic presentation of Jesus as "the king of the Jews[24]".

II. JESUS AS "THE KING OF THE JEWS"

John has six instances of this title (18,33.39; 19,3.19.21 *bis*). In view of the Synoptic parallels, the title and the immediate contexts in which it occurs are surely traditional:

Pilate	John 18,33	= Mark 15,2 (Matt 27,1; Luke 23,2)
Barabbas	John 18,39	= Mark 15,9
Mocking	John 19,3	= Mark 15,18 (Matt 27,29)
Titulus	John 19,19	= Mark 15,26 (Matt 27,37; Luke 23,38)

The two instances in John 19,21 do not have Synoptic parallels[25].

In the four passages listed above, the title is used only by Pilate and his soldiers[26]. Furthermore, there are two passages, unique to John, in

---

23. Given the multiple attestation of this motif in all the Gospels (see note 14 above), there may be an element of historical truth in this portrait, though that is not our primary concern here.

24. The issue here is thus not whether Pilate is a "weak" or a "strong" character, i.e., a "good guy" or a "bad guy," but the *uses* to which John puts the character within the given constraints of tradition. Along similar lines, DIEBOLD-SCHEUERMANN writes that "Pilatus ist in der Darstellung des Evangelisten eine Figur, durch die dieser eine bestimmte Botschaft vermittelt. Die Textanalyse und die Auseinandersetzung mit der Forschung konnten, was die Rolle des Pilatus betrifft, deutlich machen, dass der Autor Pilatus mit einer ganz bestimmten Absicht *im Blick auf* den Aussagegehalt seines Verhörs zeigt und dass es dabei *nicht* um die *Motive des Pilatus* in der Auseinandersetzung mit den Juden gehen kann. So ist der Tatsache, dass der Evangelist Pilatus benutzt nicht zu zweifeln, denn der Autor stellt hier von Anfang an das Vorhaben der Juden, Jesus zu kreuzigen, und den *Werkzeugcharacter des Pilatus* heraus (vgl. 18,31b) und verfolgt es konsequent. Daraus folgt sowohl von der historischen Gegebenheit wie auch von der Exposition der Verhörs her, dass Pilatus Jesus verurteilen muss" (*Jesus vor Pilatus* [n. 10], p. 217; emphasis original).

25. There are five instances of the title "the king of the Jews" in Mark (15,2.9.12.18.26), three in Matthew (27,11.29.37), and three in Luke (23,2.37.38). The instances in Mark 15,12 and Luke 23,37 do not have parallels in John (or the other Synoptic Gospels). Both Mark (15,32) and Matthew (27,42) also refer to Jesus as "the king of Israel" at the crucifixion. Jesus is acknowledged as "the king of Israel" earlier in John (1,49; 12,13; cf. 12,15; 6,15). In the passion narrative, however, he is characterized only as "the king of the Jews," as in Luke. This is important, as we shall see.

26. The two instances in 19,21 are not real exceptions since they narrate the Jewish complaint to Pilate about *his* wording of the titulus placed on Jesus' cross. They say to him: "Do not write, 'The King of the Jews', but, 'This man said, I am the King of the Jews'."

which Pilate presents Jesus to the Jews as "*your* king," i.e., as the king of the Jews (19,14 and 19,15a)[27].

The issue in John's passion narrative is whether, *and in what sense*, Jesus is "the king *of the Jews*." The focus in John 18-19 is not on Jesus' kingship as such[28] but on his being "the king *of the Jews*." Jesus as "the king *of Israel*" (1,49; 12,13; cf. 12,15; 6,15) is a different matter, being closely linked to the disciples' faith in him as "the Christ, the Son of God" (1,49; 20,30-31)[29]. "The Jews" over whom Jesus in his crucifixion now becomes king ("the king of the Jews") have no such faith in him at all. Jesus is their king, i.e., "the king of the Jews," whether they like it or not – that is the import of 19,21-22.

It is well known that there are in John many references (about 70) to "the Jews" and that "the Jews" are cast in much of John as Jesus' opponents with hostile, even murderous intentions (about half the total)[30]. "The Jews" are so depicted in John's passion narrative (cf. 18,31.36.38; 19,7.12.20.21.31.38). "The Jews" here refer at one and the same time to "the chief priests" (whose leader is the high priest; cf. esp. 18,35; 19,6.15.21)[31], and to "the Pharisees" (18,3)[32]. In 18,12, "the officers of the chief priests and of the Pharisees" of 18,3 become simply "the officers of the Jews[33]". "The Jews" in John's passion narrative are thus not the Jewish people in general (after all Jesus and his disciples are themselves ethnic Jews)[34] but those Jewish authorities or leaders who (a) seek

27. In addition, the word "king" is twice applied to Jesus in 18,37 (in Jesus' conversation with Pilate), again in 19,12 (Jesus is charged with "making himself [their] king" by Jewish leaders), and by implication in 19,15b (where the Jews claim to have "no king but Caesar", thereby rejecting Jesus as their king). Again, these passages are without Synoptic parallels. John has twice as many references (twelve) to Jesus' kingship in the passion narrative as does Mark in his (there are four in Matt, three in Luke).
28. Cf. TUCKETT's claim (above p. 134) that "the focus is throughout on Jesus' kingship." For the wide currency of this view, see DIEBOLD-SCHEUERMANN, *Jesus vor Pilatus*, pp. 291-292, who shares it.
29. Even so this title plays a minor role in the whole presentation of Jesus in the Gospel's final form.
30. See the discussion with bibliography in my *Johannine Perspectives* (n. 4), pp. 69-70.
31. Also 18,3.10.13.15(bis).16.19.22.24.26; cf. 7,32.45; 11,47.49.51.57; 12,10.
32. Cf. 1.24; 3,1; 4,1; 7,32(bis).45.47.48; 8,13; 9,13.15.16.40; 11,46.47.57; 12,19.42.
33. The character of John as a two-level drama clearly comes into view here (cf. my *Johannine Perspectives*, pp. 53-55, with reference to the well-known work of MARTYN, *History and Theology* (n. 4), pp. 37, 84-85). The chief priests are Jewish leaders hostile to Jesus (the first level of the Johannine drama), the Pharisees are Jewish leaders hostile to Johannine Jewish Christians in the post-Easter period (the second level of the Johannine drama). By referring simply to "the Jews" John can implicitly merge the two levels of the drama, in order to enable the Johannine reader to see that the two levels correspond.
34. As are John and Johannine readers. For such reasons, among others, John is not antisemitic. Antisemitic uses of the Gospel must be resisted and condemned. I treat this

to speak and to act for the Jewish "nation" (ἔθνος) (11,50-52; 18,35)[35] and (b) express hostility toward the Jewish Jesus as well as toward Jewish believers in him as the Jewish Messiah and Son of God (cf. e.g., 5,18; 9,22; 12,10.42; 16,2). The characterization of Jesus as "the king *of the Jews*" in John must, I think, be understood in this light, especially when considered from a narrative-critical perspective. In chs. 18-19, John exploits the significance of the tradition that Jesus was crucified on the charge of being "the king of the Jews." The issue is thus the kingship of Jesus *over opponents who have murderous intentions* towards him and his followers (cf. 19,38).

III. Pilate's Role

Pilate's first words to Jesus are the same in all four Gospels:

Mark 15,2   And Pilate *asked* him,   'You are the king of the Jews?'
Matt 27,11 And he *asked* him,   'You are the king of the Jews?'
Luke 23,3   And Pilate *asked* him, saying,   'You are the king of the Jews?'
John 18,33 Pilate… *said* to him,   'You are the king of the Jews'.

John's difference from the other three, however, is readily apparent. In the Synoptics, Pilate's words to Jesus are *clearly* a question (ἐπηρώτησεν, or ἠρώτησεν, "he asked"), whereas the matter is not clear in John (εἶπεν, "he said"). John commonly uses ἐρωτάω (sometimes ἐπερωτάω) to introduce questions (about 30 instances), but it is also true that the Gospel frequently uses εἶπεν (or other forms of this verb, e.g., λέγει, εἶπαν) to introduce questions (notable examples may be found in 18,37.38; 19,9.10.15)[36]. When John does use εἶπεν, however, there are markers in the context to indicate that what follows is to be construed as a question (e.g., the word order, an interrogative particle or pronoun)[37]. There are no such markers in John 18,33. Scholars and biblical transla-

---

matter further in my article *The Depiction of "the Jews" in John's Gospel: Matters of Behavior and Identity* (forthcoming).

35. Note that in 19,21 John refers to "the chief priests of the Jews." The Gospel's references to "the Jews" often seems to contain an element of sarcasm, which is a form of irony. These sarcastic references to the Jewish authorities as "the Jews" is probably an ironic acknowledgement of their claim to be the authoritative arbiters of a genuinely Jewish identity, a claim which Johannine Jewish Christians reject. See my *Johannine Perspectives*, p. 57.

36. See further, e.g., 1,21.38.46.48.50; 2,4.18; 2,20; 3,4.

37. In 18,37, e.g., it is the word order which indicates that a question is in view, βασιλεὺς εἶ σύ, in contrast to 18,33 where the word order is that of a statement, σὺ εἶ ὁ βασιλεύς. The word οὐκοῦν itself can be either inferential or interrogative depending on the context (cf. BAGD; BDR §451,1; BDF §451,1) or accenting (cf. LSJ).

tors routinely assume that Pilate's statement must be a question[38], undoubtedly under the influence of the Synoptic parallels. Jesus' response to Pilate, however, confirms that in 18,33 the Johannine Pilate has probably made a statement, not posed a question: "Jesus answered, 'Do you *say* (λέγεις) this from yourself or have others *said* (εἶπαν) this to you concerning me?'" (18,34). Pilate's response in 18,35 ("I'm not a Jew, am I? Your nation and the chief priests handed you over to me") implies that the Jewish leaders ("the chief priests") are the source of his information[39]. His further question ("What have you done?") anticipates his thrice repeated declaration that he can find no capital case against the Jesus who stands in front of him. It needs to be noted here for the sake of precision that the Johannine Pilate does not declare Jesus "innocent" or "not guilty" of the charge of being "the king of the Jews" (or some other supposed wrongdoing). John only has Pilate emphatically and repeatedly declare that he can find "no legal grounds" (οὐδεμίαν αἰτίαν) for executing Jesus precisely *as* "the king of the Jews."[40] John evidently cannot have Pilate's first words to Jesus presented as a question in 18,33, since for John Jesus *is* "the king of the Jews." The matter is not subject to debate.

John goes on to use Pilate to affirm that claim again and again:

> 18,39 He went out to the Jews again and told them, '... Do you want me to release for you the king of the Jews?'.

The Johannine Pilate here assumes that Jesus is "the king of the Jews," as he does in the following passages (contrast Mark 15,12).

> 19,14 He said to the Jews, 'Here is your king!'.
> 19,15 Pilate asked them, 'Shall I crucify your king?'.
> 19,19 Pilate also wrote an inscription and put it upon the cross[41]. It read, 'Jesus the Nazorean, the king of the Jews'.

---

38. But see M. DE JONGE, *Jesus: Stranger from Heaven and Son of God*, Missoula, MN, Scholars Press, 1977, pp. 68 and 76 n. 69 ("A statement, not a question").

39. In view of 19,21, the Jewish authorities have probably said to Pilate: "This man says that he is the king of the Jews." John's Pilate is untroubled by this charge against Jesus (as we see below), to the exasperation of "the Jews" in John.

40. On αἰτία (18,38; 19,4.6) as a technical legal term, see BAGD, αἰτία, 2. According to DIEBOLD-SCHEUERMANN, whose analysis extends only through 19,16a, "das Königsthema" in the trial before Pilate is primarily "das Vehikel, mit welchem der Autor ... die Schuldlosigkeit Jesu bestätigen lässt" (appealing to 18,36.37 with 18,38b and 19,1-3) (*Jesus vor Pilatus*, p. 293). For the Johannine Pilate however, Jesus is not so much "innocent" as harmless (19,1-2). The distinction is important, since the Johannine Pilate can affirm Jesus as "the king of the Jews" without difficulty, as we shall see momentarily.

41. So a literal translation. This is normally understood to mean that "Pilate also *had* an inscription written and (had it) put upon the cross" (so NRSV). That may well be the meaning though the Greek stills calls attention to Pilate's own role and use of the title.

Most interesting is the exchange between Pilate and "the Jews" which immediately follows:

> 19,21-22 Then the chief priests of the Jews said to Pilate, 'Do not write, "The king of the Jews," but "This man said, I am the king of the Jews"'. Pilate answered, 'What I have written, I have written'.

In all these passages the Johannine Pilate forthrightly affirms what "the Jews" do not, that Jesus the Nazorean is "the king of the Jews."

As noted above, Pilate sees no grounds for condemning Jesus to death for being "the king of the Jews" and he would not have done so had he not been placed in an impossible situation by Jewish leaders ("If you release this man, you are no friend of Caesar. Everyone who claims to be a king sets himself against Caesar"). Thus Pilate condemns Jesus to death on the charge of being "the king of the Jews" but he also has no problem with calling *Jesus* that. The issue is: In what specific sense and to what Johannine end does he do so?

The Johannine reader does *not*, however, think that Pilate is making a declaration of faith or has become a believer in any (Johannine) sense of the term[42]. And this is so for two reasons.

(1) Pilate affirms that Jesus is the king *of the Jews*[43]; he does not accept or embrace Jesus as *his* king. Jesus is not "the king of Pilate" or "the king of the Romans." The issue here is not Jesus' kingship over all and sundry[44], but his kingship *of the Jews*[45]. Pilate accepts and affirms Jesus as "the king of the Jews" from beginning to end (18,33; 19,22). But John's Pilate does so without being fully aware who it is he affirms as "the king of the Jews," anymore than "the Jews" fully realize who it is they reject as their king. Only John and his Johannine readers know[46].

---

42. TUCKETT writes (apparently in response to an earlier draft of this essay) that the inscription placed on the cross by Pilate is not "an affirmation of truth by the Pilate of the story, *for it is the charge on which Pilate is condemning Jesus to death*! It cannot be a claim which John's Pilate regards in any way positively" (above p. 139; TUCKETT's emphasis). So "neither Pilate nor the Jews believe that Jesus is the King of Jews." But this line of argument assumes that Pilate's affirmative use of the title would constitute some sort of belief in Jesus, a confession of faith by Pilate akin to 20,30-31. But that is not so. The Johannine Pilate is made to understand the title within his own Roman frame of reference, as we see further below.

43. In 18,35-38, John portrays Jesus' kingship as a Jewish matter ("Am I a Jew?"), of no real concern to a Roman and unintelligible to him ("What is truth?").

44. See n. 28 above.

45. This is so even in 18,36-37 which is sandwiched by Pilate's use of the title in 18,33 and 18,39.

46. M. DE JONGE writes that "the Jews" of John operate with "an earthly conception" of the title "the king of the Jews" (*Jesus* [n. 38], p. 67; cf. p. 58). So does Pilate. For Pilate, however, the application of the title "the king of the Jews" *to Jesus* is a matter of indifference, which is not the case for "the Jews" for whom the title could (and, in the case of Jesus, would) also have messianic overtones. See n. 53, and further below on 18,37.

(2) The title "the king of the Jews" is not in any case a matter of faith in John. Believers embrace Jesus as "the Messiah, the Son of God" (20,30-31), or as "the king of Israel" (1,49; 12,13), but not as "the king of the Jews." The title "the king of the Jews" only occurs on the lips of Pilate or his soldiers, never on the lips of Jesus or his followers[47]. Nor is it used by John in commentary on the narrative[48]. Jesus is thus "the king of the Jews" in chs. 18-19 in a special and limited sense, not as an object of faith but as *an item of ironic fact* (that is, it is an ironic fact for John that Jesus, whose execution "the Jews" bring about, is publicly and permanently confirmed as their king precisely in and through the crucifixion by the Roman governor).

Before we pursue this point further, we need to ask how plausible the Johannine Pilate's emphatic and repeated affirmation of Jesus as "the king of the Jews" really is. Does it have any verisimilitude? The question of history aside (what did the historical Pilate actually say and do?), there are two ways in which John's portrayal achieves some measure of verisimilitude for the Johannine reader.

(1) The title "the king of the Jews" was a Roman (or a Gentile) designation for the kings of Judea (cf. Josephus, *Ant.* 14.3.1 §36; 15.10.5 §373; 16.10.2 §11[49]; Matt 2,1-11)[50]. This is consistent with the fact that the title appears only on the lips of Pilate and his Roman soldiers in the Gospels, including John. On the lips of the historical Pilate, the title could have meant simply "the king of the Judeans." On the lips of the Johannine Pilate, and in the context of the Johannine passion narrative, it probably means "the king of the Jews."

(2) John has Jesus tell Pilate that his kingship, i.e., his being "the king of the Jews," is "not from this world" (18,36). Jesus explains that if it were from this world his "followers would be fighting to keep me from

---

47. Cf. DIEBOLD-SCHEUERMANN, *Jesus vor Pilatus* (n. 10), pp. 292-293. John 18,33 and 19,21 imply that the title was also used by "the Jews" in handing Jesus over to Pilate in order to give him a reason to condemn Jesus to death (see n. 50).

48. The title "the king of the Jews" is thus not used by John to give expression to Jesus' unique identity nor to his heavenly origin. For John, Jesus is (or here becomes) "the king of the Jews" because he is already the Son of God from above; he is not the Son of God because he is (or becomes) "the king of the Jews". See n. 53 below.

49. In the latter two passages, Herod the Great is called "the king of the Jews." In the first, there is a reference to "Alexander, the king of the Jews."

50. See BROWN, *Death* (n. 8), pp. 730-731. Though Jews could in conversations with Gentiles very well have referred to their king as "the king of the Jews", amongst themselves they would presumably have referred to him (or to the Messiah) as "the king of Israel" (cf. John 1,49; Mark 15,42; Matt 27,42).

51. For the translation "kingship" (instead of the more common "kingdom"), cf. G.R. BEASLEY-MURRAY, *John* (Word Biblical Commentary, 36), Waco TX, Word Books, 1987, pp. 330-331.

being handed over to the Jews. But as it is, my kingship (βασιλεία)[51] is not from here." This explanation tells Pilate that Jesus' kingship is no threat to the Romans[52]. As noted above, Pilate subsequently goes out to "the Jews" to say to them with great emphasis that he finds "no case" against Jesus at all (18,38). The Johannine Pilate can thus accept and declare Jesus to be "the king of the Jews"[53] for the simple reason that Jesus' kingship is presented to Pilate as containing no political threat to him or to the Roman Empire he represents (18,33-18,38b).

For these two reasons, then, John's presentation of Pilate's acceptance and affirmation of Jesus as "the king of the Jews" is a plausible element in the story for the Johannine reader. We may once again point out that Pilate does not thereby embrace Jesus as *his* king, nor does he in any way become a believer.

But what about 18,37? Pilate here asks Jesus, "So then you are a king?". This is not a hostile question and implies an affirmative answer. Jesus replies, "You *say* (σὺ λέγεις)[54] that I am a king. For this I was born, and for this I came into the world, to testify to the truth. Everyone who belongs to the truth listens to my voice." Pilate then says to him, "What is truth?" Pilate's question implies that since he is not "from the truth" himself, he can have no idea what "truth" is (cf. 14,6). But there is irony in the question John has placed into the mouth of the uncomprehending Pilate: the Johannine Pilate actually does know (though he does not understand) what that truth is to which Jesus has

---

52. Since Jesus exercises his kingship (i.e., his kingship "of the Jews") precisely in his crucifixion (19,21), John turns the "earthly conception" (n. 47) of Jesus' kingship shared by Pilate and "the Jews" upside down and inside out; Jesus' kingship is "not from here" (18,36), that is, because it is not a political or military form of kingship, it subverts both Roman and Jewish expectations of who and what an earthly king of the Jews might be and do. However, while Jesus' kingship may not be "from this world" (= "from here") for John, it is still exercised, or becomes effective, on the earthly plane of existence and could thus have profound political and military implications for the Johannine reader. See BEASLEY-MURRAY, *John* (n. 51), p. 331; E. HAENCHEN, *John 2*, Philadelphia, Fortress, 1984, p. 179: "Here it becomes evident that the expression ['the king of the Jews'] did not suit the Evangelist. He did indeed take it over but reinterpreted it. Jesus first of all bases his claim on the fact that he would have used force to prevent his deliverance to the Jews, were his kingship an earthly one... Christianity, as the Evangelist understands it, is not a political movement and therefore makes no use of political means."

53. We may recall that Herod the Great was "the king of the Jews" only with Roman permission and sufferance. See Josephus, *Jewish War*, 1.282-285.

54. These two words, which also appear in v. 34, are taken from tradition, being found in all three Synoptics as a response to Pilate's question, "Are you the king of the Jews?". In John, the repetition of these words (along with the context) emphasizes what Pilate has declared Jesus to be, namely, "the king of the Jews", though Jesus now goes on to give his own indication of what this kingship really signifies for him and thus also for John and the Johannine reader.

come to testify in the context of the passion narrative[55]. That truth is found on his own lips and he utters it again and again, namely, that Jesus is "the king of the Jews." For John, Pilate functions in the narrative as the mouthpiece of a truth Pilate does not, indeed cannot, fully comprehend.

This becomes clear in what follows. Pilate seeks to make it possible to release Jesus, first by appealing to a custom of releasing someone at Passover (18,39-40). Pilate proposes "the king of the Jews," but to no avail. He then has Jesus scourged and mocked as "the king of the Jews," the soldiers' brutal action demonstrating that Jesus' kingship is no threat to Roman authority or control. Pilate then brings Jesus out to "the Jews" wearing his mock crown and royal robe "to let you know that I find no case against him" (19,1-5). The scene is sandwiched by Pilate's repeated declaration that he finds "no case against him" (18,38; 19,6), a declaration found in the scene itself (19,4). For the Johannine Pilate, "the king of the Jews" is a pathetic and harmless figure[56].

In 19,7-12 the situation momentarily changes. The reason why Jesus must be put to death is after all not that he is or claims to be "the king of the Jews" but that he supposedly "made himself Son of God" (19,7). The charge that he is "the king of the Jews" is simply a smokescreen. Upon hearing this, Pilate "became rather afraid" (19,8) and he asks Jesus, "Where are you from?" (19,9)[57]. Jesus does not answer (Pilate will not understand the answer to the question and the Johannine reader already does). In what follows, Jesus makes it plain to Pilate that his destiny is not finally in Pilate's control anyway (19,10-11). The Johannine reader then learns that Pilate "was seeking to release him" (19,12a). In 19,12b, "the Jews" attempt to convince Pilate that the religious charge that Jesus "made himself Son of God" really means that he was "mak-

---

55. Pilate's question has provoked considerable speculation. The context indicates that it must be interpreted in relation to the issue of Jesus' kingship, i.e., his function as "the king of the Jews."

56. For this reason, Pilate's repeated references to Jesus as "the king of the Jews" or as "your king" could be construed as instances of sarcasm tinged with incredulity and contempt: e.g., 18,39, "Do you want me to release for you the [so-called] 'king of the Jews'?"; 19,14, "Here is your [so-called] 'king'!" If so, Pilate is (being portrayed as) attempting to taunt or humiliate "the Jews". But it is difficult to attribute to Pilate as a character of the narrative the ironic sensibility and intentionality of John. The Johannine Pilate uses the title without irony; for him it is simply an acceptable fact, one he can live with, even if "the Jews" cannot.

57. Cf. HAENCHEN, *John* (n. 52), p. 182: "That means [in the mouth of Pilate]: are you a heavenly being, a god?". This questions occurs repeatedly in the Fourth Gospel (cf. 3:2.31; 6,42; 7,26-29.42-43.52; 8,23.42; 9,29-30; 13,3; 16,27-28.30). See my *Johannine Perspectives* (n. 4), pp. 105-111.

ing himself [our] king" which in turn means (and this is the important point) that he "opposes Caesar." The Johannine Pilate now has a plausible reason (opposition to Caesar), one that could and should concern him as a Roman governor, to condemn Jesus to death from the βῆμα (19,13).

Here again, however, Pilate "says to the Jews, 'See, here is your king'" (19,14)[58]. They once again, as they have before (18,40; 19,6), demand that he be crucified (19,15a). Pilate then asks, "*Your king* shall I crucify[59]"? The Johannine reader is probably meant to understand Pilate asking this question with a tone of incredulity: "Do you mean you want me to crucify your very own king?" "The high priests" tell the Roman governor, "We have no king but Caesar" (19,15)[60]. Pilate is only allowed by the evangelist to proceed to Jesus' crucifixion (as he must since that is a datum given by the tradition) once "the Jews" have explicitly repudiated Jesus as their king, even if Pilate has not[61].

Beyond 19,22, Pilate appears twice more in the narrative, to give his (implied) consent to the request of "the Jews" that the bones of the three crucified men be broken and their bodies removed (19,31) and to allow Joseph of Arimathea to remove the body of Jesus for burial (19,38). Here Pilate, as a character of the Johannine narrative, shows his sensitivity to Jewish customs and concerns (cf. 18,28-29.39; 19,31.40), but only as a tool of the theological agenda of the evangelist. That is, John allows Pilate repeatedly to affirm, in both word and deed, that Jesus is indeed "the king *of the Jews.*"

In making use of Pilate in this way, John brings some terrible ironies to the fore: Pilate and the Romans, the recognized deadly enemies of the nation (cf. 11,48), declare Jesus to be "the king of the Jews" without reserve, whereas "the Jews" themselves emphatically reject him as such. In rejecting Jesus as their king, "the Jews" embrace instead their own enemy (king Caesar). In bringing about Jesus' crucifixion, "the Jews" think that they have successfully disposed of Jesus as their putative king, but the reverse is true: he is now their king forever. "The Jews" publicly repudiate Jesus as their king, yet Jesus becomes their king for all the world to see on a Roman cross. This last irony is vividly

---

58. Cf. BROWN, *Death* (n. 8), pp. 848, 1391-92: The intention of this scene is to make "the Jews" take responsibility for executing Jesus.

59. This translation reflects the word order of the Greek text.

60. Thus, it is not Pilate who is implicitly "a Jew," as TUCKETT (above p. 135) claims in an interpretation of 18,35. Rather, "the Jews" are implicitly Romans, i.e., part and parcel of "this world" which Pilate represents. This is shown by their embrace of Caesar which is a reflex of their rejection of Jesus.

61. They also repudiate God as their king in the process. Cf. BROWN, *Death*, p. 849.

on narrative display in the crucifixion scene (19,16b-22). The notice put on the cross declaring Jesus to be "the king of the Jews" is written in three languages, a fact which is often taken to mean that the gospel is now universalized and has a Gentile mission in view. But in 19,20, John reports that "many *of the Jews*" read this trilingual notice and were offended by its content. Jesus is here being declared "the king *of the Jews*" for all the world to see and to understand[62]. Pilate is made to affirm this in a striking manner, refusing to change the wording of the notice: "What I have written, I have written." It cannot be changed. Jesus *is* "the king of the Jews" for all the world to see[63]. It serves John's purpose to have Pilate affirm this solemnly one last time. John thereby underscores the ironic factuality of it all.

IV. Conclusion

In his portrayal of Pilate, John has a specific agenda. John uses this particular character to affirm repeatedly that Jesus is indeed "the king of the Jews" even though "the Jews" of John's narrative themselves expressly reject him as their king[64].

For John, the real reason "the Jews" sought to do away with Jesus is that he supposedly "made himself Son of God." Because of the constraints of tradition, however, John must portray Jesus as having being crucified as "the king of the Jews" by Pilate and the Romans. Confronted with these constraints, John exploits the ironic implications of the crucifixion of Jesus as "the king of the Jews" for the Johannine reader. Jesus comes to function as the king *of the Jews* precisely in their successful campaign to have him killed on that very charge[65]. John uses

---

62. Jesus for John is also king in some other sense for (non-Jewish as well as Jewish) believers; my point is that that is not what is said expressly here, in this particular scene, where the issue is Jesus' kingship "of the Jews."

63. Cf. BROWN, *Death* (n. 8), p. 966: The words "Jesus the Nazorean" which accompany the words "the king of the Jews" in the trilingual titulus placed by Pilate on Jesus' cross have "all the formality of 'Tiberius Caesar,' and the trilingualism increases the imperial or regal atmosphere." BROWN continues: "We may compare Pilate's present role to that of Caiaphas in John 11:49-52; 18:14. High priest that year and therefore someone who could prophesy, Caiaphas was brought by God unknowingly to speak the truth about Jesus: 'It is better that one man die for the people.' Having encountered truth (Jesus), Pilate is brought to make an imperial proclamation prophetically true in its wording."

64. It is also part of the agenda of the evangelist to portray "the Jews" as repeatedly rejecting Jesus. Each time Pilate is made to affirm Jesus as "the king of the Jews," the Jewish leaders are made to repudiate this affirmation. But Pilate is given the last word: "what I have written, I have written." This is actually the last word of the Fourth Gospel on the matter.

65. If Pilate does seat Jesus on the βῆμα in 19,13 (one possible reading, though probably the less likely, as shown by BROWN, *Death*, pp. 1388-1393), it is so that he can func-

Pilate, the uncomprehending, unbelieving, and reluctant participant in the events leading to Jesus' crucifixion, as a narrative vehicle for this terrible and tragic irony[66]. The Johannine Pilate's repeated affirmation of Jesus as "the king of the Jews[67]", culminating in the unchangeable titulus he finally places on Jesus' cross, serves a larger narrative purpose: it allows John to portray the Johannine Jesus hanging on a Roman cross to be what "the Jews" of the narrative expressly do not want him to be, namely, their king[68].

ABSTRACT

In an extended dramatic presentation, John presents Pilate as an extremely reluctant participant in the drama of Jesus' trial and crucifixion (John 18,28-19,22; cf. 19,31.38). Pilate's decision to hand Jesus over for crucifixion is brought about by "the Jews" of the narrative; they, not Pilate, are made to bear moral responsibility for Jesus' crucifixion. But what is the narrative function of the *extended* and *dramatic* portrayal of Pilate in John 18-19? An answer is sought in the fact that the Johannine Pilate repeatedly refers to Jesus as "the king of the Jews", i.e., of those who have all along sought to kill him and eventually succeed by forcing Pilate to hand Jesus over for crucifixion. The issue in Jesus' encounter with Pilate is not the kingship of Jesus over all and sundry, but quite specifically his kingship "of the Jews". The Pilate of the Johannine narrative functions as a mouthpiece of a truth he does not, indeed cannot, understand (he does not embrace Jesus as *his* king, nor does he in any way become a be-

---

tion as judge of "the Jews." Pilate immediately presents Jesus to "the Jews" as their king (19,14). Cf. the word of judgment from Jesus' lips in 19,11: "the one who handed me over to you (Pilate) has greater sin." See above.

66. I agree with TUCKETT when he claims that John may have "tears in his eyes" (following CULPEPPER) because of the Jewish rejection of Jesus (above pp. 133, 139). But that is not because Pilate has driven "the Jews" to kill Jesus, but because they themselves have brought about his execution: "He came to what was his own, and his own people did not accept him" (1,11).

67. To repeat a crucial point made earlier: Pilate's affirmation of Jesus as "the king of the Jews" is not intended to be construed as a confession of faith on his part. See discussion above.

68. The theological implications bear further investigation. Here I can only cite some observations by J.L. MARTYN in his essay *John and Paul on the Subject of Gospel and Scripture*, in *Theological Issues in the Letters of Paul*, Edinburgh, T&T Clark, 1997, p. 215: "John finds that the story of Jesus contains numerous geological faults (Verwerfungen), radical disjunctures that cause the gospel story to be a landscape over which it is impossible for human beings to walk... One does not walk into the community of the redeemed across the terrain that reaches from the past into the present, for there seem to be no bridges that reach over the geological fault created by the advent of Christ, the Stranger from Heaven." One of those geological faults in John may then be his depiction of Jesus as the crucified "king of the Jews" in chs. 18-19.

liever). The Johannine Pilate repeatedly affirms what "the Jews" of the narrative reject, namely, that Jesus is in fact their king, whether they like it or not (cf. 19,21-22).

For John, the real reason "the Jews" sought to kill Jesus is that he supposedly "made himself Son of God" (19,7). Because of the constraints of tradition, however, John must portray Jesus as having been crucified as "the king of the Jews" by Pilate and the Romans. Confronted with these constraints, John exploits the ironic implications of the crucifixion of Jesus as "king of the Jews" for the Johannine reader. Jesus comes to function as the king *of the Jews* precisely in their successful campaign to have him killed on that very charge. John uses Pilate, the uncomprehending, unbelieving, and reluctant participant in the events leading to Jesus' crucifixion, as a narrative vehicle for this terrible and tragic irony. The Johannine Pilate's repeated affirmation of Jesus as "the king of the Jews", culminating in the unchangeable titulus he finally places on Jesus' cross, serves a larger narrative purpose: it allows John to portray the Johannine Jesus hanging on a Roman cross to be what "the Jews" of the narrative expressly do not want him to be, namely, their king.

RÉSUMÉ

Dans un récit dramatique et détaillé, Jean présente le personnage de Pilate comme participant à contrecoeur au drame du procès et de la crucifixion de Jésus (Jean 18,28-19,22; cf 19,31.38). Si Pilate décide de livrer Jésus pour qu'il soit crucifié, c'est parce qu'il y est poussé par "les Juifs" du récit; ce sont eux, et non Pilate, qui portent la responsabilité morale de la crucifixion de Jésus. Quelle est alors la fonction narrative du portrait *détaillé* et *dramatique* de Pilate en Jean 18-19? La réponse est à chercher dans le fait que, dans le récit johannique, Pilate désigne fréquemment Jésus comme "le roi des Juifs" (cf. 18,33.39; 19,14.15.19.21-22). Jean utilise Pilate comme moyen narratif pour montrer de manière emphatique que Jésus est le roi *des Juifs*, c'est-à-dire de ceux qui, tout au long du récit, ont cherché à le tuer et qui y parviennent finalement en contraignant Pilate à le livrer pour qu'il soit crucifié. La question qui est au centre de la rencontre de Jésus avec Pilate n'est pas celle de sa royauté sur tout un chacun, mais celle, très spécifique, de sa royauté sur "les Juifs". Le Pilate du récit johannique a pour fonction d'être le porte-parole d'une vérité que lui-même ne comprend pas, qu'en fait il ne peut pas comprendre (il ne reconnaît pas Jésus comme *son* roi, il ne devient nullement croyant). Le Pilate de Jean affirme à de nombreuses reprises ce que "les Juifs" du récit rejettent, à savoir que Jésus est en réalité leur roi, que cela leur plaise ou non (cf. 19,21-22).

Pour Jean, la raison véritable qui fait que "les Juifs" cherchent à tuer Jésus est que, selon eux, "il s'est fait Fils de Dieu" (19,7). Mais Jean, à cause des contraintes de la tradition, est tenu de montrer que Jésus a été crucifié par Pilate et par les Romains en tant que "roi des Juifs". Confronté à ces contraintes, Jean exploite les implications ironiques de la crucifixion de Jésus comme "roi des Juifs" pour le lecteur johannique. Jésus en vient à assumer la fonction de roi *des*

Juifs précisément parce que ces derniers réussissent à le faire mettre à mort sur la base de cette accusation. Jean utilise Pilate – celui qui ne comprend pas, qui ne croit pas, qui participe à contrecoeur aux événements menant à la crucifixion de Jésus – comme véhicule narratif de cette ironie terrible et tragique. L'affirmation réitérée du Pilate de Jean, selon laquelle Jésus est "le roi des Juifs", culmine dans l'inscription immuable qu'il fait placer sur la croix; cette affirmation est au service d'un but narratif plus large: elle permet à Jean de présenter Jésus, crucifié sur une croix romaine, comme étant ce que "les Juifs" du récit ne voulaient justement pas qu'il soit, à savoir leur roi.

Faculteit der Godgeleerdheid	Martinus C. DE BOER
Vrije Universiteit	
De Boelelaan 1105	
1081 HV Amsterdam	
The Netherlands	

11

THE GOD OF THE BOOK OF ACTS

What image of God does the author of Luke-Acts offer his readers[1]? In the small number of studies consecrated to this question, the majority offer an analysis of the contents, enumerating the characteristics that Luke uses to attire the God of his narrative[2]: God, the agent of salvation history, Jesus as the mirror of the Father's action, the joy of God at the return of the lost, the universal God that Peter discovers (Acts 10-11), the providential God of the sermon in Athens, etc. Hence there emerges the portrait of a God who is faithful to what He promised, a God that tends towards a universal program, and quite bluntly intervenes in guiding history.

However, this type of analysis and enumeration which consists in extracting from the Lukan text a discourse on God merits a questioning of his method. In forcing the text of Luke into a quest for divine statements, we accumulate a mixture of parables and visions, logia and ecstasies, human discourses and angelic revelations. Whereas, the study of semiotics has taught us that form makes meaning. Along the same lines, narratology teaches us to distinguish the narrative authorities a narrator uses to communicate his information to the reader[3].

I will explore this line, dealing particularly with the manner in which the author of the book of Acts constructs his image of God. How does the narrator express, throughout the narrative, the action and the word of

---

1. A French version of this text appeared in A. MARCHADOUR (ed.), *L'Évangile exploré. Mélanges offerts à S. Légasse* (LD, 166), Paris, Cerf, 1996, pp. 301-331. Translation: K. MCKINNEY and G.D. LAUGHERY.

2. In this tendency, I note: G. SCHNEIDER, *Gott und Christus als Kyrios nach der Apostelgeschichte*, in *Begegnung mit dem Wort*, FS H. Zimmermann (BBB, 53), 1980, pp. 161-174; ID., *Lukas, Theologe der Heilsgeschichte* (BBB, 59), 1985, pp. 213ss.; R.F. O'TOOLE, *The Unity of Luke's Theology. An Analysis of Luke-Acts*, Wilmington, DE, Michael Glazier, 1984; F. BOVON, *The God of Luke*, in *New Testament Traditions and Apocryphal Narratives*, Allison Park, Pickwick, 1995, pp. 67-80; R.L. BRAWLEY, *Centering on God. Method and Message in Luke-Acts*, Louisville, Westminster – John Knox, 1990, pp. 107-124; L.M. MALONEY, *"All that God had Done with Them". The Narration of the Works of God in the Early Christian Community as Described in the Acts of the Apostles*, New York – Bern, Lang, 1991.

3. To be consulted: M.A. POWELL, *What is Narrative Criticism?*, Minneapolis, Fortress, 1990, or J.-N. ALETTI, *L'art de raconter Jésus-Christ* (Parole de Dieu, 27), Paris, Seuil, 1989.

God? How does he communicate what he knows of God and how does he make it known to his readers[4]?

The *first* part of this essay will attempt to differentiate the two modalities of the Lukan discourse concerning God; we will note that a theologically coherent narrative strategy, hardly noticed until recently, rigorously controls the divine statements in Acts. A *second* section will adopt a more syntagmatic perspective, with the intention of recognizing the functions which divine intervention fulfills in the plot of the Acts of the Apostles; the typology that emerges from this analysis allows us to distinguish a programmatic function, a performative function and an interpretative function. A *conclusion* briefly summarizes the characteristics of the God of Acts which our study has elucidated[5].

I. Two languages to say God

One of the most abrupt and unforeseeable turning points in the Pauline mission takes place just after the Jerusalem Council. Paul had begun what we used to call his second missionary journey (Acts 15,36) and he is travelling through Cilicia with Silas, when one after the other, three events radically reorient his itinerary: the Holy Spirit prevents (κωλυθέντες) them from going into Asia (16,6), the Spirit of Jesus does not allow (οὐκ εἴασεν) them to go to Bithynia (16,7); in a night vision, Paul sees a Macedonian pleading for him to come and help (16,9). For the reader of the Book of Acts familiar with the language of the Septuagint, each of these interventions bears the signature of God: the intervention of the Holy Spirit (or the Spirit of Jesus: the only occur-

---

4. Several works opened the way. I have in mind the statistical studies of R.L. Mowery, *Direct Statements Concerning God's Activity in Acts*, in *SBL 1990 Seminar Papers*, pp. 196-211; Id., *God the Father in Luke-Acts*, in E. Richard (ed.), *New Views on Luke and Acts*, Collegeville, Liturgical Press, 1990, pp. 124-132; Id., *Lord, God, and Father: Theological Language in Luke-Acts*, in *SBL 1995 Seminar Papers*, pp. 82-101; see also the contribution of K. Löning, *Das Gottesbild der Apostelgeschichte im Spannungsfeld von Frühjudentum und Fremdreligionen*, in H.-J. Klauck (ed.), *Monotheismus und Christologie. Zur Gottesfrage im hellenistischen Judentum und im Urchristentum* (QD, 138), Freiburg, Herder, 1992, pp. 88-117. Narrative reading by J.-N. Aletti, *Quand Luc raconte. Le récit comme théologie* (Lire la Bible 115), Paris, Cerf, 1998, p. 19-69.

5. The exhaustive portrait of God in Luke remains to be painted. As M. Dumais comments, "on n'a pas encore vraiment élaboré une 'théologie' lucanienne au sens premier du terme, c'est-à-dire un discours systématique sur la conception de Dieu dans l'œuvre de Luc"; M. Dumais, *Les Actes des Apôtres. Bilan et orientations*, in ACEBAC (ed.), *De bien des manières. La recherche biblique aux abords du XXIe siècle* (LD, 163), Montréal – Paris, Fides – Cerf, 1995, pp. 307-364, quotation 328-329. In any case, this effort cannot avoid considering the manner Luke constructs his discourse concerning God in the narrative, as sketched out in this study.

rence in Acts) and the vision are part of the traditional theophanic code. The decoding of these theophanic signs doesn't pose a bigger problem for the reader than to attribute to God the origin of the coming of the Spirit at Pentecost (2,1-11). The only surprising thing is the rapid succession of events; this signals an inhabitual pressure of God on human history.

Just after the mention of the threefold reorientaling of the Pauline itinerary, we have the first of four "We-passages" (16,10-17), which names the invisible author of the three interventions and deciphers the underlying intention: *"...we immediately tried to cross over to Macedonia, being convinced that God had called us to proclaim the good news to them"* (16,10)[6].

This narrative sequence illustrates clearly that speaking of God in the book of Acts requires observing these two different modalities: on the one hand, the explicit discourse where God is directly named (16,10), and on the other hand, the implicit discourse where God manifests himself through theophanic mediations whose code is known to the readers (16,6f.9). Both constitute the theo-logy of the book of Acts.

These two modes that Luke borrows to speak of God conform to the religious language of his time in two ways. First, for the Jewish tradition as for the Greco-Roman culture of the first century, the God of heaven uses intermediaries when he wants to reach people. Second, Luke knows how to unfold a discourse in which God is explicitly named and called by his titles: θεός, κύριος, πατήρ. What relationship does the narrator establish between these two forms of language for God (one implicit and the other explicit)?

1. The implicit language corresponds to the theophanies of the LXX

God transmits his messages through angels sent to the apostles (1,10f; 5,19f), to Philip (8,26), to Peter (12,7-10), to Herod (12,23), to Cornelius (10,3-6.22.30-32; 11,13f), to Paul (27,23f; cf. 23,9). God gives visions or ecstasies to Stephen (7,55f), to Peter (10,10-16; 11,5-10), to Paul (9,3-8, cf. 22,17-21 and 26,13-18; 16,9). These visions can be appearances of Jesus (1,3-11; 7,56; 18,9f; 22,17-21; cf. 9,7). We know also of double visions, highly valued by the Greeks and the Romans (9,10-12; 10,1-23). The casting of lots can also signify God's action (1,26), but the action of the Spirit is more frequently directed to the apostles (2,1-11), to Philip (8,29.39), to Cornelius (10,44-46; 11,15), to the community (13,2), to Peter (10,19f; 11,12) or Paul (16,6f). We also witness wonders: earthquakes (4,31; 16,26), miraculous deliverances from prison

---

6. Biblical quotations are generally taken from the NRSV.

(5,19f; 12,6-10; 16,26), rescues from storms (27,9-44). The power of the apostles also signals the divine, when they heal, exorcise, reanimate the dead, punish cheats and escape from vipers[7].

We witness an extraordinary diversity of the ways God intervenes. Luke, who is a fine manager of the vocabulary, applies the adequate wording[8] for every occurrence. However, we should note: from Luke's point of view, the greatest intervention of God in history is surely the resurrection of Jesus. It not only overshadows his narrative but also carries the thaumaturgical power of the apostles in its flow: *"Jesus Christ that you crucified, God has raised from the dead"* (4,10; 2,23f; 3,14f; 13,29f; etc.).

This inventory of divine interferences calls for three remarks.

Primo. God's interventions, in such diversity, do not have their equal in the gospel of Luke, with the exception of the two extremities: the infancy narrative (Lk 1-2) and the paschal cycle (Lk 24)[9]. As soon as Jesus comes on the scene (Lk 2,40), he monopolizes the divine, so that the appearances of angels, ecstasies and irruptions of the Spirit are reserved for him alone[10]. This impressive christological concentration of the gospel makes way in Acts for a theology offering a better repartition between a christological (the resurrection kerygma and miracles), pneumatological (the launch of missions), and theological (God as an agent in the history of salvation) triad.

Secundo. The divine interventions are not uniformly distributed in the flow of the narrative. There is a concentration of ecstatic manifestations or collective wonders in the first section of the book (Acts 1-7), while as the narrative reaches its end, the divine materializes essentially in favor of individuals, especially Paul (18,9f; 20,9-12; 22,6-11.17-21;23,9; 26,13-18;27,23f; 28,3-6). One major exception is the rescue at sea (27,9-44). Does this evolution mean that the closer the account gets to

---

7. Healings and exorcisms: 3,1-10; 9,17f., 32-35; 14,8-10; 16,16-18; 28,7f. Raisings of the dead: 9,36-42; 20,7-12. Punitive acts: 5,1-11; 13,9-12; 19,13-17. Paul escapes from a viper: 28,3-6. Healing summaries: 2,43; 5,12.15f.; 6,8; 8,6f.13; 14,3; 19,11f.; 28,9. The Acts links miracles to christology (they concretize the power of the "name of the Lord") rather than to theo-logy.

8. The care with which Luke chooses his technical terminology is manifest, for example in the diversity of his vocabulary of the vision: ὁράω, ὅραμα, θεωρέω, ἀκούω, ἔκστασις, φῶς, φωνή. On the other hand, he avoids ὄναρ and ὄνειρος (dream).

9. Trances and epiphanies abound at the beginning of the gospel: Lk 1,11-20.26-38.41.64.67; 2,9-14.27 and visions come back in force in the paschal cycle: Lk 24,4-7.31.36-51.

10. The only exception is the Transfiguration which narrativizes the ecstatic visions of a group of disciples (Lk 9,28-36).

the author's time, the more the narrator has conformed the divine manifestation to what characterizes the historic present of the Christianity to whom he writes? Whatever the case, the most spectacular epiphanies, the ones that lit the fire of the community, are confined to the "Golden Age" (2,1-11; 4,31; 5,15; 7,55f; 8,39)[11].

Tertio. Luke is not reluctant to requisition for his narrative all the available forms of the divine, in order to impress and convince his readers. Independently of the marked taste for the spectacular in popular Hellenistic faith (see the Greek novel), the Simon episode (8,9-12. 18-24) as well as that of Bar-Jesus (13,6-11) signal that Luke lived in a world where magical practice and religious competitions had set off an open debate concerning the proper handling of the divine. From his perspective the author of Acts clearly fights against syncretism[12]. The decisive question becomes the interpretation of the theophanic signs and it is to this task that the author of Acts will apply himself.

2. *An explicit language to name God*

Along side the implicit language in the narrative runs an explicit language that names God: θεός, κύριος, πατήρ[13]. As the subject of a verbal syntagma, θεός appears 61 times in Acts, κύριος 9 times and πατήρ once[14].

How does Luke use these divine titles as subjects? A first indication immediately attracts our attention: the massive presence of the titles in the speeches (52 out of 61 times for θεός; 4 of the 9 occurrences of κύριος). The priority of the explicit language for God is given to the speech register and not the narrative. It participates in the rhetorical aim of the Lukan speeches, which is to interpret the action of the narrative to his readers. But let us go further in the analysis. What can be said of the uses of the divine titles as subject in the narrative register? The answer

11. I have shown elsewhere that this evolution of the manifestations of the Spirit throughout the Acts differentiates the pneumatic experiences of the "Golden Age" (Acts 1-8) and the inspiration of the Spirit on individuals (end of Acts); D. MARGUERAT, *La première histoire du christianisme (Les Actes des apôtres)* (LD, 180), Paris, Cerf, 1999, pp. 151-155.
12. Luke's critical relationship to polytheism and magic has been studied by B. WILDHABER, *Paganisme populaire et prédication apostolique* (Le Monde de la Bible, 15), Genève, Labor et Fides, 1987 and by H.-J. KLAUCK, *With Paul in Paphos and Lystra. Magic and Paganism in the Acts of the Apostles*, in *Neotestamentica* 28 (1994), pp. 93-108 and *Magie und Heidentum in der Apostelgeschichte des Lukas* (SBS, 167), Stuttgart, KBW, 1996.
13. We have left aside the annex appellations (ὕψιστος: 7,48; 16,17) which do not modify the bottom line of the analysis.
14. The inventory of these mentions will not be repeated here; it has been established by R.L. MOWERY, *Direct Statements* (n. 4) and *Lord, God, and Father* (n. 4); see also K. LÖNING, *Gottesbild der Apostelgeschichte* (n. 4), pp. 95f.

is enlightening: God never appears as a figure of the narrative world, but only in the words attributed to someone[15]. Except for a few rare occasions, the narrator never directly ascribes the action of the narrative to God.

In other words, God never becomes the subject except in the word of a character. It is the angel who tells Peter: *"What God has made clean, you must not call profane"* (10,15); or Peter who recognizes the hand of God in his evasion of prison (12,11) and then confesses this to his brothers: *"He ... described how the Lord had brought him out of prison"* (12,17); or again Paul who says to the high priest Ananias: *"God will strike you"* (23,3). God is designated as the active subject solely in the frame of a direct discourse (1,7; 10,15.28; 11,18; 12,11; 23,3), or in an indirect discourse introduced by a communication verb (12,17; 14,27; 15,4.12; 21,19)[16], or at the most, when the narrator describes the inner conviction of a character (16,10)[17]. The only exceptions, if we set aside the introductory frame of a Scripture quotation (13,47), concern two summaries (2,47 and 19,11) and two ambiguous mentions of κύριος that could be christological (16,14; 18,9)[18]. This is too little evidence to contradict the overwhelming Lukan tendency to quote God nominally only in the words exchanged between two characters in the narrative world. The result: to name God is not so obvious; only the word of the witness can designate the author of the events that direct the story. As R.L. Mowery has shown, the same language game takes place between the Passion-Ressurection in the gospel (Lk 22-24), which never names the divine instigator of the events, and the speeches in Acts, where Peter and Paul do not cease to attribute to God the raising of Christ from the dead[19].

We shall conclude in the following way. The examination of the language for God in the book of Acts reveals a systematic control on the part of the narrator: he chooses narrative language when God manifests himself by a mediation which conceals him, and he chooses the discursive language when God is mentioned by name as an agent of history. To say the same thing in the technical terms of narrative criticism: the

---

15. See K. LÖNING, *Gottesbild der Apostelgeschichte* (n. 4), p. 95: "Von Gott ist immer nur die Rede zwischen den Figuren der erzählten Welt".
16. ἀναγγέλλω (14,27; 15,4), ἐξηγέομαι (15,2; 21,19), διηγέομαι (12,17).
17. συμβιβάζοντες ὅτι (16,10).
18. In 16,14, we do not know for sure if κύριος designates God (cf. v. 14a) or Jesus (v. 15b); it is also the case in 18,9 where κύριος refers back to Jesus by attraction to v. 8.
19. *Lord, God, and Father* (n. 4), pp. 98-101. Luke designates God indirectly by a divine passive (ἠγέρθη 24,6.34), by the theological δεῖ (24,7.26.44) or the Scriptural reference (24,46). On the other hand, the explicit mention of God as the author of the raising of Jesus becomes a stereotype in the speeches of Acts (2,24.32; 3,15.22.26; 4,10; 5,30; 10,40; 13,30.33f.37; 17,31; 26,8). From the same author: *The Divine Hand and the Divine Plan in the Lukan Passion*, in *SBL 1991 Seminar Paper*, pp. 558-575.

implicit language is reserved for the narrator (extradiegetic), while the explicit language characterizes the discourse of the characters of the story-world (intradiegetic)[20].

This division of languages lays out the problem in which the analysis of the image of God in the Acts fits. Visibly, Luke refuses to describe God as metamorphosing and mixing incognito with the affairs of men, in the style of a Yahvist or a Homer. However, beyond the respect for the holiness of God, which refuses vulgar anthropomorphisms, what role does Luke give to the discourse about God in the outline of his narrative? How does the explicit discourse that names God participate in the plot of Acts and engender a movement forward? In order to deal with this question it is necessary to advance case by case, following the function that the divine statements exercise in the narrative. We shall examine this in the next section.

II. WHAT IS THE LINK BETWEEN A HISTORY OF GOD AND HUMAN HISTORY?

Recently, it has been affirmed, and not without reason, that the central theme of the book of Acts is "the plan of God"[21]. Speaking of God in the book of Acts can be reduced to asking oneself how God intervenes to direct history according to his plan. What is the connection between a history of God and human history (or if one prefers, divine will and human freedom) in Acts?

Within the plot of the narrative, the divine interventions can have three distinct functions[22]. Sometimes they precede the events and take on a *programmatic* function (in the form of a vision, a dream or an oracle). For example, when Paul is lead off to Macedonia (16,6-10). On other occasions they exercise a *performative* function, when God intervenes by saving, punishing or guiding the course of the events. What happens on the road to Damascus (9,1-19a) is an example. Then again they can have an *interpretative* function, when they are situated after the events in order to indicate their meaning or to justify them for example with Stephen's vision (7,55f.). We shall see how Luke, in the composition of his narrative, artistically combines these three functions, which when taken together account for the irruption of the divine into history.

---

20. The reader interested in this differentiation of narrative authorities should consult the manual: D. MARGUERAT and Y. BOURQUIN, *How to Read Bible Stories*, London, SCM, 1999, pp. 25-28.

21. J.T. SQUIRES, *The Plan of God in Luke-Acts* (SNTS.MS, 76), Cambridge, Cambridge University Press, 1993.

22. This classification of the functions was inspired by the illuminating study of J.N. ALETTI, *Quand Luc raconte* (n. 4), pp. 21-26.

1. The programmatic function: God precedes history

The narrative procedure that Luke prefers is the programmatic statement, which announces and anticipates what follows in the narrative. The most well known are the promise of the resurrected One in Acts 1,8 and the prediction of the destiny of Paul in 9,15f. This type of proleptic formulation concretizes the notion of divine guidance in history so essential to Luke[23]. The programmatic statement can be revealed in a dream, as in 23,11 where by a night vision, the Lord informs Paul of his future: *"For you have testified for me in Jerusalem, so you must bear witness also in Rome"*. It can be delivered through the sermon of Agabus: *"This is the way the Jews in Jerusalem will bind the man who owns this belt and will hand him over to the Gentiles"* (21,11).

In the framework of the discourse concerning God, three programmatic statements – 5,38-39; 16,10 and 27,23-25 – merit our consideration; they are all in explicit language.

1. In the Lukan narrative the programmatic expression functions according to what I shall refer to as the "Gamaliel principle". Gamaliel was the Pharisee that persuaded the Sanhedrin not to mistreat the apostles by proposing the following rule: "… let them alone; because if this plan or undertaking is of human origin, it will fall; but if it is of God, you will not be able to overthrow them …" (5,38b-39a)[24]. But is there any evidence which allows one to verify if the work of the apostles is indeed "of God"? Only the narrative of their actions allows verification that their works will not disappear and this is exactly why Luke indissociably links the description of the plan of God with the life of the witnesses. The Lukan narrative becomes this irreplaceable theological medium of verification offered to its readers[25].

The interest in the Gamaliel principle for our subject is that it links the recognition of the divine will with the destiny of the group who witness to Jesus. No other mirror is offered. One who wants to discern the ways of God has only a narrative recounting the joys and more often the misfortunes of a group of believers. When applying the Gamaliel principle, the reading of Acts becomes the link for the perception of God. Only the narrative teaches the reader what "work" the Holy Spirit calls Paul and

---

23. The notion of providence in Hellenistic historiography and in Luke has been examined by SQUIRES, *Plan of God* (n. 21), esp. pp. 103-154.

24. This rule corresponds to a Hellenistic topos, as SQUIRES reminds us (*Plan of God* [n. 21], p. 176, note 109).

25. "Luke writes Acts to prove Gamaliel's hunch correct." (R. STRELAN, *Gamaliel's Hunch*, in *ABR* 47 (1999), pp. 53-69, quotation p. 53).

Barnabas to (13,2) or how the prophecy of Agabus will come to pass (21,11).

The programmatic statements disseminated throughout the narrative orient the reading, functioning as advance signals inserted by the narrator to guide the deciphering of the story. The prolepsis of Acts 16,10 will help us to understand how such a signal works.

2. Acts 16,10 belongs to the episode cited above where two interventions of the Spirit blocking the road of Paul and Silas precede the vision of the Macedonian calling for the help of the apostles (16,6-9). The deciphering of these divine interventions, or if one prefers, the passage from an implicit language about God to an explicit one, is the fruit of the group into which the narrator inserts himself, the group of "we"[26]; its interpretative work ends by redirecting the missionary itinerary toward Macedonia, for "*we immediately tried to cross over to Macedonia, being convinced that God had called us to proclaim the good news to them*" (16,10). The programmatic value of this proleptic declaration cannot be doubted: the call for help by the Macedonian is understood as coming from God in order to change the direction of the diffusion of the Word towards the West. The evangelization of Macedonia begins, preparing for Greece (Acts 17-18).

But how can the validity of this interpretation be verified? The narrator does not force the reader to wait long: a few verses later, in Philippi, the preaching of the apostles meets the attentive ears of Lydia who "*was listening to us ... The Lord opened her heart to listen eagerly to what was said by Paul*" (16,14). A little later, the miraculous deliverance from prison of Peter and Silas (16,25-26) confirms that the apostles' work is truly "from God". The Gamaliel principle worked.

3. The term θεός appears four times in the narrative of the storm (Acts 27), whereas κύριος is absent. The fourth use comes during the eucharistic type meal that Paul organizes on the ship (v. 35). The three other uses are concentrated in the verses 23-25, where Paul communicates to his companions what an angel of the Lord revealed to him dur-

---

26. I cannot resolve the question of the "We-passages" here, but I would point out that the purely literary solutions (Robbins) or the purely historical ones (Bruce) are not commendable; the alternative is not one of a simple effect of style or the physical presence of Luke at the side of Paul. One must keep two factors in mind: 1) it is difficult to deny that the introduction of "we" aims to integrate the narrator into the story and thus to validate his testimony to the reader; 2) it is undeniable that the use of "we" in the sea voyage accounts has become a literary procedure from the time of the Odyssey (cf. K. BERGER, *Hellenistische Gattungen im Neuen Testament*, in *ARNW* II/25 (1984), pp. 1031-1432, here p. 1274).

ing a vision: *"Do not be afraid, Paul; you must stand before the emperor; and indeed, God has granted safety to all those who are sailing with you"* (v. 24).

This sequence plays a decisive role in the narrative. After the unfortunate decision of the crew (against Paul's advice! vv. 9-12) and the assault of the storm (vv. 13-20), the apostle appears as the true hero of the story, by a word act[27]. His discourse is not even his own, but his reporting of the angel's declaration: *"For last night there stood before me an angel of the God, to whom I belong and whom I worship, and he said ..."* (v. 23). In this formulation, the double motif vision/hearing attests to the revealed character of the apostle's knowledge. A theological reading of the event unfolds, which not only signals that the journey remains under the divine δεῖ (*"you must stand before the emperor"*) but also predicts its happy ending. This declaration will materialize with the symbolic act of the meal on the morning of the landing in Malta, which anticipates in the εὐχαριστεῖν τῷ θεῷ (v. 35) the end of the drama and the favorable result of the voyage.

The narrative function of the Pauline discourse in the economy of Acts 27 appears clearly now. Emerging after the dramatic report of the storm and its consequence, and the despair of the passengers (v. 20), the explicit language of God has a double effect, revelatory and programmatic. Revelatory: Paul names God as the ultimate (and paradoxical) agent of the event. Programmatic: the apostle interprets the rescue of the ship as a grace included in the plan of God in favor of his messenger. The divine origin of the rescue is unveiled nowhere else; but the reader of the Septuagint will verify the precision by calling upon the theme of the Creator, master of the waters[28], while the reader of Hellenistic culture will remember the classic motif of divine protection of the innocent[29] (the story of the viper 28,3-6 and the brief mention of the Dioscuri 28,11c[30] will confirm he is right).

27. Paul is the only person in Acts 27 to act by word. The verbs used are: παραινέω and λέγων (vv. 9b-10), λέγω (v. 21), παρακαλέω (vv. 33.34), λέγω (v. 35).

28. Beside the classic references in Jonah and the Psalms, see Lk 5,4-8; 8,22-25. The rabbinical literature also ties the storm with the anger of God, e.g. in the miraculous liberation of Rabbi Gamaliel (*bBab. Mes* 59b) or in relating the fright of Titus shaken by the waves upon his return to Rome after the devastation of Jerusalem (*ARN* 7).

29. References in G.B. MILES, G. TROMPF, *Luke and Antiphon: The Theology of Acts 27-28 in Light of Pagan Beliefs about Divine Retribution, Pollution, and Shipwreck*, in *HThR* 69 (1976), pp. 259-267 and D. LADOUCEUR, *Hellenistic Preconceptions of Shipwreck and Pollution as a Content for Acts 27-28*, in *HThR* 73 (1980), pp. 435-449.

30. The celestial twins, Castor and Pollux, are renown as protectors of sailors, but also as the guardians of the truth and the punishers of perjurers. Concerning the Jewish and Hellenistic concepts which are at work in the account of Acts 27, see my article *The End of Acts (28,16-31) and the Rhetoric of Silence*, in S.E. PORTER and Th.H. OLBRICHT

Let us conclude. In Acts, the anticipated announcement of the plan of God by the mediation of a vision or a prediction intends to program the theological reading of the narrative. Following the "Gamaliel principle" (5,38-39), it assigns to the reader in its everyday story a place to discover and celebrate the ways of God.

2. *The performative function: God changes history*

The God of the book of Acts is interventionist. Luke describes him as continually breaking into the narrative with miracles, shaking up his community by the sending of the Spirit, opening prison doors, converting the persecutor of Christ, saving his messengers from all dangers, blinding the fake magicians, striking Herod, saving the 276 passengers on a ship so that his messenger can arrive safely ... From the beginning to the end of the narrative, the God of Acts dismantles obstacles that hinder the success of his plan: the spreading of the Word[31].

However, we must point out that the Acts of Luke are not the apocryphal Acts of the apostles, where the missionaries' successes open pagan temples and destroy idols[32]. At Luke's time, we are not yet that far along: the Synagogue effectively opposes the Pauline mission; the Greco-Roman cults bristle up before the Christian competition (Lystra, Philippi, Athens, Ephesus); God's protection does not prevent his messengers from failure, humiliation, flagellation and martyrdom. In contrast to a triumphal progression, the route of the missionaries is a path overshadowed by the cross.

On several occasions, this route will be modified by the interventions of the God who changes history. We have already seen this in the episode of the Macedonian (16,6-10). We shall deal with it in three other texts: Acts 8,26-40, Acts 9 and Acts 10-11. These texts will allow us to discover more precisely how Luke proceeds. Only the word of the witness deciphers after the fact the intervention of God and designates its author while the (explicit) discourse of the witness always follows the (implicit) language of the narrator. Why did Luke choose this sequence?

1. The encounter of Philip and the Ethiopian eunuch (8,26-40) is arranged by God: the angel of the Lord orders Philip to take the road from

---

(eds.), *Rhetoric and the New Testament* (JSNT.SS, 90), Sheffield, Sheffield Academic Press, 1993, pp. 74-89, esp. 82-86 or *The Enigma of the Silent Closing of Acts (28.16-31)*, in D.P. MOESSNER (ed.), *Jesus and the Heritage of Israel*, Harrisburg, Trinity Press International, 1999, esp. pp. 293-297.

31. From my viewpoint, the theme of the book of Acts is neither the Spirit nor the relations with Israel (even if this question is identitary for Lukan Christianity), but rather the launching of the Word into the world.

32. This motif occurs in some second century apocrypha (*Acts of John* 37-45; *Acts of Paul*, PHeid, pp. 35-39) and then more frequently from the third century on.

Jerusalem to Gaza ... which is deserted (v. 26). Then (the second initiative) the Spirit tells him: *"Go over to the chariot and join it"* (v. 29). The reader is thus prepared for the miraculous and foreseen interview, whose outcome will follow the plan of God. Finally, the mysterious snatching away of Philip by the Spirit confirms this point of view (v. 39): Philip has played the role God ascribed to him: he can disappear, from the sight of the eunuch as well as from the narrative of Acts[33].

This text has one striking particularity. At both ends of the story there are two initial impulsions (vv. 26 and 29) and a final vanishing act (v. 39) that frame the encounter. In between the two, where the essential of the story takes place (the catechism of the eunuch, his request and baptism), there is no trace of divine intervention. What does this structure mean?

Firstly. The theophanic interventions provoke the incredible: a eunuch, excluded from the cult according to Deut 23,2 LXX, is welcomed with his desire to understand the Scriptures and to join the people of the covenant through baptism[34]. Massive divine manipulation affirms that the breaking of Mosaic legislation is not Christian impertinence; it is the work of God.

Secondly. Once in the eunuch's presence, Philip acts alone. Overshadowed by the injunction of the Spirit (v. 29), which signifies his ability to witness[35]. Nevertheless he acts alone. There is no light, no angel to whisper his announcement of the "good news of Jesus" (v. 35). No trance dictates his decision to baptize the eunuch. Philip's initiative as witness is his own. His preaching (v. 35) relies on the text of Isa 53,7-8 which has just been quoted, but he witnesses on his own authority. In Acts, God never dictates the message of the messengers. His pressure on events can be forceful, but the word of the missionaries comes forth from their own responsibility[36].

---

33. Concerning the role of the eunuch in the missionary strategy which underlies the plot of Acts, see E. DINKLER, *Philippus und der ANHP AIΘIOΨ (Apg 8,26-40). Historische und geographische Bemerkungen zum Missionsablauf nach Lukas*, in *Jesus und Paulus. FS W.G. Kümmel*, Göttingen, Vandenhoeck & Ruprecht, 1975, pp. 85-95; C.J. MARTIN, *The Function of Acts 8,26-40 within the Narrative Structure of the Book of Acts. The Significance of the Eunuch's Provenance for Acts 1,8c*, Dissertation, Duke University, 1986; F. SCOTT SPENCER, *The Portrait of Philip in Acts: A Study of Roles and Relations* (JSNT.SS, 67), Sheffield, Sheffield Academic Press, 1992, pp. 128-187.

34. The ostracizing of eunuchs for ritual impurity (cf. also Lev 21,20; 22, 24) is confirmed by Josephus (*Ant.* 4,290-291) and Philo (*Spec. Leg.* 1,324-325). Hope for their inclusion into the eschatological community is present in Isa 56,3-8 and Wis 3,14-15; Acts 8 fits into this line.

35. Concerning the Spirit as ability to witness in Acts, see my reflexions in *La première histoire du christianisme* (n. 11), pp. 149-174.

36. This is not the case in apocalyptic literature, where the word of the witness/seer is legitimated by the process of dictation: see 4 Esra 14,37-49; 2 Enoch 22,28; the mes-

To summarize, the theophanic interventions create a totally unexpected framing in which the responsibility of the witness plays a role as he interprets the event and names its author. It all happens as if the God of Acts, after having organized the encounter by supernatural means, withdraws to leave for the witness. The story only becomes salvation history when men and women accept to enter into the role that God indicates, without ever taking away the responsibility of the word or action of the witnesses. The pericope of the meeting of Peter and Cornelius and the conversion of Paul on Damascus road fit well into this perspective.

2. In composing the narrative of the encounter of Peter and Cornelius (Acts 10,1-11,18; 15,7-11), Luke has pushed his narrative art to its highest standard of excellence. This can be measured by the density of applied narrative techniques: the intertwining of the paths of two persons, realized by means of crossed discourses (10,1-33); the visionary encounter anticipating the "face-à-face" of Peter and Cornelius (10,5-6.22); Peter's progressive awareness of the meaning of the event becoming evident through the four times that he speaks (10,28-30; 10,34-43; 11,5-17; 15,7-11)[37].

This excellence in the construction of the narrative can be explained by the play of the pericope in the plot of the book: God lets Peter know, by a vision which mixes all sorts of animals, that he is pulling down the millenial barrier between pure and impure (10,13-15). To legitimate the outrageousness of the divine choice which opens the covenant to Gentiles, Luke is not reluctant to refer to supernatural means: a vision (10,3), a trance (10,10), a message of the Spirit (10,19) and the descent of the Spirit himself (10,44.46), all the former being necessary to shatter Peter's resistance[38].

This narrative sequence should be brought together with the conversion of Saul in chapter 9 and its rereadings in chapters 22 and 26. The same narrative technique is at work in the construction of the account: intertwining (9,10-17), double vision (9,10-12), successive readings of the event by Paul (9,20; 22,6-21; 26,12-23)[39].

sages committed to Enoch the "scribe of justice"(1 En 12,4; 15,1). As well as Rev 1,9; 10,4; 14,13; 19,9; 21,5; 22,19.

37. Concerning the narrative construction of Acts 10-11, see the seminal study of R.C. TANNEHILL, *The Narrative Unity of Luke-Acts. A Literary Interpretation*, vol. 2, Minneapolis, Fortress, 1990, pp. 128-145. The process of redundancy is analyzed by R.D. WITHERUP, *Cornelius Over and Over and Over Again: "Functional Redundancy" in the Acts of the Apostles*, in *JSNT* 49 (1993), pp. 45-66. Cf. also W.S. KURZ, *Reading Luke-Acts*, Louisville, Westminster – John Knox, 1993, p. 131.

38. See the eloquent study of B.R. GAVENTA, *From Darkness to Light. Aspects of Conversion in the New Testament*, Philadelphia, Fortress, 1986, pp. 107-125.

39. Concerning the texts, see GAVENTA, *From Darkness*, pp. 52-95 and TANNEHILL, *Narrative Unity* (n. 37), esp. pp. 114-122, 275-277, 321-322. The process of narrative re-

But bringing these two stories together is necessary above all for reasons of thematic affinity. On both sides there is:

- an unheard of and staggering choice of God: Saul, the enemy of Christ; Cornelius, the non-Jew;
- a theophanic manifestation with no immediate follow-up, which leaves the individuel stunned (9,9) or confused (10,17);
- a new initiative of God, by the sending of messengers (9,17; 10,17b-20) delegated by a vision (9,10-12; 10,5-8):
- a resistance to the divine initiative arriving from where it was unexpected: from Ananias and Peter, representatives of the believing community (9,10.13-14; 10,17);
- an integration into the community of the marginal chosen by God.

The two endings move toward different goals:

- the call of Saul is unveiled to Ananias, but not to him (9,15-16); it will unfold in the narrative; whereas Peter draws the inference of the integration of Cornelius before the Jerusalem Council (15,7-11);
- Saul will know the reversal of his destiny, and the persecutor will become the persecuted (9,19b-30), while Peter's initiative will be confirmed by the descending of the Spirit (10,44-48).

In both cases, God turns history around by a surprising choice which has to overcome the resistance of the Church and whose consequences are enormous for the pursuit of the plot. As F. Bovon has said, "Luke is alone in the New Testament to relate *narratively* how the God of the fathers has become the universal God"[40]. But how does this theological reading take place? How are these astonishing events interpreted as the coming of God to each and all?

Here again, the passage from the implicit to the explicit is assured by the speech of the witness. I will show it first in Acts 10-11, before noting the presence of a similar scenario in Acts 9, 22 and 26.

10,13-14   Upon the order *"Kill and eat"*, Peter answers with a pious refusal.

10,15.17   The declaration of the celestial voice *"What God has made clean, you must not call profane"* does not convince Peter but plunges him into confusion.

---

dundancy has been studied by R.D. WITHERUP, *Functional Redundancy in the Acts of the Apostles. A Case Study*, in *JSNT* 48 (1992), pp. 67-86 and W.S. KURZ, *Reading Luke-Acts*, pp. 125-131; see also my study: *Saul's Conversion (Acts 9-22-29) and the Multiplication of Narrative in Acts*, in C.M. TUCKETT (ed.), *Luke's Literary Achievement* (JSNT.SS, 115), Sheffield, Academic Press, 1995, pp. 127-155.

40. F. BOVON, *God of Luke* (n. 2), p. 78.

10,22   The messengers of Cornelius declare that a holy angel revealed to them that they would hear the ῥήματα (words and events) from Peter (diff. v. 5!); but which ones?

The word of Peter will progressively interpret the event:

10,28   Peter, discovering (εὑρίσκει v. 27b) a large crowd, applies his vision to human relations: *"God has shown me that I should not call anyone profane or unclean"*.

10,34   Peter broadens the concept of the universality of God to whoever practices justice in any nation: *"I truly understand that God is not προσωπολήμπτης"*.

10,47   Peter interprets the glossolalia in the house of Cornelius as the sign of the Spirit authorizing their baptism.

11,17   Peter assimilates the work of the Spirit with *"the same gift that he gave us..."*.

15,8   Peter again develops the motif of the purification of the heart by faith.

Summary:

1) Peter passes from the implicit to the explicit by naming God; this procedure is manifest in the syntax which imposes θεός as the subject of the statements in Peter's discourse[41].
2) Peter's word progressively gains in theological intensity.
3) The theological elaboration takes place through the exchange of persons and the responsibility of the witness.

If we observe Acts 9, 22 and 26, a similar scenario can be noticed[42]:

9,3-8   A theophanic shock knocks Saul to the ground and blinds him.
9,9   The shock places Saul in a state of total dispossession.
9,17   Ananias lays hands on him to heal his blindness and to fill him with the Holy Spirit; but for what?

Paul's discourse will progressively interpret the event:

9,20.22   Saul proclaims Jesus Son of God and Messiah.
(9,27   Barnabas tells how Saul saw the Lord who spoke to him).

---

41. This is the case in 10,28.34.38.40; 15,7.8.
42. For more details see my study *Saul's Conversion* (n. 39).

22,14   Paul tells the people of Jerusalem that the God of the fathers has given him the vocation to be witness before all men.

22,18.21   Paul tells how the Lord appeared to him in the Temple to send him to the nations.

26,16-18   Paul declares before Agrippa that Jesus revealed the reason of his appearance: to send him to convert the nations to believe in him.

Summary:

1) Paul passes from the implicit to the explicit by naming Jesus; this procedure is translated narratively by the increasingly active role that is given to Jesus in the dialogue with Paul (22,10.17-21; 26,15-18).
2) The call of Paul is affirmed more clearly in passing from 9,15f to 22,14f.18-21 and 26,16-18.
3) The concentration on the dialogue between Paul and Jesus goes hand in hand with the progressive fading out of the role of Ananias (9,10-17; 22,12-16; absence in ch. 26)[43].

This succession of a theophany and then a discourse that explains it is clearly shown in the example of Acts 10-11 and Acts 9, 22-26. From Luke's point of view is this a simple narrative procedure or a theological structure? I prefer the second and will now show why.

3. In the succession that presents the theophany and the word of the witness, each element has its own function. The theophany signals that the initiative comes from God; it presents an unexpected character, sometimes outlandish in his choices, but also enigmatic, requiring the reading of a believer. It is striking that the narrator never says "God did" or "God said"; he lets one of the persons in the narrative say it, not without having shown the "non-evidence" of the reading of the event. Here we have the discretion of God, an indicator of the source from which Luke draws his theology: **a theology of the hidden God**, who reveals himself by veiling himself. The word of the witness must pierce the uncertainty. This is not a theology of mystery but a theology of revelation which brings Luke close to the wisdom-apocalyptic stream of the Q source[44]. The name of God is not pronounced until after the

---

43. The literary and thematic shifts perceivable between the narrative of Acts 9 and its successive repetitions in Paul's autobiographical speeches (Acts 22 and 26) have been explained either by their location in the narrative of Acts and in the effect on the reader (Tannehill), or by the change of audience (Gaventa), or by the change of speakers (Kurz). The dimension of progressive elucidation in the word of the witness must also be taken into account.

44. See the Lukan reception of the logia of Q concerning the wisdom of God, particularly Lk 13,34-35; see also 19,41-44 (theme of hidden/revealed) and 21,20-24 (diff Mk

event, not immediately but by the mediation of a word that designates his naming.

This concentration in the word of the witnesses about God is connected with another phenomenon, not often noticed: the consistant theocentrism of the speeches in the book of Acts. This is because the theology which animates the discourses in Acts is not christocentric, as we would expect: when the Christ is mentioned, the speech generally points to the action of God[45]. In Acts 2, Peter's speech celebrates the God who revealed Jesus, whose resurrection David predicted. In Acts 3, the word points to God who establishes a time of refreshing through Christ. Stephen (Acts 7) speaks of the God of Abraham, Joseph and Moses constantly enduring the unfaithfulness of his people. In 10,34-43, Peter announces the God who is partial to none. In Acts 13, Paul announces in Antioch the God who fulfils the promises made to the fathers by giving them judges, kings and a Savior. In Lystra (Acts 14), it is the Creator God who fills with his good-will. In Athens (Acts 17), it is God the giver of life, that should not be sought among idols.

The main aim of the speeches of Acts is to promote faith in the God who has ultimately unveiled his mercy (his εὐδοκία) to Israel, according to the promises in the Scriptures, in the sending and resurrection of his Son. The orators of the book of Acts call for conversion, not to Christ but to God[46].

But from what must one convert? A single term applies to the Jews (3,17; 13,27) as well as to the pagans (17,30): ἄγνοια. This is not ignorance, but a mistake concerning God. ἄγνοια is a soteriological category in Luke; it characterizes both the Jewish mistake concerning the Messiah (3,17) and the bewilderment of the Hellenistic religious quest (17,30), and so of all people. Concerning all people we must say, not only that they "know not what they do" (Lk 23,34), but that they know not God. The Lukan ἄγνοια then does not represent a passing deficiency, but a soteriological lack. It gives rise to the speech of the witness with its hermeneutic of God who reveals his eschatological action in the person of Jesus.

Let us conclude. With the action of Philip in Samaria (Acts 8), with the conversion of Saul (Acts 9) and with the encounter of Peter and Cornelius (Acts 10-11), Luke shows how God advances history by jolts

13,14-20). Concerning this see LÖNING, *Gottesbild der Apostelgeschichte* (n. 4), pp. 100-101.

45. In the speeches of Acts, the christology is carried by the reference to God who raised Jesus from the dead: 2,22-24.32-33; 3,13.15.18.25-26; 4,10; 10,40.42; 13,37; 17,31. In qualification of this fact, my colleagues of the "Luke-Acts Seminar" (SBL Annual Meeting, Philadelphia, 1995) prefer to speak of a theocentric christology in Luke.

46. μετανοέω: 2,38; 3,19; 17,30; ἐπιστρέφω: 3,19; 14,15; 26,20.

intentionally opening the word of salvation to all people. In conformity with Jewish historiography, the author of Acts describes a God who allows himself to be known, while at the same time hiding in the events of history. "God" does not speak, he is revealed by the language of the witness. This explains why Luke deploys a theology of the word; through the speeches of the witnesses, he can lift God's incognito and move from misunderstanding to knowledge. This alternance of the narrative, which describes history and the speech which deciphers the action of God within history narratively concretizes the movement of the Lukan mission, putting in evidence the role of the confession of faith by the witness, which alone can decipher the signs of the eschatological work of God in the chaos of history.

3. The interpretative function: God reveals the meaning of history

Divine interventions in the book of Acts above all serve the two functions that have just been examined: programmatic and performative. More rarely, they situate events to justify or confirm them or to indicate their importance. At the level of the narrative, these analepsis[47] initiate a process of veridiction or verification for the reader.

1. We have already mentioned several retrospective divine irruptions. After the baptism of the Ethiopian eunuch, Philip is seized by the Spirit and disappears (8,39). This remarkable event does not just simply satisfy a taste for the marvelous, it confirms for the reader a decree of God, which is even more astonishing: the eunuch's integration into the covenant. Another retrospective intervention: the interruption of Peter at the house of Cornelius by the irruption of the Spirit (10,44-45); in the eyes of Peter's Jewish entourage, this noisy divine approval concretizes Peter's speech, which allows the benefit of the forgiveness of sins (10,43) to pagans; with the decision to baptize then coming to ratify the divine decree (10,47).

In Acts 8 as in Acts 10, the theophanic intervention after the event validates retrospectively a paradoxical logic, the logic of the ways of God. Hence Philip and Peter participate in the transgression of the limits already initiated by the supernatural interventions that we have seen above (cf. pp. 169-174). This transgression is only confirmed afterwards, offering the reader the certainty that the process of extension of the covenant is willed and accomplished by God himself through witnesses.

---

47. By analepsis, we mean the return of a narrative to an element that is chronologically anterior; the inverse movement (the reference to a future event) is called prolepsis. See G. GENETTE, *Figures III*, Paris, Seuil, 1972, pp. 90-115.

2. The vision of Stephen at his martyrdom, another validating function, is also at the service of a paradoxical logic: *"Look, I see the heavens opened and the Son of Man at the right hand of God"* (7,56)[48]. But why do the heavens open up? Here we must differentiate at two levels[49]. At the story level, Stephen's vision sets in motion the murderous fury of the members of the Sanhedrin who "cover their ears" and drag him out of the city to stone him (7,57-58); Stephen's trance announces the resurrection of the Crucified. On the narrative level, the anachronic use of the title υἱὸς τοῦ ἀνθρώπου echoes Jesus' declaration during his trial (Lk 22,69). However, the vision does not immediately provide its "raison d'être". A few verses later, two of Stephen's words reinforce the parallelism of the two martyrs: *"Lord Jesus, receive my spirit"* (7,59b; Lk 23,46) and *"Lord, do not hold this sin against them"* (7,60b; Lk 23,34). One can measure the extent of the paradox: the evocation of the exaltation of Jesus at the right hand of God does not help the witness to escape death, but rather leads him to it, confirming Stephen's thesis concerning the constant resistance of his Jewish listeners to the Holy Spirit (7,51).

Stephen's death then, which accentuates the open crisis between the Jerusalem authorities and the apostles (Acts 3-7)[50], is at the same time paradigmatic of the condition of the witness of Jesus. The reader now knows that a proclamation of the Gospel does not offer any different a destiny from that of the Master. Stephen's trance certifies the conformity of his martyrdom to the passion of Jesus (Stephen does not only die *for* Jesus, he dies *like* him). But this effect of veridiction extends to the rest of the narrative, as it sets up a divine logic of testimony: those who proclaim the Gospel must expect to suffer.

Saul of Tarsus, who moves from the role of the persecutor to that of the persecuted will immediately experience this (9,19b-30). The vision of the Lord that he receives in Jerusalem (23,11) functions analeptically (*"Keep up your courage! For just as you have testified for me in Jerusalem ..."*) and proleptically (*"... so you must bear witness also*

---

48. See M. SABBE, *The Son of Man Saying in Acts 7,56*, in J. KREMER (ed.), *Les Actes des Apôtres* (BETL, 48), Gembloux-Leuven, Duculot-University Press, 1979, pp. 241-279; R. PESCH, *Die Vision des Stephanus. Apg 7,55-56 im Rahmen der Apostelgeschichte* (SBS, 12), Stuttgart, KBW, 1966.

49. In what follows, I rely on the differentiation set out by S. Chatman between story and discourse; the first corresponds to the *what* of the narrative and the second to the *how*, that is to the narrative rhetoric. (Cf. S. CHATMAN, *Story and Discourse*, Ithaca, Cornell University Press, 1978 or D. MARGUERAT and Y. BOURQUIN, *How to Read Bible Stories* [n. 20], pp. 18-28).

50. Concerning the rise of the crisis between the Christian community and the Jerusalem authorities in chapters 1-7, see my article *La mort d'Ananias et Saphira (Ac 5,1-11) dans la stratégie narrative de Luc*, in *NTS* 39 (1993) 209-226, esp. pp. 211-217.

in Rome"). On the one hand, this message confirms the validity of Paul's two speeches in Jerusalem (22,1-21; 23,6), in spite of the confusion they set off. On the other hand, it signals Paul's appeal to Caesar (25,11) through inscribing it, by anticipation, in the plan of God[51].

3. Up to this point, divine programming of the events has appeared overly forceful since it envelops the events of history (before, during and after). In contrast, as already noted above (pp. 169-175), the responsibility of the witness in the elaboration of his testimony appears to be total. How does Luke handle this tension? Is the freedom of the witness only charade?

Luke offers no systematic reflection on the matter, but an observation of the narrative provides a few indications. Peter legitimizes the baptism of the Gentiles at Cornelius' house by saying: *"... who was I to hinder God?"* (11,17b; already in 10,47). The same κωλύειν was used by the eunuch in 8,36: τί κωλύει με βαπτισθῆναι; On the stage of history, the roles are clearly distributed: God takes the initiative and human action follows. The apostles are aware of having a place in the divine economy, which will be explained to the pagans in terms of providence (17,26-28)[52] and to the Jews in the words of the Scriptures. In Antioch, Paul legitimizes his right to announce the promise of salvation to the non-Jews with the help of Isa 49,6: *"I have set you to be a light to the Gentiles, so that you may bring salvation to the ends of the earth"* (13,47). In Jerusalem, Paul and Barnabas present "all the signs and wonders that *God had done through them* among the Gentiles" (15,12), which with the help of Amos 9,11-12 will allow James to see the opening up to the Gentiles as the expression of God's unchanging will. The Scripture plays the role of retrospective confirmation. We see, however, that it comes in secondarily like an ultimate instance, after the theophanic signs have taken place.

This putting together of the roles of the Scriptures and the theophanic signs allows us to consider the importance of their *retrospective* character. Each has a balancing effect on the programmatic interventions, in

---

51. Same procedure in 18,9-10: the epiphany of Christ which Paul had already experienced prior to his appearance before Gallio, presents two sides, one analeptic (*"Do not be afraid, but speak and do not be silent"*), the other proleptic (*"for I am with you, and no one will lay a hand on you to harm you, for there are many in this city who are my people"*). The first validates the attitude adopted by Paul up to this point while the second outlines the program of Paul's stay in Corinth, foreseeing the failure of the denunciation before the proconsul.

52. The Lukan understanding of the notion of providence has been illuminated by J.H. NEYREY, *Acts 17, Epicureans, and Theodicy. A Study in Stereotypes*, in *Greeks, Romans and Christians. Essays in Honor of A.J. Malherbe*, Minneapolis, Fortress, 1990, pp. 118-134. More widely: J.T. SQUIRES, *Plan of God* (n. 21).

letting the action of the witnesses take place beforehand. Luke sets divine intrusion into history and human decision side by side, without seeing any contradiction. In two successive verses he can speak of the departure of Paul and Barnabas as a delegation of the Antiochean community (13,3) and as a sending of the Holy Spirit (13,4). The Spirit does not short-circuit the human connection, but uses human mediations, which through prayer are open to his impulsions (13,3)[53].

Furthermore, even the resistance to the Gospel is included in God's plan. This is masterfully illustrated by the quote of Isa 6,9-10 at the end of the book of Acts (28,26-27). However from chapter 3 on, the narrative exposes how the Jews systematically refuse to listen to the objurgations of the apostles, be it Peter, Stephen or Paul. The end of Acts does not describe the liberty of the adversaries as a charade, but rather shows that Paul's failure in his mission to the Jews (a) fits into a prophetic failure tradition in the midst of his people[54], and (b) serves God's plan to offer salvation beyond Israel (28,28). With this example, we perceive how Luke succeeds in aligning the omnipotence of God and human freedom, without the one eliminating the other, without providence crushing the individual's responsibility. Human freedom remains, a freedom even to say no.

Perhaps it is because of this principle that Luke leaves open the question of Israel at the end of his work[55]; the failure of the mission to the Jews is signified (28,28); hope to unify the λαός around Jesus is gone (28,25); but the future of the people of Abraham is left in suspense. At the end of Acts, the Church takes on the character of Paul's house: it is open to "all who entered" (28,30), to those who, in reliance on the Hebrew Scriptures, seek in this history to know how the old proclamation of the "Kingdom of God" is united with the new message "about the Lord Jesus Christ" (28,31).

---

53. On the theme of the mediations in Lukan theology, we must return to F. BOVON's initiatory study, *The Importance of Mediations in Luke's Theological Plan*, in *New Testament and Apocryphal Narratives*, Allison Park, Pickwick, 1995, pp. 51-66.

54. Attention must be paid to the commission given to the prophet in the introduction to the quotation of Isa 6,9f (28, 26a): "*Go to this people and say...*". This mention, unique in the quotations of Isa 6, 9f in the NT, aligns Paul's mission with that of the prophet by assimilating his failure in the mission to the Jews to Isaiah's failure. The Pauline incapacity to assemble Israel around the name of Jesus from this point on fits retrospectively in a tradition attested by the Scriptures.

55. Concerning the question of the relations with Judaism in Luke-Acts, see my article *Juifs et chrétiens selon Luc-Actes*, in D. MARGUERAT (ed.), *Le déchirement. Juifs et chrétiens au premier siècle* (Le Monde de la Bible, 32) Genève, Labor et Fides, 1996, pp. 151-178.

Conclusion

Three characteristics of the God of the Acts of the Apostles have been put forth in this study: the "non-evidence" of God, the interaction of human and divine, and the irony of God.

Firstly. In the book of Acts, God is never immediately evident or visible. The author uses two languages to speak of God: one (implicit) refers back to God through theophanic signs; the other names God explicitly, but it only comes into the narrative through the believing word. A theology of the hidden God permeates the story: the way to this God is encumbered by misunderstanding (ἄγνοια) and requires the mediation of a revealing word. God comes to the world through the words of his messengers. Therefore, to tell the story of God, the author of Acts has no other means except to tell it through the story of his messengers.

Secondly. Luke's God redirects history in order to mold it into his plan, which is the offer of salvation to all. The initiative to change the direction of history is always in God's hands, the witness' responsibility is to enter into his logic of salvation. Yet for Luke, human freedom, even when it resists these divine intrusions, is never abrogated. This explains the astonishing dialectic of the narrative of Acts where the divine and the human never cease to meet and mix in varying mediations, in order to transform history into salvation history.

Thirdly. Every page of the book of Acts displays the irony of God. If people remain free to act, they also remain ignorant of the consequences of their action. Neither Gamaliel, when he pleads in favor of the liberation of the apostles, nor the magistrates of Philippi when they imprison Paul and Silas, nor even Claudius the tribune, when he leads Paul to Caesarea under escort, realize their collaboration with the divine plan. The irony of God consists in integrating even the actions of his enemies, in order to make them contribute to the advancement of the word "to the ends of the earth" (1,8).

ABSTRACT

This study investigates the way in which the author of the Book of Acts constructs his picture of God as a thread in his narrative account. Luke employs two languages with regard to God: one is implicit and reflects the character of theophanies, the other is explicit, in which God is named, but this occurs solely in the speeches of his messengers. It is possible to construct a typology of divine interventions in the scheme of the plot and to discern three functions: programmatic, performative and interpretative. It is particularly notable that the plot of Acts is marked by a theology of the hidden God, and by a corresponding dialectical tension between direct divine initiative and the human responsibility of those who witness to divine activity.

RÉSUMÉ

L'étude porte sur la manière dont l'auteur du livre des Actes construit son image de Dieu au fil de son récit. Luc emploie à la fois un langage implicite, qui renvoie à Dieu au travers des théophanies, et un langage explicite, où Dieu est nommé, mais uniquement dans les discours de ses messagers. Une typologie des interventions divines dans l'intrigue du récit permet de distinguer trois fonctions, programmatique, performative et interprétative. Il en ressort notamment que le récit des Actes est marqué par une théologie du Dieu caché, ainsi que par une tension dialectique entre initiative divine et responsabilité humaine des témoins.

Université de Lausanne
Faculté de théologie
BFSH 2
CH-1015 Lausanne

Daniel MARGUERAT

RELATED TEXTS

12

JOSEPH, ASENETH, AND LÉVI-STRAUSS

I. INTRODUCTION

The narrative of Joseph and Aseneth is replete with interpretative problems. Who should have conceived such an elaborate story to expound a single scriptural verse (Gen. 41,45) from which it is learnt that the great hero of the tribes of Israel has married out? As C. Burchard has put it: "How could Joseph – the model of chastity, piety, and statesmanship – marry a foreign Hamitic girl, daughter of an idolatrous priest?"[1] What might the principal purpose of the story be: to convince Jewish boys that if they have eyes for a Gentile girl, they must insist that she convert before he even dares his first kiss, or is it to warn Gentile girls that should they be taken with a Jewish boy, they must first convert, if ever they intend marriage? But if conversion is the subject matter, then why is there no mention of Torah and its accompanying customary practices? Who wrote this attractive tale, when and why?

There have been many answers to these questions[2] and the interest in Joseph and Aseneth does not seem to be dwindling. Amongst the more recent attempts at answers are several suggestions which have differing implications for the genre of the work. R.S. Kraemer has argued that the

---

1. C. BURCHARD, *Joseph and Aseneth* in J.H. CHARLESWORTH (ed.), *The Old Testament Pseudepigrapha*, London, Darton, Longman and Todd, 1985, vol. 2, p. 177.
    This study treats Joseph and Aseneth as a literary unity and follows closely the English translation of the text as established by BURCHARD. BURCHARD's version which depends on an eclectic text is based largely on the *b* group of manuscripts. BURCHARD stands against those who would assert that the textual evidence allows scholars to see that a short text was gradually expanded, since he argues that the manuscripts containing the shorter text often contain inferior readings and show signs of omissions. If BURCHARD's arguments are taken seriously, then any analysis of the different purposes of the various editions must remain very tentative. Thus, the proposals of A. STANDHARTINGER, *From Fictional Text to Socio-Historical Context: Some Considerations from a Textcritical Perspective on Joseph and Aseneth*, in *SBL 1996 Seminar Papers*, 1966, pp. 303-318, must be treated very cautiously.
2. Note the comment by A. MOMIGLIANO, *Alien Wisdom: The Limits of Hellenization*, Cambridge, University Press, 1975, p. 117: "Classical scholars have suddenly suspected that *Joseph and Aseneth* may be the oldest Greek novel in existence. New Testament scholars have found it relevant to the question of the nature of the Last Supper. And more generally the seekers of symbols have found a new text to interpret on their own level".

story is from the third or fourth century CE, a Jewish composition which was subsequently edited by Christians[3]. Kraemer proposes that three paradigms undergird the story, the midrashic, the magical, and the mystical. These paradigms are definitions of the genre of the story on the basis of content: the midrashic makes the story interpretative of various biblical passages, the magical stresses that the principal sub-genre at the focus of the story enables the adjurations of the angel, and the mystical underlines that the story line has as its principal character the "prototypical soul who seeks and attains restoration to a primordial angelic identity"[4]. Against this attention to the defining role of content, R.D. Chesnutt has argued that Joseph and Aseneth is defined by its function which was "to enhance the status of Gentile converts in the Jewish community"[5]. Chesnutt is concerned to stress that the work is about conversion and that it is more particularly written to persuade "Jewish readers who had reservations about the full integration of converts"[6] that conversion is a worthwhile practice. For Chesnutt the purpose of the tale in addressing a single issue in a particular context results in the work being a kind of an apologia: it is a story to defend a point of view[7]. In a rather different vein J.C. O'Neill has argued that Joseph and Aseneth is really an allegory about apostate Israel: Israel "is won back to God the Father by Joseph who stands for the Messiah, the Son of God, who is bridegroom to Israel, his bride, and who bestows the Holy Spirit on her. She becomes a city of refuge for all who repent, including the Gentiles"[8]. Or again, G. Bohak has tried to show that Joseph and Aseneth is "a fictional history which 'foretells,' and justifies, the establishment of the

---

3. R.S. KRAEMER, *The Book of Aseneth*, in E. SCHÜSSLER FIORENZA (ed.), *Searching the Scriptures: A Feminist Commentary*, New York, Crossroad Publishing, 1994, pp. 859-888.

4. *The Book of Aseneth*, p. 861.

5. R.D. CHESNUTT, *From Death to Life: Conversion in Joseph and Aseneth* (JSP Supplement, 16), Sheffield, Sheffield Academic Press, p. 264. CHESNUTT defends his approach methodologically in *From Text to Context: The Social Matrix of Joseph and Aseneth*, in *SBL 1996 Seminar Papers*, 1996, pp. 285-302.

6. *From Text to Context: The Social Matrix of Joseph and Aseneth*, p. 301. See also his essay on the same theme *The Social Setting and Purpose of Joseph and Aseneth*, in *Journal for the Study of the Pseudepigrapha* 2 (1988) 21-48, esp. p. 43.

7. In this CHESNUTT takes further the proposals of D. SÄNGER, *Antikes Judentum und die Mysterien: Religionsgeschichtliche Untersuchungen zu Joseph und Aseneth* (WUNT, 2/5), Tübingen, Mohr, 1980, pp. 209-215, who has concluded as follows: "So scheint mir JosAs ein Beispiel dafür zu sein, wie grundlegende Anliegen einer jüdischen Minorität angesichts einer Umgebung, deren Haltung ihr gegenüber von freundlich über indifferent bis latent-aggresiv ging, in Apologetik, Werbung nach außen und einiger Identitätsfindung konkretisiert werden konnten".

8. J.C. O'NEILL, *What is Joseph and Aseneth about?*, in *Henoch* 16/2-3 (1994) 189-98, esp. p. 197.

Jewish temple in Heliopolis"[9]. To determine the setting of the story is to determine its character and purpose.

Over against these and other recent opinions about Joseph and Aseneth, the starting point for appreciating the composition seems to me to lie in taking seriously the generic classification of the narrative which is offered by G.W.E. Nickelsburg. Whereas Burchard is satisfied to define the tale as "a romance in the wider sense of the word"[10], Nickelsburg after careful use of vague terms like narrative and story finally opts for defining the work as myth. For Nickelsburg applying the term myth to Joseph and Aseneth means that the story is to be viewed as explaining the origin of proselytism. Nickelsburg further clarifies his definition as follows: "In creating his myth the author portrays Joseph and Aseneth as larger-than-life figures with special characteristics that befit their archetypal status. The elaborate rituals may also function to underscore the special, prototypical nature of Aseneth's conversion and need not imply that such rituals were employed in the author's community"[11].

But myth is a polyvalent term; how does it assist in the understanding of the narrative of Joseph and Aseneth? Should myth be understood as another way of talking about aetiology, or are there other matters to which the label can point? Prompted by Nickelsburg's use of the term myth, it is the purpose of this chapter to investigate the suitable use of the term in relation to Joseph and Aseneth from the angle of the reading of narrative texts associated with the structural anthropologists, and chief amongst them Claude Lévi-Strauss himself[12]. Given that an archangel has a major role in the story, and thus the heavenly realm impinges directly on the development of the plot, we may use the term myth of the tale with some measure of suitability. But it is the approach

---

9. G. BOHAK, *Joseph and Aseneth and the Jewish Temple in Heliopolis* (SBL Early Judaism and Its Literature, 10), Atlanta, Scholars Press, 1996, p. 102. BOHAK has defended his methodological approach in his essay *From Fiction to History: Contextualizing Joseph and Aseneth*, in *SBL 1996 Seminar Papers*, 1996, pp. 273-284.

10. C. BURCHARD, *Joseph and Aseneth* (n. 1), p. 186; followed recently by J.M.G. BARCLAY, *Jews in the Mediterranean Diaspora from Alexander to Trajan (323 BCE-117 CE)*, Edinburgh, T. & T. Clark, 1996, pp. 204-205.

11. G.W.E. NICKELSBURG, *Jewish Literature between the Bible and the Mishnah*, Philadelphia - London, Fortress Press - SCM Press, 1981, pp. 262-263. He writes similarly in *Stories of Biblical and Early Post-Biblical Times*, in M.E. STONE (ed.), *Jewish Writings of the Second Temple Period: Apocrypha, Pseudepigrapha, Qumran Sectarian Writings, Philo, Josephus* (CRINT, 2/2), Assen - Philadelphia, Van Gorcum - Fortress Press, 1984, p. 70.

12. This study thus approaches Joseph and Aseneth as myth in terms different from those used by critics who are interested in ancient narratives from a more literary perspective. For such a perspective and with a helpful classification of literary myth, see N. FRYE, *The Great Code: The Bible and Literature*, Orlando, Harcourt Brace Jovanovich, 1982, pp. 31-52.

of Lévi-Strauss in defining myth that really illuminates this narrative in intriguing ways.

Much has been written about Lévi-Strauss' approach to myth. The chief characteristic of myth according to Lévi-Strauss is opposition, and the function of myths is to describe, control, transform and resolve oppositions. This can be grasped most readily, not from his more theoretical works, but from his book entitled *Paroles Données*, which is a collection of the annual reports he made to the Collège de France between 1951 and 1982[13]. In a report from 1961-1962 entitled *The Raw and the Cooked* he wrote as follows:

> The myths examined deal – either directly or indirectly – with the discovery of fire, and hence of cooking; the latter is symbolic in indigenous thought of the transition from Nature to Culture. The starting point was a group of Bororo myths collected and published by Albisetti and Colbacchini, which were shown to represent variations on a single theme. These variants have been classified and subdivided along several dimensions, and parallels were sought in the mythical thought of both the Ge and the Tupi.
>
> It appeared that all these myths made use of the same code, constructed from terms which, for all that they are qualitative and intimately associated with concrete experience, are none the less conceptual tools allowing the combination or separation of significant properties according to logical rules of compatibility and incompatibility, and in relation to cultural differences between the various groups, as discerned by the anthropologist.
>
> In fact, all the myths examined relate to the origin of cookery. Another common feature is their opposition of this mode of nourishment to that found in carnivorous animals, consumers of raw meat, and in scavengers, who eat rotten meat. Certain myths even evoke, directly or indirectly, a fourth alimentary regime in cannibalism, sometimes conceived as terrestrial (the ogres), and sometimes as aquatic (the *piranha* fish).
>
> In every case, consequently we encounter a double opposition, on the one hand between raw and cooked, on the other between fresh and rotten. The axis that joins the raw and the cooked is characteristic of the transition to Culture; that joining the raw and the rotten, of the return to Nature. Thus cooking brings about the cultural transformation of the raw, just as putrefaction brings about a natural transformation[14].

According to this description, myth certainly has to do with origins but it also has to do with the suitable categorization of experience into a system of oppositions, which archetypically for Lévi-Strauss in this instance as in many others can be characterized chiefly as the opposition between Culture and Nature. The two realms are complex entities in need of careful analysis to disclose their full significance. Nor is it sim-

---

13. C. LÉVI-STRAUSS, *Paroles données*, Paris, Librarie Plon, 1984; English translation by R. WILLIS: *Anthropology and Myth: Lectures 1951-1982*, Oxford, Blackwell, 1987.

14. *Anthropology and Myth*, pp. 39-40.

ply a matter of describing something static. There is movement and process: most obviously in the example quoted the act of cooking is the process whereby transformation from one realm to another takes place.

It is this definition of myth which this study will briefly apply to the narrative of Joseph and Aseneth since the story presents in a non-threatening way the resolution of several basic oppositions. The story of Joseph and Aseneth does indeed have many of the ingredients of the Greek novels, but it seems to fall short of them in narrative power[15]. J. Barclay has expressed it as follows: "Even the most sympathetic reader of *Joseph and Aseneth* would have to acknowledge some aesthetic disappointment in comparing this story with the tales to be found in the romances ... The real cause of the failure of the narrative as romance is that it has been overwhelmed by the theme, and the elongated depiction, of Aseneth's conversion"[16]. But this dissatisfaction is in fact the key to appreciating Joseph and Aseneth as myth. The conversion of Aseneth is the process of the overcoming of oppositions; through her conversion she is transformed from the "raw" to the "cooked", from Nature to Culture. It is exactly this kind of transformation which is at the centre of what distinguishes one group from another[17].

II. Mythical Polarities in Joseph and Aseneth

1. Life-death

It is often pointed out that until her moment of transformation Aseneth resides in the realm of death, cut off from the living God. In chapter 8 Joseph meets Aseneth:

> And Joseph said to Aseneth, "May the Lord God who gives life to all things bless you." And Pentephres said to Aseneth, "Go up and kiss your brother." And as Aseneth went up to kiss Joseph, Joseph stretched out his right hand and put it on her chest between her two breasts, and her breasts were already standing upright like handsome apples. And Joseph said, "It is not fitting for a man who worships God, who will bless with his mouth the living God and eat blessed bread of life and drink a blessed cup of im-

---

15. M. Philonenko, *Joseph et Aseneth: introduction, texte critique, traduction et notes* (SPB, 13), Leiden, Brill, 1968, p. 48, describes the work as follows: "De qualité littéraire médiocre, *Joseph et Aseneth* n'en apparaît pas moins comme une des oeuvres les plus curieuses de la littérature romanesque de l'antiquité".

16. *Jews in the Mediterranean Diaspora* (n. 10), p. 205.

17. This has been shown convincingly from an anthropological viewpoint through the application of the ideas of A. van Gennep, V. Turner and B. Lincoln to Joseph and Aseneth by R.C. Douglas, *Liminality and Conversion in Joseph and Aseneth*, in *Journal for the Study of the Pseudepigrapha* 3 (1988) 31-42.

mortality and anoint himself with blessed ointment of incorruptibility to kiss a strange woman who will bless with her mouth dead and dumb idols and eat from their table of strangulation and drink from their libation cup of insidiousness and anoint herself with ointment of destruction" (8,5)[18].

Aseneth is unkissable because she is associated with death, dead idols, strangulation, insidiousness, and destruction. Her conversion leads her from death to life. The conversion begins with Aseneth dressing in her black tunic for mourning (10,9-10), taking her idols, grinding them to pieces, and throwing the dust out of the window (10,10-13), then mourning for seven days. Then after her soliloquies the chief of the angels appears to her and commands her to put off her black tunic of mourning and to wash her face and hands in "living water" (14,12). After she has complied, the angel declares "For behold, your name was written in the book of the living in heaven; in the beginning of the book, as the very first of all, your name was written by my finger, and it will not be erased forever. Behold, from today, you will be renewed and formed anew and made alive again, and you will eat blessed bread of life, and drink a blessed cup of immortality". Then when Joseph first kisses Aseneth he gives her the spirit of life (19,11); in his subsequent kisses he bestows the spirit of wisdom and the spirit of truth.

But that is not all, because there needs to be some proof that Aseneth is truly of the realm of life. Such proof comes in 21,8-9 where the life-death opposition is played once again. The Pharaoh gives a marriage feast for Joseph and Aseneth and declares: "Every man who does any work during the seven days of Joseph's and Aseneth's wedding shall surely die". This death sentence is followed immediately in the narrative by the statement, "And it happened after this, Joseph went in to Aseneth, and Aseneth conceived from Joseph, and gave birth to Manasseh and Ephraim, his brother, in Joseph's house". Aseneth is in the abode of life, Joseph's house, and herself gives birth.

Aseneth's conversion is the story of her transformation from death to life. The opposition between the two is overcome through the conversion process. It is intriguing to note that in this conversion even Lévi-Strauss' interpretation of the raw and the cooked features indirectly. In the realm of death Aseneth can merely participate at the table of strangulation, raw dead meat, but once transformed she can eat the blessed

---

18. Trans. C. BURCHARD, *Joseph and Aseneth*, pp. 211-212. BURCHARD includes on these pages an extensive note on the bread, the cup and the ointment with a detailed bibliography to which can be added B. LINDARS, *Joseph and Asenath and the Eucharist* in B.P. THOMPSON (ed.), *Scripture: Meaning and Method: Essays Presented to Anthony Tyrrel Hanson*, Hull, University Press, 1987, pp. 181-199.

bread of life, which of course has been cooked. In Lévi-Strauss' terms Aseneth has moved from Nature to Culture. There is also something archetypal in her converted state. The angel declares to her that her name was written in the book of the living in heaven, in the beginning of the book, as the very first of all. Aseneth's transformation was always anticipated in the heavenly realm. The story as myth reveals how the heavenly realm can materialize in everyday reality.

2. Pure-impure

The demarcation of the opposition that is so obviously described in terms of life and death is clarified and reinforced by attention to the distinction between the pure and the impure. As has already been noted along with the description of Aseneth's idols as dead, come associated descriptions of corruptibility, insidiousness, and destruction. Aseneth belongs in the realm of abomination. When Joseph arrives at the house of Pentephres, his feet are washed and a table is set for him all by himself, "because Joseph never ate with the Egyptians, for this was an abomination to him" (7,1). Joseph sees Aseneth at the window and despises her, putting her in the same category as all the wives and daughters of the noblemen and the satraps of the whole land of Egypt who "used to molest him (wanting) to sleep with him" (7,3). Joseph recalls the advice of his father that one must avoid "associating with a strange woman, for association with her is destruction and corruption" (7,5).

When Pentephres responds to Joseph that the girl at the window is his daughter, he describes her as "a virgin hating every man, and there is not any other man who has ever seen her except you alone today. And if you will, she will come and address you, because our daughter is like a sister to you" (7,7). In this Pentephres suggests that virginity makes people of different religions into siblings. Thus the reader is informed of one aspect of how the conversion becomes possible. Though in the realm of corruption, Aseneth is herself a pure virgin, ripe for transformation. Aseneth's virginity is the potential state for resolving the opposition between her own association with idols and Joseph's righteous innocence. Joseph therefore prays to God, "Bless this virgin, and renew her by your spirit" (8,10).

As the start of the conversion is depicted Aseneth is surrounded by virgins (10,1), but the importance of her virginity comes in the words of the archangel after he has commanded her to wash in living water: "Dress in a new linen robe (as yet) untouched and distinguished and gird your waist (with) the new twin girdle of your virginity" (14,12).

When she comes before him washed and changed, he first requests her to remove her veil, addressing her as "a chaste virgin" (15,2), and then he continues by encouraging her, "Courage, Aseneth, chaste virgin," a form of address which is repeated three times in his speech to her (15,2-6). When Joseph finally returns to take Aseneth as his wife, he copies the angel and addresses Aseneth as "chaste virgin" (19,9). All through the story the outward sign of her chastity and virginity is her great beauty which even she is surprised at, when finally she comes to see herself after her conversion (18,7-9).

A small motif confirms this matter, the purity of her bed. The reader is told about it in 2,8-9: "And there was a golden bed standing in the chamber, (a bed) that looked toward the window (looking) east, and the bed was laid with gold-woven purple stuff, interwoven with violet, purple, and white. And in this bed Aseneth slept, alone; and a man or another woman never sat on it, only Aseneth alone". Then when alone with the angel, Aseneth invites him as follows: "I beg you, Lord, sit down a little on this bed, because this bed is pure and undefiled, and a man or woman never sat on it". The meal with the honeycomb follows; this is pure breakfast-in-bed from start to finish. The invitation to the angel to sit on the bed carries no risk of defilement, since the angel does not and cannot eat anything; rather his presence is the guarantee from the heavenly realm that Aseneth's purity is a reflection of the Culture to which she truly belongs, a culture in which purity is the hallmark of the ongoing realization of divine pleasure and purpose through right worship.

3. God-Satan

A third polarity in Joseph and Aseneth is that between God and Satan. This is most obvious in Aseneth's soliloquies. In her prayers she takes the risk of seeking refuge with the "Lord God of the ages who created all things and gave life to them" (12,1). Aseneth herself characterizes the opposition. On the one hand there is God whom she addresses as "father of the orphans" and "protector of the persecuted" and "helper of the afflicted" (12,13). She prays that the Lord will be "a sweet and good and gentle father. What father is sweet as you, Lord, and who (is) as quick in mercy as you, Lord, and who (is as) long-suffering toward our sins as you, Lord?" (12,15).

Compared with the merciful Lord, Aseneth characterizes Satan as "the old wild lion" who persecutes her. "He is the father of the gods of the Egyptians, and his children are the gods of the idol maniacs. And I have come to hate them, because they are the lion's children, and have thrown all of them from me and destroyed them. And the lion their father furiously persecutes me" (12,9-10). She prays that God will deliver her from this lion's mouth, "lest he carry me off like a lion, and tear me up and throw me into the flame of fire, and the fire will throw me into the hurricane, and the hurricane (will) wrap me up in darkness and throw me out into the deep of the sea, and the big sea monster who (exists) since eternity will swallow me, and I will be destroyed for ever (and) ever" (12,11).

In this opposition something of the continuing threat of voracious death beyond the moment of conversion is to be seen. Overall the narrative allows the reader to recognize that the conversion of Aseneth is not a sentimental journey from nastiness to niceness. Once converted, threatening situations will recur, as the concluding chapters of the work make plain. Thus the soliloquies serve not only as expressions of Aseneth's confession of faith, but as demonstrations for how the religious life can constantly keep the voracious lion at bay. It is through prayer addressed to the merciful God that protection is continuously available[19]. To be transformed to and to remain on God's side is to be constantly enclosed in cultural processes. But Satan represents the constant threat that the process can go the other way. As Lévi-Strauss would put it in relation to the cooked, the raw and the rotten, myths which combine the raw and the rotten are generally about the return to nature. So as Satan is identified with the processes of destruction, he represents the return to starkest nature.

As listeners hear the prayer of Aseneth and identify with her in saying it, they endorse that controlled universe of which they are part. They stand over against that process of consumption which moves from wild land animals, to the violence and unpredictability of natural forces, to the threat of darkness, to the terror of the deep and the voracious sea monster. Whether on land or sea, Satan is depicted in terms which are all-consuming. God sustains and protects, Satan devours and destroys. Listeners can receive Aseneth's prayer as an amulet which preserves them in the care of God. It is difficult to decide whether this would apply especially to converts to Judaism who by hearing the story would be reminded of all the benefits of their own transformation or whether this prayer belongs more to those who have been Jews from birth and so are having their Jewishness confirmed. Perhaps it does not matter; whoever hears the story will be reminded of the character of the God who is both

---

19. As Susanna also knows, when she appeals directly to God for protection and deliverance.

their maker and sustainer and the threat of Satan who can yet be kept at bay.

4. Parent-child (father-daughter)

The prayer of Aseneth addressed to God as father reflects another polarity which runs through the conversion process. This is the opposition between parent and child. When Joseph is about to visit Pentephres' house, Pentephres seizes the opportunity to suggest to Aseneth that she could do no better than be married to him. She will have none of it, and answers her father "daringly and with boastfulness and anger" (4,12) as teenage daughters have done throughout the ages. She rushes out of the room and goes to her tower where she looks out of the window and realizes that her father might have been right after all (as teenage daughters have realized throughout the ages!). "And Aseneth saw Joseph on his chariot and was strongly cut (to the heart), and her soul was crushed, and her knees were paralyzed, and her entire body trembled, and she was filled with great fear. And she sighed" (6,1) and admits to herself that she has made a big mistake.

However, rather than setting things right with her father and asking him to set the match up, she has to see her declaration of independence through. This separation from her father is underlined throughout her prayers during the conversion process by the repeated stress on her state as an orphan. "With whom shall I take refuge, or what shall I speak, I the virgin and an orphan and desolate and abandoned and hated?" (11,3; cf. 12,5). She describes to God how she is orphaned because she has rejected her parents' gods: "Rescue me, Lord, the desolate and solitary, because my father and my mother disowned me and said, 'Aseneth is not our daughter'... I am now an orphan and desolate" (12,12-13).

The angel confirms that indeed God is her father. Part of this confirmation seems to belong to the episode of the name-change. No longer is she named Aseneth, but City of Refuge because "in you many nations will take refuge with the Lord God, the Most High, and under your wings many peoples trusting in the Lord God will be sheltered, and behind your walls will be guarded those who attach themselves to the Most High God in the name of Repentance" (15,7). Repentance is loved by the "Most High Father" (15,8). God's fatherhood compensates for Aseneth's orphan state.

The narrative reinforces the distance between father and daughter which is both necessary as Aseneth changes marital status and so, somewhat ironically, achieves her father's ambition for her. This same distance between father and daughter is also the necessary distance from all that Pentephres symbolizes as priest in Heliopolis. After the angel has left, it is a servant, not Pentephres, who announces Joseph's impending arrival, and it is her foster-father who helps her prepare herself to meet him (18,11).

To add insult to injury, when Pentephres offers permission for the wedding and to underwrite the celebrations, Joseph refuses and claims that he must defer to Pharaoh.

> And Pentephres said to Joseph, "Tomorrow I will call all the noblemen and the satraps of the whole land of Egypt and give a marriage feast for you, and you will take my daughter Aseneth for (your) wife." And Joseph said, "I will go tomorrow to Pharaoh the king, because he is like a father to me and appointed me chief of the whole land of Egypt, and I will speak about Aseneth into his ears, and he himself will give her to me for (my) wife." And Pentephres said to him, "Go in peace" (20,8-10).

Thus it is Pharaoh himself who marries them and throws the party. Aseneth's conversion, her transformation from nature to culture prevents her father from having any major role in her subsequent marriage ceremonies; Pharaoh becomes the agent through whom Joseph's God blesses what happens. Whereas Pentephres remains on the outside as one who belongs to the realm of death and corruption, Pharaoh's credentials are established by virtue of his knowledge that Aseneth has been betrothed to Joseph since eternity (21,3), his declaration that the Lord, the God of Joseph, had chosen her as Joseph's bride, and by his ability to call Joseph "the firstborn son of God" (21,4). When the silent Pentephres stands her before Pharaoh, Pharaoh says, "May the Lord, the God of Joseph bless you, child" (21,4), and the marriage is sealed through a further blessing which Pharaoh also declares: "May the Lord God the Most High bless you and multiply you and magnify and glorify you forever" (21,6). No Egyptian priest of Heliopolis could have uttered with credibility such benedictions.

5. *Fear-safety*

There is yet another set of polarities which is resolved as the narrative is developed. This set revolves around the issue of fear and safety, insecurity and security. The theme is presented most awkwardly and strikingly in the incident of the bees[20]. When Aseneth sets the table before

---

20. Several of the features of the following description are highlighted well by G. BOHAK, *Joseph and Aseneth and the Jewish Temple of Heliopolis* (n. 9), pp. 1-18, but he is concerned to draw attention particularly to the priestly character of the bees, arguing that as they move from the first honeycomb to form another on Aseneth's mouth, they represent the priesthood which has left Jerusalem to set up a new Temple at Heliopolis.

the angel, he says to her, "Bring me a honeycomb" (16,2). This itself causes Aseneth consternation as she has no honeycomb to offer. However, the angel knows there is one in the storeroom: "And the comb was big and white as snow and full of honey. And that honey was like dew from heaven and its exhalation like breath of life" (16,8). The angel mocks Aseneth by reminding her how she had insisted that she did not have a honeycomb. And she is afraid. This first fear is dissipated by the angel. He smiles at her understanding that the honeycomb must have come from him.

But then Aseneth is afraid a second time as he takes her head in his right hand. "And Aseneth was afraid of the man's hand, because sparks shot forth from his hand as from bubbling (melted) iron" (16,13). The angel then explains about the honeycomb in more detail. "The bees of the paradise of delight have made this from the dew of the roses of life that are in the paradise of God"; this is angels' food and "everyone who eats of it will not die for ever (and) ever" (16,14). The honeycomb is the source of eternal life. Then the angel brings myriads of bees out of it. They have sharp stings and though the reader is assured that they will not injure anyone (16,19), they encircle Aseneth's mouth and make a comb on it and eat it. They seem to be of two kinds, some eat of the comb and then fly away to heaven but others are a real threat: "those who wanted to injure Aseneth fell to the ground and died" (16,22). The first comb from which the bees have come is then consumed by fire; the life-giving, yet harmful threat, is removed. The angel has performed the right tricks to ensure Aseneth's survival.

But the motifs of fear and security are present also in the need to domesticate Aseneth. For this reason, if for no other, it seems likely that the narrative was written by a man[21]. For the various parts of the tale to work she has to be portrayed as stunningly beautiful and gorgeously arrayed. Though Joseph is her match in looks (7,4), as the leading character in the story she presents a sexual threat to the reader[22]. This threat must be overcome. Indeed, Aseneth's sexuality is tamed. From being potentially the object of desire, she is turned into the universal archetypal Jewish mother figure. This is even hinted at the outset: Aseneth is

---

21. R.S. KRAEMER is now inclined to think that the author and certainly subsequent redactor(s) were male: "Though I have elsewhere argued that the shorter version of *Aseneth* could have been authored by a woman, I am somewhat less inclined to think this so. The redactor(s) of the longer version seem to me almost certainly to be male, on the basis of their revisions of passages that are particularly concerned with constructions of gender" (*The Book of Aseneth* [n. 3], p. 860).

22. Both male and female; male inasmuch as she may elicit sexual arousal, female inasmuch as she may create an unreal role model.

"tall as Sarah and handsome as Rebecca and beautiful as Rachel... and the fame of her beauty spread all over that land and to the ends of the inhabited world" (1,6). Once converted, though still beautiful (18,9), she becomes the City of Refuge and loses all her overt sexual allure in the process; she moves from stunning virgin to archetypal security blanket. However, in one sense this domestication merely embraces what may have been overtly erotic and threatening and turns it into the subversive sexuality present in any household where parents and children of opposite sexes (or even the same) reside in close quarters. The raw nature of her sexuality is enculturated in Jewish motherhood.

6. Human-divine

A sixth polarity may be discernible in the opposition between the human and the divine, or at least between the human and the angelic. Here the polarity of death and life is worked out in a rather particular way, since humans are generally on the side of mortality and the angels on the side of the immortal. R.S. Kraemer has convincingly highlighted a remarkable feature of the incident of the honeycomb through which the overcoming of the opposition between the human and the angelic is depicted. For Kraemer in several ways the passage in Joseph and Aseneth 16 is a play on and reversal of the story of Adam and Eve in the garden. In Genesis 2-3 it is Eve who instructs Adam to eat and because disobedience is involved their food ensures their mortality. In Joseph and Aseneth the angel instructs the woman to eat the food of immortality. "And the bees of the paradise of delight have made this from the dew of the roses of life that are in the paradise of God. And all the angels of God eat of it and all the chosen of God and all the sons of the Most High, because this is a comb of life, and everyone who eats of it will not die for ever (and) ever" (16,14).

In Joseph and Aseneth 16 it is the encounter between the angel and Aseneth which is the first indication of the resolution of the polarity between the human and the divine. However, it needs to be remembered that the reader or listener has been prepared for this resolution much earlier. The description of Joseph in chapter 5 is very detailed. He is dressed in royal attire which is somewhat ambiguous, having features which recall the figure of Helios, but which could also be understood as standing in the Jewish priestly tradition. In chapter 14 when Aseneth raises her head to see the angel, the narrator remarks: "And behold, there was a man in every respect similar to Joseph, by the robe and the crown and the royal staff, except that his face was like lightning, and his eyes like sunshine, and the hairs of his head like a flame of fire of a burning torch, and hands and feet like iron shining forth from a fire, and sparks shot forth from his hands and feet" (14,9). It is the angel who commands Aseneth to eat, rather than Joseph, but since the two figures are described in a very similar way, one doubles for the other. Through Aseneth as the City of Refuge, the elect will become angelic, immortal, the very condition which can be deemed an opportunity for Adam and Eve in the garden before disobedience forced them into mortality. "It appears that the divine couple of Joseph and Aseneth restore the damage done by Adam and Eve, affording human beings a means to return to their original angelic state and, indeed, acquiring precisely the immortality which God feared Adam and Eve might acquire had they remained in Eden (Gen 3:22-24)"[23]. It is important to note, however, that although Joseph and Aseneth together resolve this opposition between the divine or angelic and the human, the resolution does not take the form of a complete reversal of Eden. Though sharing in immortality, Joseph and Aseneth retain their sexuality, as the narrative requires.

III. CONCLUSIONS

Some matters are worth noting by way of conclusion. In the first place this reading of Joseph and Aseneth as myth as understood and explicated by Lévi-Strauss is an approach to many of the features of the story at the level of archetypes. Reading the story in this way draws attention to features with universal implications, a fact which may partially explain why scholars find this story so difficult to provide with an accurate and convincing particular setting in life. But this kind of reading of the story does not exclude other ways of reading it[24]. It is still worth looking for particular settings where the story would have made sense, such as at Heliopolis, or amongst the Therapeutae, or in the Christian communities of the third or fourth centuries CE.

In the second place, it is striking that for all its interest in the figures of Joseph and Aseneth, the narrative as myth does not especially address the polarity of gender issues themselves. Hence, there is no paragraph in this short study which tries to suggest that the male-female distinction is overcome in any way. Aseneth is distinctively portrayed as having a

---

23. R.S. KRAEMER, *The Book of Aseneth* (n. 3), p. 880.
24. M. PHILONENKO, *Joseph et Aseneth* (n. 15), pp. 53-98, has offered a way of reading the story at three different levels: "le roman missionnaire", "le roman à clef", and "le roman mystique", the last having characteristics of allegory, gnostic drama and initiatory liturgy.

salvific role as City of Refuge, and so represents one of very few female figures who occupy such a position in antiquity[25]. But overall, as Kraemer has adeptly concluded, the texts of Joseph and Aseneth "don't manifest much tension around issues of gender"[26].

In the third place this brief survey of six polarities discernible in the myth of Joseph and Aseneth provides some important clues for the better understanding of the narrative. Most significantly it shows why so much attention is paid to the process of Aseneth's conversion. In terms of contemporary romances, this seems tedious, but when viewed as myth the process is the means of her passing from death to life, from impurity to purity, from threat to security, from daughter to mother, from mere human to near angel. But, as myth, the whole story allows the reader to recognize polarities at several different levels; this is most obvious in the way Aseneth's prayers are a recognition of the continuing presence of the voracious lion, a presence which is presented narratively in the final section of the tale (22-29) in which Pharaoh's son attempts to kidnap Aseneth and rise to power in Egypt. For the reader the polarities are resolved and yet the polarities remain. Joseph has risked an encounter with Nature, he has married out, but only so that in its very telling the story of his bride's conversion can demonstrate that Judaism (even without the Law) is the very apogee of all Culture.

ABSTRACT

This study is an exploration of the story of Joseph and Aseneth using the definition of myth established by C. Lévi-Strauss. He argued that myth does not only deal with origins, but also categorizes human experience through a system of oppositions which archetypically can be characterized in the opposition between Culture and Nature. Myth serves to resolve the oppositions appropriately. In the narrative of Joseph and Aseneth there are several readily discernible polarities: between life and death, between purity and impurity, between God and Satan, between parent and child, and between insecurity and security. Aseneth's conversion is not so much an object lesson in conversion per se, but is rather the focus of the resolution of these opposites: it is her passage from death to life, from impurity to purity, from the realm of Satan, from daughterhood to motherhood, from threat to security. Overall the narrative is about how Joseph risks an

---

25. C. BURCHARD argues that this attention to Aseneth should not cause any surprise: "The Sion tradition, at least when taken up directly, paved the way for this portrayal (cf. also Gal 4:21-31). This portrait may also reflect the fact that more women than men became full proselytes, and that a relatively liberal status was accorded to women in some quarters of Jewish Hellenism" (*Joseph and Aseneth* [n. 1], p. 190).

26. *The Book of Aseneth* (n. 3), p. 886.

encounter with Nature, he has courted a Gentile, but only so that in the telling of the story of his bride's pre-marital conversion, Judaism (even without explicit mention of the Law) can be seen as the very apogee of Culture.

RÉSUMÉ

La présente étude explore le récit de Joseph et Aséneth en utilisant la définition du mythe proposée par C. Lévi-Strauss. Pour ce dernier, le mythe traite non seulement des origines. mais sert aussi à organiser l'expérience humaine selon un système d'oppositions, qui peut être caractérisé de manière archétypique par l'opposition entre Nature et Culture. Le mythe a pour fonction de donner à ces oppositions la solution qui convient. Dans le récit de Joseph et Aséneth, on peut facilement repérer plusieurs exemples de polarités: polarité entre la vie et la mort, entre la pureté et l'impureté, entre Dieu et Satan, entre parents et enfant, entre insécurité et sécurité. La conversion d'Aséneth n'est pas tant un enseignement sur la conversion en elle-même, mais est plutôt centrée sur la manière dont ces oppositions sont résolues: on y voit Aséneth passer de la mort à la vie, de l'impureté à la pureté, du règne de Satan à celui de Dieu, du statut de fille à celui de mère, de la menace à la sécurité. Le récit dans son ensemble traite de la manière dont Joseph prend le risque d'une rencontre avec la Nature. Il courtise certes une païenne, mais il le fait de manière à ce que, par le récit de la conversion de sa femme avant même son mariage, le judaïsme (même sans aucune mention explicite de la Loi) puisse être considéré comme l'apogée même de la Culture.

Department of Religions and Theology George J. BROOKE
University of Manchester
Manchester M13 9PL

13

L'USAGE DU NARRATIF DANS LE *TESTAMENT DE JOSEPH*

La recherche sur les *Testaments des Douze Patriarches* (*T12P*) est confrontée à plusieurs grandes questions. En matière de critique textuelle, elle doit se prononcer sur le classement et la valeur respective des principaux témoins (une quinzaine de manuscrits grecs et une version arménienne). Grâce à l'édition de M. de Jonge, nous disposons aujourd'hui d'un texte qui repose sur une classification de l'ensemble des témoins – même si la préférence donnée aux mss. b et k (famille I) n'est pas toujours entièrement convaincante et si l'on aurait souhaité un apparat critique différent, positif et plus lisible[1]. L'analyse de la composition littéraire des *T12P*, qui est inséparable de la détermination de leur milieu d'origine, est appelée à trancher le problème suivant: est-il possible d'identifier des étapes rédactionnelles et des passages interpolés dans le texte actuel de l'écrit?

Sur cette question essentielle, la recherche actuelle est divisée entre deux grandes tendances. La première considère les *T12P* comme une œuvre fondamentalement juive, enrichie par des interpolations chrétiennes. Elle trouve sa meilleure illustration dans l'analyse littéraire de J. Becker, qui distingue trois stades dans la composition des *T12P*: (a) un écrit de base («Grundstock»), d'origine juive hellénistique, rédigé dans les trois premières décennies du 2e siècle avant J.-C.; (b) un accroissement progressif de cet écrit de base au sein du judaïsme hellénistique, entre le 2e siècle avant et le 1er siècle après J.-C.; (c) enfin, une troisième couche, constituée par les adjonctions chrétiennes, à partir du début du 2e siècle de notre ère[2]. Les représentants de la seconde tendance estiment que la cohérence de l'écrit rend impossible toute distinction nette entre couches rédactionnelles juives et chrétiennes; ils inclinent à situer la composition des *T12P* dans des milieux chrétiens, durant la seconde moitié du 2e siècle. Cette position est défendue notamment par M. de Jonge et H.W. Hollander[3].

1. M. DE JONGE, *The Testaments of the Twelve Patriarchs. A Critical Edition of the Greek Text* (PVTG, 1,2), Leiden, Brill, 1978.
2. J. BECKER, *Untersuchungen zur Entstehungsgeschichte der Testamente der zwölf Patriarchen* (AGJU, 8), Leiden, Brill, 1970.
3. Voir surtout M. DE JONGE, *The Testaments of the Twelve Patriarchs. A Study of their Text, Composition and Origin*, Assen/Amsterdam, van Gorcum, 1975² (1953), ainsi

Ces points de vue divergents sur la composition de l'ouvrage se reflètent naturellement dans l'analyse du *Testament de Joseph* (*TJos*). Mais ce dernier présente plusieurs particularités qui le distinguent des autres pièces du recueil[4]. Il se distingue surtout par le fait qu'il contient deux évocations narratives de la vie du patriarche, qui servent à illustrer, dans les parties parénétiques, deux vertus différentes.

Le premier morceau biographique (*TJos* 3,1-9,5) est centré sur la résistance de Joseph face aux nombreuses tentatives de séduction de l'Égyptienne, femme du chef cuisinier de Pharaon; il débouche, dans la parénèse qui suit (10,1-4), sur une exhortation à «rechercher la chasteté et la pureté» (10,2). La seconde section biographique (*TJos* 11,2-16,6) rapporte des épisodes liés à la condition servile de Joseph et à sa vente par les Ismaélites à Petephrès, fonctionnaire de Pharaon; elle illustre la conduite exemplaire de Joseph qui, en taisant sa véritable origine, évite de couvrir de honte ses frères et manifeste ainsi son amour pour eux.

La question que je me propose d'examiner est la suivante: quel est le rapport entre ces deux «histoires» de Joseph? Ont-elles une visée différente et doivent-elles être attribuées à deux étapes distinctes de la rédaction des *T12P*? Ou bien sont-elles liées par une thématique commune et appartiennent-elles dès l'origine au *TJos*? Je commencerai par évaluer les arguments avancés en faveur de l'origine indépendante des deux parties du *TJos*. Je dirai ensuite pourquoi je me rallie à l'autre explication, en m'appuyant notamment sur les travaux de H.W. Hollander. Je formulerai enfin quelques observations sur la composition de *TJos* 3-9 et sur la fonction narrative commune aux deux sections.

---

que les études réunies dans M. DE JONGE ET ALII, *Studies on the Testaments of the Twelve Patriarchs. Text and Interpretation* (SVTP, 3), Leiden, Brill, 1975; H.W. HOLLANDER – M. DE JONGE, *The Testaments of the Twelve Patriarchs. A Commentary* (SVTP, 8) Leiden, Brill, 1985 (en particulier pp. 82-85).

4. Dans chaque Testament, on retrouve les mêmes éléments constitutifs. Une introduction et une conclusion narrative servent à encadrer le discours d'adieu que chacun des patriarches, à l'approche de sa mort, adresse à ses fils et petits-fils. À l'intérieur de ce discours, qui constitue l'essentiel de chaque Testament, on distingue trois composantes: (1) un rappel biographique de certains événements de la vie du patriarche, qui se raccroche à des données du texte biblique et les amplifie; (2) une parénèse, qui reprend les éléments du rappel biographique pour illustrer un comportement éthique, positif ou négatif; (3) une annonce prophétique des événements qui se produiront dans l'avenir et affecteront la destinée de la tribu ou d'Israël dans son ensemble (ces prophéties suivent généralement le schéma «péché» – «exil» – «restauration» et comportent souvent aussi un développement sur la prééminence de Lévi et de Juda). Dans le *TJos*, ce dernier élément n'occupe que peu de place et est présenté sous la forme particulière d'un rêve; son contenu est fortement marqué par une perspective christologique.

I. La thèse de l'hétérogénéité des deux sections narratives

Les auteurs qui attribuent les ch. 3-9 et les ch. 11-16 à deux mains différentes s'appuient sur plusieurs observations. D'abord, l'orientation des deux récits n'est pas la même. Le premier (ch. 3-9) est centré sur le thème de la chasteté, que Joseph défend héroïquement contre les assauts répétés de l'Égyptienne, alors que le second (ch. 11-16) est dominé par le thème de l'amour des frères, que Joseph met en pratique en subissant sa condition d'esclave et en dissimulant son origine noble. Deuxièmement, les personnages reçoivent des noms différents: dans le premier récit, le maître de Joseph est appelé «l'Égyptien» (3,4; 4,5; 5,1; 7,2; 8,4) et sa femme «l'Égyptienne» (3,1; 4,3; 8,1; 8,5), alors que le second le nomme «Petephrès» ou «Pentephrès» (12,1; 13,1; 13,4; 15,6), et appelle sa femme «la Memphite» (ἡ Μεμφία ou ἡ Μέμφις: 12,1; 14,1; 14,5; 16,1)[5]. Enfin, on relève que la succession des deux morceaux ne suit pas la chronologie des événements. S'ils avaient été composés en même temps, les épisodes liés à la vente de Joseph par ses frères auraient dû être placés avant l'évocation des tentatives de séduction de l'Égyptienne. Ces observations conduisent à attribuer les deux sections à deux phases différentes de la composition des *T12P*.

La question est alors de savoir laquelle des deux sections appartient à la rédaction primitive du *TJos*. Selon R.H. Charles, c'est le récit des démêlés de Joseph avec la femme de Potiphar qui remonte à l'auteur des *T12P*, alors que le morceau qui va de 10,5 au ch. 18 est une addition postérieure[6].

La position inverse est défendue par J. Becker, sur la base d'une argumentation nettement plus étoffée que celle de Charles. Becker invoque d'abord la transition abrupte entre l'exhortation de 10,1-4, qui tire la leçon de l'affrontement entre Joseph et l'Égyptienne, et l'introduction en 10,5 d'un nouveau développement, centré sur les relations de Joseph avec ses frères. La mention de l'amour de Jacob pour Joseph en 10,5 («Mes frères savaient combien mon père m'aimait») montre que ce développement devait à l'origine suivre directement l'ouverture du discours d'adieu en 1,2 («Ecoutez Joseph, le *bien-aimé d'Israël*»). Le fait

---

5. La règle souffre quelques exceptions: en 3,6, on trouve «Memphia l'Égyptienne» et en 16,5 simplement «l'Égyptienne». De plus, au ch. 2, qui se rattache étroitement aux ch. 3-9, le chef cuisinier du Pharaon est appelé «Photimar» (leçon du ms. b en 2,1).

6. R.H. Charles, *The Testaments of the Twelve Patriarchs, Translated... with Notes*, Londres, A. & C. Black, 1908, p. 173; Idem, *The Apocrypha and Pseudepigrapha of the Old Testament*, Oxford, Clarendon Press, 1913, vol. 2, p. 290. Dans le même sens, M. Braun, *History and Romance in Graeco-Oriental Literature*, Oxford, Blackwell, 1938 (réimpr. New York – Londres, Garland, 1987), pp. 47-48.

que 10,5 ss. commence par évoquer la jeunesse de Joseph au pays de Canaan et sa vente par ses frères s'accorde bien avec la structure d'autres Testaments, qui s'ouvrent par un rappel biographique analogue. *TJos* 1,3-10,4 est donc un morceau indépendant, qui a été inséré après coup dans le texte premier du discours d'adieu de Joseph (1,2; 10,5 ss.).

Selon Becker, le contraste entre les deux parties est profond. En 1,3-10,4, Joseph est présenté comme le héros qui combat pour la chasteté avec les armes du jeûne et de la prière; il s'apparente par certains traits à un θεῖος ἀνήρ, manifestant dans ses actes une puissance surhumaine (par ex. 6,6-8, où il absorbe impunément une potion magique). Au contraire, dans le texte de 10,5 ss., il n'est qu'un homme comme les autres, qui obéit aux exigences de la Loi et pratique l'amour des frères de façon humble et tranquille[7].

II. LES ARGUMENTS EN FAVEUR DE L'UNITÉ DES DEUX PARTIES

A cette analyse qui accentue l'hétérogénéité des deux parties du *Testament de Joseph*, on peut opposer plusieurs observations qui vont dans le sens contraire. Un premier argument est fourni par l'analyse de la section initiale du *TJos* (1,3-2,7), Comme Hollander l'a montré de manière convaincante, cette section, qui s'apparente par sa forme et son contenu à un psaume d'action de grâce individuelle, sert d'introduction à l'ensemble du Testament – et pas seulement aux ch. 3-9[8]. A côté de renvois évidents à la première histoire, elle contient aussi des termes et des expressions qui se réfèrent à la seconde seulement, et d'autres qui reviennent dans les deux parties.

Un lien particulièrement fort est établi par la notion d'«endurance» (ὑπομονή, ὑπομένω), qui réapparaît dans trois passages «stratégiques»

---

7. La position de J. Becker est adoptée par E. VON NORDHEIM, *Die Lehre der Alten. I. Das Testament als Literaturgattung im Judentum der hellenistisch-römischen Zeit* (ALGHJ, 13), Leiden, Brill, 1980, pp. 71-80. Elle est même présentée comme tellement évidente qu'elle n'a pas besoin d'être rediscutée: «Da heute von niemandem ernsthaft bestritten wird, dass die beiden Darstellungen des Geschicks Josephs voneinander zu unterscheiden und unabhängig sind und inhaltlich nicht zusammengehören, erübrigt es sich hier, auf diese Frage näher zu gehen» (pp. 73-74). Cette affirmation péremptoire est surprenante car, dans la note qui l'accompagne (p. 74, n. 174), von Nordheim renvoie, pour une argumentation détaillée, non seulement à J. Becker, mais aussi à l'étude de H.W. Hollander parue en 1975 (voir notre note 8), qui défend l'unité des deux parties de manière très «sérieuse».

8. H.W. HOLLANDER, *The Ethical Character of the Patriarch Joseph*, in G.W.E. NICKELSBURG (éd.), *Studies on the Testament of Joseph* (SBL, Septuagint and Cognates Studies, 5), Missoula, Scholars Press, 1975, pp. 47-104; voir aussi, du même auteur, *Joseph as an Ethical Model in the Testaments of the Twelve Patriarchs* (SVTP, 6), Leiden, Brill, 1981.

du *TJos*. Elle figure d'abord en 2,7, juste avant la première histoire: «Par dix tentations, il me mit à l'épreuve, et dans toutes ces (tentations) je fis preuve de patience (ἐμακροθύμησα); car la patience (ἡ μακροθυμία) est un grand remède, et l'endurance (ἡ ὑπομονή) donne de nombreux biens». Elle se retrouve ensuite au début de la parénèse qui conclut chacune des parties narratives: «Voyez donc, mes enfants, tout ce que produisent l'endurance (ἡ ὑπομονή) et la prière jointe au jeûne» (10,1); «Voyez, mes enfants, tout ce que j'ai enduré (πόσα ὑπέμεινα) pour ne pas couvrir de honte mes frères» (17,1). Dans cette récurrence, il faut certainement voir la trace d'une même rédaction, qui a voulu illustrer l'endurance de Joseph dans l'une et l'autre des sections narratives.

C'est dans la même perspective qu'il faut relire l'histoire du «combat» de Joseph avec l'Égyptienne (cf. 2,2: «j'ai combattu contre une femme impudente qui me poussait à violer la Loi avec celle»). Comme l'a justement relevé Hollander, la réaction de Joseph face aux assauts répétés de la séductrice correspond à celle du juste persécuté par ses ennemis, telle qu'elle s'exprime en particulier dans les psaumes de lamentation individuelle. Il prie (3,3; 4,3; 4,8; 6,7; 7,4; 8,1); il jeûne (3,4-5; 4,8; 6,3); il s'humilie en revêtant le sac (4,3); il pleure et se lamente (3,6; 3,9; 6,3; 8,1). Il ne faut donc pas voir en Joseph un héros ou un «homme divin», qui utilise l'arme de la prière et du jeûne pour faire triompher la vertu de chasteté. Son comportement dans ces chapitres est celui du juste qui affronte une situation de détresse et qui demande à Dieu de le délivrer.

Le thème de l'exaltation, corollaire de celui de l'endurance, est également commun aux deux parties narratives. Dans la parénèse qui suit les ch. 3-9, on lit que le Seigneur habite en celui qui recherche la chasteté, même s'il est victime de la jalousie, de l'esclavage ou de la calomnie: «non seulement il le délivre du mal, mais il l'élève (ὑψοῖ) et le glorifie (δοξάζει) comme (il l'a fait) pour moi» (10,2-3). La même idée se retrouve dans la parénèse qui conclut la seconde histoire: «Si donc, vous aussi, vous marchez dans les commandements du Seigneur, Dieu vous élèvera (ὑψώσει) ensuite et il vous bénira (εὐλογήσει) de biens pour toujours (…) et vous serez rachetés de tout mal par le Seigneur» (18,1-2).

Le verbe ὑψοῦν sert d'ailleurs de charnière entre les deux parties. De l'élévation de l'homme par Dieu, mentionnée en 10,3, on passe en 10,5 à l'idée contraire de l'auto-élévation de l'homme: «Mes frères savaient combien mon père m'aimait, et je ne m'élevais pas en mon cœur» (οὐχ ὑψούμην ἐν τῇ καρδίᾳ μου). On ne saurait donc parler d'une rupture abrupte entre 10,4 et 10,5. De plus, la mention de l'humilité de Joseph, qui introduit le récit de son comportement vis-à-vis de ses frères, se rencontre aussi dans la conclusion de 17,8: «Je ne m'élevai pas moi-même (οὐχ ὕψωσα ἐμαυτόν) parmi eux, par vantardise, à cause de ma gloire en ce monde, mais j'étais parmi eux comme l'un des plus petits».

Dans le deuxième récit, l'endurance de Joseph est mise en relation avec l'amour et le respect qu'il voue à ses frères (10,6; 11,1; 17,2-3). Concrètement, elle se manifeste dans le fait qu'il «garde le silence», qu'il dissimule sa véritable condition pour sauver leur réputation: «Une fois arrivé chez les Indocolpites avec les Ismaélites, ils m'interrogeaient, et moi je leur dis: "Je suis leur esclave, né dans leur maison", pour ne pas couvrir mes frères de honte. Le plus âgé d'entre eux me dit: "Tu n'es pas un esclave, car ton apparence même révèle ce qu'il en est de toi"; et il me menaçait de mort. Mais moi je leur disais que j'étais leur esclave» (11,2-3). Ni les menaces de mort, ni les coups, ni la prison ne peuvent rien contre la détermination de Joseph de ne pas couvir de honte ses frères (dans la suite du récit, voir 14,2; 15,3). Cette attitude le pousse même à ne pas dévoiler la malhonnêteté de l'eunuque qui, l'ayant acheté pour quatre-vingts pièces d'or, déclare faussement à sa maîtresse qu'il en a dépensé cent: «Bien que je fusse au courant, je gardai le silence pour que l'eunuque ne fût pas démasqué» (16,6).

Ce motif du silence n'est pas totalement absent dans la première partie. On le rencontre dans l'avant-dernier épisode (9,4): «Que de fois, alors qu'elle était malade, elle descendait vers moi à une heure indue et entendait ma voix quand je priais. Et moi, me rendant compte de ses gémissements, je gardais le silence» (ἐσιώπων). Le texte veut-il simplement dire que Joseph arrêtait de prier lorsqu'il entendait les soupirs de la femme? L'interprétation suggérée par Hollander me semble plus pertinente: Joseph, bien qu'il connaisse la passion coupable de la femme, n'en dit rien à personne pour ne pas la déshonorer. L'auteur ferait ainsi place, à la fin de la première partie, au motif du silence, qui joue un rôle central dans la seconde partie.

Quoi qu'il en soit de ce dernier indice, j'estime que les points communs entre les deux parties narratives du *TJos* suffisent à établir, contre la thèse de Becker, leur appartenance à une même rédaction. Elles présentent certes des différences; mais celles-ci ont leur origine dans les traditions utilisées par l'auteur du *TJos* et s'expliquent par les relations particulières que les deux histoires entretiennent avec le texte biblique.

III. Joseph et la femme égyptienne (TJos 3-9):
un développement haggadique de Gn 39,10-20

Pour faciliter l'analyse de ces chapitres, il est utile de les subdiviser en une série d'«épisodes». Le découpage que je propose est le suivant[9].

(1) 3,1-5   Elle lui offre de devenir le maître de la maison.
(2) 3,6-10   Elle l'embrasse comme s'il était son fils.
(3) 4,1-3   Elle offre de tirer profit en secret de sa chasteté, qu'elle vante publiquement.
(4) 4,4-8   Elle propose de renoncer aux idoles et de se convertir.
(5) 5,1-4   Elle menace d'empoisonner son mari.
(6) 6,1-8   Elle cherche à lui faire boire une potion magique.
(7) 7,1-8,1 Elle menace de se suicider.
(8) 8,2-5   Elle veut lui faire violence et s'empare de ses vêtements.
(9) 9,1-3   Elle offre de le faire sortir de prison.
(10) 9,4   Elle se rend à la prison à une heure indue et gémit.
(11) 9,5   Elle se dénude devant Joseph.

Comme l'a bien montré M. Braun, bon nombre des moyens de pression utilisés par l'Égyptienne ont des parallèles dans la littérature hellénistique, en particulier dans la légende de Phèdre[10]. Braun en a conclu à juste titre que *TJos* 3-9 a repris à son compte, en les judaïsant, des motifs narratifs empruntés à l'hellénisme. En revanche, il a sans doute fait fausse route dans l'identification du genre littéraire de notre texte; il a voulu y reconnaître un exemple de «roman populaire», stade intermédiaire dans une évolution conduisant de la «nouvelle» au roman d'amour hellénistique. Pour expliquer l'absence évidente de cohérence dans la chronologie de la narration de *TJos* 3-9, Braun a été obligé d'incriminer à plusieurs reprises la maladresse de l'auteur. Sur ce point, son analyse a été soumise à une critique très pertinente par R.I. Pervo, dont je cite ici la conclusion:

> TJos 3-9 n'est donc pas un récit continu. Il contient des histoires, mais n'est pas une "histoire". Il n'y a pas de séquence logique; le caractère des personnages manque de consistance; la préférence va aux scènes typiques, et non aux événements singuliers; il n'y a pas de gradation, pas de point culminant (*climax*). Ces "défauts" ne sont pas dus à ce qu'il faudrait consi-

---

9. Ce découpage corrrespond pour l'esssentiel à ceux de J. Becker (n. 2), pp. 234-235 et du commentaire de H.W. Hollander - M. de Jonge (n. 3), pp. 372-390. La principale différence concerne la fin du morceau, où je considère 9,4 et 9,5 comme deux unités distinctes, ayant chacune une valeur récapitulative.
10. M. Braun, *History and Romance* (n. 6).

dérer comme un manque déplorable de capacité narrative ou éditoriale; ils sont plutôt l'indice d'une forme différente. Le candidat le plus probable semble être le sermon ou, plus justement, un style homilétique[11].

À mes yeux, l'étude de Pervo apporte une contribution décisive à la compréhension de la forme et de la fonction de notre texte. Ma lecture du *TJos* m'amène simplement à lui apporter quelques nuances et prolongements.

Le caractère typique des scènes est confirmé par le fait qu'elles sont plusieurs fois introduites par les adverbes ποσάκις (3,1; 4,1; 9,4) ou πολλάκις (9,1), et surtout par la prédominance des verbes à l'imparfait. En revanche, je suis moins convaincu par la remarque de Pervo sur l'absence de gradation et de point culminant.

Il ne fait pas de doute, comme l'a relevé le savant nord-américain, que le caractère répétitif des tentations de Joseph vise à éclairer le texte de Gn 39,10: «Jour après jour, elle parlait à Joseph de se coucher à côté d'elle et de s'unir à elle, mais il ne l'écoutait pas»[12]. Ce verset est effectivement à l'arrière-plan des sept premières tentations (3,1-8,1), comme je vais le montrer de manière plus précise. Mais la huitième tentation, elle, se rattache au récit de Gn 39,11-20. C'est pourquoi je suis d'avis qu'elle marque un tournant dans l'affrontement de Joseph avec l'Égyptienne et qu'elle constitue bien une sorte de point culminant, qui me semble signalé par l'emploi de l'adverbe τέλος en 8,2.

Dans chacun des sept premiers épisodes, on trouve en effet un reflet des diverses composantes de Gn 39,10, ce qui n'est pas le cas des épisodes suivants.

- «Jour après jour». Cette indication de temps est à l'origine de la multiplicité et de la répétition des tentatives de séduction de la femme. Elle permet de comprendre l'absence d'enchaînement chronologique. Elle explique aussi la prédominance des imparfaits dans le récit des tentations: celles-ci ne se situent pas à un moment précis, mais se répètent régulièrement, «chaque jour».

---

11. R.I. PERVO, *The Testament of Joseph and Greek Romance*, in G.W.E. NICKELSBURG (éd.), *Studies on the Testament of Joseph* (SBL, Septuagint and Cognates Studies, 5), Missoula, Scholars Press, 1975, pp. 15-28. Citation p. 22: «T Jos 3-9, then, is not a continuous narrative. Although it contains stories, it is not itself a "story". Logical sequence is absent, consistency of character is lacking, typical scenes are preferred to specific incidents and the climax is ignored. These "flaws" do not stem from what would have to be the most woeful absence of narrative or editorial acumen; they do point to a different form. The most likely candidate appears to be the sermon or, more properly, a homiletic style.»

12. TM: וַיְהִ֕י כְּדַבְּרָ֥הּ אֶל־יוֹסֵ֖ף י֣וֹם ׀ י֑וֹם וְלֹא־שָׁמַ֥ע אֵלֶ֛יהָ לִשְׁכַּ֥ב אֶצְלָ֖הּ לִהְי֥וֹת עִמָּֽהּ׃ LXX: ἡνίκα δὲ ἐλάλει τῷ Ιωσηφ ἡμέραν ἐξ ἡμέρας, καὶ οὐχ ὑπήκουσεν αὐτῇ καθεύδειν μετ' αὐτῆς τοῦ συγγενέσθαι αὐτῇ.

- «elle parlait à Joseph». La femme s'efforce de gagner la faveur de Joseph par la parole; elle parle avec lui chaque jour. Cet aspect du texte biblique est repris et développé dans six des sept premières tentations, qui rapportent au discours direct une parole de la femme à Joseph (voir les ἔλεγέ μοι ou λέγει μοι de 3,1; 4,2; 4,5; 5,1; 6,4; 7,3); seule la deuxième tentation n'est pas associée à un «dire» de la femme, mais seulement à un «faire».

- «de se coucher à côté d'elle et de s'unir à elle». Le but des assauts répétés de la femme, formulé dans le verset biblique par deux expressions synonymes, trouve un écho dans chaque tentation, mais y est exprimé de manière diverse[13].

- «mais il ne l'écoutait pas». La résistance victorieuse de Joseph aux attaques de la séductrice est exprimée par une variété de verbes d'action à la première personne, souvent soulignés par ἐγώ. Le refus de Joseph s'exprime de manière active et visible. Il réagit à la manière d'un juste persécuté: il prie, il jeûne, il se lamente, il s'humilie en revêtant le sac.

La huitième tentation, introduite par l'adverbe τέλος (8,2-5), a un caractère différent des sept premières, parce qu'elle a un autre rapport avec le texte scripturaire. On passe des assauts répétés «jour après jour», suggérées par Gn 39,10 (יוֹם יוֹם), à l'attaque finale et ponctuelle racontée en Gn 39,11 ss., qui a lieu «le jour où il vint à la maison» (וַיְהִי כְּהַיּוֹם הַזֶּה וַיָּבֹא הַבַּיְתָה). On relèvera ici que le potentiel dramatique de Gn 39,11-20 n'est pas du tout exploité dans le *TJos*: le récit biblique est supposé connu et ne fait l'objet que d'une brève évocation[14].

L'emprisonnement de Joseph crée une situation nouvelle. Dans Gn 39, il signifie la fin des manœuvres de la femme, qui disparaît du récit. Dans le *TJos* au contraire, la passion de l'Égyptienne subsiste et s'aggrave même, une fois Joseph jeté en prison par suite de sa dénonciation mensongère. Elle tombe malade de chagrin[15]. Mais à la différence des scènes précédentes, elle n'a plus la possibilité d'«être avec» Joseph, de lui parler: elle doit se contenter d'écouter sa voix de l'extérieur de la

---

13. (1) «aller avec elle» (3,1); «si tu te donnes à moi» (3,2). (2) «de nuit elle entrait chez moi sous prétexte de me rendre visite» (3,6). (3) «voulant, quand nous étions seuls (καταμόνας), me faire trébucher» (4,1). (4) «sous prétexte d'instruction religieuse elle venait chez moi» (4,4); «unis-toi à moi», συμπείσθητί μοι (4,5). (5) «Si tu ne veux pas commettre l'adultère, je tuerai l'Égyptien et ainsi je te prendrai légalement pour mari» (5,1). (6) «Le lendemain, venant chez moi...» (6,4). (7) «Alors elle se précipita chez moi, alors que son mari était toujours dehors» (7,3); «Je me pends, ou je me jette dans un puits ou un précipice, si tu ne t'unis pas à moi».

14. Comme le relève justement PERVO (n. 10), p. 21: «T Jos supplies details where Genesis summarizes and summarizes where Genesis gives detailed information».

15. La situation décrite en 7,1-3 (épisode 7) se répète, mais il ne peut plus s'agir cette fois d'une maladie feinte.

prison (la «maison de ténèbres»). Elle l'entend chanter un hymne et glorifier Dieu parce qu'il a «été délivré de l'Égyptienne grâce à une mauvaise raison». Cette prière de louange contraste avec les réactions de Joseph dans les épisodes précédents. Elle confirme que la huitième tentation entraîne un changement de situation: les appels à l'aide de Joseph ont été entendus; Dieu l'a délivré de l'Égyptienne.

La neuvième tentation (9,1-3) se situe pendant que Joseph est prisonnier. La femme lui fait savoir qu'elle le fera sortir de prison s'il consent à combler son désir. Le *TJos* présuppose donc que l'emprisonnement de Joseph n'a pas mis fin aux assauts de la «tentatrice». Mais ici encore, la réaction de Joseph n'est pas la même que dans les sept premiers cas: ni prière, ni lamentation, ni jeûne, mais un simple «mais moi, même pas en pensée, je ne me tournai vers elle», suivi d'une réflexion sur Dieu, qui prépare déjà la parénèse de 10,1-4. En prison, Joseph est désormais à l'abri des attaques de la femme.

Les deux dernières scènes (9,4 et 9,5) ne contredisent pas l'idée que l'emprisonnement de Joseph marque un aboutissement. Selon moi, elles ont une fonction récapitulative. Elles évoquent deux situations typiques. La première, dont nous avons déjà parlé, reprend des éléments de 8,5 et a donc pour cadre la prison[16]. La seconde nous ramène au temps des sept premières tentations; elle dépeint une dernière fois la gravité du danger auquel Joseph a été exposé et rappelle qu'il est redevable de son salut à la protection de Dieu: «Quand j'étais dans sa maison, elle mettait à nu ses bras, sa poitrine, ses jambes, pour que j'aie des rapports avec elle. Car elle était très belle, toute parée pour me séduire. Et le Seigneur m'a gardé de ses attaques» (9,5).

Ces quelques observations montrent que le texte de *TJos* 3-9 n'est pas dépourvu de toute «séquence logique» et de toute «gradation». L'ordre des épisodes n'est pas entièrement fortuit. Le combat de Joseph avec la femme égyptienne passe par deux moments distincts: celui des tentatives répétées et de la résistance de Joseph «jour après jour» (Gn 39,10) et celui de la tentative finale qui conduit à son emprisonnement et à sa délivrance (Gn 39,11-20).

IV. UNE TECHNIQUE NARRATIVE ENRACINÉE DANS L'HOMÉLIE: UNE HYPOTHÈSE VALABLE POUR LES DEUX PARTIES DU TJOS

Etudier en détail la composition de la seconde section narrative du *TJos* (ch. 11-17) excèderait le cadre de cette contribution. Je me limite-

---

16. *TJos* 9,4 est traduit plus haut p. 206.

rai à quelques remarques, qui suggèrent que cette partie pourrait bien relever du même style homilétique que Pervo attribue aux ch. 3-9.

Dans les épisodes racontés dans les ch. 11-16, nous avons aussi affaire à l'expansion haggadique d'un texte biblique. Le texte de départ est ici Gn 39,1: «Joseph, étant descendu en Égypte, Potiphar, eunuque de Pharaon, le grand sommelier, un Égyptien, l'acquit des mains des Ismaélites qui l'y avaient amené».

Ce passage est développé en une série d'épisodes qui s'enchaînent selon un ordre chronologique. Le début de chaque épisode est marqué par une notation de caractère temporel.
- 11,2 «Une fois arrivé chez les Indocolpites avec les Ismaélites».
- 11,5 «Lorsque nous arrivâmes en Égypte». Confié à un marchand, Joseph demeurera chez lui «trois mois et cinq jours».
- 12,1 «En ce temps-là».
- 15,1 «Après vingt-quatre jours, les Ismaélites arrivèrent».

Mais la succession de ces épisodes ne constitue pas à proprement parler une intrigue menant à un dénouement. Le narrateur rapporte une série d'événements exemplaires, qui démontrent l'amour de Joseph pour ses frères.

Le caractère non linéaire du récit est confirmé par une autre singularité. L'évocation biographique s'interrompt en 16,6 (Joseph acheté aux Ismaélites pour le compte de Petephrès) pour reprendre ensuite, après une brève parénèse (17,1-3), en 17,4-8. L'amour de Joseph pour ses frères est alors illustré par deux exemples supplémentaires, tirés de la suite de son histoire (17,4: «Lorsque mes frères vinrent en Égypte...»; 17,5: «Après la mort de Jacob notre père...»).

Cette manière de raconter n'est pas sans analogie avec celle de la première partie. Comme l'a suggéré Pervo, elle s'apparente au style d'une homélie. Il ne s'agit pas pour l'auteur de raconter une histoire indépendante, mais d'enchaîner, sans souci de progression, une suite d'événements exemplaires. Les deux sections narratives du *TJos* se caractérisent ainsi par une même visée: les épisodes racontés, par leur caractère répétitif, ont pour but d'amener l'auditoire à adopter et à pratiquer les valeurs morales dont Joseph est le modèle.

RÉSUMÉ

La présence dans le *Testament de Joseph* de deux sections narratives évoquant la vie du patriarche fait problème. On considère le plus souvent que ces deux "histoires" de Joseph sont hétérogènes et appartiennent à deux phases différentes de la composition des *Testaments des Douzes Patriarches*. Mais les thèmes et les expressions qui les relient entre elles montrent qu'elles se rattachent à une même rédaction. Elles ne développent pas une intrigue menant à un dénouement, mais accumulent une suite d'épisodes exemplaires, dans le style de l'homélie. Cependant, l'analyse des scènes qui décrivent les "tentations" de Joseph par la femme égyptienne (ch. 3-9) permet de distinguer deux phases distinctes: les tentatives de séduction qui se répètent "jour après jour" (développement de Gn 39,10) et l'assaut final (correspondant à Gn 39,11-20).

ABSTRACT

The presence in the *Testament of Joseph* of two narrative sections which evoke the life of the patriarch is problematic. Most often these two narrative histories about Joseph are considered to be heterogeneous, belonging to two different phases in the history of the composition of the *Testaments of the Twelve Patriarchs*. But the themes and expressions which occur in both show that it is more likely that they belong to a single redaction. They do not develop a coherent plot leading to a climax, but are a series of exemplary episodes, in the style of a homily. However, an analysis of the scenes which describe the trials of Joseph by the Egyptian woman (ch. 3-9) makes it possible for two distinct exegetical phases to be distinguished: the attempts at seduction which are repeated "day after day" (developing Gen 39,10) and the final assault (corresponding with Gen 39,11-20).

Université de Lausanne Jean-Daniel KAESTLI
Institut romand des sciences bibliques
CH–1015 Lausanne

14

THE LITERARY FUNCTION OF PONTIUS PILATE IN JOSEPHUS' NARRATIVES

Josephus' remarks regarding Pontius Pilate have been repeatedly scrutinised by historians engaged in piecing together a picture of the political-social context in which Christianity first emerged. The texts, preserved in both the *Jewish War* and the *Antiquities of the Jews*, are generally isolated from their literary context and individually subjected to rigorous historical inquiry. Read in this way, a rather negative picture of Pilate's term of office begins to emerge; a time characterised by clashes between the governor and the people. We see Pilate introducing iconic standards into Jerusalem, appropriating temple funds for an aqueduct, executing Jesus of Nazareth, and eventually being recalled to Rome after subjugating a messianic uprising amongst the Samaritans. We can even begin to fill in some of the gaps, to suggest motives for Pilate's behaviour and to surmise historically plausible explanations for the people's resentment of his apparently heavy-handed conduct[1].

But, I would like to suggest, this kind of *exclusively* historical approach does not do justice either to the historical Pilate or to Josephus' narrative. Historical accuracy was certainly important to Josephus (and I would not for one moment want to deny that these stories are rich in historical material)[2], but his writings are first and foremost literary works designed to produce specific effects and emotions on their readers. Everything about the narrative – the juxtaposition of particular stories, the way characters are presented, and the author's own asides – are all designed to further Josephus' apologetic concerns. What Josephus wants to say about Pilate, therefore, can only be understood if the stories about the prefect are seen as part of the larger narrative. What I would like to

---

1. See for example the treatments of Pilate in E. SCHÜRER, *The History of the Jewish People in the Age of Jesus Christ*, Edinburgh, T&T Clark, 1973, vol. 1 revised, pp. 383-387; J. P. LÉMONON, *Pilate et le gouvernement de la Judée*, Paris, Gabalda, 1981; B.C. MCGING, *Pontius Pilate and the Sources*, in *CBQ* 53 (1991) 416-38.

2. For Josephus' attempt at historical accuracy see *Antiquities* 20.157, *War* 1.3,16 and 7.455. Modern archaeology has confirmed the veracity of many of Josephus' descriptions of places and buildings whilst research into his use of sources suggests that he adhered closely to their substance and main contents. For a survey of modern research into Josephus' value as a historian see especially P. BILDE, *Flavius Josephus between Jerusalem and Rome*, Sheffield, Academic Press, 1988, pp. 191-200.

do in this paper is to look at Pilate as a literary character in Josephus' two works, to see what role he plays in each and how he furthers the individual plots.

I. THE JEWISH WAR

The first question we need to ask is why was the *Jewish War* written? And what effect did Josephus want it to have on his readers? Writing after the Jewish Revolt and under Flavian patronage, the Jewish writer had several motives in writing his account – to explain the tragedy befalling his people, particularly the destruction of the temple; to improve the strained relations between Jews and Romans; and, most importantly (at least as far as his Roman patrons were concerned), to impress on other nations the futility of revolt against Rome[3].

Josephus stresses that the Jewish Revolt, caused by the agitation of a few brigands and exacerbated by the corrupt government of the last two Roman procurators[4], was doomed to failure from the start. Quite simply, Rome was just too powerful. The military might of the imperial forces is stressed throughout the work, from the superiority of its army to the tactics of its victorious generals[5]. But what seals the invincibility of Rome is that it has God as an ally, guiding its glorious destiny[6]. Revolt against Rome is therefore revolt against God, as Josephus' speech to his besieged countrymen makes plain (5.362-419)[7]. The message of the *Jewish War* is clear: the Jews should have quietly put their trust in God rather than attempted to alter his guidance of history by taking up arms. The

---

3. For a fuller description of Josephus' aims, see BILDE, *Flavius*, pp. 75-78.
4. The Jewish nationalists are variously described as "tyrants" and "bandits", τύραννοι, λῃσταί. See for example 1.4,10,24,27. BILDE suggests that the *War* lays an immediate cause of the revolt at the feet of the ever poorer administration of Palestine by the Romans which led to the growth of the war party and tensions between Jews and non-Jews (*Flavius*, p. 74). See also T. RAJAK, *Josephus: the Historian and his Society*, London, Duckworth, 1983, p. 79. S. J. D. COHEN however correctly notes that only the procurators Albinus and Festus are seen as external factors in *War*'s description of the revolt and not a gradual disintegration of governors (*Josephus in Galilee and Rome*, Leiden, Brill, 1979, p. 154). See especially 2.276, 293, 299, 318, 333.
5. 1.21-22, 142; 2.72, 199, 354, 357, 362, 373; 3.70-109, 244; 5.269, 348ff; 6.22; the Gauls were overawed by the strength of Rome (2.362-379), as were other great nations (2.365-379,577; 3.31). Titus' speech in 3.472-484 makes the same point. The pictures in the triumphal procession in Rome show the might of the Roman troops taking Jerusalem (7.139).
6. God is behind Roman successes in Palestine: 3.293,404,494; 4.297,323,370; 5.2,39,343; 6.39ff,110,250,399,401; 7.32,319.
7. See also Agrippa's speech shortly before the outbreak of revolt (2.345-404), and its counterpart, that of Eleazar to his fellow Zealots on Masada (7.323-336).

detailed description of the *passive protest* against Gaius' proposed statue illustrates at an early stage the effectiveness of non-violence and placid trust in God (2.184-203). The story of the revolt itself, on the other hand, is a graphic illustration of what happens when a subject nation rises up and takes on the power of Rome and is a dire warning to others of the tragic consequences to which such action leads.

How does Pilate fit into all of this? The first one and a half books of the *Jewish War* give an extended prologue to the revolt, filling in the historical context for the reader. We learn in some detail of the rise and fall of the Hasmonaean dynasty, of repressive peace under Herod I, of the brutal reign of his son Archelaus, and the people's request to Augustus that they be placed under direct Roman rule. Of the next thirty years, until the reign of Agrippa I (AD 41-44), Josephus reports virtually nothing. The general impression is that they were stable years when the majority of the population were content with Roman rule. In fact, the bulk of the narrative at this point is given over to a description of Jewish "philosophies": the Pharisees, Sadducees and Essenes.

Into this period of relative peace and tranquillity, Josephus presents us with two stories from the governorship of Pilate. The first describes the prefect's stealthy introduction of iconic military standards into Jerusalem, the indignation of the Jewish people, their peaceful six day protest outside the governor's residence at Caesarea and the eventual removal of the offending standards (2.169-164). The second recounts Pilate's appropriation of Temple funds to build an aqueduct in Jerusalem, an angry uproar amongst the people and their subsequent violent death at the hands of Pilate's soldiers (2.175-177). The two stories are quite striking: first in the amount of detail that they contain; and second in the fact that Pilate is introduced abruptly with no extraneous biographical detail. We are told nothing about when he came to the province nor when he left, only rather vaguely that he was the "governor" (ἐπίτροπος). The effect of this is that the reader's attention is drawn not to Pilate's governorship itself but to the events of the two stories.

A closer look at the two stories shows that they have two characteristics in common. The first is their structure, built around cause and effect[8]. An action of Pilate provokes the people causing a Jewish reaction which in turn provokes a counter-reaction from Pilate. This scheme is developed furthest in the episode of the standards; throughout the narrative we are continually presented with a series of actions and reactions between the two actors in the drama, Pilate and the people.

---

8. This was also noticed by LÉMONON, *Pilate* (n. 1), p. 146.

The second common characteristic is that in both narratives the emphasis is not so much on Pilate's *initial action* as the subsequent *Jewish reaction* and what this leads to. In both, Pilate's initial offences are described briefly and serve primarily as catalysts that spark off Jewish reactions. Josephus does not waste time telling us why Pilate wanted to alter the Jerusalem garrison, or how he acquired temple money for the aqueduct. These details are passed over in great haste so that the reader's attention is directed squarely onto the way in which the people react[9].

In fact, the two stories present two completely different reactions. In the first, the people are entirely peaceful and passive; without any hint of aggression they implore Pilate to remove the standards, embracing death rather than the violation of their laws. Pilate, astonished by their religious devotion, has the standards removed. This narrative shows that a passive demonstration showing respect for and submission to the governor could achieve its aim. The reaction occasioned by the aqueduct, however, was completely different. The people showed aggression towards Pilate, surrounding his tribunal and besieging him "with angry clamour". This angry protest with its attempt to intimidate the governor produced a massacre; many were killed by the prefect's troops, others were horrifyingly trampled to death by their compatriots. The final line is heavily dramatic: "cowed by the fate of the victims, the multitude was reduced to silence". This second story shows that an angry protest cannot succeed and will only end in bloodshed and disaster for the people.

It is no coincidence that these two incidents together illustrate the most important apologetic purpose of the *War*: opposition in the form of riots or angry tumults is useless, Rome is much too strong. Only a passive respectful protest can hope to succeed. Josephus repeats this technique later when he juxtaposes two incidents from the governorship of Cumanus, one involving a violent protest in which more than thirty thousand people were killed (2.223-227), the other non-militant and therefore successful (2.228-232)[10]. Later the moral of these pairs of stories under Pilate and Cumanus is given verbal expression by Agrippa in his speech attempting to stall the outbreak of the revolt (2.345-404): even if a governor rules badly "the powers that be should be conciliated by flattery, not irritated", "there is nothing to check blows like submis-

---

9. This is made even clearer by the opening sentence of the aqueduct narrative: "On a later occasion he provoked a fresh uproar..." (μετὰ δὲ ταῦτα ταραχὴν ἑτέραν ἐκίνει...); it is clearly the Jewish response, in this case an uproar, which is the focus of attention.

10. In all, Josephus describes three incidents which occurred under Cumanus' governorship. The third describes a conflict between Galileans and Samaritans which, due to his tardiness in dealing with the problem, led to Cumanus' banishment (2.232-245).

sion and the resignation of the wronged victim puts the wrongdoer to confusion" (§§ 350f).

The two incidents in Pilate's governorship, coming at a time of relative peace, seem therefore to highlight the two options open not only to Jews but to all subjects of the Roman empire: accept Roman rule peacefully and its governors will show consideration, or resort to violence and risk certain annihilation at the hands of Roman troops.

The very next clash between the Jewish people and Rome in the *War* concerns Gaius' statue (2.184-203). Here the Jewish protest has close parallels with that occasioned by the standards. The people peacefully appealed *en masse* to the legate, Petronius, offering to die rather than transgress their laws. This behaviour favourably impressed Petronius, as it had Pilate earlier, and he resolved to delay the statue. With God's help the demonstration finally succeeded (2.186). In this incident the people seem to have heeded the lesson of the episodes in Pilate's administration. The affair of the aqueduct, however, remains in the reader's mind as a warning against more aggressive action. It is this policy, rather than the successful peaceful protests of the standards and Gaius' statue, which is eventually employed by members of the war party with disastrous results for the nation.

These two stories about Pilate probably go back to genuine historical events, but they are presented and exaggerated in such a way that their primary purpose is to underscore the message of the *Jewish War*. Josephus was not interested in giving an account of Pilate's governorship, but was intent on presenting the reader with the two options open to subject peoples – aquiesce to Roman rule and see your ancestral laws safeguarded, or take up arms and suffer the consequences. Quite probably Josephus could have told us many more stories from the time of Pilate had he wanted to[11], but literary considerations meant that he needed only two. The stories are not really about Pilate at all, but revolve around two different Jewish reactions to Roman intervention. Consequently, we learn virtually nothing about the prefect himself. The two stories stand out starkly from the preceeding narrative and dramatically emphasise the major theme of the *Jewish War*.

THE ANTIQUITIES OF THE JEWS

But what about Josephus' other major work, the *Antiquities of the Jews*? What purpose does Pilate serve in this narrative? Is it the same,

11. He was born only a year or two after Pilate's dismissal (AD 37/8 acording to *Life* 5) and was a native of Jerusalem (*War* 1.3). Presumably he would have heard stories about Pilate's governorship from his family and older contemporaries in Judaea.

or is Josephus presenting him in a different way? Again, we need to start by considering why the work was written. Composed almost two decades after the *Jewish War*, the *Antiquities of the Jews* chronicles the history of the Jewish race, presenting a record of its ancient and glorious past to the Graeco-Roman world. Anxious to subdue hostilities after the revolt, Josephus impressed upon his readers the antiquity of Judaism, its Scriptures and the Law, and the respect and favour shown towards it by earlier Roman rulers[12]. The revolt itself is portrayed as a brief interlude in a history dominated by religious tolerance between Israel and its gentile overlords. As in the *War*, the revolt was not something which the Jewish people themselves had welcomed, but was forced onto them by external factors. In this work, however, a much wider set of circumstances and people are held to blame – responsibility lay not only with brigands and the procurators Albinus and Florus, as in the *War*, but also with dissention amongst the High Priests and aristocracy (20.179-181, 213); King Agrippa (20.216-218); a rescript of the emperor Nero (20.184); pagan troops (19.366); and the Roman governors of Judaea. This last group, by continually offending against the Jewish law, are implicated in the rise of brigandage and play a significant part in the country's descent into revolt.

Behind the entire narrative lies a strong deuteronomistic conception of guilt and fate in which the pious are rewarded whilst the unrighteous who do not obey God's law are punished. Josephus is at pains to bring this out right from the very beginning of his narrative; in 1.14 he states that the lesson to be drawn from the *Antiquities* is that "men who conform to the will of God, and do not venture to transgress laws that have been excellently laid down, prosper in all things beyond belief, and for their reward are offered by God felicity; whereas, in proportion as they depart from the strict observance of these laws, things (else) practicable become impracticable, and whatever imaginary good thing they strive to do ends in irretrievable disasters"[13]. Characters such as Abraham (1.256), Isaac (1.346), Hyrcanus (13.299-300), Izates of Adiabene (20.46-48) and many others are praised for their piety and righteousness towards God and are rewarded by long lives and prosperity. Characters who transgress the law, however, are punished – the Sodomites (1.194-195, 202-203), the insolent Hebrews in the wilderness (3.311ff), Saul (6.104, 141-151, 334-336, 378), Solomon (8.190ff), Haman (11.209-

---

12. See especially 1.5, 16, 24; 3.223; 10.218; 11.120ff, 332ff; 12.45-50; 16.31-57; 18.266ff. for the antiquitiy of Judaism and its Law, and 14.185-9; 16.174 for decrees and edicts from Roman rulers showing favour towards Judaism.
13. See also 1.20; 2.28, 107; 6.307; 8.314; 18.127-129.

269), Antiochus Epiphanes (12.248-359), the emperor Gaius (18.306, 19.1-113) and others. Not only individual characters but the whole Jewish race are warned that afflictions would come upon them should they transgress God's law[14].

Again, what part does Pilate play in all of this? The prefect is much more prominent in the *Antiquities* than he was in the *War*. We are told the precise times of his arrival and departure from the province (18.35, 89), and also four events which took place during his governorship. This particular section of the narrative is structured as a series of five disturbances (θόρυβοι) or events which broke out simultaneously amongst Jews in Judaea and Rome and amongst the Samaritans. The first three are linked to Pilate – his introduction of the standards, his building of the aqueduct, and his execution of Jesus, "a wise man". Next, Josephus turns his attention away from Pilate to Rome, first narrating a scandal involving Isis worship and then "another outrage" (ἕτερόν τι δεινόν) – Tiberius' expulsion of all the Jews from the city. The final disturbance returns to Judaea, describing how Pilate put down a Samaritan uprising; an event which led to Vitellius' intervention and Pilate's removal from the province[15].

The accounts of the standards and the aqueduct have not been simply lifted from the earlier work but have been completely rewritten, giving certain themes a very different emphasis[16]. In particular, the strong sequence of cause and effect, and the attention to the Jewish reactions which characterised the accounts in the *War*, have been minimised[17]. Instead, the story of the standards concentrates on Pilate and his actions[18], describing him in extremely negative terms. He is charged with consciously and deliberately breaking the Jewish law by introducing standards with effigies of Caesar into Jerusalem (18.55-56). By this act, Pilate is compared unfavourably with preceding governors and aligns himself with other characters who attempted to destroy (καταλύω) the Jewish

---

14. E.g., 4.312ff; 5.179-180, 185, 200; 6.305; 8.314.
15. Pilate is referred to again briefly in 18.177, a passage mentioning only that Gratus and Pilate were the only governors appointed to Judaea under Tiberius.
16. This has been demonstrated by COHEN, *Josephus* (n. 4), pp. 58-65; he writes, "the natural assumption of continual and detailed consultation of BJ by AJ is unjustified" (p. 65).
17. For example, the initial Jewish reaction to the standards, which took 9 lines to describe in the *War*, has been shortened to 3 lines in the *Antiquities* (using the Loeb edition).
18. The *War* described Pilate's introduction of the iconic standards in just over 3 lines, the *Antiquities* however narrates it in 11. By moving up the phrase "for our law forbids the making of images" in *Antiquities*, Josephus has made it into an enlargement upon Pilate's crime rather than an explanation of the people's outrage.

law such as Antiochus Epiphanes (12.322), Herod I (15.274,281,388; 16.1)[19], or the people of Dora who attempted to place Caesar's statue in the synagogue (19.301).

At Caesarea, Pilate gives a reason for his refusal to remove the standards: "to do so would be an outrage (ὕβρις) to the emperor" (18.57). Although Josephus does not condemn due honour being shown to the emperor it must not impinge upon or supersede honour shown to God and his laws[20]. The ensuing narrative describes a clash between Pilate's stubborn and aggressive determination to honour Caesar, irrespective of Jewish sensitivities, and the determination of the Jews not to allow the governor to jeopardize the peace of the nation by transgressing the law. Pagan innovations could involve the whole nation and not just the perpetrator in divine retribution and so it was worth suffering, even dying, in an attempt to prevent them[21].

The cumulative effect of these details is that it is no longer the Jewish reaction which primarily engages the reader's attention. Although the Jewish willingness to die rather than to transgress ancestral law is still a dominant motif, Pilate himself has become much more important, both his activities and motivation. This ties up with the interest in the *Antiquities* not only in national history but in the personal histories of individuals who played a part in shaping the nation's fortunes[22]. In this incident therefore Josephus shows an interest in Pilate himself as a Roman governor of Judaea. In particular his attitude to the Jewish law is important; an attitude which, in common with other characters in the *Antiquities*, will ultimately determine his fate.

---

19. There are close similarities between Pilate's actions here and an incident in the reign of Herod I recounted in 15.267-291 in which the king introduced games into Judaea and decorated the theatre in Jerusalem with war trophies. In the belief that these trophies were images surrounded by weapons, the people became extremely indignant. Even when the trophies were dismantled and shown to contain no images, however, a group of Jews formed a conspiracy against Herod in the belief that his violation of their national customs would bring disaster upon the whole nation.

20. In his description of Herod I's reign, Josephus shows that by flattering the emperor and influential Romans (here by founding cities and temples) Herod "was forced to depart from the customs (of the Jews) and to alter many of their regulations" (15.328). After they have pulled down Herod's eagle, Judas and Matthias tell Herod that it is less important to observe his decrees (here specifically accepting the Roman eagle above the temple) than the laws given by God to Moses. Later, Petronius felt a similar tension, this time between following the orders of the emperor (Gaius) and respecting Jewish customs (18.265ff). The Jews reply that by transgressing the law they would "incur God's severe wrath – and He even in your eyes must be accounted a higher power than Gaius" (§ 268).

21. See 15.280ff.

22. For example the stories of King Izates of Adiabene and his mother Helena (20.17-48) or the death of Gaius (19.113).

Throughout the following scenes Pilate retreats to some extent. In the account of the aqueduct, the prefect's actions give way to a description of the brutality of the pagan troops and the courage of the people in the face of this aggresssion; both important apologetic points for Josephus. After the so-called *Testimonium Flavianum*, the two incidents in Rome and the incident with the Samaritan messianic activist, Pilate once again takes centre stage. He is called to account for his crimes, his ὕβρις (18.88)[23]. Although this is linked chronologically to the Samaritan incident, it is a sequel to Pilate's administration generally and his actions with the standards in particular. The narrative of the *Antiquities* has repeatedly stressed that an unpleasant fate awaits those who attempt to tamper with the Jewish law. Now, ordered to Rome by Vitellius, Pilate is called to account for his crimes. There is an interesting textual variant in § 89 which reads Ἰουδαῖοι for Σαμαρεῖται[24]. This would have Pilate sent to account to the emperor regarding matters with which he was charged by the *Jews*. Although this does not fit the context and clearly it is the Samaritans who are meant, the textual variant gives the correct "theological sense". For Josephus it is fundamentally because of his crimes against the Jewish nation and its law that Pilate loses his position and only incidentally because of a dispute with the Samaritans.

The subsequent fate of Pilate is left untold. Josephus notes only that Pilate reached Rome to find Tiberius already dead. Gaius, his successor, he tells us, "devised countless attacks upon the *equites*" (to which social group Pilate belonged), "he deprived (them) of their privileges and expelled them from Rome or put them to death and robbed them of their wealth" (19.3). Whatever happened to Pilate, he did not return to Judaea and Marullus is sent to replace him (18.237).

Read in the context of the *Antiquities* as a whole, then, Pilate is portrayed in negative terms as one of the characters in Jewish history whose impiety and insensitivity agitated the people and played its part in fostering the anti-Roman feeling which eventually manifested itself in open revolt. Josephus' insertion of Tiberius' expulsion of the Jews from Rome into the account of Pilate's governorship gives the impression that these years were turbulent and difficult ones for Jews throughout the whole of the empire. Finally, in keeping with the *Antiquities*' deute-

---

23. ὕβρις is often used in Jewish literature of one who will incur God's wrath and suffer divine retribution. For example, Philo of Alexandria uses this word to describe the behaviour of Pilate (*Legatio* 302), the Alexandrian mob (*In Flaccum* 40, 95, 136) and Flaccus (*In Flaccum* 77)

24. MS., MWE Lat; see L. H. FELDMAN, *Jewish Antiquities* (LCL, IX), London, Harvard University Press, 1969, p. 64, n. 1.

ronomistic conception of guilt and the punishment which impious behaviour incurs, Pilate is ordered to Rome to account for his crimes.

When Josephus' reports concerning Pilate are seen in their literary context, therefore, it is clear that they have been selected, edited and arranged in such a way as to enhance the apologetic themes of both the *Jewish War* and the *Antiquities of the Jews*. Although they have some relation to actual historical events, their primary purpose in Josephus' narratives are literary and apologetic.

ABSTRACT

This paper examines Pilate's role as a literary character within Josephus' two major works, the *Jewish War* and the *Antiquities*. In each the presentation of Pilate conforms perfectly to the rhetorical themes of the work as a whole. The two stories involving Pilate in the *War* tell us virtually nothing about the historical prefect; instead, they highlight two possible reactions to Pilate's activities – passivity and protest – and, in so doing, dramatically emphasize the book's major theme. Turning to the longer account in the *Antiquities*, the Jewish reaction is no longer of paramount interest. Pilate himself, both his activities and motivation, have become much more prominent. His hostile attitude towards the Jewish Law is especially important, an attitude which, in common with other characters within the *Antiquities*, will ultimately determine his fate. This ties in with the *Antiquities*' interest not only in national history but also in the personal histories of those who played a part in shaping the nation's fortunes. When seen in their literary context, it is clear that Josephus' reports concerning Pilate have been selected, edited and arranged in order to enhance the apologetic and rhetorical interests of each book.

RÉSUMÉ

Cette étude examine le rôle de Pilate comme personnage littéraire dans les deux oeuvres majeures de Flavius Josèphe, la *Guerre juive* et les *Antiquités*. Dans un cas comme dans l'autre, la présentation de Pilate se conforme parfaitement aux thèmes rhétoriques de chaque ouvrage dans son entier. Les deux histoires dont Pilate est le sujet dans la *Guerre* ne nous apprennent pratiquement rien au sujet du préfet historique; elles servent plutôt à mettre en évidence deux réactions possibles face aux activités de Pilate: la passivité et la protestation; ce faisant, elles soulignent de façon dramatique le thème majeur de l'ouvrage. Lorsqu'on se tourne vers le récit plus développé des *Antiquités*, on constate que la réaction des Juifs n'est plus au centre de l'intérêt. Une place beaucoup plus grande est donnée à Pilate lui-même, à ses activités aussi bien qu'à sa motivation. Son attitude hostile à l'égard de la Loi juive est particulièrement importante; c'est cette attitude qui, à l'instar de celle d'autres personnages des *Antiquités*, déterminera en dernier ressort le destin de Pilate. Cela s'accorde avec l'intérêt que les *Antiquités* portent non seulement à l'histoire nationale, mais aussi à l'histoire personnelle des personnages qui ont contribué à forger la destinée de la nation. Lorsqu'on étudie les récits de Josèphe sur Pilate dans leur contexte littéraire, il est clair qu'ils ont été choisis, édités et agencés afin de mettre en valeur les intérêts apologétiques et rhétoriques de chacun des ouvrages.

Faculty of Divinity Helen K. BOND
New College
Mound Place
Edinburgh EHI 2LX

15

NARRATIVE AS A STRATEGIC RESOURCE FOR RESISTANCE
READING THE *ACTS OF THECLA*
FOR ITS POLITICAL PURPOSES

I

In the forgotten world of the Old Roman Empire, a young woman finds before her all that society has to offer. Anticipating marriage to the city's leading man she becomes captive to the spell of a travelling preacher. Rejecting marriage with its promise of wealth and respect, she vows religious virginity. Enraging her intended, and later humiliating her would-be suitor, she stirs up political persecution against herself. Twice she faces public execution; twice she is miraculously delivered. Spurning the pleasures of riches she travels the ancient world in search of the one who has captured her affection. Adopting his message and life-style she lives out her chaste life as a wandering Christian preacher.

What might be taken to be the plot of a pulp romance is in fact the account of an early Christian, saint Thecla. Her story in the *Acts of Thecla (AThl)*[1] (*ca.* 185-195 CE) has been the focus of critical research for over a century, and while recent work has been informed by contemporary theological issues, concern has focused largely on locating *AThl* within the lived experience of an individual or a community. A more recent trend of inquiry has stirred the debate to consider how readers in late antiquity may have actually responded to this narrative. It is clear that from the beginning reader response to the narrative was ambiguous. For example, Tertullian, the earliest witness to *AThl*, indicates how it was exploited by some to legitimise a practise[2]. In Tertullian's view it was illicit to attribute the text to St Paul in order

---

1. The abbreviation *AThl* is used throughout to indicate that section in the *Apocryphal Acts of Paul* relating the story of Paul and Thecla. See E. HENNECKE & W. SCHNEEMELCHER (eds.), *New Testament Apocrypha*, London, SCM Press, 1974, pp. 353-364; J.K. ELLIOTT (ed.), *The Apocryphal New Testament*, Oxford, Clarendon Press, 1993, 364-374 (numbers which follow, e.g. *AThl* 4, refer to the subsections of the text).

2. "But if they claim writings which are wrongly inscribed with Paul's name – I mean the example of Thecla – in support of women's freedom to teach and baptize, let them know that a presbyter in Asia, who put together that book, heaping up a narrative as it were from his own materials under Paul's name, when after conviction he confessed that he had done it from love of Paul, resigned his position": TERTULLIAN, *On Baptism*, 17 in J. STEVENSON, *A New Eusebius: Documents Illustrating the History of the Church to AD 337*, London, SPCK, 1987, p. 172.

to underwrite the practise of "women's freedom to teach and baptize". Given the trend of "officially" sanctioned reading, and the variety of contemporary interpretations, the question for us concerns how such a narrative could be treated so ambiguously. What enabled certain groups to read *AThl* "in support of women's freedom to preach and baptize", namely, for the political purpose of gaining access to power?

To answer this question I want to propose a reading strategy open to the complex relations of power at work within the narrative. Here I shall draw on Michel Foucault and his work on the socio-political positioning of the subject within the structures of power relations (what Foucault terms the "discourse of power"). This will allow me to suggest two possible readings: one which reads the relations of power as concerned with conserving male privilege (albeit in a new register), the other reading the relations of power as an attempt at the radical resistance of that privilege. Such a strategy will facilitate a number of insights: the possibilities which exist within the narrative for political readings; the place of the narrative in the subtle negotiations of subject positioning – the way certain narratives offer the reader a picture of the social order which subtly shapes their understanding of themselves within that order; and the possibilities for using the narrative as a strategic *cite* of resistance, and by extension as a potential resource within contemporary theology. It will be clear that by reading with attention to power relations, from the perspective of reader-response, this strategy will not be dependent on establishing authorial intent. It is my conviction that it is this very independence which will yield insights into both the use of narratives in ancient theological debates and the use of ancient narratives in contemporary theological debate.

II. READERS RESPOND WHERE AUTHORS INTEND

Lynne Boughton has distinguished two lines of inquiry in recent Thecla research. One line, typified by Elisabeth Schüssler Fiorenza, proposed that the popular and liturgical use of *AThl* between the third and fifth centuries showed that the narrative was regarded as revealed and considered canonical. Fiorenza's primary concern has been to redress theologically the political status of women within early Christian communities, and she maintains *AThl*, together with other similar narratives suggest women's leadership was regarded as canonical even in the mainstream churches, to the extent that "In many regions this book was regarded as canonical in the first three centuries"[3]. The other line of inquiry concentrated on the possible means of transmission from the apostolic age of a model of female leadership. Like Fiorenza, Steven L. Davies has been concerned to locate precedents for contemporary feminist theology, and he finds in the apocryphal Acts generally a link with actual early Christian experience, "[these works] are not simply disguised homilies composed by individuals. They seem to have arisen out of the experience of some Christians with itinerant wonder-working Christian preachers"[4]. Thus he concludes that communities of widows preserved in oral (and written?) form stories of relevance to themselves.

This recent, "theologically orientated" work has opened up interesting and creative avenues of research, locating a species of proto-feminism in the earliest period of church history (cf. Fiorenza). However, while it has been suggestive of radical possibilities, in the end it has not been possible to tie the speculation firmly to the external evidence. The result has beeen a challenge by "historical" writers on the grounds that the author was probably more conservative than these readings of resistance will allow. This challenge has sought new possibilities in the appropriation, by some, of reader-response theory. Several scholars could be cited here[5], but I shall choose Dennis R. MacDonald and Kate Cooper as representing two approaches which reach very different conclusions.

MacDonald, impressed with recent research in folklore, has argued that it is possible to read *AThl* as the written form of oral traditions. While this approach is to some degree compatible with Davies, MacDonald differs, not so much in his concern with oral traditions and their disputed *Sitz im Leben*, but in his steering research away from the search for historical evidence and towards literary associations[6].

---

3. Elisabeth SCHÜSSLER FIORENZA, *In Memory of Her: a Feminist Theological Reconstruction of Christian Origins*, London, SCM Press, 1983, p. 173. Against this BOUGHTON points out that only communities accepting the authority of the bishop were part of the Catholic Church, and no community fitting that definition listed *AThl* as undisputed text of scripture.

4. Steven L. DAVIES, *The Revolt of the Widows: The Social World of the Apocryphal Acts*, Carbondale and Edwardsville, South Illinois University Press, 1980, p. 104.

5. Jean-Daniel KAESTLI (cited in Virginia BURRUS, *Chastity as Autonomy: Women in the Stories of the Apocryphal Acts*, in Dennis Ronald MACDONALD (ed.), *The Apocryphal Acts of Apostles, Semeia* 38 [1986] 101-135) links MACDONALD with DAVIES and BURRUS; Peter DUNN, *Women's Liberation, the Acts of Paul, and other Apocryphal Acts of the Apostles*, in *Apocrypha* 4, 1993, p. 255, includes Birte CARLE, *Thekla. En Kvindeskikklelse i tidlig fortoellekunst*, Copenhagen, Delta, 1980, in a group whose "unanimous conclusion is that the texts attest to women's liberation in early Christianity".

6. Dennis Ronald MACDONALD, *The Legend and the Apostle*, Philadelphia, The Westminster Press, 1983. MACDONALD's thesis is that both *AThl* and the Pastoral Epistles represent competing branches of second century Pauline Christianity, and that when the deutero-Pauline author writes: "Have nothing to do with profane myths and old wives' tales" (1 Tim 4,7), reference is being made to the oral traditions that underlie *AThl*.

MacDonald finds literary parallels to Thecla in the Hagnodice legend, a tale which gives prominence to women and is antagonistic to men: "Both clearly were oral tales about women who broke traditional barriers against their professional pursuits"[7]. Borrowing heavily from Alex Olrik's *Epic Laws of Folk Narrative* (1965), MacDonald locates *AThl* as redacted oral tradition, and proceeds to consider the gender of the storytellers. While the external evidence is weak, his rehearsal of the internal evidence is more convincing: in *AThl* those who hear Paul are "women and the young", or "women and virgins"; the Iconians complain that Paul beguiled their wives; Thecla's mother asks the governor to burn Thecla so "that all the women who have been taught by this man may be afraid". In other words, the text constructs its ideal reader/listener as female, and given the text's sensitivity to women and contempt of men, "If the contents of any early Christian story suggests that its tellers were women, it is this one"[8].

Another approach which considers literary associations is that offered recently by Cooper. She contends that the apocryphal Acts generally and *AThl* in particular contain strong parallels to the ancient romance novels[9]. Now the position of the romantic hero is usurped by the apostle in what becomes a spiritual triangle of husband/lover-woman-apostle. Cooper argues that the conversion of Thecla to continence in *AThl* is, in the wider context of the *Acts of Paul*, a narrative device which propels the conflict between apostle and the symbolic representative of the ruling class of the cities he visits. If MacDonald's structuralism arrives at a women's audience, Cooper's leads her to claim *AThl* is directed at men:

> The challenge by the apostle to the householder is the urgent message of these narratives, and it is essentially a conflict *between men*. The challenge posed here by Christianity is not really about women, or even about sexual continence, but about authority and the social order. In this way, tales of continence use the narrative momentum of romance, and the enticement of the romantic heroine, to mask a contest for authority, encoded in the contest between two pretenders to the heroine's allegiance[10].

---

7. MACDONALD, *The Legend and the Apostle*, p. 20.
8. *Ibid.*, p. 36.
9. Kate COOPER, *The Virgin and the Bride: Idealized Woman in Late Antiquity*, Cambridge, Mass., Harvard University Press, 1996. Against this view BURRUS finds the structures of the chastity stories in the apocryphal Acts of the Apostles to have important differences from Hellenistic romance narrative structure. Significantly she also notes the divergence of attitude expressed to the social order: "the novel and the Christian chastity story ... take extremely different stances, and chastity in particular has a dramatically different social significance in the two groups" (*Chastity as Autonomy*, p. 107). I am very grateful to Dr Cooper for generously making available to me material from her book in manuscript form, and for her constructive criticism of what was originally a postgraduate research paper.
10. COOPER, *The Virgin and the Bride*, p. 55.

Cooper claims that such rhetorical analysis exposes accounts of ascetic practice as performance designed to elicit new allegiances from its audience, in this case men who read of "a virtuous heroine for literary, rhetorical, and even quasi-pornographic reasons"[11]. Despite her claim that contemporary theories of reading[12] may explain how women came to own Thecla as heroine, it is difficult to see why, since Cooper's rhetorical analysis has reduced Thecla to a listening cipher, whose body is strategically inscribed with ascetic values in order to challenge a social order constructed in the image of patriarchy. On the other hand, rhetorical analysis does return us to the ambiguity in the exchange between an author's intention and a reader's response.

Prior concerns mean that MacDonald and Cooper reach widely divergent conclusions. Was it the product of a community concerned with the place of women in an oppressive power relationship? Was it directed at consolidating a new social order in the hearts of a male readership? Locating *AThl* within the literary flow of late antiquity, either as the condensing of oral traditions to writing, or as the intentional mimicking of romance novels, may offer a firmer historical base to the author's theological intent. However, it still fails to explain what it implies, namely the possibility of reader responding to the narrative to underwrite political aims; the issue of Tertullian's censure and a site of contemporary dispute. This, then, is the moment to explore the relations of power within the narrative, and to enlist Foucault to help locate the narrative as a strategic resource for resistance in a way independent of establishing authorial intent[13].

III. POWER RELATIONS: STRUGGLE AND DEVIANCE

The focus of concern in Foucault's project has been the analysis of power and power relationships at work in the modern state. To this end Merquior describes him as an "historian of the present", seeking the conceptual underpinnings of key practices in modern culture, and placing them in historical perspective[14]. Foucault dealt with the specialised

---

11. *Ibid.*, p. 63.
12. COOPER cites Jonathan CULLER, *Readers and Reading: Reading as a Woman*, in his *On Deconstruction: Theory and Criticism after Structuralism*, Ithaca, NY, Cornell University Press, 1982, pp. 43-64.
13. See Michel FOUCAULT, *What is an Author?*, in Paul RABINOW (ed.), *The Foucault Reader: an Introduction to Foucault's Thought*, Harmondsworth, Penguin, 1991, pp. 101-120.
14. J.G. MERQUIOR, *Foucault*, London, Fontana Press, Modern Masters, 1991, pp. 15, 16.

"languages" constructed by those who claim to know, and who by their knowledge wield power over others; a power/knowledge exercised through their ability to define and position "the other". However, he did not occupy himself with these "discourses of power" as ends in themselves; his prior concern has been with the human subject placed in the complex relations of power which through language act to shape an individual's perception of themselves as a subject – their subjectivity. Foucault announced, "it is not power, but the subject, which is the general theme of my research"[15]. This concern with power/knowledge and subjectivity proves useful in considering *AThl*, as the characters in the story may be read as so many subjects captured within a discourse of power which is productive of both their social context and themselves as subjects. Clearly some characters are at odds with this discourse, and their resistance to its demands becomes a dynamic moment, concentrated, for example, in Thecla's assertion of the right to define herself by the canons of another discursive power; a challenge which itself becomes a further moment in the shaping of subjectivity. I shall suggest that Foucault's notion of the struggle which lies at the heart of power relations, linked with his idea of the deviant, the one defined by power/knowledge as other, will focus attention on the relations of power within the text. This will reveal the potential of the narrative to offer divergent reading positions, which are themselves implicated in the subtle negotiations of subject positioning, and thereby locate the narrative as a strategic resource for resistance in the ancient world and for contemporary theology.

Foucault set his face against either a metaphysics or an ontology of power. For Foucault, power is not an essence, a thing in itself; it has no independent existence; it is only ever a function of relation. Power does not precede a relationship, but it is coexistensive with it. Power is denotative. "Clearly it is necessary to be nominalist: power is not an institution, a structure, or a certain force with which certain people are endowed: it's the name given to a complex strategic situation in a given society!"[16] Power is a term for the actions in relationships between partners. Characteristic of the exercise of power is the way the actions of one partner modify the actions of the other. With echoes of Hegel and Kojève, Foucault writes:

15. Michel FOUCAULT, *Afterword: the Subject and Power*, in Hubert L. DREYFUS & Paul RABINOW, *Michel Foucault: Beyond Structuralism and Hermeneutics*, Hemel Hempstead, The Harvester Press, 1982, p. 209.
16. FOUCAULT, cited by Colin GORDON, *Birth of the Subject – Foucault*, in Roy EDGLEY & Richard OSBORNE (eds.), *Radical Philosophy Reader*, London, Verso, 1985, p. 73.

a power relationship can only be articulated on the basis of two elements which are each indispensable if it is really to be a power relationship: that "the other" (the one over whom power is exercised) be thoroughly recognised and maintained to the very end as a person who acts; and that, faced with a relationship of power, a whole field of responses, reactions, results, and possible inventions may open up[17].

There is no need to discuss here how this definition might deal with questions about the place of power in the exercise of violence or the economy of slavery. What is important is that Foucault maintains the necessity for "the other" to be free to act as an essential ingredient in the relationship of power. So he writes:

> At the very heart of the power relationship, and constantly provoking it, are the recalcitrance of the will and the intransigence of freedom. Rather than speaking of an essential freedom, it would be better to speak of an "agōnism"[18] – of a relationship which is at the same time reciprocal incitation and struggle; less of a face-to-face confrontation which paralyses both sides than a permanent provocation[19].

The concept of "agōnism" is important in that it recognises that the power relation is constituted in struggle; it is the struggle against a power/knowledge which is determinative of the construction of subjectivity.

It is at the point of struggle, within the strategies of confrontation, or forms of resistance, that Foucault finds the starting place for an analysis of power relations. In our own history the experience of struggle is embodied in such power oppositions as male/female, child/parent, psychiatry/mental illness, medicine/population, which commonly embrace struggles about the status of individuals both to assert their right to be different, and to attack that which ties them as individuals to their own identity. These are struggles to oppose the effects of power linked with knowledge, competence, and qualification. These are struggles which revolve about the question "Who are we?" In short these are struggles against "a technique, a form of power", that

> applies itself to immediate everyday life which categorizes the individual, marks him by his own individuality, attaches him to his own identity, imposes a law of truth on him which he must recognize and which others have to recognize in him. It is a form of power which makes individuals subjects[20].

17. FOUCAULT, *Afterword* (n. 15), p. 220.
18. From *agōnisma* (Greek) meaning "a combat". DREYFUS & RABINOW note the term implies a "contest in which the opponents develop a strategy of reaction and of mutual taunting, as in a wrestling match" (*Michel Foucault* [n. 15], p. 209).
19. FOUCAULT, *Afterword*, pp. 221, 222.
20. *Ibid.*, p. 212.

So it is by knowledge and the authority to define subjectivity (the way in which an individual is to be rightly understood) that subjects are produced and power is claimed over them in one swift move.

In *Discipline and Punish* and *The History of Sexuality* Foucault developed his general theory of power into specific investigations concerning the actual operations of power and the forms in which power appears. Both books take as the object of power the individual body in society and its inscription by power/knowledge; the former, through institutional surveillance and discipline, the latter, through the systematic questioning and supervision of the individual's sexuality. In both cases the regime maximises power through the production of knowledge about the individual; in both cases Foucault links the dynamics of discursive power to the production and articulation of knowledge.

In *The History of Sexuality* Foucault argues that until the Enlightenment three major and explicit codes – canonical law, the Christian pastoral, and the civic law – governed sexual practice, patroling the boundary between licit and illicit. All had their centre in matrimonial relations. It was with the discursive explosion of the eighteenth and nineteenth centuries that the category of the "unnatural", the perverse, became a specific dimension implanted in the discourse of sexuality. Crucial in the emergence of this category was that it represented a form of power articulated through the discourse of sexuality grounded in a knowledge about the individual. Foucault distinguished the implantations of perversion, of which the campaign against child masturbation is illustrative. In prohibiting the practise of an activity by denying it as "natural" the campaign constituted its pleasure a perversity, and compelled the "deviant" child to conceal its action. The entry of doctors and educators into the tracking of deviance, and their recruitment of parents, impelled both the family and the child's sexuality into a medico-sexual discourse, where,

> The child's vice was not so much an enemy as a support; it may have been designated as the evil to be eliminated, but the extraordinary effort that went into the task that was bound to fail leads one to suspect that what was demanded of it was to persevere .... Always relying on this support, power advanced, multiplied its relays and its effects ... all around the child, indefinite *lines of penetration* were disposed[21].

Thus a standard was raised, in this case a knowledge about adult (hetero)sexuality, which denied the sexuality of the child, reducing it to

---

21. Michel FOUCAULT, *The History of Sexuality: an Introduction*, Harmondsworth, Penguin, 1981, p. 42.

a perversion in need of remedy. The arrival of medics, educators, and ultimately psychiatrists, with their discourses of expertise, implied the production and impartation of knowledge about healthy and perverse child development, against which the child's subjectivity could both measure itself and be measured by those exercising power.

It must be kept in mind that Foucault's critique is directed at the modern period and the mechanisms of capitalist society. Even so, comparable "technologies of the self" can be detected in other periods, reinforcing "both the relations and the forces of social production, manufacturing, at the concrete physical level, docile utilizable social individuals and, at the 'ideological' level, constituting individuals as subjects"[22]. It is also the case that while the specifics in which power is manifest historically may differ, Foucault has laid bare the operations and forms by which power is felt. By constituting "agōnism" at the core of the power relation, and coupling this idea with that of the deviant held captive by power/knowledge, Foucault offers a means of exposing the processes instinctually operating when subjects resist their positioning by rereading their narratives in search of an alternate position. This new awareness accounts for the disjunction between authorial intention and reader-response, in which *AThl* may be decoded and read politically, and it locates Tertullian's censure as a response from within a now threatened position of dominance in the power relation. Such rereading would yield what Foucault would term a strategy of resistance.

IV. Reading Thecla after Foucault

Tertullian's reaction suggests that reading *AThl* as strategic resistance was not only possible but actual in certain communities of his day; clearly the narrative was surrounded with ambiguity from the beginning. To explore this ambiguity I want, firstly, to sketch the general cultural setting of the work in terms of its power relations, before advancing two possible "Foucauldian" readings of *AThl* – one reading the relations of power as concerned with conserving male privilege (in a new register), the other reading the relations of power as an attempt at the radical resistance of that privilege. These readings will plausibly account for the ambiguity of reaction to *AThl*, both ancient and contemporary.

(a) *Power Relations*

Thecla's story is not uncomfortable in its world of wealth, culture and the cruel exercise of power. Her story opens a window to a society or-

22. GORDON, *Birth of the Subject – Foucault* (n. 16), pp. 71, 72.

dered around relationships of privilege. It is a society whose coinage is exclusion and loyalty; on the obverse, opposing the threat, real or imagined, posed by the unfamiliar outsider (Thamyris, *AThl* 15), on the reverse, peopled with dutiful citizens upholding civic values, bonded by the commitments of family ties (Theocleia, *AThl* 20).

Thecla's story is also structured around privilege, with its high ranking officials (Castellius, *AThl* 15), powerful men (Alexander, *AThl* 26) and influential women (queen Tryphaena, *AThl* 36). Typically, wealth in Iconium is named and privileged over anonymous poverty, the mass of unnamed extras are barely visible in the spectacle. It is wealthy Iconian males of high rank who are the cultural icons, those who command the position of strategic strength in the hierarchy of power relations. And it is the preservation of this dominant structure of oppression in the hands of wealthy males that is the objective of the exercise of a power wielded by threat. The turning of Iconian women towards the outsider's message of monotheism and continence challenges the value system of the dominating patriarchal structure (*AThl* 11,15), which in turn threatens the bodies of potential deviants – those whom the dominant power/knowledge defines as "other". This response itself exposes the extent to which the customs and traditions have become institutionalised within the social hierarchy. The presumptions of sexual rights are secure in male minds, and fearfully unquestioned by key female characters (notably Theocleia, *AThl* 20). It is in this way that the institutionalising of sexual customs, so acutely privileging of men, generates a discourse of sexuality, a way of speaking about women which inscribes their bodies such that Iconian men possess their women body and soul. This is the sexuality of political oppression, an oppression which surfaces in the Pauline writings of Ephesians 5 and the Pastorals (arguably writings contemporary with *AThl*).

And so to begin reading after Foucault.

(b) *Reading to Conserve*

Against this backdrop the Apostle Paul takes the stage. For narrative effect he is played firstly, opposite Demas and Hermogenes, and then Onesiphorus; and the contrasts are marked. Paul's travelling companions are "full of hypocrisy and flattered Paul as if they loved him" (*AThl* 1), while Paul "sought to make sweet to them all the words of the Gospel". Onesiphorus, the Iconian, welcomes Paul but sees the truth about Demas and Hermogenes (*AThl* 4). Already the major lines of division are drawn. Paul is recognised by the privileged Iconian as charismatic, stamped with spiritual authority, while he also recognises the lack in the false teachers, who, jealous of Paul, and sensing their lack which he represents, will seek his downfall through the structures of political power.

Enter Thecla (*AThl* 7). Like Onesiphorurs, she recognises Paul's spiritual authority and responds to it. Both Theocleia, her mother, and Thamyris, her intended, are rendered powerless by Paul's charisma (*AThl* 10), and through the innocent virgin the power struggle moves from the arena of the personal to the political. Intending harm, Thamyris seeks knowledge about the stranger and finds in Demas and Hermogenes co-conspirators, willing to expose Paul as a false teacher (*AThl* 11-14). For them the alluring mix of religion and power politics is seductive. But it is no more empowering than political power alone, and in the contest of powers, symbolised now in the battle to control Thecla, strength lies with the spiritual; Thecla remains "bound with [Paul] in affection" (*AThl* 19).

The threat to the body politic compels it to act decisively on the actions of the deviant; the full weight of political power must be exercised on the body, and Paul is scourged and driven from the city. Yet it is Thecla who has come to embody the success of the outsider; the challenge to political power has now become physical in her flesh, and from her flesh it must be eradicated. In refusing the offer to return to Thamyris she condemns herself, and the governor weeps at the inevitability of her punishment (*AThl* 22).

Thecla's deliverance from execution demonstrates the triumph of spiritual authority over political power. In her reunion with Paul (*AThl* 24), spiritual power gains its trophy and its vindication; it has inscribed its followers with a new allegiance, liberating them from the constraints of the prevailing social order, and triumphing over the present godlessness. Thecla's journey with Paul to Antioch, her attempted rape by Alexander (*AThl* 26), her condemnation (*AThl* 27), failed execution and release (*AThl* 37,38) all serve to assure the reader of the ultimate triumph of spiritual authority.

If this represents the texture of a "Foucauldian" reading of *AThl* concerned to conserve male privilege, now in the new register of spiritual authority, what would a reading that radically resists that privilege feel like?

(c) *Reading to Resist*

When Thecla is introduced (*AThl* 7) she is firmly located within an economy of political power, and defined by her gendered status as daughter and wife(-to-be). Her desire for Paul is initially difficult to comprehend; "a man small of stature, with a bald head and crooked legs" (*AThl* 3), he hardly seems the answer to a maiden's prayer. In any case she first encounters only his voice, and the message of the "virgin life". But it is this message which seems to answer to a deep, possibly unacknowledged, desire; Paul becomes the metonymic displacement of her hoped for emancipation; and Thecla comes to pursue Paul, seeking to possess the embodiment of her desire.

Continence was vital to Thecla, not for eternal salvation alone, but for temporal emancipation. The malevolent characters of both Demas and Hermogenes, perform as important literary devices for establishing continence as the heart of the message to which Thecla responds. Contrasted as they are with Paul, they represent the fruit of a short-circuit gospel; they are deceivers, exploiters, oppressors, who underwrite the dominant structure of power, while Paul's beneficient character is the fruit of the gospel of continence, refusing the way of oppression. Continence appears as Thecla's route to freedom; a means by which the oppression of male dominance may be cast off, an important technique of power in a limited female arsenal. This is made explicit by her mother's chilling call to Castellius to "Burn the lawless one! Burn her that is no bride in the midst of the theatre, that all the women who have been taught by this man may be afraid!" (*AThl* 20).

Thecla's refusal to adopt the socially prescribed role of wife is taken for what it in fact is: the rejection of the socially imposed parameters of legitimate womanly behaviour; a rejection that brings with it the inevitable expression of power political (*AThl* 21,22). So, to rescue the perceived rights of privilege, and thereby maintain the social order, Thecla must be sacrificed to the god of the dominant structure of oppression. Yet it is Thecla's God who triumphs. The "single God", who desires continence, delivers a faithful daughter, vindicates her commitment, and underwrites her struggle against the culture of male dominance.

Paul and Thecla are reunited, only for him to abandon her to the capricious Alexander (*AThl* 26), who at turns bids for her love, attempts rape, and finally, "partly out of love for her"(!), has her condemned to "the beasts" (*AThl* 27). Thecla, champion of women's emancipation, is ultimately betrayed by males both of culture and of nature as in the arena she is attacked by male beasts.

If in the first reading Thecla was the catalyst for the struggle between Apostle and state, in this second reading she has become the very site of struggle, embodying in her own flesh the contest for freedom. Her body, inscribed by gender definitions, has been assaulted in attempts to crush the revolt; but her body, inscribed by spiritual resistance, has fought back and stands now as a palpable symbol of resistance.

(d) *Dealing with Ambiguity*

Tertullian's response to the (ab)use of this narrative indicates the plausibility of these readings. His view, that it was illicit to attribute the text to St Paul in order to underwrite the practise of "women's freedom to teach and baptise", lies on an opposite trajectory to any reading in which Thecla's body may have been taken as site of struggle against patriarchy. On the other hand, Tertullian's view is itself on a trajectory of reading in which the holy Apostle is read as challenge to the secular state. Foucault's notions of struggle and deviance help to account for the ambiguity attached to the opposing reading trajectories that were not only possible but appear to have been actual in certain Christian communities of late antiquity.

It is in the context of this ambiguity that the importance of the narrative in the negotiations of subject positioning needs to be considered. How do such readings offer the reader a picture of the social order which is able to subtly shape their understanding of themselves within that order?

Initially it is important to recognise that while the first reading professes to overthrow patriarchy, it in fact colonises it, shrouds its techniques of oppression in the discourse of spirituality, and returns them in the continued oppression of women. In this reading Thecla is reduced to *spolia opima*, the spoil taken in battle by a leader from a leader. It is the second reading that gives her a meaningful role, one in which she herself struggles, and where she becomes her own subject.

Given the way in which Iconian society names and knows its wealthy, high ranking males, it is illuminating to see how Paul and Thecla are isolated as objects of knowledge in order to become objects of exercised power. Little is recorded about any of the major players in the story. Thamyris' wealth is suggested by his self-honouring description as "first man of the city", his offer of much money to Demas and Hermogenes, his impromptu and "sumptuous banquet, with much wine, great wealth and a splendid table" (*AThl* 12,13), and his free access to the governor, Castellius (*AThl* 15). Information is also gleaned incidentally about Onesiphorus, Alexander and queen Tryphaena, but it is the interest attracted by those who would normally be marginal figures, unknown and unnoticed, that intrigues. It is from *AThl* that we have the famous description of Paul, small, bald, with crooked legs, eyebrows meeting and hooked nose, "full of friendliness" (*AThl* 3), incidental detail offered about no other character in the story, attention warranted by no other outsider. Again Thecla, one who should, even would, be another faceless virgin, is called to step forward, to be known by patriarchy. She is defined in terms of her sexual/marital and therefore political status, held in the discourse of politico-sexuality from which she struggles to deviate. The facts about Paul and Thecla are recounted precisely because they deviate, and their deviance positions them within the discourse. In other words, the power of the discourse to define normalcy holds Paul and Thecla captive as deviants, and engages them within the structures of the power relation. Power/knowledge recognises them as "other", as acting (non)subjects on whose actions acting subjects may act. By knowledge power gains purchase and control is extended.

Yet in this struggle it is necessary to inquire where the true power relation is located. Foucault insists that power is exercised only over free subjects, and while Paul may be free, Thecla's freedom (in the first of my readings) is in doubt. And if she can not be described as free, she will not qualify to be described as subject.

AThl narrates an explicit system of power which senses itself under threat, both from the ideas of the outsider and the body of the insider. It is a system of power held in the grip of patriarchy; a system which is male, which installs sexuality within the political discourse, and which exercises its power by threats of actual harm to the bodies of the deviant. However, there is in *AThl* a second power system; an implicit system, traceable through the text, at work in the gaps left by patriarchy, which it seeks to subvert and transcend. It is a power equally manipulative, installing sexuality within the discourse of spirituality. Foucault terms it "pastoral power", "an old power technique which originated in Christian institutions"[23] and contrasts it with political/state power. Foucault's argument that the modern Western state has integrated this old power into a new political shape need not concern us here. What is of interest is his characterisation of pastoral power as a form aimed ultimately at assuring individual salvation in the next world and implying "a knowledge of the conscience and an ability to direct it".

> This form of power is salvation oriented (as opposed to political power). It is oblative (as opposed to the principle of sovereignty); it is individualising (as opposed to legal power); it is coextensive and continuous with life; it is linked with a production of truth – the truth of the individual himself[24].

---

23. FOUCAULT, *Afterword* (n. 15), p. 213.
24. *Ibid.*, p. 214.

Under the Iconian hegemony Thecla represents the status of all women. Held in the power relation constructed by patriarchy she stands as "other", the subject who is not a subject on whose actions acting subjects act. Denied access to power, and stripped of subjectivity, Thecla, and those she represents have become (non)subjects, the objects of power, now seen to be acting in a (non)power relation. It is not so much Thecla's refusal to marry that challenges the political power of Iconium as the arrival of the outsider, it is his pastoral power which facilitates her resistance[25].

Thecla's (non)subjectivity finds champion, and political power finds genuine "other", in the advent of pastoral power, which confronts political power on two flanks. Firstly, as genuine "other" it stands independent of the thoughts and values of patriarchy. It has not been in any sense determined by the Iconium system, and it stands in place for a genuinely free and resistant subject. Secondly, if this is an ideological and external challenge then the palpable power of the pastoral threat (and the genius of Christianity) lies in its capacity to produce genuine subjects, who challenge patriarchy from within.

For the construction of subjectivity *AThl* supplies a twofold strategy of uncoupling.

Firstly, Paul's gospel of monotheism and continence removes sexuality into the discourse of spirituality. By offering individual salvation contingent on individual sexual praxis, Paul strategically uncouples sexuality from the political discourse, inserting it into the discourse of spirituality, only to return it once more to the political, now charged with subversive energy. The personal becomes political and is oppressed in the mundane; but the personal becomes spiritual, transcends the mundane, and returns to resist the political. It is this implication of pastoral power in "a knowledge of the conscience and an ability to direct it" which initiates the process of consciousness raising. This in turn opens the path to genuine subjectivity, and with it the possibility of genuine resistance.

Secondly, the women in Thecla's society provide the practical means to facilitate the uncoupling of sexuality from the economic bonds which tied resistance and maintained the power of patriarchy. Davies and MacDonald both draw attention to the way *AThl* is sympathetic to the issues of women and contemptuous of men: Davies writes of the story

---

25. From this it may be objected that "pastoral power" is to be constructed heterosexual, theistic, and masculine. However, against this I want to argue that pastoral power is not so ideologically specific, and that, for example, it is possible to see a form of pastoral power emerging between the characters of Celie and Shug Avery in Alice WALKER's *The Colour Purple*, London, The Woman's Press Limited, 1992. In this case pastoral power is black, lesbian, panentheist, and feminist.

revealing someone deeply resentful of the male sex and highly sensitive to the difficulties of women[26]. Indeed, men distrust and reject her (Paul is suspicious of her desire to follow him and to teach, abandoning her in Antioch); abuse her publicly (Alexander takes her as a prostitute); and condemn her to public humiliation and execution. Those who might protect her (including Paul) fail, and her family (both actual, Theocleia, and prospective, Thamyris) disown her. Yet Thecla finds a new home and a new family in the shape of continent women, in particular queen Tryphaena, whose dead daughter, Falconilla, Thecla replaces.

V. CONCLUSION

The value of these readings of *AThl* is obviously open for debate. But Tertullian's reaction to the narrative's reception demonstrates that, regardless of whether these dynamics were at work within the narrative, they were certainly at work in the communities which read Thecla's story. It also demonstrates how the ambiguity of divergent readings expresses the highly ambiguous nature of pastoral power. On the one hand, while professing liberation, pastoral power occupies the structures of patriarchy, making opaque its techniques within the discourse of spirituality. On the other hand, the dynamic of the spiritual resists the political and engenders in those whom Thecla represents the strength to refuse. She allowed her body, once inscribed by patriarchy, to be rewritten by the discourse of sexual-spirituality. As such her performance of the rewritten text of her body becomes a site of resistance, in the same way that the subsequent reading of the written text which is her story becomes a strategic resource for resistance (told, perhaps even written, by women storytellers[27]). Whether this resistance was for catharsis or conversion[28] it was a strategy which had, and retains, the potential to be deployed for the benefit of women readers/listeners. It is as such a strategic resource for resistance, liberated from the constraints of authorial intent, that Thecla may be read as a continuing resource for theology[29].

In this essay I set out to consider the complex relations of power captured within *AThl*, and thereby to explore political readings possible from within the narrative. I have avoided making any attempt at retrac-

26. DAVIES, *The Revolt of the Widows* (n. 4), p. 107.
27. *Ibid.*, p. 50.
28. BURRUS, *Chastity as Autonomy* (n. 5), p. 114.
29. See for example Karen ARMSTRONG, *The Gospel According to Woman*, London, Elm Tree, 1986, reproduced in Ann LOADES (ed.), *Feminist Theology: a Reader*, London, SPCK, 1990, pp. 83-88, for her appropriation of *The Acts of Paul and Thecla*.

ing the author's original intention. Instead, using Foucault's ideas of struggle and deviance, I have tried to account for the kind of political reading response which would have provoked Tertullian's censure, and at the same time find ground on which the narrative may be claimed as a "text of resistance" for contemporary theology. Analysing the readings in this way has uncovered their operation in the subtle negotiations of subject positioning. The reading which seeks to conserve male privilege, taking Thecla as the catalyst for the struggle between Apostle and state, betrays its claims of resistance as the colonising of dominant structures and the continued oppression of women in the register of spirituality. Such a reading offers women the subject position of *spolia opima*, and has the intention of producing "docile utilizable social individuals". The reading which radically resists this privilege reads Thecla herself as the site of struggle, her own flesh becomes the palpable symbol of resistance. Now she becomes her own subject, worthy of being offered to women as a subject position able to facilitate resistance. The irony is that both readings are predicated on the operations of pastoral power.

ABSTRACT

This essay considers the power relations portrayed in the *Acts of Thecla*, exploring the narrative's political reading possibilities. A review of recent scholarship gives particular attention to MacDonald's (structuralist) and Cooper's (feminist) approaches; however, neither adequately explains the possibilities for the politically motivated reader response they each imply. Foucault's ideas of struggle and deviance help to account for a politically motivated reading response, such as Tertullian's censure at the narrative's use in support of "women's freedom to teach and baptize". The analysis offers to uncover the narrative's operation in the subtle negotiations of subject positioning, and helps ground claims for the narrative as a "text of resistance" in contemporary theology. Two political readings are offered. Firstly, a reading which seeks to conserve male privilege, and takes Thecla as the catalyst for the struggle between (male) Apostle and state, continuing women's oppression in the register of spirituality. Secondly, a reading which radically resists this privilege, and reads Thecla herself as the site of struggle, her own flesh the palpable symbol of resistance. These readings are illuminated by and in turn illuminate Foucault's concept of "pastoral power".

RÉSUMÉ

Cette étude a pour objet les relations de pouvoir reflétées dans les *Actes de Thècle* et explore les possibilités d'une lecture politique du récit. Elle passe en revue des travaux récents et accorde une attention particulière à l'approche (structuraliste) de MacDonald et à l'approche (féministe) de Cooper. Cependant, aucune de ces approches ne développe de façon adéquate les possibilités qu'elles impliquent d'une réponse politiquement motivée du lecteur. Les idées de Foucault à propos de la lutte et de la déviance aident à expliciter ce qu'est une réponse politiquement motivée; un exemple nous est donné par Tertullien, qui censure l'utilisation faite des Act*es de Thècle* pour appuyer "le droit des femmes à enseigner et à baptiser". L'analyse met à jour le fonctionnement du récit dans les négociations subtiles qui servent à situer le sujet; elle contribue à montrer que le récit peut à bon droit être considéré comme un "texte de résistance" dans le contexte de la théologie contemporaine. Deux types de lecture politique sont proposées. Premièrement, il y a une lecture qui cherche à préserver le privilège masculin et qui fait de Thècle le catalyseur de la lutte entre l'Apôtre (masculin) et l'État, tout en maintenant l'oppression des femmes dans le registre de la spiritualité. Deuxièmement, il y a une lecture qui rejette radicalement ce privilège masculin et qui voit dans la personne même de Thècle le "lieu" du combat, et dans sa chair elle-même le symbole tangible de la résistance. Ces lectures sont éclairées par la notion de "pouvoir pastoral" chez Foucault, et elles éclairent à leur tour cette notion.

Department of Religions and Theology Steve NOLAN
University of Manchester
Manchester M13 9PL

16

MATTHIDIA'S WISH:
DIVISION, REUNION, AND THE EARLY CHRISTIAN FAMILY
IN THE PSEUDO-CLEMENTINE *RECOGNITIONS*

The Pseudo-Clementine *Recognitions*[1], apparently written in Greek in the third century C. E., record, in the first-person style of ancient romance, the adventures of the aristocratic youth Clement of Rome, a kinsman of the emperor[2]. When his philosophical curiosity brings him to Palestine, Clement encounters the eminently respectable religious teacher Peter, a man of wisdom and no few words. Head of what seems to be a messianic sect of Judaism, Peter is in the midst of preparing for an important debate with his local arch-rival, Simon, whom the reader is meant to recognize as the Simon Magus of the Book of Acts. As Clement tells it, the contrast between the two men is discernible immediately. Their private lives tell the story in short-hand form: Simon swans around in the company of an illegitimate mistress, Luna, asserting that he himself is a power above God the creator while Luna has descended from the higher heavens as an avatar of Wisdom, the mother of all things, over whom the Greeks and the Barbarians contend. Peter, by

---

1. I am grateful for discussion of oral versions of the present material to a number of colleagues. In addition to the Manchester-Lausanne seminar, I would particularly like to thank members of the Philadelphia Seminar on Christian Origins and its 1996-97 organizer Leigh Gibson, and members of the Early Christian Literature master-theme of the International Congress of Patristic Studies held at Oxford in 1995, especially Richard Norris, Bernard Pouderon, and Virginia Burrus. I have benefited greatly from discussions with Loveday Alexander, Conrad Leyser, and Susan Stephens, although none of the above bears responsibility for what follows.

2. The Greek original is now lost; various versions survive in translation. Most influential for the West has been the fifth-century translation by Rufinus of Aquileia; on the date of Rufinus' translation, see C.P. HAMMOND, *The Last Ten Years of Rufinus' Life and the Date of his Move South from Aquileia*, in *Journal of Theological Studies* n. s. 28 (1977), 372-429, at p. 428, and now F.S. JONES, *An Ancient Jewish-Christian Source on the History of Christianity: Pseudo-Clementine Recognitions 1.27-71* (Texts and Translations, 37; Christian Apocrypha Series, 2), Atlanta, GA, Scholars Press, 1995, p. 43, n. 14. The date of the original is discussed by M. EDWARDS, *The Clementina: A Christian Response to the Pagan Novel*, in *Classical Quarterly* 42 (1992), pp. 459-471, particularly at pp. 463-464, and J. IRMSCHER and G. STRECKER, *The Pseudo-Clementines*, in W. SCHNEEMELCHER (ed.), *New Testament Apocrypha*, Vol. II, *Writings Relating to the Apostles, Apocalypses and Related Subjects*, trans. ed. R.McL. WILSON, Cambridge, James Clark and co., 1992, pp. 483-541, who give a bibliography and selections from both the *Recognitions* and their sister text, the *Homilies*.

contrast, is accompanied by a legitimate wife so modest that her name is not mentioned, and she appears in the text only when a female guest of the entourage is in need of a respectable chaperone.

The *Recognitions* form half of a Peter-centred didactic diptych, whose complex inter-relationship has puzzled scholars for centuries[3]. At issue, among other things, is the question of whether the *Recognitions* pre- or post-date their partner text, known to scholars as the *Homilies*, which follow a similar and at times identical narrative skeleton, but articulate it very differently as a series of highly developed set-piece theological speeches connected by a tentative narrative thread. The present essay is designed to offer a new approach to the diptych, arguing that if our focus is shifted from source-critical investigation of the philosophical debates which constitute the bulk of the text (and which have attracted the lion's share of scholarly attention), and conferred instead on Clement's own story of reunion with long-lost parents and siblings (which unfolds during the course of the philosophical debate), we may begin to discern in the frame-story of Clement's family drama a device calculated not only to furnish dramatic interest, but also to emphasize the absolute nature of the apostle's truth.

Because the genre conventions in question are those of the ancient romance, the present study is centred on the *Recognitions* as the version of the Clementine narrative which has the clearest ties to the genre. One of the most significant differences between the two versions is the elaboration in the *Recognitions* of the romance of Clement and his family, centred on Books 7-9, which bears a striking resemblance to pagan and Jewish romance, perhaps particularly to late versions of the genre such as Heliodoros' *Aethiopica* or the *History of Apollonius, King of Tyre*[4]. By paying close attention to this generic context I will argue that al-

---

3. In addition to the contributions of JONES, IRMSCHER and STRECKER in the previous note, see F.S. JONES, *The Pseudo-Clementines: A History of Research*, in *The Second Century* 2 (1982), pp. 1-33 and 63-96, reprinted in E. FERGUSON (ed.), *Studies in Early Christianity*, Vol. II, *Literature of the Early Church*, New York and London, Garland, 1993, pp. 195-262.

4. Recent scholarship on the *Clementina* has called attention to this link. M. EDWARDS has argued (*The Clementina*, p. 459) that the cursory treatment shown by synthetic treatments of the novel such as those of B.E. PERRY (*The Ancient Romances*, Berkeley, University of California Press, 1967) and T. HÄGG (*The Novel in Antiquity*, Oxford, Oxford University Press, 1983) is ill-deserved: their somewhat idiosyncratic refraction of the romance sensibility, fused with a curiosity regarding magico-religious arcana, is itself worthy of interest to the literary historian of later antiquity. (N.B. while Edwards follows Hägg in referring to "the ancient novel", the present article adopts Perry's older term, "ancient romance"; I have, however, followed Edwards in using the term "Clementina" to designate the Pseudo-Clementine material, as these are only two of a number of unrelated texts travelling under the name of Clement in the manuscript tradition.)

though the literary art of the *Recognitions* is by no means breath-taking, its author (or redactor?) has nonetheless made a sophisticated use of genre conventions, proposing in the *Recognitions* a family romance which uses to an apologetic end the romance's narrative convention of signalling narrative closure by the reunion of hero and heroine.

This reading sheds new light on one of the most intriguing aspects of the Clementine family romance: the fact that it celebrates the values of the earthly family, standing boldly against the radical break with the ancient family proposed by its closest Christian literary parallels, the *Apocryphal Acts of the Apostles*. Here, the importance of blood kinship as the central unit of social solidarity is asserted in a way which would be far more familiar to a reader of pagan or Jewish romance than their Christian counterparts. One senses that the author of the *Recognitions* could only have been pleased by the stress laid on the sober head of household as the model for ecclesiastical authority which is proposed in the Pastoral Epistles and reflected in other early Christian texts such as the Letters to the Ephesians or Colossians. What we have here is perhaps best described as a conflation of the form and narrative strategy of the *Apocryphal Acts* with the content and social strategy of a more conservative stripe of early Christian literature.

I. THREE CHARACTERS IN SEARCH OF AN AUTHOR

An aspect of the *Recognitions* which has contributed to the view held by many scholars that it cannot be an original piece of literature but must be a somewhat hastily revised elaboration of the *Homilies*, is its striking and somewhat awkward use of first-person speeches to serve the purposes of narrative exposition. The story-within-a-story of Clement's family's disintegration is a case in point. It is revealed to the reader through first-person speeches made by the story's principal characters, each coming onstage just in time to deliver his or her version of events as it is needed. In fact, though it is not handled with any elegance, this is a device which would have been familiar enough to readers of the ancient novel[5]. The summary below will preserve the technique of exposi-

---

5. For discussion of ironic interest in the first-person narrative persona in Greek romance, see K. COOPER, *The Virgin and the Bride: Idealized Womanhood in Late Antiquity*, Cambridge, MA, Harvard University Press, 1996, pp. 32ff. On related issues, see S. BARTSCH, *Decoding the Ancient Novel: The Reader and the Role of Description in Heliodoros and Achilles Tatius*, Princeton, Princeton University Press, 1989, and S. GOLDHILL, *Foucault's Virginity: Ancient Erotic Fiction and the History of Sexuality*, Cambridge, Cambridge University Press, 1995.

tion by reporting these speeches more or less in full, but it should be remembered the an ancient audience would have found the mannered elaboration less jarring – in fact more pleasing – than it sounds to a modern ear.

Very soon we are in the territory of the studied set piece, but the initial opening for the narrative seems innocent enough. When the apostle Peter, having made reference to his own status as an orphan, asks his new friend Clement, arch-narrator of the *Recognitions,* about his own family, Clement reports his own answer back to the reader in first person.

> Then said Peter, "Is there no one of your family surviving?" I answered, "There are indeed many powerful men, coming from the stock of Caesar; for Caesar himself gave a wife to my father, as being his relative, and educated along with him, and of a suitably noble family. By her my father had twin sons, born before me, not very like one another, as my father told me, for I never knew them. But indeed I have not a distinct recollection even of my mother; but I cherish the remembrance of her face, as if I had seen it in a dream. My mother's name was Matthidia, my father's Faustinianus; my brothers', Faustinus and Faustus. Now, when I was barely five years old, my mother saw a vision – so I learned from my father – by which she was warned that, unless she speedily left the city with her twin sons, and was absent for ten years, she and her children should perish by a miserable fate" (R VII, 8)[6].

With an immediacy that betrays an incomplete grasp of the narrative art on the part of our author, Peter is separated from Clement directly after this conversation, and encounters the beggar-woman Matthidia, whom he berates for her unwillingness to work for a living.

Moving to another level of narrative remove, the arch-narrator reports the following story of Matthidia's family tragedy in her own words, although Clement would not have been present when she told it to Peter. As she speaks, the reader immediately "places" her version of the story in relation to what has already been recounted:

> Being born of noble parents, and having become the wife of a suitably powerful man, I had two twin sons, and after them one other. But my husband's brother was vehemently inflamed with unlawful love towards me;

---

6. Citations from the *Recognitions* here and below are taken from the translation of T. SMITH, *The Ante-Nicene Fathers,* vol. VIII, repr. Grand Rapids, Mich., William B. Eerdmans, 1978, pp. 73-211. For the sake of the wider readership I have drawn citations from the best and most recent existing translations throughout the present article. The standard edition of the *Recognitions* is B. REHM, *Die Pseudoklementinen. II. Rekognitionen, in Rufins Übersetzung,* 2nd ed. rev. G. STRECKER, Berlin, Akademie Verlag, 1994. On the textual basis of Rehm's edition, see JONES, *An Ancient Jewish Christian Source* (n. 2), p. 39, n. 1; Jones also offers an assessment of the textual basis of Smith's translation at p. 31, n. 141.

> and as I valued chastity above all things, and would neither consent to so great wickedness, nor wished to disclose the business of his brother, I considered whether in any way I could escape unpolluted, and yet not set brother against brother, and so bring the whole race of a noble family to disgrace. I made up my mind, therefore, to leave my country with my two twins, until the incestuous love should subside, which the sight of me was fostering and inflaming; and I thought our other son should remain to comfort his father to some extent (R VII, 15).

What happens next will come as no surprise. Not only does Peter bring Matthidia to the ship where Clement is waiting, and reunite the two, but into the bargain he discovers that two of his other disciples are in fact the twins, whom she had lost sight of during her adventures.

There is only one unfortunate aspect of the recovery, Peter confesses: now that the three young noblemen have accepted baptism, they are no longer able to eat at the table of the gentiles and thus there can be no banquet of family reunion. Matthidia, however, counters this setback by urging that she be baptized as quickly as possible, since while the gods of the Romans have caused her only misery, the God of the Hebrews has restored to her her lost sons.

The story takes on yet another facet on the morning after Matthidia's baptism, when Peter and the three brothers befriend Faustinianus, an old workman of astrological inclinations, who wishes to engage them in a discussion of providence and determinism. To illustrate the truth of his position, he brings into discussion the astrological chart of his long-lost wife.

> "...She had Mars with Venus above the centre, and the moon setting in the houses of Mars and the confines of Saturn. Now this configuration leads women to be adulteresses, and to love their own slaves, and to end their days in foreign travel and in waters. And this has so come to pass. For she fell in love with her slave, and fearing at once danger and reproach, she fled with him, and going abroad, where she satisfied her love, she perished in the sea." Then I answered, "How do you know that she cohabited with her slave abroad, and died in his society?" Then the old man said, "I know it with perfect certainty; not indeed that she was married to the slave, as indeed I had not even discovered that she loved him. But after she was gone, my brother gave me the whole story, telling me that first she had loved himself; but he, being honourable as a brother, would not pollute his brother's bed with the stain of incest. But she, being both afraid of me, and unable to bear the unhappy reproaches (and yet she should not be blamed for that to which her genesis compelled her), pretended a dream, and said to me, "Some one stood by me in a vision, who ordered me to leave the city without delay with my two twins." When I heard this, being anxious for her safety and for that of my sons, I immediately sent her away and the children, retaining with myself one who was younger. For this she said that he had permitted who had given her warning in her sleep (R IX, 32-33).

There are two tensions here. First, that between the workman's version of the family saga and those to which the reader is already privy. Secondly, the tension between his commitment to what the text presents as the learned nonsense of astral determinism and the reader's ironic knowledge that the patent falsity of his understanding of events mimics the falsity of the determinism to which he is so fervently committed. Peter, Clement, and the reader are all aware that Matthidia's story is not at all what her husband believes it to be.

But Peter's reaction to the story makes a peculiarly Christian use of the irony. In his unwillingness to allow a direct encounter between Clement and the workman, Peter sharpens our author's focus on the issue of mediated and unmediated narrative, which has characterized the presentation of first- and second-hand refractions to which the reader has already been exposed. It is an intervention calculated to assert the apostle's privilege as mediator of truth:

> Then I, Clement, understanding that he perchance was my father, was drowned in tears, and my brothers also were ready to rush forward and disclose the matter; but Peter restrained them, saying, "Be quiet, until I give you permission." Therefore Peter, answering, said to the old man, "What was the name of your younger son?" And he said, "Clement." Then Peter: "If I shall this day restore to you your most chaste wife and your three sons, will you believe that a modest mind can overcome unreasonable impulses, and that all things that have been spoken by us are true, and that genesis is nothing?" Then said the old man: "As it is impossible for you to perform what you have promised, so it is impossible that anything can take place apart from genesis" (R IX, 34).

Drawing on the kaleidoscope of stories he, and we, have already heard, Peter takes advantage of the audience gathered for his debate with the old astrologer to stage the most dramatic of the "recognitions" which lend their title to the larger text.

> He turned to the crowds, and thus began: "This person whom you see, O men, in this poor garb, is a citizen of the city of Rome, descended of the stock of Caesar himself. His name is Faustinianus, He obtained as his wife a woman of the highest rank, Matthidia by name. By her he had two sons, two of whom were twins; and the one who was the younger, whose name was Clement, is this man!" When he said this, he pointed to me with his finger.....But as soon as Peter pronounced our names, all the old man's limbs weakened, and he fell down in a swoon (R IX, 35).

Thus, most graphically and intimately, does Peter demonstrate to Faustinianus that he has misunderstood not only the truth about his wife's disappearance, but the wider philosophical truth of divine providence as the mechanism governing the universe. The artificiality of the scene reflects in microcosm the contrived quality of the *Recognitions* as a didactic text.

As we will see below, the approach here to division and reunion within the family draws copiously on the narrative devices of pagan and Jewish romance, particularly in its use of marital reunion to signal narrative closure. Broadly speaking, the narrative of a married or betrothed couple of high rank from one of the great cities of the Roman empire, who are separated through shipwreck, a prophetic dream, flight from incest, mistaken identity, or a combination thereof, constitutes the narrative core of Greek romance[7]. Not even the religious and philosophical debate of the *Recognitions* distinguishes it from its pagan counterparts if we remember the philosophical debates of the Egyptian priest Kalasiris in Heliodoros' *Aethiopica*, a text to which we will return below.

All of the Greek romances, with the exception of Longus' second-century *Daphnis and Chloe*, contain the same kinds of travel, including, typically, shipwreck, capture by bandits, sale into slavery, adoption of a false identity, and repeated attempts to evade the sexual advances of a powerful suitor, that we have seen above. In each of these cases, the hero or heroine's sexual magnetism and near-escape from seduction (or, in the particularly salacious tales, failure to escape) serve to heighten the reader's anticipation of the nuptial reunion at the story's close.

A number of texts share the mechanism of the "recognition", well-suited as it is to the exploration of how the self fragments and is re-integrated as the protagonist passes out of, and returns to, the context in which his or her identity is grounded and has meaning. Classic is the ending of Longus' *Daphnis and Chloe*, in which Daphnis, a shepherd from the hinterland of Mytilene, discovers that he had been exposed as an infant, and is restored to his rightful parents, one of the noblest families of the locality. A search is made for the parents of his heroine, the shepherdess Chloe, in hope that his new-found high status will not prove an obstacle to their union in marriage. All the gentry of Mytilene are invited to a banquet, at which the birth tokens which were left with Chloe when she was exposed, are carried about on a tray for "the best of the Mytileneans" to study, in hope that some may recognize them. Indeed, the honourable Megacles admits to being her father, and sends for his wife so that mother and daughter may be reunited; this in turn means that Chloe and Daphnis are able to make an honourable marriage on the following day[8].

---

7. A succinct definition of the genre is given by B.P. REARDON in his edited volume of *Collected Ancient Greek Novels*, Berkeley, University of California Press, 1989, p. 2.

8. LONGUS, *Daphnis and Chloe*, 4, 36 and 4, 39.

The narrative closure of marriage in romance also expresses a public and civic function. This is perhaps best visible in Chariton's *Chaereas and Callirhoe*, thought by many to have been the first of the Greek romances, written perhaps as early as the first century B.C.E., which describes the public rejoicing that explodes when the two rival great men of the city of Syracuse allow their children to wed:

> The whole meeting rushed from the theatre; the young men went off to find Chaereas, the council and archons escorted Hermocrates, and the Syracusans' wives too went to his house to attend the bride. The sound of the marriage hymn pervaded the city, the streets were filled with garlands and torches, porches were wet with wine and perfume. The Syracusans celebrated this day even more joyously than the day of their victory[9].

This is precisely the ideology of civic marriage to which texts such as the *Apocryphal Acts* show hostility, but which the *Clementina* seem delighted to invoke without comment, smoothing over the tension between the faith group and the family group as competing claimants on the loyalty of the individual. We will see below that the issue of allegiance to, and reunion with, the earthly family is a point of divergence in early Christian fiction, attesting the elasticity[10] of the genre, and our own uncertainty about how its apologetic strategies should be understood.

II. Matthidia's Wish

Although each member of Clement's family must make the crossing from the gentile to the faithful fold independently and of his or her own accord, each of the five looks for reunion spiritual as well as material with the rest of the family, as their identities are progressively revealed. Discovery and "recognition" here have an allegorical, gnostic meaning, as each in turn discovers his or her true identity more or less at the point of crossing the divide. It is not that the narrative requires us to be unaware of the tension between family and faith group, but rather that the tension is inverted, with the earthly family standing as a multi-valent double for the "family" of faith. In Book Six, more or less directly before the recognitions begin, Peter sets the stage for the *Recognitions*' ironic treatment of the distinction between heavenly and earthly families

---

9. Chariton, *Chaereas and Callirhoe*, 1, 1, 12-13 (tr. Reardon, in *Collected Ancient Greek Novels* [n. 7]).
10. "Substantial fluidity" is how R.I. Pervo, *Early Christian Fiction*, in J.R. Morgan and R. Stoneman, *Greek Fiction: The Greek Novel in Context*, London, Routledge, 1994, pp. 239-254, puts it, at p. 252.

by including, in his teaching on the knowledge and love of God, the following caution:

> Then let us consider carefully in the next place, what reason we have for loving our parents. For this cause, it is said, we love them, because they seem to be the authors of our life. But our parents are not the authors of our life, but the means of it. For they do not bestow life, but afford the means of entering this life; while the one and sole author of life is God (R VI, 6).

The way this substitution of God for parent as primary claimant is handled is gently humorous rather than harshly dramatic. Thus, for example, a scene in which Clement and his brothers, having met but not yet recognized the old man who will be revealed to be their biological father, become entangled in a progressively complicated series of *parapraxes* while attempting to engage him in debate over providence and determinism:

> When the old man had said this, I Clement said to him: "Hear, my father: if my brother Niceta bring you to acknowledge that the world was not governed without the providence of God, I shall be able to answer you in that part which remains concerning the genesis; for I am well acquainted with this doctrine." And when I had thus spoken, my brother Aquila said: "What is the use of our calling him father, when we are commanded to call no man father upon earth?" (cf. Matt. 23, 9) Then, looking to the old man, he said, "Do not take it amiss, my father, that I have found fault with my brother for calling you father, for we have a precept not to call anyone by that name." When Aquila said that, all the assembly of the bystanders, as well as the old man and Peter, laughed. And when Aquila asked the reason of their all laughing, I said to him: "Because you yourself do the very thing which you find fault with in another; for you called the old man father." But he denied it, saying: "I am not aware that I called him father." Meantime Peter was moved with certain suspicions, as he told us afterwards; and looking to Niceta, he said, "Go on with what you have proposed" (R VIII, 8).

The triangle here between biological father and father in heaven is made explicit by the reference to Matthew 23, 9. At the same time, the progressive recognition of the biological father Faustinianus serves as a metaphor for the slow progress of the soul toward a recognition of the heavenly father, although the reader has already been warned at *Recognitions* 6, 6 that the knowledge of god is more difficult and arduous than the knowledge of mere earthly parents. The metaphor is complicated even further by the presence of Peter, the spiritual father, who signals his own superior understanding of what is at stake in the scene, but, acting as mediator in the family's process of self-recognition, waits to reveal his own knowledge for a more opportune moment.

Similarly, a positive if slightly chiding model is offered for how family members should view one another's status with regard to baptism both implicitly, through the story of Clement's family as each new member is discovered and encouraged to be reunited with the others in baptism, and explicitly, through Peter's comment on Matthidia's own view of baptism, when she first asks immediately to be united with the God who has reunited her to her son, and adds that she would like to request baptism equally for a kind woman of Judea who took her in when she was lost and distressed. Our narrator, Clement, reports Peter's pleasure in Matthidia's great faith, and adds,

> Then said I: "I pray you, my lord Peter, tell me what is the declaration which you say afforded you evidence of her faith?" Then Peter: "It is her asking that her hostess, whose kindnesses she wish to requite, may be baptised along with her. Now she would not ask that this grace be bestowed upon her whom she loves, unless she believed that there is some great boon in baptism. Whence, also, I find fault with very many, who, when they are themselves baptised and believe, yet do nothing worthy of faith with those whom they love, such as wives, or children, or friends, whom they do not exhort to that which they themselves have attained as they would do if indeed they believed that eternal life is thereby bestowed" (R VII, 35).

Thus Matthidia's innocent readiness to see her own Roman paganism and her friend's Judaism assimilated to the faith of her long-lost sons is seen as a sign both of her capacity for friendship and of her faith in the *reality* of the salvation which has already come to Clement and his brothers. The reader is invited to imagine that the boundaries which the new religious affiliation exacts are only serious obstacles to those who are unwilling or unable to see matters according to the trusting, affectionate zealotry exemplified by Matthidia.

But by his very praise of Matthidia, Peter reminds the reader that not all Christians are able to co-mingle the fellowship of faith with the preexisting network of family and friendship. However well-accepted the "family values" of the Pastoral Epistles or the Letter to the Ephesians may have been in practice, the Christian literary imagination was well-saturated with the implications of Mark 10, 29-30 and its parallels: "I promise you, everyone who has forsaken home, or brothers, or sisters, or mother, or children, or lands for my sake and for the sake of the gospel ... in the world to come, he will receive eternal life" (*RSV*; cf. Mt 19, 29-30; Lk 18, 29-30)[11].

---

11. On the role of *enkrateia* in the apocryphal acts, see Y. TISSOT, *Encratisme et Actes apocryphes*, in F. BOVON ET ALII (eds.), *Les Actes apocryphes des Apôtres: Christianisme et monde païen*, Geneva, Labor et Fides, 1981, pp. 109-119. Now historiographically central is the hypothesis of V. BURRUS (*Chastity as Autonomy: Women in the Stories of the Apocryphal Acts*, Lewiston, NY and Queenston, Ontario, Edwin Mellen Press, 1987) in

The *Apocryphal Acts* evince in its most pointed form the view that when faced by the polarity between heavenly and earthly families the Christian should turn away from the affections, and even the well-being, of pagan family members. Across the *Apocryphal Acts*, the recurrent pattern of conversion to Christianity, in which a spiritual triangle forms between a woman, her husband or suitor, and the apostle whose preaching she wishes to follow, serves as an emblem of the transfer of allegiance from the pagan family to the Christian "family". At issue in these triangles is usually the woman's rejection of the earthly advances of her husband/suitor: she prefers to show her spiritual loyalty to Christ and to his representative, her spiritual mentor, by eschewing carnality (in the form of marital chastity) for continence. I have argued elsewhere that whatever the encratite or other views of the particular authors or communities who may have produced them, the rivalry between apostle and marriage-partner (husband or fiancé) over the allegiance of the heroine has less to do with virginity than with apologetics – that is to say, with an invitation to a reader to follow the heroine in transferring his or her allegiance from the civic leadership of the ancient city to the Christian bishop and his clergy[12].

The relatively benign version of the phenomenon can be seen in the second-century *Acts of Paul and Thecla*, in which Theocleia, Thecla's mother, is mocked for siding with her daughter's jilted fiancé, when the daughter falls in love with the preaching of Paul of Tarsus, and refuses an advantageous marriage[13]. When mother and fiancé realize the gravity of what Thecla intends, the response of the girl herself is supremely uninterested:

> And those who were in the house wept bitterly, Thamyris for the loss of a wife, Theocleia for that of a daughter, the maidservants for that of a mistress. So there was a great confusion of mourning in the house. And while all this was going on (all around her) Thecla did not turn away, but gave her whole attention to Paul's word[14].

---

dialogue with the work of S.L. DAVIES (*The Revolt of the Widows: The Social World of the Apocryphal Acts*, Carbondale and Edwardsville, Southern Illinois University Press, 1980) and D.R. MACDONALD (*The Legend and the Apostle: The Battle for Paul in Story and Canon*, Philadelphia, Westminster Press, 1983). A recent and commented bibliography on women and continence in the Apocryphal Acts, including responses to Burrus, runs through the footnotes of J. BREMMER, *Women in the Apocryphal Acts of John*, in ID. (ed.), *The Apocryphal Acts of John*, Kampen, Kok Pharos, 1995, pp. 38-56.

12. This hypothesis is discussed at greater length in COOPER, *The Virgin and the Bride* (n. 5), pp. 65-67.

13. *Acts of Paul and Thecla*, 8-9. The standard Greek text is that of R.A. LIPSIUS and M. BONNET, *Acta Apostolorum Apocrypha*, vol. I, Leipzig, Mendelssohn, 1891, pp. 235-272, here, pp. 241-242.

14. *Acts of Paul and Thecla*, 10 (tr. SCHNEEMELCHER, in SCHNEEMELCHER, *New Testament Apocrypha* [n. 2], p. 241; LIPSIUS-BONNET I, 242-243).

There is little interest here for a mother's sense of loss at her daughter's betrayal; certainly we are far from the affectionate Matthidia's attempt to reconcile conflicting claims through a policy of mass conversion.

Similarly, the third-century *Acts of Andrew* record the heroine Maximilla's pointed lack of sympathy for her husband Aegeates, as he plagues her with anxious questions in order to find out what has gone wrong with their marriage. His attempt to discover why she has refused the conjugal bed, once she has been converted to the continent life without consulting her husband thanks to the preaching of the apostle Andrew, meets with an icy refusal even to attempt to share with him the joys of her new-found conversion. The language in which she expresses her conversion ("I am in love, Aegeates") draws on the same idea of divine *erôs* that is present in the Hellenistic Jewish novel of Joseph and Aseneth, to which we will return below, but in this case it is made fairly clear that if there is an earthly embodiment of her otherworldly love, it is not her legitimate husband but the unmarried visitor, Andrew.

But the hostility to the family in these texts can also take a more poisonous form. More austere, for example, is a later instance in the saga of Maximilla and Aegeates, in which, in a touch of magic realism, Aegeates discovers that his newly continent wife has been paying a servant girl to impersonate her in the marriage bed over a period of months, without his ever suspecting. First Aegeates begs Maximilla abjectly to return to him: "I cling to your feet, I who have been your husband now for twelve years, who always revered you as a goddess and still do." Maximilla, however, shows little pity for her husband, and even less for the servant girl whom she had taken as an accomplice when, in a bizarre attempt to repair his marriage, the husband has the girl subjected to a slow and painful death by dismemberment on hearing that she has begun to tell insulting tales about her mistress in the scullery[15]. Gregory of Tours' Epitome of the *Acts of Andrew* adds a similarly bleak episode: when the Christian youth Sostratus comes to him to complain of a mother whose affections towards him have taken an incestuous turn, the apostle sees to it that the offending parent is struck by lightning[16].

The gratuitous violence of these scenes jars the modern sensibility, but it is presumably an attempt to counter Christian fears about the

---

15. *Passion of Andrew* 22, tr. MacDonald, text and translation in D.R. MacDonald, *The Acts of Andrew and the Acts of Andrew and Matthias in the City of the Cannibals* (Texts and Translations, 33; Christian Apocrypha Series, 1), Atlanta, Ga, Scholars Press, 1990, here, p. 35. See also J.-M. Prieur and W. Schneemelcher, *The Acts of Andrew*, in Schneemelcher, *New Testament Apocrypha* (n. 2), pp. 101-151.

16. Gregory of Tours, *Liber de miraculis* 4 (B. H. L. 430), text and translation in MacDonald, *Acts*, pp. 190-195.

collision of allegiances which many faced in reality. That the agonizing tension between earthly and heavenly families was not merely a figure of the imagination is clear from the prison journal of the literate Christian convert Vibia Perpetua, composed circa 203 at Carthage. The journal records the attempt made by the father of a Christian laywoman in her early twenties, held in prison awaiting martyrdom, to persuade his daughter to recant, in the knowledge that a gruesome execution is her lot if she refuses. Perpetua's response is obdurate. Pointing to a water-vessel, she argues that she can no more cease being called a Christian than the water-vessel can cease to be called what it is. Perpetua claims a certainty about her identity which might have surprised the author of the *Recognitions*, and which prompts her anxious father to rage. Only after the event does she betray a passing hint of compassion for his anxiety: "I was sorry for my father's sake because he alone of all my family would be unhappy to see me suffer"[17]. Matthidia's glib willingness to suppress religious difference – indeed, to dispense altogether with inconvenient religious identities – for the sake of family affect and friendship, can perhaps best be understood as the opposite side of the same coin. Matthidia's is a wishful reconciliation, in which the father happily follows his offspring to Christian certainty, rather than confronting the bewildering abyss faced by the father of Perpetua.

Matthidia's (fictional) certainty is equal to Perpetua's, yet she seems blissfully unaware of the hostility of the *Apocryphal Acts* to the earthly family's bonds and obediences, or the painful certainty of Perpetua that the conflicting allegiances can never be reconciled. Her artless confidence that the two *can* be reconciled, if only the non-Christians would be pleasant and give way, might best be understood as the sugar on the mildly sinister pill of a Christian totalizing discourse, about which Averil Cameron has so eloquently spoken[18]. But the light-hearted tying up of loose ends characterizes non-Christian romance as well. More specifically, we shall see below that the *Recognitions* form part of a wider tradition, at home in both pagan and Jewish romance, of mingling religious change with the delights and pieties of marriage bed and hearth.

---

17. *Acts of Perpetua and Felicitas* 5, text and translation in H. MUSURILLO, *The Acts of the Christian Martyrs*, Oxford, Clarendon Press, 1972, pp. 106-131; here, pp. 112-113. Presumably the rest of Perpetua's family was already Christian, and could be expected to share her positive view of the impending martyrdom.

18. A. CAMERON, *Christianity and the Rhetoric of Empire*, Cambridge, University Press, 1990.

III. Heavenly and Earthly Families: "Recognition" and Religious Conversion

The "Recognition" scenes of the *Recognitions* evoke one of romance's most dramatic (and implausible) mechanisms for achieving the union of the marital couple, and thus narrative closure. This is the *coup de théâtre* of revealed identities in which long-parted family members discover, through birth tokens or intersecting narratives, that they have found one another again. That the characters do not recognize each other is often due to a separation in infancy, or the wearing effect of the long years of travel and sea salt.

While the theme of reunion is clear, the spontaneous self-revelation scenes of the *Recognitions* are not formal and systematic along the lines of the search for the girl's parents which we have seen above in *Daphnis and Chloe*. Another family romance, the *History of Apollonius, King of Tyre*[19], preserves a closer parallel. The *History of Apollonius* is an intergenerational narrative in which the married couple, now mature and themselves parents, are separated and struggle to reconstitute the family unit. (The couple's daughter, Tarsia, is herself of a marriageable age, and her restoration to her rightful father, like Chloe's, allows her to return from servile to noble status and thus to be given in marriage to an aristocratic suitor.)

The circumstances of the reunion of father and daughter in the *History of Apollonius* are strikingly different to those of the *Recognitions*, but the underlying mechanism is similar, in that the characters discover each other through spontaneous autobiographical outpourings, rather than through the formal search process of *Daphnis and Chloe*. Apollonius, believing his wife to be dead, had left their daughter Tarsia with friends while he travelled the Mediterranean in an attempt to forget his sorrow. Years later, the girl having grown to marriageable age, she is handed over to a servant for execution by the wicked foster-mother, but, as in the folk-tale of Snow White, the servant deputed to kill the girl has taken pity and released her. Captured by pirates and enslaved, she becomes a lyre-player in a brothel. When her father, now himself near death with grief after being informed of her death by the foster-parents, brings his ship to Mytilene, her new home, the girl is summoned to distract him from his grief. When she is unsuccessful, Tarsia pours out her own story

---

19. A text preserved in Latin but perhaps deriving from a Greek original, believed by its most recent editor to date from the third century. For a recent text and translation, and well-informed discussion of dating problems, see E. ARCHIBALD, *Apollonius of Tyre: Medieval and Renaissance Themes and Variations* Cambridge, D.S. Brewer, 1991.

of woe to her client, thinking him a complete stranger. Hearing her story, Apollonius recognizes that the girl is his own daughter, and the daughter, who has maintained her virginity despite living in a brothel, finds an honourable marriage. Father and daughter then travel to Ephesus to give thanks to the great goddess Artemis, whose priestess, it emerges, is none other than the long-lost mother.

A third- or fourth-century pagan text, the *Aethiopica* of Heliodoros, provides a useful foil to the above examples, linking "recognition" with religious innovation[20]. It shares with the *Recognitions* and *Apocryphal Acts* a number of narrative elements, including an exuberant interest in religious and philosophical discourse, a daughter who refuses to marry as the point of origin for a story of travel and adventure, and a near-martyrdom at least as extravagant as Thecla's, but it leads to shipwreck and marriage in the usual way. Book Two of the text introduces the religious dimension, a strand of the narrative which reads at times like a parody of the *Apocryphal Acts*. Two pagan priests, Charikles, priest of Apollo at Delphi, and the Egyptian priest Kalasiris, put their heads together to discuss Charikles' adoptive daughter Charikleia, who has dedicated herself to the sacred service of Artemis and is now intent on hunting, archery practice, and the preservation of her virginity[21]. Charikles begs Kalasiris to use "all his Egyptian arts" to sway the girl towards marriage. The plea could not be more humorously timed, since it is spoken on the morning of the religious festival at which the heroine Charikleia will encounter her hero, Theagenes. Religious solemnity and the cult of *erôs* co-mingle as Kalasiris tells the story:

> Theagenes made to take the fire, and in that instant it was revealed to us, Knemon, that the soul is something divine and partakes in the nature of heaven. For at the moment when they set eyes on one another, the young pair fell in love, as if the soul recognized its kin at the very first encounter...[22]

Heliodoros delights in the inability of Kalasiris to unscramble the heavenliness of love with the divine purpose of the rites of Pythian Apollo: we are not far, as we listen to Kalasiris' lengthy discourses on fate throughout the *Aethiopica*, from the evident delight of the author of the

---

20. For discussion of the date of the *Aethiopica*, see the introduction to J. MORGAN's translation in REARDON, *Collected Ancient Greek Novels* (n. 7), along with S. SWAIN's appendix, *The Dating of the Greek Novels*, in IDEM, *Hellenism and Empire: Language, Classicism and Power in the Greek World*, Oxford, Clarendon Press, 1996. A number of the *Proceedings of the Cambridge Philological Society* on Heliodoros, edited by R. HUNTER, will shed new light and is currently in press.

21. HELIODOROS, *Aethiopica* 2, 33.

22. HELIODOROS, *Aethiopica* 3, 5 (tr. MORGAN, in REARDON, *Collected Ancient Greek Novels*, p. 414).

Recognitions at Faustinianus' pedantic astrological explanation for a story which the reader knows to be untrue[23].

Like the *Recognitions*, the *Aethiopica* gives a religious turn to the family reunion which is central to the narrative. After long travels, Charikleia is brought as a prisoner of war to Meroe, capital city of Ethiopia, where her birth parents are King and Queen. Before her identity can be revealed, however, she is designated as a human sacrifice to give thanks for the Ethiopian victory to which she owes her capture. When the people of the royal city discover that the luminously beautiful maiden is in fact the king's daughter they refuse to allow the girl to be sacrificed; the king in turn ordains a ban on human sacrifice forevermore, to bring the Ethiopian state religion into line with the sensibilities of his subjects. Although the religious element here is less than central to the larger narrative, it reveals the civic and ideological charge which filial and familial piety were understood to carry, and confirms the notion that love and religious piety could be understood to reinforce one another, rather than being set at odds as in the *Apocryphal Acts*.

More striking is the role of religious conversion in the anonymous Jewish romance of *Joseph and Aseneth*[24]. Here, a sometimes heightened eroticism takes its place comfortably both with filial piety and with chastity in its classical sense of fertile, legitimate, monogamous consummation (rather than repudiation of the marriage bed), while religious conversion takes its place with romance at the centre of the narrative.

The Egyptian Aseneth, the daughter of Pentephres, priest of Heliopolis and chief of all the satraps and noblemen of Pharaoh, is raised to so extraordinary a standard of virginal modesty that she has never laid eyes on a man. When her parents propose to her a marriage alliance with Joseph, she refuses the alliance, appropriate to her noble station, saying she prefers to be married to the first-born son of Pharaoh, who himself is betrothed in turn to a woman of his own station, the daughter of the king of Moab. However, upon seeing Joseph arrive at her father's house

23. EDWARDS, *The Clementina* (n. 2), pp. 466-467, puts the *Recognitions*' interest in determinism and Providence into the wider context of the play of fortune in the Greek romance.

24. According to the introduction to C. BURCHARD's translation in J.H. CHARLESWORTH, ed., *The Old Testament Pseudepigrapha*, Garden City, NY, Doubleday, 1985, vol. II, pp. 177-247, at p. 187, the date and provenance of *Joseph and Aseneth* are uncertain, but it is likely to belong to the first or second century B.C.E or C.E. – a wide field. R. KRAEMER, *When Aseneth Met Joseph: A Late Antique Tale of the Biblical Patriarch and his Egyptian Wife*, New York, Oxford University Press, 1998, places the text at the late end of this spectrum, or even later. On the context of Jewish romance, see L.M. WILLS, *The Jewish Novellas*, in MORGAN and STONEMAN, *Greek Fiction* (n. 10), pp. 223-238, and ID., *The Jewish Novel in the Ancient World*, Ithaca, NY, Cornell University Press, 1995.

through the window of her bedroom, her heart is struck and she decides to adopt the God of Israel in order to be united with Joseph. After they are introduced, she fasts, in sackcloth and ashes, for seven days and seven nights, to purify herself for his return, and the period of contemplation brings her a visit from the chief of the angels of heaven.

This transfer of allegiance from the gods of her parents to the God of her husband is viewed as unproblematic, the logical result of her parents' wish that she marry Pharaoh's Hebrew protegé. A national holiday is called to celebrate the union of Joseph and Aseneth, which takes place in the palace of Pharaoh, and the union is immediately blessed with the conception of legitimate offspring. When, some time later, the first-born son of Pharaoh, himself struck to the heart by Aseneth's queenly beauty, attempts to kidnap the young bride, Aseneth repudiates him, the brothers of Joseph rescue her, and the son of Pharaoh is fatally wounded in the attempt. Thus the assimilation of the Egyptian Aseneth into the family of Joseph is sealed, Joseph is made the heir to the throne of Pharaoh, and Aseneth's original reluctance to act on the suggestion of her father is expiated. While the world of *Joseph and Aseneth* is a world of high drama, the values of filial piety, fertility, and religious truth are mutually reinforcing.

What emerges here, is that, while the *Recognitions* do not precisely fit the narrative paradigm of any of the pagan or Jewish novels, they nonetheless share important characteristics with a number of them, and can safely be said to partake of the same array of narrative possibilities and commitments. Even the element of religious conversion finds its parallels; though the *Recognitions* may perhaps be said to handle the issue of religious commitment less gracefully than the other texts, it is the lack of literary sophistication, rather than the interest in religious matters, which distinguishes it from its pagan and Jewish counterparts.

IV. The Apologetic Family and the Varieties of Early Christian Discourse

A number of questions remain for future scholars. Should the pro-family approach of the *Recognitions* be read as reflecting a Jewish (or broader Greco-Roman) emphasis on the family as opposed to a Christian predilection for *enkrateia*? This view would hold that the *Recognitions* have so much in common with pagan and Jewish versions of the romance genre precisely because they themselves spring from a Jewish-Christian milieu (as evinced, for example, by Peter's advice to Matthidia that her now-Christian sons will have to eat separately from her until she is baptized)[25]. On this line of argument, the seemingly encratite views of the *Apocryphal Acts* are just the beginning of what will be a growing tendency within Patristic Christianity to privilege the perspective of Mark 10, 29-30 over the perspective of the Pastoral Epistles, a tendency which will culminate in the full-fledged cult of virginity of the late fourth century onwards.

An alternate line of argument, however, would hold that the common ground between the *Recognitions* and the Pastoral Epistles, the notion that a temperate and devoted family life is a meaningful index of progress in Christian virtue, was in fact the early Christian middle ground. This line of argument would find support in work that is currently being done in the later patristic period to suggest that the separatist-ascetic views of late fourth-century writers like Jerome and Ambrose were far from widely accepted by a clergy and laity steeped in the civic Christianity of the Pastoral Epistles[26]. Support for this reading can be drawn from the values expressed, for example, by early Christian funerary inscriptions, which reveal notions of family closely interdependent with those of their pagan and Jewish counterparts[27], or indeed from the social milieu of the *Recognitions*' fourth-century translator Rufinus of Aquileia, known for his interest in providing edifying reading for the married Christian laity[28].

Attention to a final "recognition" scene, however, may help to establish that the Christian literary imagination drew deeply on the intercultural currents of romance, delighting in its ability to accommodate (and indeed confuse) a variety of social messages, ranging from the encratite to the ardently domestic. In the *Life of Mary, Niece of Abraham of Qidun*, an anonymous fifth-century Syriac text, we see that even an ex-

---

25. Principal investigations of the Jewish Christian context of the *Clementina*, in addition to JONES (n. 2), are O. CULLMANN, *Le problème littéraire et historique du roman pseudo-Clémentin: Étude sur le rapport entre le gnosticisme et le Judéo-Christianisme* (Études d'histoire et de philosophie religieuses publiées par la Faculté de théologie protestante de l'Université de Strasbourg, 23), Paris, Librairie Félix Alcan, 1930, and G. STRECKER, *Das Judenchristentum in den Pseudoklementinen* (Texte und Untersuchungen, 70), 2nd (rev.) ed., Berlin, Akademie Verlag, 1981.

26. D. HUNTER, *Resistance to the Virginal Ideal in Late Fourth-Century Rome: The Case of Jovinian*, in *Theological Studies* 48 (1987), 45-64.

27. J. JANSSENS, S.J., *Vita e morte del cristiano negli epitaffi di Roma anteriori al sec VII*, Rome, Università Gregoriana Editrice, 1981, and COOPER, *The Virgin and the Bride* (n. 5), pp. 97-101.

28. Rufinus' translation of the Pythagorean *Sentences of Sextus*, for example, is dedicated to the married couple Avita and Apronianus, as a manual of spiritual formation for Avita "so plain-spoken that a girl whose mind is distracted may not give as an excuse to her reader that she is unable to follow the meaning" (RUFINUS, *Praefatio in Sexti Sententias*, in *Corpus Christianorum, Series Latina*, 20, p. 259, translation my own).

plicitly ascetic vision could mobilize romance's association of family reunion with narrative closure. One of a number of texts in the repentant prostitute tradition best known in texts such as the *Penitence of Pelagia* and the *Life of Mary of Egypt*, the Syriac *Life of Mary* recounts the story of an orphan who is raised by her father's brother, the venerable hermit Abraham of Qidun, a historical figure attested in the sixth-century *Chronicle of Edessa*[29].

From the age of seven, Mary lives as an acolyte of Abraham, in the outer part of his house, her dedication to the ascetic way of life a source of delight to the holy man. Some years later, however, the girl has grown into a woman, and is seduced by a false monk who sees her through a window when visiting Abraham. In shame, Mary departs from Qidun, and establishes herself as a prostitute in another town. After a long search, Abraham finds out where she is living, and poses as a potential client in order to secure an opportunity to speak to his niece in private. When he sees her dressed in her finery, he attempts to hide his distress. The girl draws near him and does not recognize his face because of the soldier's helmet which he has implausibly worn into the tavern where he meets her[30], but the odour of sanctity on his blessed body assaults her outer and inner senses, and she begins to lament her own lost ascetic youth. Abraham finally reveals himself when the two are alone together, taking off his helmet and pleading with her to return to Qidun.

The moral of the story of Mary is certainly different to that of the *Recognitions*: Mary's recognition of her uncle, and return to his protection, is an allegorical sign to the reader that God works as a hidden presence to bring back to himself all who stray. In the words of the hagiographer, "Who was so hard-hearted that he failed to praise God when he heard her lamenting her sins? Compared with hers, our repentance is a mere shadow; compared with hers, our supplications are just as dreamlike"[31]. What the texts have in common is not so much a message as the choice of a reconciliation between earthly kin, rather than the repudiation of earthly kinship, as the narrative medium through which the mes-

---

29. Both Mary and Abraham have a place in the Syrian hymnaries: Abraham as the subject of thirteen hymns of praise, while some of the MS versions of the Syrian Orthodox festal hymnary contain an acrostic lament of Mary. S.P. BROCK and S.A. HARVEY, *Holy Women of the Syrian Orient*, Berkeley, University of California Press, 1987, p. 185.

30. "God who alone is wise and loves mankind saw to it that she did not recognize him and so run away in panic" (*Life of Mary, Niece of Abraham of Qidun* 22, trans. BROCK and HARVEY, *Holy Women*, p. 33).

31. *Life of Mary, Niece of Abraham of Qidun* 25 (trans. BROCK and HARVEY, *Holy Women*, p. 26).

sage of each is expressed. It is of course possible to argue that this view of the demands of the earthly family as compatible with those of its heavenly counterpart can be accounted for by geography, building on Susan Ashbrook Harvey's recent work on how Syriac hagiography reflects family-based institutions within Syriac asceticism[32]. But we are dealing here with a classic instance of a literary trope which has not been found in part because it has not been looked for: medieval copyists and modern scholars alike have tended to alight with particular interest on ascetic themes and concerns. As the apologetic use of family unity and reunion surfaces in an ever-increasing variety of Christian texts – the fifth- or sixth-century Roman *Acts of Marius, Martha, and their Children,* for example,[33] or the fourth-century *Martyrdom of Marian and James*[34] – we may begin to be dissatisfied with a paradigm that dismisses it as an exception to the rule.

The broader conclusion to be drawn from our investigation is one about Christian diversity in the multi-cultural society of the later Roman Empire. It no longer makes sense to look for "the Christian view" of the family, as against "the pagan" or "the Jewish view". Rather, we can see that not only did Christians often disagree with one another over matters of social polity or rhetorical strategy more rather than less seriously than they disagreed with their pagan or Jewish neighbours: they also expressed a variety of views depending on the context which occasioned the expression. Put simply, there *was* no single, stable "Christian" view of the family. Perpetua's boldness in the face of her father's anxiety was not intrinsically inimical to Matthidia's wish to see her family reunited around the dinner table. What separates the flesh-and-blood Perpetua from the fictional Matthidia is certainly not the divergence between "encratite" and "pro-family" visions of Christianity: Perpetua herself was a married woman, sexually active, and mother of at least one infant. The difference in this case, and in many cases, may have been nothing more than the difference between a romance heroine's ability to speak for an elusive ideal of unity that confounds the boundaries of religious affiliation, and the historical Christian's exigency of tempering hope through the harsh demands of the possible.

---

32. S.A. HARVEY, *Sacred Bonding: Mothers and Daughters in Early Syriac Hagiography,* in *Journal of Early Christian Studies* 4 (1996), 27-56.

33. *Acta Marii, Marthae et filiorum* (B. H. L. 5543, Acta Sanctorum Ian. II., pp. 216-219).

34. *The Martyrdom of Saints Marian and James* 13, in MUSURILLO, *Acts* (n. 17), pp. 212-213.

ABSTRACT

This analysis is centred on the Pseudo-Clementine *Recognitions* as the version of the Clementine narrative which has the closest ties to the genre of the ancient romance. In particular the attention in Books 7-9 on Clement and his family bears some striking resemblances to pagan and Jewish romance especially Heliodorus' *Aethiopica* or the *History of Apollonius, King of Tyre*. Attention to this genre shows that, although they are not a very well crafted narrative, the *Recognitions* do use genre conventions suitably for a particular apologetic purpose. That purpose is to celebrate the values of the earthly family. The *Recognitions* thus stand against the radical break with the ancient family proposed by its closest Christian literary counterparts, the *Apocryphal Acts*. The *Recognitions* assert the importance of blood kinship as the basic ingredient of social solidarity and so stand in the conservative mould of the Pastoral Epistles and the Letters to the Ephesians and Colossians. The study discusses the roles and characterization of Peter, Clement and Matthidia, and notes in detail how in the recognition scenes of the *Recognitions* the apologetic for the earthly family is made. Comparison with other similar early Christian literature shows clearly that there was considerable diversity amongst Christians in the multi-cultural society of the later Roman Empire. The narrative of the *Recognitions* argues for just one view of the family amongst many that were possible for Christians to hold.

RÉSUMÉ

Cette étude a pour objet les *Reconnaissances pseudo-clémentines*, c'est-à-dire la version latine de l'ouvrage du pseudo-Clément qui entretient les liens les plus étroits avec le genre du roman antique. Lorsqu'on examine les livres 7 à 9, qui parlent de Clément et de sa famille, on relève de fortes ressemblances avec le roman païen et le roman juif, en particulier avec les *Aethiopica* d'Héliodore et l'*Histoire d'Apollonius, roi de Tyre*. La comparaison avec ce genre littéraire montre que, si les *Reconnaissances* ne présentent pas un récit très bien construit, elles n'en utilisent pas moins avec habileté les conventions du genre, ceci dans un but apologétique particulier. Le but en question est de célébrer les valeurs de la famille terrestre. Les *Reconnaissances* s'opposent ainsi à la rupture radicale avec la famille traditionnelle, préconisée dans les textes chrétiens qui sont les plus proches des *Reconnaissances*, les Actes apocryphes des apôtres. Les *Reconnaissances* affirment l'importance des liens de sang en tant qu'ingrédient de base de la solidarité sociale, et se conforment de la sorte au modèle conservateur des Épîtres pastorales ou des Lettres aux Éphésiens et aux Colossiens. La présente étude examine les rôles et la caractérisation de Pierre, de Clément et de Matthidia; elle relève en détail, dans les scènes de reconnaissance des *Reconnaissances*, la façon dont le récit fait l'apologie de la famille terrestre. La comparaison avec d'autres oeuvres littéraires du christianisme ancien montre clairement qu'il y avait une diversité considérable parmi les chrétiens au sein de la société multi-culturelle de l'Antiquité tardive. Le récit des *Reconnaissances* propose seulement une vision de la famille, parmi les nombreuses autres que les chrétiens pouvaient avoir alors.

Department of Religions and Theology   Kate COOPER
University of Manchester
Manchester M13 9PL

17

THE MIRACULOUS DISCOVERY OF THE HIDDEN MANUSCRIPT, OR THE PARA-TEXTUAL FUNCTION OF THE PROLOGUE TO THE *APOCALYPSE OF PAUL*[*]

From the edict of Thessalonica on February 28, 380, until the conversion to Christianity of more than six hundred members of the Roman aristocracy in 389, and from the anti-pagan legislation of the years 391-392 to the victory of the Cold River on September 6, 394, the reign of Theodosius I (379-395)[1] marked the definitive victory of the Nicene form of Christian monotheism over Roman polytheism, as the official religion of the Roman Empire. This turning-point in history was not only the result, but also the cause of an actual revolution in the mentality of the period, and, in regard to Christians, in the very way they looked at the world, society and mundane values[2]. It is true that the great representatives of this crisis were primarily Ambrose, Augustine, and Pru-

---

[*] This study stems from the work of the research team for the edition of the *Apocalypse of Paul*, to be published in the *Corpus Christanorum – Series Apocryphorum* (Turnhout, Brepols) under the auspices of the AELAC ("Association pour l'étude de la littérature apocryphe chrétienne", Genève – Lausanne – Paris). It is a revised version of a preliminary article in French, published in J.-D. DUBOIS – B. ROUSSEL (eds.), *Entrer en matière. Les prologues* (Patrimoines – Religions du Livre), Paris, Cerf, 1998, pp. 111-124. My thanks are due to George J. Brooke (Manchester University), Kirsti Copeland (Princeton University), Jean-Daniel Dubois (École pratique des hautes études, Paris), Rémi Gounelle (Université de Lausanne), and Jean-Daniel Kaestli (Institut romand des sciences bibliques, Lausanne) for their helpful remarks and observations. I feel also especially grateful to Richard Van De Water (Université de Fribourg), who carried out the painful task of translating the French text.

1. On Theodosius I and his religious policy, see N.Q. KING, *The Emperor Theodosius and the Establishment of Christianity*, London, SCM, 1961; A. LIPPOLD, *Theodosius der Grosse und seine Zeit*, München, C.H. Beck, 1980[2]; S. WILLIAMS – G. FRIELL, *Theodosius. The Empire at Bay*, London, B.T. Batsford, 1994; R. LIZZI TESTA, *La politica religiosa di Teodosio I. Miti storiografici e realtà storica*, in *Rend. Mor. Acc. Lincei* 9.7 (1996) 323-361.

2. On this period, see the excellent synthesis of P. BROWN, *The Body and Society. Men, Women and Sexual Renunciation in Early Christianity*, London – Boston, Faber and Faber, 1988, esp. parts II and III; cf. also the recent works of R.A. MARKUS, *The End of Ancient Christianity*, Cambridge, Cambridge University, 1990, though the point of view adopted by this author is too occidental (Latin Christianity), intellectual (Augustine), and official (according to the list of sources used, the Christians of the period would not have read "apocryphal" texts!); A. CAMERON, *The Mediterranean World in Late Antiquity AD 395-600*, London – New York, Routledge, 1993; Ch. PIETRI – L. PIETRI (eds.), *Histoire du christianisme des origines à nos jours*, II, *Naissance d'une chrétienté (250-430)*, Paris, Desclée, 1995, esp. parts III and IV.

dence in the Latin Occident[3], and Gregory of Nazianzus, Gregory of Nyssus, and John Chrysostom in the Greek Orient. But the one who in reality achieved the most delicate task, the general reorganization of an interim afterlife and an otherworldly geography adapted to the new necessities of the triumphant Church, was neither a theologian, nor a committed intellectual, but the unknown author who chose to present and impose the ideas of the "perfect" Christian society of his time under the guise of a fictitious apostolic revelation, the *Apocalypse of Paul*[4].

I. THE INTERIM AFTERLIFE IN THE *APOCALYPSE OF PAUL*

The eschatology of the *Apocalypse of Paul* is centered, not on the modalities of the last Judgment, but on the condition of souls between death and resurrection. This change of perspectives is expressed clearly from the beginning, in a series of responses that the Lord gives to the choir of the elements (chaps. 3-6)[5]: "I know all that. In effect, my eye

---

3. On the attitude of occidental Christian intellectuals towards the imperial power, see recently F. HEIM, *La théologie de la victoire de Constantin à Théodose* (ThH, 89), Paris, Beauchesne, 1992.

4. See in general M. GEERARD, *Clavis Apocryphorum Novi Testamenti*, Turnhout, Brepols, 1992, pp. 203-209, n° 325. For the arguments that have led us to date this text between 395 and 416, see P. PIOVANELLI, *Les origines de l'"Apocalypse de Paul" reconsidérées*, in *Apocrypha* 4 (1993) 25-64, esp. 45-59. New editions of the manuscripts of Paris (P) and Saint-Gall (StG), the two most important witnesses of the complete Latin version (Latin 1), together with the manuscripts of Graz (Gz), Zurich (Z), and Vienna (F), belonging to an abridged reworking (Latin 2) of the first Latin version, have been published by C. CAROZZI, *Eschatologie et Au-delà. Recherches sur l'"Apocalypse de Paul"*, Aix-en-Provence, Université de Provence, 1994, pp. 179-265 (critical edition of P and StG), and 267-299 (synoptic edition of Gz, Z, and F); and by Th. SILVERSTEIN – A. HILHORST, *Apocalypse of Paul. A New Critical Edition of Three Long Latin Versions* (COr, 21), Genève, P. Cramer, 1997, pp. 65-167 (synoptic edition of P, StG, and a third new manuscript from Arnhem in the Netherlands), and 169-207 (another synoptic edition of Gz, Z, and F). These scholars still support the traditional thesis of a third century lost first edition (actually Carozzi dates it between 164-166 and 190), replaced by a new edition c. 420-428 (for a criticism of this thesis, see *infra*, n. 46). Also to be noted are the following modern translations based on the textual evidence of manuscript P (Latin 1): A. HILHORST, *De Openbaring van Paulus*, in A.F.J. KLIJN (ed.), *Apokriefen van het Nieuwe Testament*, vol. II, Kampen, J.H. Kok, 1985, pp. 210-249; H. DUENSING – A. DE SANTOS OTERO, *Apokalypse des Paulus*, in W. SCHNEEMELCHER (ed.), *Neutestamentliche Apokryphen in deutscher Übersetzung*, vol. II, Tübingen, J.C.B. Mohr, 1989[5], pp. 644-675; J.K. ELLIOTT, *The Apocalypse of Paul (Visio Pauli)*, in ID., *The Apocryphal New Testament. A Collection of Apocryphal Christian Literature in an English Translation*, Oxford, Clarendon Press, 1993, pp. 616-644; C.-C. KAPPLER – R. KAPPLER, *Apocalypse de Paul*, in F. BOVON – P. GEOLTRAIN (eds.), *Écrits apocryphes chrétiens*, vol. I (Pléiade, 442), Paris, Gallimard, 1997, pp. 775-826. We are preparing the translation of a critically reconstructed text, according to all the most important witnesses, to be published in the *Collection de poche de l'AELAC* (Turnhout, Brepols).

5. Cf. CAROZZI, *Eschatologie* (n. 4), pp. 53-58, who stresses the "evocation of the catastrophe, delayed only by God's patience" (p. 57; cf. also p. 169). In our opinion, how-

sees and my ear hears, but my patience supports them (the human beings) until they convert and repent" (chap. 4)[6]. But even if the general resurrection and the definitive Judgment are deferred *sine die*, this delay would not authorize the non-believers to proclaim: "Nothing new in this world: I eat, drink, and enjoy the things of this world! For is there anyone who has descended to Hell and has returned to tell us that there is a judgment there?" (chap. 15)[7]. It is God himself who presides over the tribunal charged with examining and judging souls after they have left the body (chaps. 14-18)[8].

At the outset of this process, the blessed, of whom the first are the ascetics, are escorted by Michael to the "Paradise of exultation" (chap. 14), corresponding to "the Promised Land" and "the City of Christ", found beyond the Ocean, to the East of the inhabited world (chaps. 22-31). There, they will be able to profit immediately from the prerogatives of the messianic age (chap. 21)[9]. While all the damned, beginning with "those who are neither hot nor cold", are entrusted to the angel Tartaruchos to be left and punished in "the outer darkness" (chap. 16), in "the prison of Hell" (chap. 18), a region situated beyond the Ocean, to the West of the inhabited world (chaps. 31-42)[10]. The sinners are con-

---

ever, the notion of a "delay" granted to the human race is more significant than the danger of a no longer topical "catastrophe".

6. This invitation to conversion and repentance, reiterated five times (chaps. 5, 6 [three times], and 10) with minimal variations, gives this first part a marked homiletical slant; cf. CAROZZI, *Eschatologie* (n. 4), p. 35. The motive of divine patience recurs in chap. 33; that of repentance in chaps. 16 (repentance and penance), 17 (penance and conversion), 22 (conversion, repentance, and penance), 43, 44, and 50.

7. Cf. Rom 10,6-7: "Do not say in your heart, 'Who will ascend into heaven?' (...) or 'Who will descend into the abyss?'" In chap. 44, the damned are too late in regretting: "And if we had known clearly that this situation (i.e. the infernal sufferings) is reserved for those who sin..." The function of the *Apocalypse of Paul*, however, is to inform the faithful exactly and without any equivocation ("What you [Paul] must tell and report publically" [chap. 21]) of the consequences in the otherworld of their conduct on earth.

8. Cf. CAROZZI, *Eschatologie* (n. 4), pp. 58-70, who concludes that "in the primitive version figured only the ascension of the souls of the righteous and the wicked, each ascension finishing by an adoration before God, exactly as in *4th Ezra*" (p. 69). However, in the versions/recensions of the *Apocalypse of Paul* which are at our disposal, actual judgments are portrayed, not mere adorations. In Christianity, moreover, the notion of the existence of a heavenly tribunal *post mortem* dates from the late-fourth or early-fifth century (for references, see PIOVANELLI, *Les origines* [n. 4], p. 47, n. 69).

9. This explains the astonishment of Paul and his question: "Will this (promised) land thus be manifested before the time (of the Parousia)?" (*ibid.*).

10. The author of the short and later *Apology* preceding the text of the first Syriac recension (Syriac 1) held a different opinion: "the blessed Paul saw in symbols all that is to come regarding retribution after the resurrection" (§22), "for, until the resurrection, there is neither joy nor torment, only this perception" (§4); see A. DESREUMAUX, *Des symboles à la réalité: la préface à l'"Apocalypse de Paul" dans la tradition syriaque*, in *Apocrypha* 4 (1993) 65-82, esp. 69-70, 73, and 76-77.

demned to endure their punishments "until the day of the great Judgment" (chaps. 16, and 18), without any hope of escaping from the places of darkness where they are stranded. The only comfort given them consists of a "rest/refreshment", a weekly respite of twenty-four hours, from nightfall on Saturday until sundown on Sunday, during which the infernal pains are temporarily suspended (chaps. 43-44)[11].

In the organization of the otherworld of the *Apocalypse of Paul*, there is no room, even in seed form, for Augustine's third category of trespassers, composed of people who are neither completely good, nor completely bad; nor for a third place, "purgatory", to receive them[12]. The only exception, more apparent than real, is situated with the blessed; it concerns the proud ascetics who, not having been admitted into the City of the Saints, must await the intercession of the righteous at the moment of the triumphal entry of Christ, at the beginning of the *millennium* (chap. 24)[13]. The time of penance on earth having ended with physical death, the souls of the departed have but two possible destinations

11. The discourse of Christ (chap. 44) mentions the "brothers" and "sisters" of the damned, "who are in the world and offer oblations"; this suggests the idea that the intercession of the living could contribute in order to obtain an extension of rest for the dead punished in Hell. This belief is also held by John Chrysostom (*3rd Homily on the Letter to the Philippians* 4). Near 402, Prudence had sung of "the vacations of pains" and the "rest" of the damned, but only during the Pascal vigil (*Cathemerinon* 5,125-127.134-137). On the contrary, the assertion that "at determined intervals, the pains of the damned receive a certain mitigation", left Augustine frankly sceptical (*Enchiridion* 29,112).

12. CAROZZI, *Eschatologie* (n. 4), pp. 121-164, holds that, in the "first edition", "the souls of those who died in the state of *dipsychia* (alternation of good and bad acts) were transferred by Christ, each year on Easter day, to Paradise, the place of the *refrigerium*", even though he admits that "the *Apocalypse of Paul* only illustrated this point (a gesture of the mercy of Christ without creating a new institution (i.e. Purgatory)" (p. 153; cf. also p. 168). As brilliant as this hypothesis may be, it has no explicit textual support: all the damned receive only a temporary respite, which includes no transfer elsewhere (cf. the beliefs of John Chrysostom, Prudence, and Augustine, cited in the preceding note). The distinction between an upper Hell (the future Purgatory) and a lower Hell (the true one) will not be accepted until the 5th Latin medieval recension (see J. LE GOFF, *La naissance du Purgatoire*, Paris, Gallimard, 1981, pp. 56-59; C. CAROZZI, *Le voyage de l'âme dans l'Au-delà d'après la littérature latine, Ve-XIIIe siècles*, Rome, École française de Rome, 1994, pp. 265-279); the true Purgatory does not appear until later, in the Spanish (Castilian) version of the *Apocalypse of Paul* (chap. 25 of the Toledo edition).

13. What is perhaps in question here is a way to restore to proper proportions the possibility of an eschatological intercession which, according to the second group of Augustine's "merciful" (*City of God* 21,18), should have been general and concerned all sinners. This motif also returns in two homilies *De die iudicii* in old English (ninth century?) which attribute the initiative of intercessions to Mary, Michael, and Peter respectively, a belief condemned as heretical by the Anglo-Saxon Aelfric (end of tenth – beginning of eleventh century); see R. FAERBER, *L'Apocalypse de Thomas en vieil-anglais*, in *Apocrypha* 4 (1993) 125-139, esp. 131-132, and 135-137; ID., *Deux homélies de Pâques en anglais ancien*, in *Apocrypha* 6 (1995) 93-126, esp. 106-107, and 122. On the idea that "pride is the root of all evils", held by John Chrysostom and Augustine, see CAROZZI, *Eschatologie* (n. 4), p. 104.

which, in spite of their interim state, prove to be definitive; whence the dramatic force of persuasion, or rather dissuasion, for all the living who read or listened to such a description of the afterlife[14].

To sum up, the setting of the otherworld in the *Apocalypse of Paul*, which was to become the Christian otherworld *par excellence*, is the result of the consciousness of an ever-increasing temporal interval separating the passion and resurrection of Christ from his Parousia and final Judgment; whence the necessity of reminding Christians that this delay does not, however, justify a lax moral order. Obviously, the eschatological perspectives of triumphant Christianity had lost much of the characteristic tension of the Christian communities before 313, still illegal and under persecution. The awareness of this major change contributed to giving rise to a new kind of otherworld, stemming from the syncretism between the Christian collective eschatology of Jewish origin, on one hand, and the pagan individual afterlife of Orphic-Pythagorean origin, on the other. Henceforth the Last Judgement had given precedence to the individual trial.

II. THE PROLOGUE TO THE *APOCALYPSE OF PAUL*

Whereas a theologian would have been able to expose this matter in a deductive manner, by way of commenting, for example, on scriptural quotations which were supposed to demonstrate the existence of an immediate judgment and retribution, the author of the *Apocalypse of Paul* preferred to have recourse to a first-person account of a voyage experienced by an illustrious figure of holy history, the apostle Paul. The difficulty of making such an authorship acceptable to the Christian public was brilliantly resolved, thanks to the redaction of an *ad hoc* Prologue, furnishing a satisfying explanation for the circumstances of the discov-

---

14. Especially in monastic circles; see C. PAUPERT, *Présence des apocryphes dans la littérature monastique occidentale ancienne*, in Apocrypha 4 (1993) 113-123, esp. 115-117, and 119; CAROZZI, *Eschatologie* (n. 4), pp. 170-173 (concerning the "second edition", described as a "monastic reworking"), and 175-178. This ascetic connotation of the *Apocalypse of Paul* should not lead to hasty identifications of the milieu in which it was composed. Actually the monks only occupy a part (granted, an important one) of the gallery of exemplary figures employed by the author. In the moral domain, his way of considering monasticism (the ascetics of chap. 9; the proud of chap. 23; the simple of spirit in chap. 29; the hypocrites of chap. 40); the priesthood (the bad ministers of chaps. 34-36), virginity (the virgins of chap. 26; the unfaithful virgins of chap. 39), and marriage (the chaste spouses of chap. 22; the adulterers of chaps. 38-39), is not incompatible with the Chrysostomian point of view (see in general BROWN, *The Body* [n. 2], pp. 305-322; and also *supra*, nn. 11, and 13; *infra*, nn. 28, and 45).

ery of an unedited Pauline text some 340 years after the death of the apostle[15].

This Prologue is conserved only in a minority of witnesses to the *Apocalypse of Paul*.

* At the beginning of the *Apocalypse of Paul* [16]:
  - in a complete form in the Latin 1 manuscript P;
  - in a developed and romanticized form in the Spanish version[17];
  - in a summarized form in the Greek text[18].
* At the end of the *Apocalypse of Paul*:
  - without the first part in the two Syriac recensions[19];
  - without the first part in the Arabic version[20].

15. To the best of our knowledge, this Prologue has been examined at some length only by W. SPEYER, in his well-documented monograph: *Bücherfunde in der Glaubenswerbung der Antike. Mit einem Ausblick auf Mittelalter und Neuzeit* (Hypomnemata, 24), Göttingen, Vandenhoeck & Ruprecht, 1970, pp. 60-65, and 130-131.

16. It must be recalled that the entire first part of the text, up to chap. 16, is lacking in the London manuscript, the only known witness for the Coptic version; it is therefore impossible to determine if this witness began with the Prologue or not (cf. PIOVANELLI, *Les origines* [n. 4], pp. 49-50; CAROZZI, *Eschatologie* [n. 4], p. 34).

17. See F. SECRET, *La Revelación de sant Pablo*, in *Sefarad* 28 (1968) 45-67, esp. 60-64. Secret has not published the last part of the Prologue, which ends in the following way in the Toledo edition, printed in 1525: [*Emperador:*] *y tuvo el sancto padre el cayado del bendito apostol y pusolo sobrel muerto diziendo le. Yo te mando enel nombre de Jesu Christo el qual ressuscito a sant Lazaro al quarto dia que era muerto del monumento / que te levantes. E luego el cuerpo se levanto vivo y hablo: y dio un gran gemido estendiendo los miembros como si se levantasse del sueño y diro cosas maravillosas alos que eran presentes del siglo venidero. Y entonces todas las gentes con grandissima devocion lloravan y gemian: y davan loores y gracias a nuestro señor Jesu Christo y al bienaventurado apostol sant Pablo. E luego en essa hora embio el emperador por todo el mundo a denunciar y publicar este miraglo: y otrosi el traslado dela revelacion suya que hallaran en la misma arca. Entonces el sancto padre otorgo grandes indulgencias y perdones a todos aquellos fieles y devotos christianos que con caridad transladassen esta revelacion y la divulgasen alas gentes la bienaventurança que despues desta vida esperan los buenos. Otrosi la danacion que esperan los malos. La qual revelacion es esta que se sigue* (fol. VI r., ll. 17-34). In this version, just before the dismissal of the angel (chap. 41), the voyage of the apostle ends with the concession to the damned of a *refrigerio* of three days per year (chap. 40, fol. LV v.) which demonstrates that its Latin model must have contained at least chaps. 1-44 of the original text.

18. The Greek text has been published by C. TISCHENDORF, *Apocalypsis Pauli*, in ID., *Apocalypses apocryphæ Mosis, Esdræ, Pauli, Iohannis, item Mariæ Dormitio, additis Evangeliorum et Actuum apocryphorum supplementis*, Lipsiæ, H. Mendelssohn, 1866, pp. XIV-XVIII, and 34-69.

19. The first Syriac recension (Syriac 1, Nestorian) has been published by G. RICCIOTTI, *Apocalypsis Pauli Syriace*, in *Or.* 2 (1933) 1-25, and 120-149; the second Syriac recension (Syriac 2, Jacobite) is still unedited.

20. A preliminary edition of an Arabic manuscript from Paris has been published by A. BAUSI, *Apocalisse di Paolo: versione araba (BN 5072). Introduzione, edizione diplomatica, traduzione*, Firenze, 1992; cf. ID., *A First Evaluation of the Arabic Version of the "Apocalypse of Paul"*, paper presented to the "International Conference on Christian Arabic Literature" held in Lund, August 15-18, 1996.

We present here an English translation followed by some textual remarks to justify our restitution.

Critical Translation

"[0,1] I will now come to the visions and revelations of the Lord. [0,2] I know a man in Christ who fourteen years ago (either in the body, I do not know, or outside the body, I do not know, God knows) was taken up in this way to the third heaven. [0,3] And I know that this man, in this way (either in the body or outside the body, I do not know, God knows), [0,4] was taken up to Paradise and heard ineffable words that men are not permitted to speak. [0,5] On behalf of this one, I will boast, but on my own behalf, I will boast nothing but my weaknesses."

[1,1] At what time was it (i.e. the *Apocalypse of Paul*) made public? In the consulship of Theodosius, the pious king, and of the very illustrious Cynegius, a very honored man was then living in the city of Tarsus, in the house of Saint Paul the apostle. [1,2] An angel of the Lord appeared to him in a dream, saying: "Destroy the foundations of this house and take out what you will find." But he thought it was an hallucination.

[2,1] The angel then returned and, a third time, obliged him to destroy the foundations. While digging, he found a small marble chest with an inscription engraved on the sides, which contained this Apocalypse and the sandals that Paul would wear when he taught the word of God. [2,2] Afraid of opening the chest, he carried it to the magistrate of the city. The magistrate saw that it was sealed with lead, and, fearing that it was something else, he sent it to Theodosius. [2,3] When the king had received it, he opened it and found the Apocalypse of Saint Paul; he had it copied and sent the original to Jerusalem. This is what is written there.

Textual Commentary

[0,1-5] The first part is obviously a literal quotation of 2 Cor 12,1-5, put in as an epigraph by Latin 1 P, Latin 2 Gz (which omits vv. 1 and 5 and ends with *et cetera*), and the eleventh Latin medieval recension (which gives only vv. 2-3)[21]. The Prologue to the Spanish version also makes four references to the "great secrets which were discovered and revealed to the blessed apostle, Saint Paul, when he was taken up and

---

21. Published by M.E. DWYER, *An Unstudied Redaction of the "Visio Pauli"*, in *Manuscripta* 32 (1988) 121-138; cf. Ch.D. WRIGHT, *Some Evidence for an Irish Origin of Redaction XI of the "Visio Pauli"*, in *Manuscripta* 34 (1990) 34-44.

carried to the third heaven (...) in body and in soul"[22]. The presence of this quotation in the original of the *Apocalypse of Paul* is confirmed by the Greek text, which summarizes it in these terms: "What was revealed to him (Paul) when he ascended to the third heaven, was taken up to Paradise and heard ineffable words" (cf. the first Slavonic version; Latin 1 P and Latin 2 Gz read "mysterious words"). Syriac 1, which has omitted this quotation and has transposed the account of the Prologue to the end of the text (chap. 52), relates first the circumstances of the hiding of the manuscript in the city of Tarsus and, after the death of Paul, the divine will allowing its rediscovery (chap. 51, absent from the Arabic version, and probably from Syriac 2 as well).

[1,1] Syriac 1 emphasizes the circumstances of the discovery: "Thus was found this Apocalypse" (cf. the Arabic version); the Greek text omits this first phrase. A number of modern translators, following Montague Rhodes James, have not corrected the error of identification of the person of the ruler, that the scribe of the Latin 1 manuscript P committed: "Theodosius Augustus *the Younger* (408-450) and (*sic*) Cynegius (consul in 388)"[23], whereas the original Latin 1 reading was probably "Theodosius Augustus (I, 379-395) and Cynegius (consuls together in 388)"[24]. In the Spanish version, the action takes place at Rome, under the reign of the "emperor Theodosius", and the second personality, now "senator" and identified as the "very honored man", is called "Caeseo". The Arabic version mentions only *Tādāsys*, "Theodosius", while Syriac 1 omits this first chronological precision. The adverb "then" is found only in Latin 1 P, which omits, on the other hand, the readings "city" and "apostle" preserved by the Greek text, Syriac 1, and the Arabic version.

[1,2] Latin 1 P omits "of the Lord"; the angel is "Gabriel" in the Spanish version, and his apparition took place "in a dream" according to Syriac 1 and the Arabic version; "at night" in Latin 1 P; "at night" and "in a dream" in the Spanish version. The Latin *apparens reuelauit*,

---

22. See SECRET, *La Revelación* (n. 17), pp. 61-64.
23. See PIOVANELLI, *Les origines* (n. 4), p. 39, n. 43. This is also the case for HILHORST, *De Openbaring* (n. 4), p. 212; DUENSING – DE SANTOS OTERO, *Apokalypse* (n. 4), p. 648; ELLIOTT, *The Apocalypse* (n. 4), p. 620; and CAROZZI, *Eschatologie* (n. 4), pp. 186-187, who accepts, moreover, p. 13, the suggestion of reading "Constantius" in place of "Cynegius", proposed by Th. SILVERSTEIN, *The Date of the "Apocalypse of Paul"*, in *Mediaeval Studies* 24 (1962) 335-348.
24. Oddly enough, SILVERSTEIN – HILHORST, *Apocalypse* (n. 4), p. 11, still defend the interpretation of the dating formula as "in the consulship of Theodosius the Younger and Flavius Constantius, that is to say, in the year 420", whereas p. 19, n. 3, they acknowledge the error of the source from which Latin 1 P stems.

"appearing, he revealed", could constitute a double translation of the Greek ἀπεκαλύφθη, "he revealed himself/he appeared". Latin 1 P is the only witness to present the injunction of the angel in indirect discourse: "to destroy the foundations of the house and to make public what he would find." Syriac 1 develops the last phrase: "But this man did not understand that, for he believed that it was a dream without basis (cf. the Arabic version), and he thought no more about it."

[2,1] In the Greek text, it is the "third vision", and the angel "obliged the very honored man"; Latin 1 P adds that "he whipped him"; Syriac 1 presents a more developed text: "and he said: 'O man, it is to you that I am speaking! Destroy all the foundations of this house (cf. the Arabic version) and inspect what you will find; take it and make it known to the men, in order that they might convert themselves from the path of evil to life.' So this man stood up very ardently and demolished that house." In Syriac 1, the uncovered box is "made of white marble", while the information of the "inscription engraved on the sides" is preserved only by Latin 1 P. The discovery of "the sandals" is omitted by the Greek text; Syriac 1 adds the finding of "his (Paul) stole, in which this Apocalypse was wrapped", and the Arabic version that of "the purchase act of the house".

[2,2] The Greek text and Syriac 1 do not mention fear and read respectively, "he took it" and "after having found these things" (cf. the Arabic version). Latin 1 P and Syriac 1 omit "of the city", but this reading of the Greek text is confirmed by the Arabic version: "(to the governor) of this country". In Syriac 1, it is the owner of the house who fears "that this was something of gold"; the Arabic version summarizes: "and the governor sent it to Theodosius, who was king". The magistrate, in Syriac 1, puts his own seal on the chest as well.

[2,3] "And this king, a believer and righteous, opened it", in Syriac 1; "when he opened it and read it, he found this Revelation", in the Arabic version; the Greek text omits the details of the opening and discovery. As for the sending of the original to Jerusalem, we follow the Greek text and the Arabic version, the latter reading: "he had it copied and sent it to Jerusalem"; in the case of Latin 1 P, it is exactly the opposite that happens: "he sent a copy of it to Jerusalem, and kept the original with him"; Syriac 1 omits the entire passage. "This is what is written there", according to the Greek text, Syriac 1 and the Spanish version, against Latin 1 P and the Arabic version, which omit this introductory formula.

III. THE LATE DISCOVERY OF AN UNKNOWN PAULINE TEXT

The Prologue is composed of two parts. The first is a quotation of 2 Cor 12,1-5, a passage from "the letter in tears" (2 Cor 10-13) sent from Ephesus, probably in 56. Paul refers there to his mystical experience fourteen years earlier[25]. The scriptural reference is indispensable in justifying the Pauline attribution of the *Apocalypse of Paul*. It is presented as a detailed and faithful account of those "visions and revelations of the Lord", a voyage across the places of rewards and punishments, which takes place between an ascension to the third heaven (chaps. 19-21) and a visit "in the body" to the earthly Paradise (chaps. 45-51). Athanasius of Alexandria had already evoked the rapture to the third heaven of 2 Cor 12, 2-4 with regard to a vision of Anthony, who had undergone, "in spirit" and with success, the examination to which the powers of the air submit the souls of the deceased[26]. Certainty had henceforth been established, even in the official circles of orthodoxy, that the apostle had gained knowledge of the mysteries of the otherworld. All that remained to be done was to situate, within an appropriate context, the late discovery of the account of his otherwordly voyage.

The second part of the Prologue thus informs us as to how the original of the *Apocalypse of Paul* was found in the foundations of the old house of the apostle, at Tarsus. This geographic location could relate, either to Paul's visit to Syria and Cilicia, from 38 to 43, or to his passing through those same regions at the beginning of his second missionary voyage, around 46[27]. For the former, fourteen years before the retrospective note in 2 Cor 12,2 would take us back to 42; Paul would have been able to be in his native town at the moment of his mystical experience, and thus to hide with ease the manuscript of the *Apocalypse*. Despite doubts that an ancient author could exhibit such a completely modern chronological

---

25. See D. MARGUERAT, *2 Corinthiens 10-13: Paul et l'expérience de Dieu*, in *ETR* 63 (1988) 497-519, esp. 511-512; C.R.A. MORRAY-JONES, *Paradise Revisited (1 Cor 12:1-12): The Jewish Mystical Background of Paul's Apostolate*, *HTR* 86 (1993) 177-217 ("Part 1: The Jewish Sources"), and 265-292 ("Part 2: Paul's Heavenly Ascent and Its Significance").

26. See *Life of Anthony* 65,2-9 (published by G.J.M. BARTELINK [ed.], *Athanase d'Alexandrie. Vie d'Antoine* [SC, 400], Paris, Cerf, 1994, pp. 304-307), a passage examined by J. DANIÉLOU, *Les démons de l'air dans la "Vie d'Antoine"*, in *Studia Anselmiana* 38 (1956) 136-147; cf. also *On the Incarnation* 25,5-6 (published by Ch. KANNENGIESSER [ed.], *Athanase d'Alexandrie. Sur l'incarnation du Verbe* [SC, 199], Paris, Cerf, 1973, pp. 356-359).

27. For the visit to Syria and Cilicia in the years 38-43, see Gal 1,21; Acts 9,30 (departure for Tarsus); 11,25 (at Tarsus). For his travel to Tarsus during the second journey, around 46, see Acts 15,41. We follow the chronology established by R. JEWETT, *Dating Paul's Life*, London, SCM, 1979.

precision, the choice of this period of Paul's life, at the outset of his first or during his second mission to the Gentiles, makes the revelations in the *Apocalypse* the turning point in the Pauline missionary thrust. For it was during this journey in the otherworld that the apostle received, among other things, confirmation of the rejection of the Jewish people from the mouth of Moses, the Lawgiver (chap. 48)[28]. It is very probable that the author intended the *Apocalypse of Paul* to be not only an authentic Pauline text, but also the foundational text for his apostolic mission, prior to the Epistles themselves.

The Miraculous Discovery

The *Apocalypse of Paul* was found thanks to an angelic intervention, the divine messenger returning three times in dreams before convincing the new owner of the house to dig in his cellar. In order to relate the circumstances of the discovery, the author thus has recourse to the "theme of the dream leading to the invention of relics". This same theme was also used by Lucian, priest of Caphargamala, near Jerusalem, in his account of the discovery of the mortal remains of Stephen, in 415[29]. Lucian had likewise been invited by an angel to dig, and the vision was repeated three times to persuade him that it was not a question of a demonic apparition. He too was told to contact the authorities, the religious rather than the civil ones, in the person of John, bishop of the Holy City. The relics of the protomartyr had likewise been transferred to Jerusalem, to the Church of Holy Zion, on December 26, 415, where they had given birth to a new cult, just as the story of the establishment of a new official

---

28. After the affair of the reconstruction of the Temple of Jerusalem, envisioned during the ephemeral reign of Julian the Apostate (361-363), the anti-Jewish controversy set in even harsher than before; see in general, for a picture of the very critical years 361-439, M. AVI-YONAH, *The Jews under Roman and Byzantine Rule. A Political History of Palestine from the Bar Kokhba War to the Arab Conquest*, Jerusalem, Magnes Press, 1984², pp. 185-231; and for the leading role played by John Chrysostom at Antioch, R.L. WILKEN, *John Chrysostom and the Jews. Rhetoric and Reality in the Late 4th Century*, Berkeley – London, University of California, 1983.

29. See V. SAXER, *Morts, martyrs, reliques, en Afrique chrétienne aux premiers siècles. Les témoignages de Tertullien, Cyprien et Augustin à la lumière de l'archéologie africaine* (ThH, 55), Paris, Beauchesne, 1980, pp. 245-246; J. AMAT, *Songes et visions. L'au-delà dans la littérature latine tardive*, Paris, Études augustiniennes, 1985, pp. 283-290. The discovery of the relics of Stephen had been preceded by the invention of those of other illustrious biblical personalities: of Habakkuk and Micah near Eleutheropolis in 385, of Samuel at Ramatha in 406, and of Zachariah in 415; all these discoveries "usually are the result of revelations received by monks, priests, bishops, or even just simple laymen; ratified by the hierarchy, they complete the survey of the holy places in fourth century" (according to P. MARAVAL [ed.], *Égérie. Journal de voyage [Itinéraire]* [SC, 296], Paris, Cerf, 1982, p. 196, n. 3; many other parallels are drawn by SPEYER, *Bücherfunde* [n. 15], pp. 63-64, n. 60).

edition of the *Apocalypse of Paul* must have supported and encouraged its diffusion.

The Emperor Theodosius

Theodosius I would have gained knowledge of the discovery of the *Apocalypse of Paul* at the peak of his power, in 388, the year of his arrival in Italy after his victory over the usurper Maximus, at Aquileia. Following this event, the emperor of the East was associated with Valentinian II, his young protégé, in the reconstruction of the Constantinian basilica of Saint Paul beyond the walls, built over the very tomb of the apostle. This gesture won for Theodosius the view of the Romans, after his death, that he was the one and only constructor of the edifice[30]. Would the Prologue to the *Apocalypse of Paul* then be the echo of an act so prestigious in the eyes of all Christians? Or did its author rather have in mind the translation of the mortal remains of another Paul, the orthodox bishop of Constantinople, who died in exile and whose body was repatriated with honors by Theodosius in 382, and would eventually have been wrongly identified with that of his apostolic namesake[31]?

Whatever the case may be, the decision to place these events under the high patronage of such a champion of Christianity was not by chance. There are other famous writings which place the discovery of other relics under the care of the same emperor: the hagiographic legend of *The Seven Sleepers of Ephesus* and the homily *On Mount Coscam*, about the discovery of the house of the Holy Family in Egypt by the patriarch Theophilus of Alexandria (385-412), zealous destroyer of the Serapeum[32]. The reappearance of archaeological treasures of Christian

---

30. See A. CHASTAGNOL, *Sur quelques documents relatifs à la basilique de Saint-Paul-hors-les-Murs*, in R. CHEVALLIER (ed.), *Mélanges d'archéologie et d'histoire offerts à André Piganiol*, vol. I, Paris, S.E.V.P.E.N., 1966, pp. 421-437 (reprinted in A. CHASTAGNOL, *Aspects de l'Antiquité tardive*, Rome, "L'Erma" di Bretschneider, 1994, pp. 309-327).

31. On the very controversial career of this figure, see W. TELFER, *Paul of Constantinople*, HTR 43 (1950) 31-92. Theodosius had his body placed in the church built by the Arian bishop Macedonius, Paul's old adversary. "This temple is very large and absolutely remarkable, and today still bears his (Paul) name; which makes many who ignore the truth, especially women (*sic*) and the masses, imagine that here lies the apostle Paul", writes Sozomen in his *Ecclesiastical History* (7,10).

32. Theodosius, travelling to Alexandria, entrusts the pagan temples to the good care of Theophilus (the event is thus claimed to take place in 391), and participates in the discovery of the treasure of Alexander the Great. In the Syriac version (see GEERARD, *Clavis* [n. 4], p. 34, n° 56; S.C. MIMOUNI, *Les "Vies de la Vierge": état de la question*, in *Apocrypha* 5 [1994] 211-248, esp. 239-240), the emperor is wrongly identified with Theodosius *the Younger*. This confusion recalls the error committed by the scribe of Latin

origins was but one of the signs of the great consideration that the faithful of the fifth century gave to the truly exceptional reign of this orthodox and pious emperor[33], who had renewed the splendour of the Constantinian period. In the case of the *Apocalypse of Paul*, this Theodosian attribution also permitted the giving of a response, however indirect, to the problem of the early disappearance of the text: as if its content had not been judged apt to be divulged by Paul during his lifetime, and it was thus necessary to await the time of the real and durable triumph of the Church for a miracle to reveal its existence.

A Literary Strategy

Of course, the convention of fictive discovery was not unknown in the ancient world. It suffices to think to the "book of the Law", found by the high priest Hilkiah in the course of work in the Temple of Jerusalem, in the eighteenth year of the reign of Josiah[34]; or the manuscript confirming the division of the world between the kings of Byzantium and Ethiopia, discovered by the patriarch Demātyos in the basilica of Saint

---

1 P (see *supra*, nn. 23, and 24). A similar case, indeed, also appears in the Prologue to the *Acts of Pilate* (or *Gospel of Nicodemus*; see GEERARD, *Clavis* [n. 4], p. 43-46, n° 62): in the Greek recension A, the discovery of the Hebrew original is explicitly dated to the eighteenth year of Theodosius II, that is, 425-426; in a manuscript of the Latin version A, on the other hand, this same discovery is dated, probably incorrectly, to the reign of Theodosius I; see R. GOUNELLE – Z. IZYDORCZYK, *L'Évangile de Nicodème, ou Les Actes faits sous Ponce Pilate (recension latine A), suivi de La lettre de Pilate à l'empereur Claude* (Collection de poche de l'AELAC, 9), Turnhout, Brepols, 1997, pp. 24-25, and 123.

33. See, for example, the enthusiastic witness of Prudence, cited by HEIM, *La théologie* (n. 3), pp. 284-285. It is worth noting that the prefect Maternus Cynegius, mentioned in the Prologue to the *Apocalypse of Paul* along with Theodosius, was himself a very zealous catholic; see WILLIAMS – FRIELL, *Theodosius* (n. 1), pp. 56, 62, and 120; SILVERSTEIN – HILHORST, *Apocalypse* (n. 4), p. 19, n. 3.

34. See 2 Kings 22,8-23,24; 2 Chron 34,14-35,19. On this episode and the literary motive of the book-finding, see B.J. DIEBNER – C. NAUERTH, *Die Inventio des ספר התורה in 2 Kön 22. Struktur, Intention und Funktion von Auffindungslegenden*, in *Dielheimer Blätter zum Alten Testament* 18 (1984) 95-118; Th. RÖMER, *Transformations in Deuteronomistic and Biblical Historiography. On "Book-Finding" and Other Literary Strategies*, in *ZAW* 109 (1997) 1-11. Even if the existence of a close dependence between this "book of the Law" and Deuteronomy is generally admitted, the book in question cannot be identified with the extant Deuteronomy, since the text we possess dates obviously from the (post)exilic period, and not from the years 622-621; see the recent reviews of Th. RÖMER, *Approches exégétiques du Deutéronome. Brève histoire de la recherche sur le Deutéronome depuis Martin Noth*, in *RHPR* 75 (1995) 153-175, esp. 161-162; Th. RÖMER – A. DE PURY, *L'historiographie deutéronomiste (HD). Histoire de la recherche et enjeux du débat*, in A. DE PURY – Th. RÖMER – J.-D. MACCHI (eds.), *Israël construit son histoire. L'historiographie deutéronomiste à la lumière des recherches récentes* (Le Monde de la Bible, 34), Genève, Labor et Fides, 1996, pp. 9-120, esp. 89-91.

Sophia in Constantinople[35]; or again the archives of Jerusalem, brought to light at the time of the emperor Justinian by Theodosius the Jew, in which could be read the record of the sentence of Jesus by the Sanhedrin[36].

Nor is the motif unknown in modern and contemporary literature. It suffices to cite some examples taken from Italian literature: the account of the vicissitudes experienced by Renzo Tramaglino and Lucia Mondella, *I promessi sposi* of Alessandro Manzoni[37]; or the memoirs of the monk Adso of Melk ("a manuscript, naturally"), who are supposed to have given the subject matter for *Il nome della rosa* of Umberto Eco; or even "the manuscripts (...), the old books and ancient maps" of Cain Groovesnore, put to use in illustrating the comic strip masterpiece that is *La ballata del mare salato* of Hugo Pratt.

The function of all these accounts of book-findings is to establish the historicity of a text claimed to be more or less ancient, the exceptional interest of which would already have justified the disclosure. If today, however, no one would believe such scenarios, which are among the most popular literary conventions of historical novels[38], the situation was somewhat different in the past, where such discoveries could even bring about even the legitimization of new practices (religious reforms, political changes) presented as ancient.

As Thomas Römer reminds us,

---

35. See chaps. 19, and 117 of the Ethiopian *Kebra Nagast*, the "Glory of the Kings". Demātyos (probably to be read "Metodyos") is claimed to present this book (which seems to refer to the *Revelations* of Pseudo-Methodius) to the three hundred eighteen orthodox Fathers of the Council of Nicea in 325, more than two centuries before the construction of the Saint Sophia basilica by Justinian I between 532 and 537; see P. PIOVANELLI, *L'épopée de Mâkedâ, reine de Saba éthiopienne*, in *Le Monde de la Bible* 95 (1995) 20-21.

36. According to the *Suidas*; see GEERARD, *Clavis* (n. 4), p. 31-33, n° 54; SECRET, *La Revelación* (n. 17), p. 52; I. BACKUS, *Guillaume Postel, Théodore Bibliander et le "Protévangile de Jacques". Introduction historique, édition et traduction française du MS. Londres, British Library, Sloane 1411, 260r-267r*, in *Apocrypha* 6 (1995) 7-65, esp. 27-28 (in 1552, Bibliander still accepted the historicity of this account). Cf. the circumstances of the discovery of the *Acts of Pilate* (*supra*, n. 32).

37. The first edition of 1825-1827, as well as the definitive edition of 1840, bear the eloquent subtitle: *Milanese Story of the Seventeenth Century, Discovered and Published by Alessandro Manzoni*.

38. The para-textual function of the Preface/Prologue-introductions in modern and contemporary literature has been examined at length by R. GENETTE, *Seuils* (Poétique), Paris, Éditions du Seuil, 1987, pp. 150-270. According to his typology, we could consider the Prologue to the *Apocalypse of Paul* as a *Préface allographe fictive*, a "fictitious allographical Preface" (pp. 265-267): the real author of the *Apocalypse of Paul* has ascribed the Prologue to a third anonymous person different from Paul, the supposed author of the *Apocalypse*.

(Wolfgang) Speyer has demonstrated that the motive of book findings in temples or holy places is a quite common literary motive in Antiquity which is mostly used "um einem gerade angefertigten Werk den Schein höheren Alters und großer Heiligkeit zu verleihen". The origin of this motive is probably to be found in the deposit of foundation tablets in Mesopotamian sanctuaries that are often "rediscovered" by later kings undertaking restoration works. (...) The discovery reports are often variations of the following diagram: 1. An important person wants to change or to "restore" important features in society. 2. He is afraid of opposition. 3. He or one of his loyal servants is sent to a holy place. 4. There he discovers a book or written oracles which are of divine origin. 5. This discovery gives divine impulse to the projects of the hero[39].

In the Prologue to the *Apocalypse of Paul*, a book of apostolic origin is miraculously discovered by a first loyal servant (the "very honored man"), and a second one (the "magistrate of the city") sends it to a very important person ("Theodosius, the pious king"). The reader, however, can only guess about the feelings and the intentions of the hero, because the real matter of the story is not the biography of a zealous Christian emperor, but the otherworldly description that follows the discovery-report ("This is what is written there").

Cooperative Readers

It is difficult to assess the impact of the Prologue to the *Apocalypse of Paul* on its ancient readers, because its primary function was, paradoxically, to try to keep itself out of the limelight on behalf of the true *Apocalypse*. In other words, readers who were convinced by the arguments of the Prologue regarded the *Apocalypse of Paul* as an authentic Pauline writing, without arguing any more about the circumstances of its discovery. Such was the case for the *Regula Magistri*, an anonymous collection of monastic rules (end of fifth – beginning of sixth century), where we can read: "as Saint Paul says in his Revelation, 'Son of men, bless the Lord unceasingly, but more especially when the sun goes down' (chap. 7)" (34,10); or for Caesarius of Arles (c. 470-542), who quotes a dozen times the sentence "the impediments of the world made them wretched" (chaps. 10, and 40), introducing it by the canonical formula "it is written"[40]; and even at the beginning of the *Commèdia*, when Dante Alighieri hesitates to undertake his journey to Hell, for (he tells Virgil) "I am not Aeneas, nor Paul" (*Inferno* 2,28-32)[41].

39. RÖMER, *Transformations* (n. 34), pp. 7-8.
40. See PAUPERT, *Présence* (n. 14), pp. 117, and 119; SILVERSTEIN – HILHORST, *Apocalypse* (n. 4), pp. 12, and 20, n. 5.
41. See the recent study of R. PENNA, *Ascendenze apocalittiche della "Divina Commedia"*, in *Henoch* 11 (1989) 41-50, esp. 42-45.

Actually the Prologue to the *Apocalypse of Paul* accomplished so well the task assigned to it by the author, that it finally disappeared from the title page in the majority of the witnesses, because the text was definitively considered as Pauline. The demonstration having been made once and for all, the large majority of the copyists and translators/editors retained only the essential of these "visions and revelations of the Lord", usually only the part concerning Hell[42].

Critical Readers

On the other hand, the fact that the Prologue constituted the heart of the apparatus fixed by the author to legitimate his pretensions is shown by the very attacks of those who challenged the authenticity of the *Apocalypse of Paul*. The first is Augustine, in his *Treatise on John* (98,8) written around 416[43]: he bitterly criticized the audacity of these "spiritual ones" who had dared to utter "ineffable words, that men are not permitted to speak". Next is Sozomen, who, having made a personal inquiry, denounced the imposture of the discovery at Tarsus, in a passage of his *Ecclesiastical History* (7,19) written around 443. It is absolutely remarkable that, on the same occasion, Sozomen contrasted the progressive disappearance of the old eschatological *Apocalypse of Peter*[44], "the totally apocryphal nature of which had been demonstrated by the ancients", with the extraordinary success in monastic circles of the new *Apocalypse of Paul*, "which none of the ancients knew" [45].

---

42. See, for instance, the 1st Latin medieval recension, translated by M.P. CICCARESE, *Un inferno apocrifo: la "Visio Pauli"*, in EAD., *Visioni dell'aldilà in Occidente. Fonti, modelli, testi* (BPat, 8), Firenze, Nardini, 1987, pp. 41-57.

43. Or after 419-420, if we follow A.-M. LA BONNARDIÈRE, *Recherches de chronologie augustinienne*, Paris, Études augustiniennes, 1965, p. 117. The same criticism would be repeated later, by the Anglo-Saxon Aelfric (see *supra*, n. 13).

44. See in general GEERARD, *Clavis* (n. 4), pp. 197-198, n° 317; and the very important study of R. BAUCKHAM, *The "Apocalypse of Peter": A Jewish Christian Apocalypse from the Time of Bar Kokhba*, in *Apocrypha* 5 (1994) 7-111. The Ethiopic text has been re-edited by D.D. BUCHHOLZ, *Your Eyes Will Be Opened. A Study of the Greek (Ethiopic) Apocalypse of Peter* (SBL.DS, 97), Atlanta (Georgia), Scholars Press, 1988; and by P. MARRASSINI, *L'Apocalisse di Pietro*, in Y. BEYENE – R. FATTOVICH – P. MARRASSINI – A. TRIULZI (eds.), *Etiopia e oltre. Studi in onore di Lanfranco Ricci*, Napoli, Istituto Universitario Orientale, 1994, pp. 171-232; see also the new French translation of R. BAUCKHAM – P. MARRASSINI, *Apocalypse de Pierre*, in BOVON – GEOLTRAIN (eds.), *Écrits apocryphes* (n. 4), pp. 745-774.

45. It is perhaps not superfluous to recall here that Paul was a first-rate figure in the theological reflection of the late-fourth century, as evidenced in Chrysostom's *Panegyrics of Saint Paul* (published by A. PIÉDAGNEL [ed.], *Jean Chrysostome. Panégyriques de saint Paul* [SC, 300], Paris, 1982). The first of these *Panegyrics* presents a series of exemplary Old Testament figures, which is not unlike that in chaps. 47-51 of the *Apocalypse of Paul*; and the Greek text, in fact, ends with an actual Panegyric of the apostle (unedited).

Lacking stronger arguments, Augustine thus chose to destroy the evil at its roots, by refuting the soundness of the first, scriptural part of the Prologue; while the Church historian preferred to discredit it on the basis of the second, factual part. Neither of the two could imagine that, one day, someone would again take seriously the witness of the Prologue to the *Apocalypse of Paul*, not in recognizing its Pauline origin, but in supporting the thesis of the existence of a first edition of the work from the third, or even second century, which would have been reworked and replaced by the extant "Tarsus edition"[46].

ABSTRACT

The *Apocalypse of Paul*, written in Greek around 400, was the basic text for the Christian "intermediary" afterlife. It foresees an immediate retribution for the souls of all the deceased, even before the final Judgment: in a place of Paradise, situated to the east of the inhabited earth, for the blessed, and in an hellish region, to the west, for the damned. The Prologue constituted the core of the ap-

---

46. See PIOVANELLI, *Les origines* (n. 4), pp. 40-45, for a critical presentation of the thesis held by several modern scholars: R.P. CASEY, *The Apocalypse of Paul*, in *JTS* 34 (1933) 1-32; SILVERSTEIN, *The Date* (n. 23); ID., *The Graz and Zürich Apocalypse of Saint Paul: An Independent Medieval Witness to the Greek*, in J.J.G. ALEXANDER – M.T. GIBSON (eds.), *Medieval Learning and Literature. Essays Presented to Richard William Hunt*, Oxford, Clarendon Press, 1976, pp. 166-180; J.-M. ROSENSTIEHL, *L'itinéraire de Paul dans l'au-delà. Contribution à l'étude de l'Apocalypse apocryphe de Paul*, in P. NAGEL (ed.), *Carl-Schmidt-Kolloquium an der Martin-Luther-Universität, Halle-Wittenberg 1988*, Halle-Wittenberg, Martin-Luther-Universität, 1990, pp. 197-212. The dating proposed by Carozzi for the "first edition" (*Eschatologie* [n. 4], pp. 165-166) runs into the following objections: (1) It is far from demonstrated that the supposed quotations of Origen come from such an edition; see PIOVANELLI, *Les origines* (n. 4), pp. 45-48. One of the two passages has recently been published by E. PRINZIVALLI (ed.), *Origene. Omelie sui Salmi. Homiliæ in Psalmos XXXVI-XXXVII-XXXVIII* (BPat, 18), Firenze, Nardini, 1991, pp. 242-245, and 446-447; L. BRÉSARD – H. CROUZEL – E. PRINZIVALLI (eds.), *Origène. Homélies sur les Psaumes 36 à 38* (SC, 411), Paris, Cerf, 1995, pp. 250-255. (2) On the other hand, it is very possible that all the witnesses at our disposal, including the Coptic version (see *supra*, n. 16), derive from one common Greek original published during the period 395-416. (3) This text contains no "allusion to the 'Laodiceans' (the Quartodecimans, thus designated because of the synod of Laodicea) and to the Pascal controversy" of the years 164-190 (*pace* CAROZZI, *Eschatologie* [n. 4], pp. 128-129), as acknowledged also by A. HILHORST, in *VigChr* 50 (1996) 94-99, esp. 95; SILVERSTEIN – HILHORST, *Apocalypse* (n. 4), p. 9. Meanwhile, our proposal of re-dating the *Apocalypse of Paul* has been agreed by C. MORESCHINI – E. NORELLI, *Storia della letteratura cristiana antica greca e latina*, II.1, *Dal concilio di Nicea agli inizi del Medioevo*, Brescia, Morcelliana, 1996, pp. 326-327; R. BAUCKHAM, *The Four Apocalypses of the Virgin Mary*, in ID., *The Fate of the Dead. Studies on the Jewish and Christian Apocalypses* (NT.S, 93), Leiden, Brill, 1998, pp. 332-362, esp. 335-336; and (hastily) rejected by A. MONACI CASTAGNO, *Apocalisse di Paolo*, in EAD., *Il diavolo e i suoi angeli: testi e traduzioni (secoli I-III)* (BPat, 28), Firenze, Nardini, 1996, pp. 286-296, esp. 294, n. 4.

paratus, which was put in place by the author to legitimate its Pauline origins, and to give a satisfactory explanation for the miraculous circumstances of its discovery, some 340 years after the death of the apostle.

RÉSUMÉ

L'*Apocalypse de Paul*, écrite en grec vers 400, fut le texte fondateur de l'au-delà chrétien "intérimaire". Elle prévoit une rétribution immédiate pour les âmes de tous les défunts avant même le Jugement dernier: dans un endroit paradisiaque, situé à l'est de la terre habitée, pour les bienheureux, et dans un endroit infernal, à l'ouest, pour les damnés. Le Prologue constituait le coeur du dispositif mis en place par l'auteur pour en légitimer la paternité paulinienne, et pour fournir une explication satisfaisante aux modalités miraculeuses de sa découverte, quelque 340 ans après la mort de l'apôtre.

University of Ottawa
Classics and Religious Studies
Ottawa, Ontario
K1N 6N5 Canada

Pierluigi PIOVANELLI

INDEXES

INDEX OF AUTHORS

ABEL, O., 20, 22, 25
ACKROYD, P.R., 69
ALETTI, J.-N., 159, 160, 165
ALEXANDER, J.J.G., 281
ALEXANDER, L.C.A., 243
ALT, A., 32, 39, 40
ALTER, R., 20, 69, 76
AMAT, J., 275
ANDERSEN, F.I., 69
ANDERSON, G., 114, 115
ANDERSON, J.C., 101
APPLEGATE, J., xvi, **69-88**, 81
ARCHIBALD, E., 256
ARMSTRONG, K., 240
ASHTON, J., 123, 133, 142
AUDET, J.-P., 41
AULD, A.G., 24, 80
AVI-YONAH, M., 275

BAARDA, T., 9.
BACKUS, I., 278
BAKHTINE, M., 120, 129, 130
BAR-AFRAT, S., 63
BARCLAY, J.M.G., 187, 189
BARRÉ, L.M., 54
BARRETT, C.K., 131, 132, 135
BARTELINK, G.J.M., 274
BARTH, G., 95
BARTSCH, S., 245
BASSLER, J.M., 120
BAUCKHAM, R.J., 280, 281
BAUSI, A., 270
BEASLEY-MURRAY, G.R., 128, 151, 152
BECHTEL, L.M., 10
BECKER, J., 201, 203, 204, 207
BENZINGER, I., 59, 60, 61
BERGER, K., 112, 167
BEYENE, Y., 280
BILDE, P., 213, 214
BLACK, C.C., 142
BLANK, J., 131
BLANKE, F., 65
BLENKINSOPP, J., 34, 41, 49
BLUM, E., 5, 6, 7, 8, 12, 20, 28
BOECKER, H.J., 17, 32, 40, 44

BOHAK, G., 186, 187, 195
BOND, H., xv, 139, **213-223**
BONNET, M., 253
BOOTH, W.C., 134
BORMANN, L., 9
BORNKAMM, G., 95
BOURQUIN, Y., xi, 165, 177
BOVON, F., 159, 172, 179, 252, 266, 280
BOWDEN, J., 69
BRAUN, M., 203, 207
BRAWLEY, R.L., 159
BREKELMANS, C., 6
BREMMER, J., 253
BREMMER, J.N., 9
BRENNER, A., 10, 37
BRÉSARD, L., 281
BRESCIANI, E., 25
BROCK, S.P., 261
BROMILEY, G.W., 55
BROOKE, G.J., **xi-xxi**, xviii, 23, 26, 31, **185-200**, 265
BROOKS THISTLETHWAITE, S., 10
BROWN, P., 265, 269
BROWN, R.E., 123, 131, 132, 133, 138, 142, 144, 145, 151, 154, 155
BROWN, W.N., 92
BRYCE, G.E., 77
BRÜSCHWEILER, F., 6
BUCHHOLZ, D.D., 280
BULTMANN, R., 91, 92, 128, 131
BURCHARD, C., 185, 187, 190, 199, 258
BURKES, S., 41
BURRIDGE, K.O.L., 74
BURRIDGE, R.A., 106, 109
BURRUS, V., 227, 228, 240, 243, 252
BUSS, M., 74

CAMERON, A., 255, 265
CAMP, C.V., 36
CARLE, B., 227
CARMICHAEL, C.M., 48
CAROZZI, C., 266, 267, 268, 269, 270, 272, 281
CASEY, R.P., 281
CATASTINI, A., 24

CHARLES, R.H., 203
CHARLESWORTH, J.H., 185, 258
CHASTAGNOL, A., 276
CHATMAN, S., 121, 177
CHESNUTT, R.D., 186
CHEVALLIER, R., 276
CHILDS, B.S., 32
CICCARESE, M.P., 280
CLARKE, A., 66
CLEMENTS, R.E., 31
COATS, G.W., 20, 70, 74
COGGINS, R.J., 69
COHEN, A., 35
COHEN, S.J.D., 214, 219
COHOON, J.W., 92
CONRAD, 49
COOPER, K., xxi, 227, 228, 229, 241, 242, **243-264**, 245, 253
COOTE, R.B., 84
CRANSTON, D., 133
CRENSHAW, J.L., 33, 38, 50
CROUZEL, H., 281
CRÜSEMANN, F., 39, 42, 44
CULLER, J., 229
CULLEY, R.C., 74
CULLMANN, O., 260
CULPEPPER, R.A., 119, 132, 133, 134, 142, 156

DANIÉLOU, J., 274
DA SILVA, A., 21
DAUBE, D., 45
DAUER, A., 132
DAVIES, S.L., 227, 239, 240, 253
DE BOER, M.C., xviii-xix, 133, **141-158**, 142, 148, 153
DE GUES, C.H.J., 4, 13
DE JONGE, M., 149, 150, 201, 202, 207
DEL TREDICI, K., 9
DE PURY, A., 5, 6, 25, 26, 277
DE SANTOS OTERO, A., 266, 272
DESREUMAUX, A., 267
DÉTIENNE, M., 22
DIEBNER, B.J., 20, 27, 277
DIEBOLD-SCHEUERMANN, C., 132, 135, 136, 137, 143, 144, 145, 146, 147, 149, 151
DIETRICH, A., 92
DIETRICH, W., 20, 21, 22, 58, 60, 61, 62
DINKLER, E., 170

DOCKX, S., 121
DODD, C.H., 131
DOLEZEL, L., 18
DONNER, H., 19
DORAN, R., 24
DOUGLAS, M., 43
DOUGLAS, R.C., 189
DOWNING, F.G., xvi, **105-118**, 108
DREYFUS, H.L., 230, 231
DRYDEN, J., 91
DUBOIS, J.-D., 265
DUCKWORTH, G.E., 112
DUENSING, H., 266, 272
DUKE, P.D., 132, 134, 135, 136, 137, 141
DUMAIS, M., 160
DWYER, M.E., 271

EDGLEY, R., 230
EDWARDS, J.R., 105, 106
EDWARDS, M., 243, 244, 258
EISING, H., 5, 6
EISSFELDT, O., 5, 69
ELLIOTT, J.K., 225, 266, 272
ELLUL, J., 55
EMERTON, J.A., 17, 74

FARBER, R., 268
FARRAR, F.W., 64, 66
FATTOVICH, R., 280
FELDMAN, L.H., 221
FENSHAM, F.C., 37
FERGUSON, E., 244
FEWEL, D.N., 11, 69
FILSON, F.V., 97
FIORENZA, E. Schüssler, 186, 226, 227
FIRMAGE, E.B., 31
FITZPATRICK-MCKINLEY, A., 35, 40
FOHRER, G., 69, 76
FONTAINE, C.R., 33, 36
FORTNA, R.T., 120, 123
FOUCAULT, M., xx, xxi, 226, 229, 230, 231, 232, 233, 234, 238, 241, 242
FREEDMAN, D.N., 69
FREYNE, S., 120
FRIEDMAN, R.E., 28
FRIELL, G., 265, 277
FRYE, N., 187
FUSS, A.M., 42

GARBE, R., 92

INDEX OF AUTHORS

GARCÍA MARTÍNEZ, F., 9
GARCIA-TRETO, F.O., 55
GAVENTA, B.R., 171
GEERARD, M., 266, 277, 278, 280
GENETTE, G., 18, 121, 176
GENETTE, R., 278
GEOLTRAIN, P., 266, 280
GERSTENBERGER, E., 44
GESE, H., 47
GIBSON, M.T., 281
GITIN, S., 48
GNILKA, J., 95
GNUSE, R., 24
GODLEY, A.D., 92
GOLDHILL, S., 245
GOLKA, F.W., 38
GOODY, J., 44
GORDON, C., 230, 233
GOTTWALD, N., 6, 13, 74, 76
GOUNELLE, R., 265, 277
GRAY, J., 59
GREEN, D., 69, 97
GRELOT, P., 24, 123
GRUNDMANN, W., 93
GUNKEL, H., 5, 7, 17, 53, 61
GUNN, D.M., 11, 69
GUNNEWEG, A.H.J., 6, 13

HAENCHEN, E., 131, 132, 134, 152, 153
HÄGG, T., 116, 244
HALPERN, B., 13
HAMMOND, C.P., 243
HARVEY, S.A., 261, 262
HAUSMANN, J., 18
HEIL, J.P., 92, 94, 102, 103
HEIM, F., 266, 277
HEITMÜLLER, W., 124, 125, 126
HELD, H.-J., 95, 99
HENNECKE, E., 225
HERGÉ, 3
HILHORST, A., 266, 272, 277, 279, 281
HOFFMANN, H.-D., 53, 58
HOFFNER, H.A., 44
HOFTIJZER, J., 37
HOLLANDER, H.W., 201, 202, 204, 207
HOUTMAN, C., 40
HUNTER, D., 260
HUNTER, R., 257

IRMSCHER, J., 243, 244

IZYDORCZYK, Z., 277

JACKSON, B.S., xv-xvi, xx, **31-51**, 31, 32, 33, 38, 42, 43, 44, 45, 46
JAKOBSON, R., 76
JAMIESON-DRAKE, D.W., 22
JANSSENS, J., 260
JANZEN, W., 80
JAPHET, S., 26, 37
JEWETT, R., 274
JONES, F.S., 243, 244, 246

KAESTLI, J.-D., **xi-xxi**, xx, **201-212**, 227, 265
KAISER, O., 69, 76
KANNENGIESSER, C., 274
KAPPLER, C.-C., 266
KAPPLER, R., 266
KASS, L.R., 10
KEBEKUS, N., 21, 22, 23
KEEFE, A.A., 10
KELLERMANN, D., 13
KENNELLY, L.B., 65
KESSLER, M., 85, 86
KEVELSON, R., 31
KEVERS, P., 5, 6, 7, 8, 12
KING, N.Q., 265
KITTEL, R., 59
KLAUCK, H.-J., 160, 163
KLIJN, A.F.J., 266
KNIERIM, R., 42
KNOX, J., 65
KRAEMER, R.S., 185, 186, 196, 198, 258
KRAUS, H.J., 23
KREMER, J., 177
KUENEN, A., 5
KUGEL, J., 9
KUNDSIN, K., 120
KURZ, W.S., 171

LA BONNARDIÈRE, A.-M., 280
LADOUCEUR, D., 168
LAMBERT, J., 18, 19, 21
LAUGHERY, G.D., 159
LE GOFF, J., 268
LEHMING, S., 5, 6, 12
LÉMONON, J.P., 213, 215
LEVINSON, B.M., 32
LÉVI-STRAUSS, C., 187, 188, 199, 200
LEWIS, I.M., 74

LEYSER, C., 243
LIEDKE, G., 42, 44
LIGHTFOOT, R.H., 120
LINCOLN, B., 189
LINDARS, B., 131, 138, 190
LINDBLOM, J., 69
LINDGREN, J.R., 31
LIPPOLD, A., 265
LIPSIUS, R.A., 253
LIZZI TESTA, R., 265
LLOYD WEBBER, A., 17
LOCHER, C., 44
LOHFINK, N., 33, 69
LONG, B.O., 74
LONGACRE, R.E., 18
LÖNING, K., 160, 163, 164, 175
LUST, J., 6
LUTHER, M., 65
LYKE, L.L., 36

MACCHI, J.-D., xvii-xviii, **3-15**, 3, 26, 277
MACDONALD, D.R., 227, 228, 229, 239, 241, 242, 253, 254
MAGNES, J., 48
MAGNESS, J.L., 106
MALBON, E. Struthers, 101, 119
MALONEY, L.M., 159
MANN, T., 17
MANUCCI, V., 119
MARAVAL, P., 275
MARCHADOUR, A., 159
MARGUERAT, D., xi, xix-xx, 119, 121, **159-181**, 163, 165, 172, 177, 179, 274
MARKUS, R.A., 265
MARRASSINI, P., 280
MARTIN, C.J., 170
MARTIN, H., 65
MARTYN, J.L., 133, 141, 147, 156
MASON, R.A., 65
MATTHEWS, V.H., 21
MAYS, J.L., 80, 81
MCBRIDE, S.D., 80
MCGING, B.C., 213
MCKANE, W., 38
MCKINNEY, K., 159
MEEKS, W.A., 120, 122, 135
MEIER, J.P., 100
MEINHOLD, A., 24
MERGAL, A.M., 65
MERLIER, O., 120

MERQUIOR, J.G., 229
MERRILL, A.L., 74
MEUNCHOW, C.A., 80
MILES, G.B., 168
MIMOUNI, S.C., 276
MINOKAMI, Y., 54, 60
MOBERLY, R.W.L., 27
MOESSNER, D.P., 169
MOLLAT, D., 120
MOLONEY, F.J., 119
MOMIGLIANO, A., 185
MONACI CASTAGNO, A., 281
MOORE, S.D., 101
MORESCHINI, C., 281
MORGAN, J.R., 250, 257, 258
MORRAY-JONES, C.R.A., 274
MOWERY, R.L., 160, 163, 164
MULZER, M., 54
MÜNTZER, T., 65
MURPHY-O'CONNOR, J., 121, 122
MURRAY, A.T., 91
MUSURILLO, H., 255, 262

NAGEL, P., 281
NAUERTH, C., 277
NEIRYNCK, F., 106
NEL, P.J., 46, 47
NEUSNER, J., 135
NEWCOMBE, C.R., 80
NEYREY, J.H., 178
NICHOLSON, E.W., 85, 86, 87
NICKELSBURG, G.W.E., 187, 204, 208
NICOL, G.G., 37
NIDITCH, S., 24
NIELSEN, E., 5, 6, 13
NOLAN, S., xx-xxi, **225-242**
NORELLI, E., 281
NORRIS, S., 243
NOTH, M., 4, 5, 6, 19, 28

OLBRICHT, T.H., 168
OLRIK, A., 228
O'NEILL, J.C., 186
OSBORNE, R., 230
O'TOOLE, L.M., 119
O'TOOLE, R.F., 159
OTTO, E., 5, 6, 44
OVERHOLT, T.W., 74, 75, 76

PASSAMANECK, S.M., 31

INDEX OF AUTHORS

PATRICK, D., 40, 42
PATRICK, S., 66
PAUL, S.M., 80
PAUPERT, C., 269, 279
PEDERSEN, J., 5, 6
PENCAK, W., 31
PENNA, R., 279
PERRY, B.E., 244
PERVO, R., 208, 209, 211, 250
PESCH, R., 177
PETERSON, D.L., 74
PHILLIPS, A., 33
PHILONENKO, M., 189, 198
PIATELLI, D., 46
PIÉDAGNEL, A., 280
PIETRI, C., 265
PIETRI, L., 265
PIOVANELLI, P., xv, **265-282**, 266, 267, 270, 272, 278, 281
POUDERON, B., 243
PORTER, S.E., 168
POTTER, R.D., 120
POWELL, M.A., 159
PRIEUR, J.-M., 254
PRINZIVALLI, E., 281
PROCKSCH, O., 5
PROVAN, I., 54
PUMMER, R., 9

RABINOW, P., 229, 230, 231
RAJAK, T., 214
RAKOTOHARINTSIFA, A., xvii, **119-130**
REARDON, B.P., 114, 115, 249, 250, 257
REDFORD, D., 17, 19, 21, 23, 24, 25
REHM, B., 246
REITZENSTEIN, R., 92
RENSBERGER, D., 132, 135, 137, 141
RICCIOTTI, G., 270
RICHARD, E., 160
RICHARDSON, P., 133
RIESNER, R., 122
RIETZSCHEL, C., 86
ROBBINS, V.K., 106
ROFÉ, A., 37, 54, 60
RÖMER, T., xiv, xviii, **17-29**, 22, 23, 25, 26, 277, 279
ROSENSTIEHL, J.-M., 281
ROUSSEL, B., 265
RUPPERT, L., 23

SABBE, M., 177

SÄNGER, D., 186
SAWYER, J.F.A., 43
SAXER, V., 275
SCHIFFMAN, L.H., 48
SCHLIER, H., 131
SCHMIDT, K.L., 122
SCHMIDT, L., 17
SCHMITT, H., 60
SCHMITT, H.-C., 21
SCHNEEMELCHER, W., 225, 243, 253, 254, 266
SCHNEIDER, G., 159
SCHULTZ, R.C., 65
SCHÜRER, E., 213
SCHWEIZER, E., 94, 97, 100
SCHWIENHORST-SCHÖNBERGER, L., 40
SCOTT, J.M.C., xviii, **91-104**
SCOTT SPENCER, F., 170
SCULLION, J.J., 70
SEBOEK, T.A., 76
SECRET, F., 270, 272, 278
SEEBASS, H., 13, 20
SEGERT, S., 44
SEGOVIA, F.F., 119
SELLIN, E., 69
SHAW, W.P., 65
SHEPERD, T., 105, 107
SHULER, P.L., 106
SILVERSTEIN, T., 266, 272, 277, 279, 281
SKA, J.L., 21, 121
SMITH, T., 246
SMYTH, F., 20, 22, 25
SOGGIN, J.A., 24, 26, 69
SPEYER, W., 270
SPRINKLE, J.M., 32, 40
SQUIRES, J.T., 165, 166, 178
STALEY, J.-L., 119
STANDHARTINGER, A., 9, 185
STECK, O.H., 60
STEHLY, R., 92
STEPHENS, S., 243
STERNBERG, M., 10, 54
STEVENSON, J., 225
STIBBE, M.W.G., 119, 132, 136, 137, 139
STONE, M.E., 187
STONEMAN, R., 250, 258
STRAUSS, H., 6
STRECKER, G., 243, 244, 246, 260
STRELAN, R., 166
STURDY, J., 69
SUGDEN, E.H., 112

Swain, S., 257

Talbert, C.H., 106
Tannehill, R.C., 171
Tasker, R.V.G., 95
Telfer, W., 276
Thompson, B.P., 190
Tischendorf, C., 270
Tissot, Y., 252
Tomes, F.R., xiv-xv, 17, 49, **53-67**
Triulzi, A., 280
Trompf, G., 168
Tuckett, C.M., xviii-xix, **131-140**, 141, 142, 143, 147, 150, 154, 156, 172
Turner, V., 189
Tuttle, G.A., 77

Ulrich, D.R., 43
Uspenskij, B.A., 123, 125, 127

van der Woude, A.S., 24
van de Water, R., 265
van Gennep, A., 189
van Houten, C., 32
Van Oyen, G., 105, 106, 107
Van Segbroeck, F., 105, 106
Van Seters, J., 5, 6, 7, 19, 21, 32
Vater, A.M., 71, 72, 73, 77, 78
Vervenne, M., 32
von Nordheim, E., 204
von Rad, G., 17, 22
von Wahlde, U., 133

Walker, A., 239
Weeks, S., 38
Weinfeld, M., 34, 40
Weiss, B.G., 31
Welch, J.W., 31
Wellhausen, J., 5, 53
Wenham, G., 40
Westermann, C., 4, 5, 7, 18, 70, 76
White, H.C., 18, 70
Whybray, R.N., 18, 33, 34, 41
Wildavsky, A., 20
Wildhaber, B., 163
Wilken, R.L., 275
Willemse, J., 120, 122
Williams, G.H., 65
Williams, S., 265, 277
Willi-Plein, I., 20, 23
Willis, R., 188
Wills, L.M., 258
Wilson, R.McL., 243
Wilson, R.R., 74
Winkler, J.J., 115
Witherup, R.D., 171, 172
Wolff, H.W., 80, 81
Wright, C.D., 271
Würthwein, E., 59, 60
Wyatt, N., 6, 10

Zobel, H.-J., 18
Zumstein, J., 119
Zwingli, H., 65

INDEX OF BIBLICAL REFERENCES

OLD TESTAMENT

Genesis		34,14-22	11	37,22	46n74
		34,14	6n8	37,28	46n74
3,22-24	198	34,15-17	11n26, 12n27	37,29	46n74
12	14	34,19	6n8	38	20, 20n14
15,12	69n4	34,20-23	11n26		(2x)
15,17	69n4	34,23	9	39-45	20
20	14, 28	34,24-26	11	39	20, 20n14
24,30	54	34,24	7n14, 11		(2x), 21, 25
26	14	34,25-29	4		(2x), 209
27,12	41n57	34,25-26	4 (2x), 7 (2x),	39,1	211
27,39-40	41n57		8n16, 11	39,10-20	207
28,6	41	34,25	5n6, 6 (2x), 7,	39,10	208 (2x), 209,
29,31-30,24	4n2, 4n3		8, 8n17, 11,		210,
30,21	3		12		212 (2x)
31,36	49	34,25b	7	39,11-20	208, 209, 210,
33,19	12	34,26	6n8, 7 (2x), 8,		212 (2x)
33,20	3		9	40	28
34,1-35,5	xvii (2x)	34,27-31	9	40,8	18
34	xvii, 4, 5, 6, 7,	34,27-29	7n14, 8 (2x)	41	24, 26
	13, 14	34,27-29	4, 5n6, 6, 7	41,14	46n74
34,1-31	3, 4		(2x), 7n13	41,16	18
34,1-26	5n6 (2x), 12	34,27	7 (2x)	41,34	23
	(2x), 14	34,27b	7, 8	41,40	28
34,1-24	5, 12	34,28	7	41,42	28
34,1-4	11	34,30	4, 6 (2x), 7,	41,45	185
34,1	4, 5n6, 6n8		7n13, 8 (2x),	42,9	23
34,2-25a	5n6		8n19, 9	42,16	46n74
34,2-3	9	34,31	4, 6, 7, 7n13	42,18	46
34,2	6n8, 10 (2x)		(2x), 9	42,24	46n74
34,3	6n8, 9, 10,	35,1	3	43,23	26
	11n25	35,2	7, 9	43,25-31	5
34,5	5n6, 7n13, 9	35,4-5	9	43,32	xiv
34,5a	7, 8	35,4	7	43,33-34	21n21
34,6-7a	11	35,5	3, 4 (2x), 7,	45	20n13
34,6	4		7n13, 8, 8n19,	45,7-8	18
34,7b	5n6, 7, 7n13,		9	46,1-5	20, 20n15
	8, 9	37-50	17, 18, 22, 29	46,8-26	23
34,8-13a	11		(2x)	46,15	4n2
34,8-10	11n26	37	20 (2x),	46,28-33	20
34,11	4, 6n8		20n14, 21, 23,	47	20
34,12	6n8		24n39, 25, 26	47,6-7	20
34,13b	5n6 (2x), 7,	37,1-2	20	47,13-26	20, 20n15
	7n13, 8, 9	37,1	23n32	47,27-28	20, 23n32

INDEX OF BIBLICAL REFERENCES

48	20	19,25	54	24,21	43
49	6, 7, 9, 20	21,10	10, 36	24,22	43
49,2	12	21,15	40, 40n55, 49	27,26	8n15
49,3-4	41n57	21,17	40, 49		
49,4	48n82	21,18-19	32n8	Numbers	
49,5-7	xvii, 4, 6 (2x), 9 (2x), 11 (2x), 12 (2x), 13, 14	21,18	44n68		
		21,20	32n9 (2x)	4,15	13n31
		21,22	32n8	4,19-20	13n31
		21,28-32	32n13	9,10-13	43
49,5-6	4 (3x), 8	21,28	8n15	14,39	54
49,6	8, 8n15	21,29	8n15	16,3	13n31
49,6b	4, 7 (3x), 8, 8n17	21,33-34	32n11	16,8	13n31
		21,33	8n15	18,1-7	13n31
49,7	4, 7, 12	21,35-36	32n13	22,7	54
49,7b	11	21,35	8n15, 33n17	27,7	42
49,29-33	20, 23n32	21,37	8n15	27,8	42n59
50	20	22,1-2	32n10	31,7-10	8n18
50,1-11	20	22,4-5	32n12	36,5	43
50,12-13	20, 23n32	22,6	33n17	36,7-9	43
50,14-21	20	22,8	33n17		
50,14	26	22,9-12	32n14	Deuteronomy	
50,17	49	22,9	33n17		
50,20	26	22,10	33n17	1,19-17	31n1
50,22-25	20, 20n15	22,13	33n17	6,2	22
50,26	20	22,25	33n17, 33n18	7,1-6	26
		22,27	33n15 (2x)	10,22	23
Exodus-2 Kings	27	23	34 (2x)	16	34 (2x)
		23,3	33n18	16,18-20	31n1
Exodus		23,4-5	33n16	16,19	34
		23,6	33n18	19,19	45
1	23	23,8	34	20,14	8n18
1,1-5a	23n32	23,11	33n18	21,15-17	47
1,5b	23n32	24,3	54	22,23-29	10n21
1,6	23n32	32,26-29	13	25,11	36n39
1,8	23n32	34,2	95n17	26,5	23
1,15-21	27	34,4	95n17	23,2 LXX	170
1,15	28				
1,17	27	Leviticus		Joshua	
1,21	27				
3	78	17,3	8n15	6,21	8, 8n15, 8n16, 8n17
3,14	95n19	21,20	170n34		
5,22-6,13	78	22,24	170n34	24,4	23
6,9	54	24,14	43		
12,46b	126	24,15	43	Judges	
13,22	10	24,16	43		
14,24	95n17	24,17	43	1,6-7	46
18,19-22	31n1	24,18	43	8,2	36n38
19,3 LXX	94n14	24,19	43, 45	14,2	46n76
19,7	54	24,20	43	14,18	46n77

14,19	46	1 Kings		9,1-13	59
14,20	46			9,1	80
15,4-6	46	11,29-39	80	9,3	59
15,6	46 (2x)	13,18	55	9,6	59
15,7-8	46	14,9	57 (2x)	9,7-10a	xiv, 53, 55, 67 (2x)
15,7	47	14,10-11	53, 57		
15,10	46	14,14	58	9,8	57
15,11	46, 46n78	14,15-16	58	9,10	53, 57
15,12-13	47	14,16	57	9,11	59 (2x)
16,18	54	15,29	57	9,12	54
21	36n38	15,30	57 (2x)	9,13	59
		16,2	57 (2x), 58	9,14-15	59
1 Samuel		16,3-4	57	9,14-15a	53
		16,4	53	9,14	63
2,2-18	78	16,7	58	9,20	59
3,18	54	16,12	57	9,22	60, 61
8,1-3	48n84	16,13	57 (2x)	9,23	63
8,10	54	16,16	58	9,24	60
10,16	55	16,20	58	9,25-26	54, 60, 61
12,8	23	18,21	64	9,27-28	63
14,34	8n15	19,10	56	9,27	60
15,3	8, 8n15, 8n16, 8n17	19,14	56	9,28-29	53
		19,15-17	56, 61	9,31	63
16,7	36n38	19,15	80	9,32	63
22,19	8, 8n15, 8n16, 8n17	19,17	56	9,34	63 (2x)
		20,11	36n38	9,36-37	53, 61
24,6	63	21	60	9,36	61
24,10	63	21,17-19	60, 61	9,37	61
24,14	36n38	21,19	57	10,1-10	54
26,9	63	21,20	57	10,1-6	64
26,11	63	21,21-22	57	10,6	63
26,23	63	21,21	57	10,9	63, 64
30,23-25	43	21,22	57 (3x)	10,10	53, 61
30,23	43	21,23	53, 57, 61	10,12-14	63
30,24	43	21,29	57	10,15-16	54, 61
30,25	43	22,38	57, 61	10,17-28	54
				10,17	53, 61
2 Samuel		2 Kings		10,18-27	54
				10,19	64
1,14	63	2,1-18	56	10,25b-27	54
11,1-12,25	106	5,7	64	10,28-31	53
11,14-15	64	8,1-15	56	10,29	62
13,11-14	10n21	8,7	80	10,30	58, 61
14	38	8,10	55	10,31	62
14,2	36	8,12	56	10,36	62
14,5-7	36	8,14	55	11	54
14,7	38n42	8,15	56, 59	13,4-5	58
14,8-17	37-38	8,29	56	14,26-27	58
20	38	9-10	53, 67	17,7-18	58

INDEX OF BIBLICAL REFERENCES

17,21-23	58	Psalms		8,4	35n31
18,13-21,19	69n3, 77n26			10,12	32n3
19,14	64	15,5	48n84	10,13	32n9
25	69n3	26,9-10	48n84	10,17	32n5
25,26	28	69,1	95	12,1	32n5
25,27-30	28 (3x)	78,12	22	12,5	32n6
25,27	28	105,18-23	23	12,10	32n14
25,28	28	106,6	22	13,8	33n18
25,29	28	107,23-30	94	13,10	32n3
		119	33n22	13,18	32n5
1 Chronicles		136,10	22	13,24	32n9, 40n52, 40n53
5,1	47, 48n82	Proverbs		14,4	32n13
5,21	8n18			14,31	33n18
7	26	1,2-6	39n46	15,10	32n5
7,29	26	1,5	35n32	15,18	32n3
		1,8	32n9, 40n51	15,31-32	32n5
2 Chronicles		1,12	32n11	16,10	32n6
		1,15	32n9	17,1	32n3
19,5-11	31n1	1,23	32n5	17,8	48n84
19,6	32n6	1,24	35n30	17,14	32n3
22,7-10	63	1,25	32n5	17,23	34
22,7	63	1,30	32n5	20,3	32n3
28,8	8n18	1,33	35n32	20.20	40, 40n54
32,1-31	69n3	2,1	32n9, 35n35	21,13	33n18
		2,2	35n33	21,14	48n84
Ezra		2,10	32n4	22,7	33n18
		3,1	32n9, 35n35	22,15	32n9, 40n53
9-10	13	3,3	32n4	22,16	33n18
9	26	3,11	32n9	22,17	35n32
		3,21	32n9	22,20	35n36
Nehemiah		3,24	42	22,22	33n18
		3,30	32n3, 41	23,13-14	32n9
10	26	4,1	32n9	23,13	40n53
		4,4	32n4, 40n50	23,15	32n9
Esther	24n39	4,10	32n9, 35n32	23,19	32n9
6,10-11	28	4,11	40n50	24,21	33n15
10,3	28	4,20	32n9, 35n33	24,24	44n68
		4,21	32n4	24,29	45
Job		5,1	32n9, 35n33	24,31	32n12
		6,1	32n9	25,7-10	32
		6,20	40n51	25,10	32n5
24,9	33n18	6,21	32n9	25,21-22	38n42
24,14	32n10	7,1	32n9	26,20-21	32n3
24,16	32n10	7,3	32n4	26,21	32n3, 33n16
29,12	33n18	7,6-27	25	26,27	32n11
29,16	33n18	7,22	32n13	27,5	32n5
31,16	33n18	7,24	35n32	27,10	33n17
31,19	33n18	8,1	35n30, 53n31	27,11	32n9

INDEX OF BIBLICAL REFERENCES

27,23	32n14	38,4	77n26	27,16-22	73n14, 74n19
28,5	32n6	38,8b-9	77n27	28	73n15, 74n19
28,8	33n18	37	73n15	28,1-10	79, 81
28,9	35n34	37,14	64	28,11-17	79, 81
28,23	32n5	43,1-13	95n19	28,17	77n27
28,24	40, 49	49,6	178	29	73n15
28,25	32n3	53,7-8	170	29,1-32	79, 83
29,14	33n18	56,3-8	170n34	29,27-28	73n14
29,15	32n9, 40n51	66,3	8n15	32,1-5	73n13, 79
30,11	40n51, 40n54			32,4-5	73n14, 79 (2x), 88 (2x)
30,17	40n51, 40n54	Jeremiah			
31,1-2	40n51			32,6-33,26	79, 83
31,9	33n18	1,4-19	78	32,8	77n27
31,26	40n51	3,6-14	79	34,1-7	79
		7,1-8,3	86n44, 87	35,1-19	73n14, 79, 83
Ecclesiastes		8,8	34	36	73n15
		13,1-11	79	36,1-32	79, 83
5,8	33n18	18	73n15	37,3-10	79, 81, 82, 88 (2x)
12,10	35n36	18,1-23	79, 81		
12,12	35n36	19,1-20,6	73n15, 79, 83	37,3-5	82
		21,1-14	79, 83	37,3	82
Isaiah		21,1-2	82n38	37,6-10	82
		25,15-38	79	37,16-21	79, 81, 82, 88 (2x)
1,23	48n84	26	76n21, 86n44, 87, 88 (2x)	37,16-17	82n38
5,23	48n84			38,1-13	79, 81
6,1-13	78	26,1-24	79, 83	38,1-6	73n13, 81, 85, 88 (2x)
6,9-10	179, 179n54 (2x)	26,1-19	73n13		
		26,1	85	38,1-3	81
7,1-24	79, 83	26,2	85	38,2-3	82
8,1-4	79, 83	26,3	85, 86	38,4-6	82
17,14	95n17	26,4-6	85, 86n44	38,4	82
20,1-6	79	26,7-9	73n14	38,5-6	82
33,15	48n84	26,7-8	73n13	38,11	82
36-39	69n3, 77n26	26,7	85	38,14-28	79, 83
36,1-37,38	79, 83	26,8b	85	38,14-16	82n38
36	73n15	26,10	85	39,1-10	69n3
36,11-12	77n26	26,11	85	40,1-6	79
36,14-16a	77n26	26,12-15	85	40,2-3	77n27
36,18	77n26	26,16	85, 86, 86n42	40,7-41,3	69n3
36,21-22	77n26	26,17-19	74n20, 85, 86	41,3b-34	69n3
37,1-7	82n38	26,18	87	42,1-43,13	79, 83
37,1-4	77n26	26,20-23	87	42,1-43,7	73n13, 83, 88 (2x)
37,8-35	82n38	26,20b	85		
37,14-20	77n26	26,24	73n13, 86, 86n42	42,1-7	83
37,17	101,30			42,1-6	82n38
37,21	77n26	27,2-7	74n19	42,7	83
37,36-38	77n27	27,9-11	73n14	42,8-22	83
38,1-22	79, 81	27,11	74n19	42,19	73n14, 83
38,2-3	77n26	27,14-15	73n14		

295

43-44	25	37,1-14	79, 83	7,10-11	73n14, 79 (2x), 80
43,1-4	73n14	37,1-3	84		
43,1-3	73n13, 83	37,1	84	7,10	80n31
43,4	83	37,4	84	7,11	80, 81n32
44	73n15	37,7a	84	7,12-17	80, 85
44,1-30	79, 81	37,7b-8	84	7,14	81
51,59-64b	79	37,9	84	7,15-17	73n14
		37,10a	84	7,15	81
Ezekiel		37,10b	84	9,11-12	178
		37,10c	84		
1,1-3,15	79, 81	37,11-14	84	Obadiah	
3,22-27	79	37,11	73n14		
8,1	82n38	37,12	85	18	22
11,2-12	73n14	38,11	73n14		
11,13a	77n27	40,1-48,35	79	Jonah	
12,1-20	79, 83	44,10-16	13 (2x)		
12,8-16	73n14	44,24-25	73n14	1,1-4,11	79, 83
12,21-25	73n14	47,13	22	1,2	83
12,26-28	73n14			3-4	73n15, 83, 88 (2x)
13,1-7	73n14	Daniel			
13,8-16	73n14			3,1-2	83
13,17	73n14	1-6	27, 28	3,3-4	83
14,1	82n38	2	24	3,5	84
18,2-18	73n14	2,48	28	3,6-9	84
18,19-24	73n14	5	24	3,10	84
18,25-32	73n14	5,29	28	4,1-5	84
20,1-44	79	6,20	101n30	4,2	84
20,1	82n38	6,26	101n30	4,6-11	84
20,5	22				
20,32	73n14	Hosea		Micah	
20,49	73n14				
22,12	48n84	1,2-3,5	79	3,11	48n84
24,15-24	79, 83	1,4	62	3,12	87
24,18b	77n27	1,10	101n30	7,3	48n84
24,25-27	77n27	2	105		
25,3	73n14	11,1	22	Haggai	
26,2	73n14				
27,3	73n14	Amos		1,1-15	83
28,2	73n14				
28,9	73n14	1,11	66	Zechariah	
29,9b	73n14	2,1	66		
33,10	73n14	6,6	22	1,4-5	73n14
33,17	73n14	7,7-17	80	1,7-6,15	79
33,20	73n14	7,7-9	80, 81, 81n32	7,1-8,23	79
33,21-22	77n27	7,9	80n31	7,2-3	82n38
33,24	73n14	7,9c	80	10,6	22
35,10	73n14	7,10-17	80 (2x), 80n31, 81, 81n32, 88 (2x)	11,4-17	79, 83
36,2	73n14				
36,20	73n14			Malachi	
37	88 (2x)			3,16-18	79 (2x)

INDEX OF BIBLICAL REFERENCES

Apocrypha

Judith		Additions to Daniel		8,23-36	105
9,2-4	9n20			8,30-33	105
		Susanna	193n19		
Wisdom				4 Ezra	
3,14-15	170n34	2 Maccabees		14,37-49	170n36

New Testament

Matthew		14,22	98	27,1	146
		14,23	94	27,11	146n25, 148
1,1-4,16	97	14,24	98	27,24-25	131n1
1,18-25	101	14,25	98	27,26-31a	143
1,23	102, 103	14,26-27	98	27,29	146, 146n25
2,1-11	151	14,28-31	98, 100	27,37	146, 146n25
2,3	95	14,30	98	27,42	146n25, 151n50
3,13-17	97	14,31	98, 100, 101, 102	27,54	99
4,1-11	97 (3x)			28,16-20	97, 101
4,8	94n14	14,32	95n21	28,16	94n14
4,15	122n9	14,33	93, 97, 98, 100, 101 (2x), 102	28,17	102 (3x)
4,17-25,46	97			28,18	102 (2x)
4,17-6,20	93			28,20	103
4,17	93, 96n23, 97	15,29	94n14		
5,1	94n14	16,8	100	Mark	
5,44	94	16,13-20	97, 100 (2x)		
6,5-15	94	16,13	100	1,4	122n8
7,28	93n11	16,14	101n29	1,5	122n8
8,5-13	95n20	16,16	100 (2x), 101 (2x)	3,20-35	108
8,18-27	94, 98 (2x)			4,1-20	106
8,18	98	16,17-19	101n29	5,21-23	108
8,19-22	98	16,20	100 (2x)	6,7-32	107
8,23-27	95n20, 97	16,21-28	101	6,7-30	108
8,24	98	16,21-26	98n26	6,14-29	105
8,25	98	16,21	93 (2x), 96n23	10,29-30	252
8,26	98			11,11-25	107, 108, 114
8,27	98	17,1-13	96n23	13,14-20	175n44
8,28-34	95n20	17,1	94n14	14,53-72	107 (2x)
8,29	99	19,1	93n11	15,2	146, 146n25
9,18-26	95n20	19,29-30	252	15,9	146, 146n25
9,27-31	95n20	20,20	102	15,12	146n25 (2x)
11,1	93n11	21,1-11	96n23	15,15-20a	143
13,53-16,20	93	23,9	251 (2x)	15,16-20	137
13,53	93	24,16	94n14	15,18	146, 146n25
14,15	94	26,1-28,20	97	15,22	148
14,22-33	xviii, 91-104, 97, 98, 100, 103, 104	26,1	93n11	15,26	146, 146n25
		26,25	135n19	15,32	146n25
		26,30	94n14		

15,42	151n50	1,15	124, 125, 125n18	1,48	148n36
				1,49	146n25, 147 (2x), 151, 151n50
Luke		1,16-18	124		
		1,17b	125		
1-2	162	1,19-28	xvii	1,50	148n36
1,11-20	162n9	1,19	122, 123, 124n16, 126, 128	2,1	122, 123
1,26-38	162n9			2,4	148n36
1,38	162n9			2,11	123, 128
1,41	162n9	1,20-28	124	2,12	122
1,64	162n9	1,21	148n36	2,13	122, 123
1,67	162n9	1,24-39	129	2,18	128
2,9-14	162n9	1,24	147n32	2,20	148n36
2,27	162n9	1,25	124	2,23	128
2,40	162	1,26	124	3,1	147n32
5,4-8	168n28	1,26b	124	3,2	128, 153n57
8,22-25	168n28	1,27	125	3,4	148n36
9,28-36	162n10	1,28-42	129	3,10-21	128
13,4-5	174n44	1,28-34	128n22	3,14	142n9
18,29-30	252	1,28-29	123 (2x), 127, 130 (2x)	3,22	122, 129
19,41-44	174n44			3,23	127
21,20-24	174n44	1,28	121 (2x), 122n8, 123, 124, 128	3,25-26	126, 130 (2x)
22-24	164			3,26	121, 123, 126, 127 (2x), 129
22,69	177				
23	131n1	1,29	122, 125 (2x), 126 (2x)	3,27-31	127
23,2	146, 146n25			3,28-30	127
23,3	148	1,29a	125	3,31	153n57
23,34	175, 177	1,29b	125	4,1-2	129
23,37	146n25 (2x)	1,30	125	4,1	147n32
23,38	146, 146n25	1,31a	125 (2x)	4,3-5	122
23,46	177	1,31c	125	4,3	123
24	162	1,32a	125	4,4-42	123
24,4-7	162n9	1,32b	125	4,22	133
24,6	164n19	1,33	124	4,29	135
24,7	164n19	1,33a	125 (2x)	4,43-54	123
24,26	164n19	1,33b	125	4,43	122
24,31	162n9	1,34	125 (2x), 125n18	4,44	122, 123
24,34	164n19			4,48	128
24,36-51	162n9	1,34a	125 (2x)	4,54	128
24,44	164n19	1,34b	125	5,1	122, 123
		1,35	126	5,18	144n13, 145, 148
John		1,36b	125		
		1,37	127, 128	5,19-47	128
1,6-8	127	1,37b	126	5,33	127
1,7	124, 124n15, 126	1,38-39	127, 130	5,35	127
		1,38	126, 148n36	5,46	133
1,11	156n66	1,38b	126	6,1	122, 123
1,12	126	1,43	121n7, 122, 123, 126	6,2	128
1,14	130			6,14	128
1,15-27	124	1,46	148n36	6,15	146n25, 147

INDEX OF BIBLICAL REFERENCES

6,26-59	128	11,7-8	123	18,22	147n31
6,26	123	11,18-20	122	18,24	147n31
6,30	128	11,45-47	145	18,26	147n31
6,42	153n57	11,46	147n32	18,28-19,22	141, 156, 157
7,1	122, 123 (2x), 144n13	11,47	128, 147n31, 147n32	18,28-19,16a	142n6
7,10	122	11,48	154	18,28-32	142, 142n6 (2x), 145n20
7,11	123	11,49 52	155n63	18,28-29	154
7,19	144n13	11,49	147n31	18,28	142n6, 144n17
7,20	144n13	11,50-52	148		
7,25	123, 144n13	11,50	128	18,30	144 (2x)
7,26-29	153n57	11,51	147n31	18,31-32	145 (3x)
7,31	128	11,53	144n13	18,31	137, 142 (2x), 144n13, 147
7,32	147n31, 147n32	11,54	122		
		11,55	123	18,31b	146n24
7,42-43	153n57	11,57	147n31, 147n32	18,32	142, 142n9, 144n18
7,45	147n31, 147n32	12,1	122	18,33-19,22	134
7,47	147n32	12,10	147n31, 148	18,33-38b	152
7,48	147n32	12,12	122	18,33-38a	142n6
7,50-51	132n5	12,13	146n25, 147, 151	18,33	134, 142n6, 143, 146 (2x), 148, 148n37, 149 (2x), 150, 150n45, 151n47
7,52	153n57				
8,13	147n32	12,15	146n25, 147		
8,22	144n13	12,19	147n32		
8,23	153n57	12,32-33	142, 145		
8,28	142n9, 144n13, 145	12,32	142n9		
		12,33	142n9	18,34-35	145
8,37	144n13	12,42	141n4, 147n32, 148	18,34	134, 149
8,40	144n13			18,35-38	150n43
8,42	153n57	13-17	129	18,35	144, 147, 148, 149, 154n60
9,13	147n32	13,3	153n57		
9,15	147n32	14,6	135, 152	18,35a	135
9,16	128, 147n32	16,2	141n4, 148	18,36-37	150n45
9,22	141n4, 148	16,27-28	153n57	18,36	135, 141, 147, 149n40, 151, 152n52
9,29-30	153n57	16,30	153n57		
9,40	147n32	18-19	147, 148, 151, 156, 156n68, 157		
10	126			18,37	135, 147n27, 148, 148n37, 149n40, 150n46, 152
10,22-24	123				
10,24-39	129	18,3	147 (2x), 147n31		
10,34-36	137				
10,39-40	123	18,10	147n31	18,37b	135
10,39	128	18,12-27	145	18,38	147, 148, 149n40, 152, 153
10,40-42	xvii, 127, 129, 130 (3x)	18,12	147		
		18,13	147n31		
10,40	121, 122n9, 123, 127, 128	18,14	155n63	18,38a	135
		18,15	140 (2x), 147n31	18,38b-40	142n6, 153
10,40c	127			18,38b	136, 143, 143n11, 149n40
10,41b	128 (2x)	18,16	147n31		
11,6	128	18,19	147n31		

18,39-40	143	19,19-22	139	3,14f	162	
18,39	136, 146 (2x), 149, 150n45, 153n56, 154	19,19	146 (2x), 149	3,15	164n19, 175n45	
		19,20	147, 155			
		19,21-22	147, 150, 157	3,17	175 (2x)	
18,40	136, 144, 154	19,21	146 (2x), 146n26, 147, 148n35, 149n39, 151n47, 152n52	3,18	175n45	
19,1-5	136, 153			3,19	175n46 (2x)	
19,1-3	142n6, 143, 149n40			3,22	164n19	
				3,25-26	175n45	
19,1-2	141, 149n40			3,26	164n19	
19,3	146 (2x)			3,29f	162	
19,4-8	142n6	19,22	150, 154	4,10	162, 164n19, 175n45	
19,4	136, 143 (2x), 149n40, 153	19,31	142n6, 147, 154 (2x), 156, 157			
				4,27	145n20	
19,5	136, 143			4,31	161, 163	
19,6	136, 137, 143 (3x), 144, 147, 149n40, 153, 154	19,36	126, 129	5,1-11	162n7	
		19,38	142n6, 147, 148, 154, 156, 157	5,12	162n7	
				5,13	162n7	
				5,15f	162n7	
19,7-12	153	19,40	154	5,15	163	
19,7	142, 144, 147, 153, 157	20,15	126	5,19f	161, 162	
		20,30-31	147, 150n42, 151	5,30	164n19	
19,8	137, 153			5,38-39	166, 169	
19,9-11	142n6	20,31	124n15, 128, 129	5,38b-39a	166	
19,9	137, 148, 153			7	175	
19,10-11	145, 153	21,5	135	7,48	163n13	
19,10	137, 148			7,55f	161, 163, 165	
19,11	138, 144, 144n18, 156n65	Acts		7,56	161, 177	
				7,57-58	177	
		1-8	163n11	7,59b	177	
19,12-16a	142n6	1-7	162, 177n50	7,60b	177	
19,12	144 (5x), 145, 147 147n27	1,3-11	161	8	175, 176	
		1,7	164	8,6f	162n7	
19,12a	153	1,8	166, 180	8,9-12	163	
19,12b	153	1,10f	161	8,13	162n7	
19,13	138, 154, 155n65	1,26	161	8,18-24	163	
		2	175	8,26-40	169 (2x)	
19,14	137, 138, 147, 149, 153n56, 154, 156n65	2,1-11	161 (2x), 163	8,26	161, 170 (2x)	
		2,22-24	175n45	8,29	161, 170 (3x)	
		2,23f	162	8,35	170 (2x)	
19,15	131, 133 (2x), 138 (2x), 142n5, 144 (2x), 145, 146, 148, 149, 154	2,24	164n19	8,36	178	
		2,32-33	175n45	8,39	161, 163, 170, 176	
		2,32	164n19			
		2,38	175n46	9	169, 171, 172, 173, 174, 174n43, 175	
		2,43	162n7			
19,15a	138, 147, 154	2,47	164			
19,15b	138, 147n27	3-7	177	9,1-19a	165	
19,15c	138	3	175	9,3-8	161, 173	
19,16a	144 (2x), 149n40	3,1-10	162n7	9,7	161	
		3,13	145n20, 175n45	9,9	172, 173	
19,16b-22	142n6, 155			9,10-17	171, 174	

INDEX OF BIBLICAL REFERENCES

9,10-12	161, 171, 172	10,44-46	161	16,10-17	161
9,10	172	10,44-45	176	16,10	161 (2x), 164, 164n17, 166, 167 (3x)
9,13-14	172	10,44	171		
9,15f	166, 174	10,46	171		
9,15-16	172	10,47	173, 176, 178	16,14	164, 164n18, 167
9,17f	162n7	11,5-17	171		
9,17	172, 173	11,5-10	161	16,14a	164n18
9,19b-30	172, 177	11,12	161	16,15b	164n18
9,20	171, 173	11,13f	161	16,16-18	162n7
9,22	173	11,15	161	16,17	163n13
9,27	173	11,17	173	16,25-26	167
9,30	274n27	11,17b	178	16,26	161, 162
9,32-35	162n7	11,18	164	17-18	167
9,36-42	162n7	11,25	274n27	17	175
10-11	159, 169, 171n37, 172, 174, 175	12,6-10	162	17,26-28	178
		12,7-10	161	17,30	175 (2x), 175n46
		12,11	164 (2x)		
10	176	12,17	164 (2x), 164n16	17,31	164n19, 175n45
10,1-33	171				
10,1-23	161	12,23	161	18,8	164n18
10,1-11	171	13	175	18,9-10	178
10,3-6	161	13,2	161, 167	18,9f	161, 162
10,3	171	13,3	179 (2x)	18,9	164, 164n18
10,5-8	172	13,4	179	19,11f	162n7
10,5-6	171	13,6-11	163	19,11	164
10,10-16	161	13,27	175	19,13-17	162n7
10,10	171	13,30	164n19	20,9-12	162
10,13-15	171	13,37	164n19, 175n45	20,7-12	162n7
10,13-14	172			21,11	166, 167
10,15	164 (2x), 172	13,47	164, 178	21,19	164, 164n16
10,17b-20	172	14	175	22	171, 172, 173, 174n43
10,17	172 (3x)	14,3	162n7		
10,18	171	14,8-10	162n7		
10,19f	161	14,15	175n46	22,1-21	178
10,19	171	14,27	164, 164n16	22,6-21	171
10,22	161, 171, 173	15,2	164n16	22,6-11	162
10,28-30	171	15,4	164, 164n16	22,10	174
10,28	164, 173, 173n41	15,7-11	171 (2x), 172	22,12-16	174
		15,7	173n41	22,14f	174
10,30-32	161	15,8	173, 173n41	22,14	174
10,34-43	171, 175	15,12	164, 178	22,17-21	161, 162, 174
10,34	173, 173n41	15,36	160	22,18-21	174
10,38	173n41	15,41	274n27	22,18	174
10,40	164n19, 173n41, 175n45	16,6f	161	22,21	174
		16,6-10	165, 169	23,3	164 (2x)
		16,6-9	167	23,6	178
10,42	175n45	16,6	160, 161	23,9	161, 162
10,43	176	16,7	160	23,11	166, 177
10,44-48	172	16,9	160, 161	23,28	145n20
				25,11	178

26	171, 172, 173, 174, 174n43	28,3-6	162, 162n7, 168	Galatians	
26,8	164n19	28,7f	162n7	1,21	274n27
26,12-23	171	28,9	162n7	4,21-31	199n25
26,13-18	161, 162	28,11c	168		
26,15-18	174	28,25	179	1 Timothy	
26,16-18	174 (2x)	28,26-27	179		
26,20	175n46	28,26a	179n54	4,7	227n6
27	167, 168, 168n30	28,28	179 (2x)	6,13	145n20
		28,30	179		
27,9-44	162 (2x)	28,31	179	Revelation	
27,9-12	168				
27,9b-10	168n27	Romans		1,9	171n36
27,13-20	168			5,12	126n19
27,20	168	10,6-7	267	10,4	171n36
27,21	168n27			14,13	171n36
27,23f	161, 162	2 Corinthians		19,9	171n36
27,23-25	166, 167			21,5	171n36
27,23	168	10-13	274	22,19	171n36
27,24	168	12,1-5	271, 274		
27,33	168n27	12,2-4	274		
27,34	168n27	12,2	274		
27,35	167, 168, 168n27				

INDEX OF CLASSICAL SOURCES

Elephantine Papyri	24	15,2-6	192		209n13
		15,2	192	3,2	209n13
Stele of Intef	38	15,7	194	3,3	205
		15,8	194	3,4-5	205
Pseudepigrapha		16	197	3,4	203
		16,2	196	3,6-10	207
1 Enoch		16,8	196	3,6	203n5, 205,
12,4	171n36	16,13	196		209n13
15,1	171n36	16,14	196, 197	3,9	205
		16,22	196	4,1-3	207
2 Enoch		18,7-9	192	4,1	208, 209n13
22,28	170n36	18,9	197	4,2	209
		18,11	195	4,3	203, 205
Joseph and Aseneth		19,9	192	4,4-8	207
	xviii, 26, 185-	19,11	190	4,4	209n13
	200, 254, 258-	20,8-10	195	4,5	203, 209,
	259	21,3	195		209n13
1,6	197	21,4	195 (2x)	4,8	205 (2x)
2,8-9	192	21,6	195	5,1-4	207
4,12	194	21,8-9	190	5,1	203, 209,
5	197	22-29	199		209n13
6,1	194			6,1-8	207
7,1	191	*Jubilees*		6,3	205 (2x)
7,3	191	30	9n20	6,4	209, 209n13
7,4	196			6,6-8	204
7,5	191	*Testaments of the Twelve*		6,7	205
7,7	191	*Patriarchs*		7,1-8,1	207
7,7	191		201, 211, 212	7,1-3	209n15
8	189			7,2	203
8,5	190	*Testament of Joseph*		7,3	209, 209n13
8,10	191		201-212	7,4	205
10,1	191	1,2	203, 204	8,1	203, 205 (2x)
10,9-10	190	1,3-10,4	204 (2x)	8,2-5	207
10,10-13	190	1,3-2,7	204	8,2	208
11,3	194	2	203n5	8,4	203
12,1	192	2,1	203n5	8,5	203, 210
12,5	194	2,2	205	9,1-3	207, 210
12,9-10	193	2,7	205	9,1	208
12,11	193	3-9	xx (2x), 202,	9,4	206, 207,
12,12-13	194		203, 203n5,		207n9, 208,
12,13	192		204, 205, 207-		210, 210n16
12,15	192		212	9,5	207, 207n9,
14	197	3,1-9,5	202		210 (2x)
14,9	198	3,1-8,1	208	10,1-4	202, 203, 210
14,12	190, 191	3,1-5	207	10,1	205
		3,1	203, 208, 209,		

INDEX OF CLASSICAL SOURCES

10,2	202	*Legatio*		15,388	220
10,2-3	205	302	221n23	16,1	220
10,3	205			16,31-57	218n12
10,4	206	*Spec. Leg*		16,174	218n12
10,5-18,1	203	1,324-325	170n34	18,35	219
10,5	203, 204 (3x), 205, 206			18,55-56	219
				18,57	220
10,6	206	Josephus	108	18,63-64	145n20
11-17	210	*Antiquities of the Jews*		18,88	221
11-16	xx, 203, 211	1,5	218n12	18,89	219, 221
11,1	206	1,6	218n12	18,127-129	218n13
11,2-16,6	202	1,20	218n13	18,177	219n15
11,2-3	206	1,24	218n12	18,226	218n12
11,2	211	1,194-195	218	18,237	221
11,5	211	1,202-203	218	18,265	220n20
12,1	203 (2x), 211	1,256	218	18,268	220n20
13,1	203	1,346	218	18,306	219
13,4	203	2,28	218n13	19,1-113	219
14,1	203	2,107	218n13	19,3	221
14,2	206	3,223	218n12	19,113	220n22
14,5	203	3,311	218	19,301	220
15,1	211	4,290-291	170n34	19,366	218
15,3	206	4,312	219n14	20,17-48	220n22
15,6	203	5,1-33	108n10	20,46-48	218
16,1	203	5,179-180	219n14	20,179-181	218
16,5	203n5	5,185	219n14	20,157	213n2
16,6	206, 211	5,200	219n14	20,184	218
17,1-3	211	6,104	218	20,213	218
17,1	205	6,141-151	218	20,216-218	218
17,2-3	206	6,305	219n14		
17,4-8	211	6,307	218n13	*Life*	
17,4	211	6,334-336	218	5	217n11
17,5	211	6,378	218		
17,8	206	8,190	218	*Jewish War*	
18,1-2	205	8,314	218n13, 219n14	1,3	213n2, 217n11
				1,4	214n4
Testament of Levi		10,218	218n12	1,10	214n4
	11n25	11,120	218n12	1,16	213n2
5-6	9n20	11,209-269	218-219	1,21-22	214n5
		12,45-50	218n12	1,24	214n4
		12,248-359	219	1,27	214n4
Philo and Josephus		12,322	220	1,282-285	152n53
		13,299-300	218	1,412	214n5
Philo		14,185-189	218n12	2,72	214n5
In Flaccum		15,267-291	220n19	2,169	215
40	221n23	15,274	220	2,175-177	215
77	221n23	15,280	220n21	2,184-203	215, 217
95	221n23	15,281	220	2,186	217
136	221n23	15,328	220n20	2,199	214n5

INDEX OF CLASSICAL SOURCES

2,223-227	216	*Talmud*		Prologue	270-273, 274, 279
2,228-232	216	b.Bab.Mes. 168n28		0,1-5	271
2,232-245	216			0,1	271
2,345-404	216	Early Christian Sources		0,5	271
2,276	214n4			0,2-3	271
2,293	214n4	*Acts of Andrew*		1,1-2	271
2,299	214n4		254	1,1	272
2,318	214n4	22	254n15	1,2	272
2,333	214n4			2,1-3	271
2,345-404	214n7	*Acts of John*		2,1	273
2,354	214n5	37-45	169n32	2,2	273
2,357	214n5			2,3	273
2,362-379	214n5	*Acts of Marius, Martha*			
2,362	214n5	*and their Children* 262			
2,365-379	214n5			Apocalypse Proper	
2,373	214n5	*Acts of Paul and Thecla*		3-6	266
2,577	214n5		xx, 116,	4	267
3,31	214n5		169n32, 225-	5	267n6
3,70-109	214n5		242, 253	6	267n6
3,244	214n5	1	234	7	279
3,293	214n6	3	236, 238	9	269n14
3,404	214n6	4	234	10	267n6
3,472-484	214n5	7	235 (2x)	14-18	267
3,494	214n6	8-9	253n13	14	267
4,297	214n6	10	235, 253n14	15	267
4,323	214n6	11-14	235	16	267, 267n6, 268
4,370	214n6	11	234	17	267n6
5,2	214n6	12	237	18	267, 268
5,39	214n6	13	237	19-21	274
5,269	214n5	15	234 (3x), 237	21	267
5,343	214n6	19	235	22-31	267
5,348	214n5	20	234 (2x), 236	22	267n6, 269n14
5,362-419	214	21	236	23	269n14
6,22	214n5	22	235, 236	24	268
6,39	214n6	24	235	26	269n14
6,110	214n6	26	234, 235, 236	29	269n14
6,250	214n6	27	235, 236	31-42	267
6,399	214n6	36	234	33	267n6
6,401	214n6	37	235	34-46	269n14
7,32	214n6	38	235	38-39	269n14
7,139	214n5			39	269n14
7,319	214n6	*Acts of Pilate*		40	269n14, 270n17
7,323-336	214n7	Prologue	277n32		
7,455	213n2			41	270n17
		Acts of Perpetua and		43-44	268
		Felicitas		43	267n6
Rabbinic Sources		5	255n17	44	267n6, 267n7, 268n11
'Abot R. Nathan		*Apocalypse of Paul*		45-51	274
7	168n28		xv, 265-282	47-51	280n45

INDEX OF CLASSICAL SOURCES

48	275
50	267n6
51	272
52	272

Apocalypse of Peter
280

Apocryphal Acts of the Apostles
245, 250, 252n11, 253, 255, 257, 260, 263

Athanasius of Alexandria
Life of Anthony
65,2-9   274n26
On the Incarnation
25,5-6   274n26

Augustine
City of God
21,18   268n13
Enchiridion
29,112   268n11
Treatise on John
98,8   280

Chronicle of Edessa   261

De die iudicii   268n13

Gregory of Tours
Liber de miraculis
4   254n16

John Chrysostom
Third Homily on Philippians
4   268n11
Panegyrics of Saint Paul
   280n45

Kebra Nagast (Ethiopic)
19   278n35
117   278n35

Life of Mary (Syriac)
   260-261
22   261n30

25	261n31

Life of Mary of Egypt   261

On Mount Coscam   276

Martyrdom of Marian and James   262
13   262n34

Origen
Homilies on the Psalms
36-38   281n46

Penitence of Pelagia
   261

Prudence
Cathemerinon
5,125-127   268n11
5,134-137   268n11

Pseudo-Clement
Homilies   244, 245
Recognitions
   xx, xxi, 116, 243-264

6	250
6,6	251 (2x)
7-9	244
7,8	246
7,15	247
7,35	252
8,8	251
9,32-33	247
9,34	248
9,35	248

Regula Magistri
34,10   279

Rufinus
Sentences of Sextus
   260, 260n28

The Seven Sleepers of Ephesus   276

Sozomen
Ecclesiastical History
7,10   276n31

7,19	280

Tertullian
On Baptism
17   225n2

Other Classical Sources

Achilles Tatius
Leucippe and Clitophon
   115-116
1,12   115

Aristotle
Rhetoric
1,ix,33 (1367b)   109n12

Chariton
Chaereas and Callirhoe
   114, 250
1,1   250n9
1,6-9   114n26
1,12-13   259n9

Dio Chrysostom
1,3,30-31 (Loeb ed.)   92

Dionysius   109
Roman Antiquities
2,32-34   110n14

Heliodorus
Aethiopica
   244, 249, 257-258, 263
2,33   257n21
3,5   257n22

Herodotus
7,33-37 (Loeb ed.)   92

History of Apollonius
244, 256-257, 263

Homer   106, 165
Odyssey   91, 167n26

Livy   109
1,10   110n14

INDEX OF CLASSICAL SOURCES

Longus
Daphnis and Chloe
    249, 256
4,36 249n7
4,39 249n7

Lucian
The Carousal
20 113
How to Write History
   108-109
28 109n11
49-50 109n11
55 109n11
True Story 112

Lucius Apuleius
The Golden Ass 112

Magical papyri 92

Philostratus 106

Plautus 111
The Two Bacchides 112

Plutarch
Lives 109, 111
Alexander
1,2 109n12
23 111n19
24,1-25,3 111n19
24,10-14 111n19
Caesar 111n20
Cicero
32,4 111n18
Demosthenes 111n20
Lycurgus 111n20
Numa 111n20
Publicola
13-14 111n17
Romulus 109
16-17 110n14
Solon
12,1-13,1 110n15

15,3-16,3 110n15
27-28 110n16
28,1 110, 110n16
Theseus
6,4-6 109n13
11,1-12,1 109n13

Tacitus
Annals
15,44 145n20

Terence 111

Thucydides 109

Virgil 106
Aeneid 91

Xenophon 106
Epehesian's Tale
   115
3,8 114n27

BIBLIOTHECA EPHEMERIDUM THEOLOGICARUM LOVANIENSIUM

Series I

* = Out of print

*1. *Miscellanea dogmatica in honorem Eximii Domini J. Bittremieux*, 1947.
*2-3. *Miscellanea moralia in honorem Eximii Domini A. Janssen*, 1948.
*4. G. Philips, *La grâce des justes de l'Ancien Testament*, 1948.
*5. G. Philips, *De ratione instituendi tractatum de gratia nostrae sanctificationis*, 1953.
6-7. *Recueil Lucien Cerfaux. Études d'exégèse et d'histoire religieuse*, 1954. 504 et 577 p. FB 1000 par tome. Cf. *infra*, n°s 18 et 71 (t. III).
8. G. Thils, *Histoire doctrinale du mouvement œcuménique*, 1955. Nouvelle édition, 1963. 338 p. FB 135.
*9. *Études sur l'Immaculée Conception*, 1955.
*10. J.A. O'Donohoe, *Tridentine Seminary Legislation*, 1957.
*11. G. Thils, *Orientations de la théologie*, 1958.
*12-13. J. Coppens, A. Descamps, É. Massaux (ed.), *Sacra Pagina. Miscellanea Biblica Congressus Internationalis Catholici de Re Biblica*, 1959.
*14. *Adrien VI, le premier Pape de la contre-réforme*, 1959.
*15. F. Claeys Bouuaert, *Les déclarations et serments imposés par la loi civile aux membres du clergé belge sous le Directoire (1795-1801)*, 1960.
*16. G. Thils, *La «Théologie œcuménique». Notion-Formes-Démarches*, 1960.
17. G. Thils, *Primauté pontificale et prérogatives épiscopales. «Potestas ordinaria» au Concile du Vatican*, 1961. 103 p. FB 50.
*18. *Recueil Lucien Cerfaux*, t. III, 1962. Cf. *infra*, n° 71.
*19. *Foi et réflexion philosophique. Mélanges F. Grégoire*, 1961.
*20. *Mélanges G. Ryckmans*, 1963.
21. G. Thils, *L'infaillibilité du peuple chrétien «in credendo»*, 1963. 67 p. FB 50.
*22. J. Férin & L. Janssens, *Progestogènes et morale conjugale*, 1963.
*23. *Collectanea Moralia in honorem Eximii Domini A. Janssen*, 1964.
24. H. Cazelles (ed.), *De Mari à Qumrân. L'Ancien Testament. Son milieu. Ses écrits. Ses relectures juives* (Hommage J. Coppens, I), 1969. 158*-370 p. FB 900.
*25. I. de la Potterie (ed.), *De Jésus aux évangiles. Tradition et rédaction dans les évangiles synoptiques* (Hommage J. Coppens, II), 1967.
26. G. Thils & R.E. Brown (ed.), *Exégèse et théologie* (Hommage J. Coppens, III), 1968. 328 p. FB 700.
27. J. Coppens (ed.), *Ecclesia a Spiritu sancto edocta. Hommage à Mgr G. Philips*, 1970. 640 p. FB 1000.
28. J. Coppens (ed.), *Sacerdoce et célibat. Études historiques et théologiques*, 1971. 740 p. FB 700.

29. M. Didier (ed.), *L'évangile selon Matthieu. Rédaction et théologie*, 1972. 432 p. FB 1000.
*30. J. Kempeneers, *Le Cardinal van Roey en son temps*, 1971.

Series II

31. F. Neirynck, *Duality in Mark. Contributions to the Study of the Markan Redaction*, 1972. Revised edition with Supplementary Notes, 1988. 252 p. FB 1200.
32. F. Neirynck (ed.), *L'évangile de Luc. Problèmes littéraires et théologiques*, 1973. *L'évangile de Luc – The Gospel of Luke*. Revised and enlarged edition, 1989. x-590 p. FB 2200.
33. C. Brekelmans (ed.), *Questions disputées d'Ancien Testament. Méthode et théologie*, 1974. *Continuing Questions in Old Testament Method and Theology*. Revised and enlarged edition by M. Vervenne, 1989. 245 p. FB 1200.
34. M. Sabbe (ed.), *L'évangile selon Marc. Tradition et rédaction*, 1974. Nouvelle édition augmentée, 1988. 601 p. FB 2400.
35. B. Willaert (ed.), *Philosophie de la religion – Godsdienstfilosofie. Miscellanea Albert Dondeyne*, 1974. Nouvelle édition, 1987. 458 p. FB 1600.
36. G. Philips, *L'union personnelle avec le Dieu vivant. Essai sur l'origine et le sens de la grâce créée*, 1974. Édition révisée, 1989. 299 p. FB 1000.
37. F. Neirynck, in collaboration with T. Hansen and F. Van Segbroeck, *The Minor Agreements of Matthew and Luke against Mark with a Cumulative List*, 1974. 330 p. FB 900.
38. J. Coppens, *Le messianisme et sa relève prophétique. Les anticipations vétérotestamentaires. Leur accomplissement en Jésus*, 1974. Édition révisée, 1989. xiii-265 p. FB 1000.
39. D. Senior, *The Passion Narrative according to Matthew. A Redactional Study*, 1975. New impression, 1982. 440 p. FB 1000.
40. J. Dupont (ed.), *Jésus aux origines de la christologie*, 1975. Nouvelle édition augmentée, 1989. 458 p. FB 1500.
41. J. Coppens (ed.), *La notion biblique de Dieu*, 1976. Réimpression, 1985. 519 p. FB 1600.
42. J. Lindemans & H. Demeester (ed.), *Liber Amicorum Monseigneur W. Onclin*, 1976. xxii-396 p. FB 1000.
43. R.E. Hoeckman (ed.), *Pluralisme et œcuménisme en recherches théologiques. Mélanges offerts au R.P. Dockx, O.P.*, 1976. 316 p. FB 1000.
44. M. de Jonge (ed.), *L'évangile de Jean. Sources, rédaction, théologie*, 1977. Réimpression, 1987. 416 p. FB 1500.
45. E.J.M. van Eijl (ed.), *Facultas S. Theologiae Lovaniensis 1432-1797. Bijdragen tot haar geschiedenis. Contributions to its History. Contributions à son histoire*, 1977. 570 p. FB 1700.
46. M. Delcor (ed.), *Qumrân. Sa piété, sa théologie et son milieu*, 1978. 432 p. FB 1700.
47. M. Caudron (ed.), *Faith and Society. Foi et société. Geloof en maatschappij. Acta Congressus Internationalis Theologici Lovaniensis 1976*, 1978. 304 p. FB 1150.

48. J. KREMER (ed.), *Les Actes des Apôtres. Traditions, rédaction, théologie*, 1979. 590 p. FB 1700.
49. F. NEIRYNCK, avec la collaboration de J. DELOBEL, T. SNOY, G. VAN BELLE, F. VAN SEGBROECK, *Jean et les Synoptiques. Examen critique de l'exégèse de M.-É. Boismard*, 1979. XII-428 p. FB 1000.
50. J. COPPENS, *La relève apocalyptique du messianisme royal. I. La royauté – Le règne – Le royaume de Dieu. Cadre de la relève apocalyptique*, 1979. 325 p. FB 1000.
51. M. GILBERT (ed.), *La Sagesse de l'Ancien Testament*, 1979. Nouvelle édition mise à jour, 1990. 455 p. FB 1500.
52. B. DEHANDSCHUTTER, *Martyrium Polycarpi. Een literair-kritische studie*, 1979. 296 p. FB 1000.
53. J. LAMBRECHT (ed.), *L'Apocalypse johannique et l'Apocalyptique dans le Nouveau Testament*, 1980. 458 p. FB 1400.
54. P.-M. BOGAERT (ed.), *Le livre de Jérémie. Le prophète et son milieu. Les oracles et leur transmission*, 1981. Nouvelle édition mise à jour, 1997. 448 p. FB 1800.
55. J. COPPENS, *La relève apocalyptique du messianisme royal. III. Le Fils de l'homme néotestamentaire*. Édition posthume par F. NEIRYNCK, 1981. XIV-192 p. FB 800.
56. J. VAN BAVEL & M. SCHRAMA (ed.), *Jansénius et le Jansénisme dans les Pays-Bas. Mélanges Lucien Ceyssens*, 1982. 247 p. FB 1000.
57. J.H. WALGRAVE, *Selected Writings – Thematische geschriften. Thomas Aquinas, J.H. Newman, Theologia Fundamentalis*. Edited by G. DE SCHRIJVER & J.J. KELLY, 1982. XLIII-425 p. FB 1000.
58. F. NEIRYNCK & F. VAN SEGBROECK, avec la collaboration de E. MANNING, *Ephemerides Theologicae Lovanienses 1924-1981. Tables générales. (Bibliotheca Ephemeridum Theologicarum Lovaniensium 1947-1981)*, 1982. 400 p. FB 1600.
59. J. DELOBEL (ed.), *Logia. Les paroles de Jésus – The Sayings of Jesus. Mémorial Joseph Coppens*, 1982. 647 p. FB 2000.
60. F. NEIRYNCK, *Evangelica. Gospel Studies – Études d'évangile. Collected Essays*. Edited by F. VAN SEGBROECK, 1982. XIX-1036 p. FB 2000.
61. J. COPPENS, *La relève apocalyptique du messianisme royal. II. Le Fils d'homme vétéro- et intertestamentaire*. Édition posthume par J. LUST, 1983. XVII-272 p. FB 1000.
62. J.J. KELLY, *Baron Friedrich von Hügel's Philosophy of Religion*, 1983. 232 p. FB 1500.
63. G. DE SCHRIJVER, *Le merveilleux accord de l'homme et de Dieu. Étude de l'analogie de l'être chez Hans Urs von Balthasar*, 1983. 344 p. FB 1500.
64. J. GROOTAERS & J.A. SELLING, *The 1980 Synod of Bishops: «On the Role of the Family». An Exposition of the Event and an Analysis of its Texts*. Preface by Prof. emeritus L. JANSSENS, 1983. 375 p. FB 1500.
65. F. NEIRYNCK & F. VAN SEGBROECK, *New Testament Vocabulary. A Companion Volume to the Concordance*, 1984. XVI-494 p. FB 2000.
66. R.F. COLLINS, *Studies on the First Letter to the Thessalonians*, 1984. XI-415 p. FB 1500.
67. A. PLUMMER, *Conversations with Dr. Döllinger 1870-1890*. Edited with Introduction and Notes by R. BOUDENS, with the collaboration of L. KENIS, 1985. LIV-360 p. FB 1800.

68. N. LOHFINK (ed.), *Das Deuteronomium. Entstehung, Gestalt und Botschaft / Deuteronomy: Origin, Form and Message*, 1985. XI-382 p. FB 2000.
69. P.F. FRANSEN, *Hermeneutics of the Councils and Other Studies*. Collected by H.E. MERTENS & F. DE GRAEVE, 1985. 543 p. FB 1800.
70. J. DUPONT, *Études sur les Évangiles synoptiques*. Présentées par F. NEIRYNCK, 1985. 2 tomes, XXI-IX-1210 p. FB 2800.
71. *Recueil Lucien Cerfaux*, t. III, 1962. Nouvelle édition revue et complétée, 1985. LXXX-458 p. FB 1600.
72. J. GROOTAERS, *Primauté et collégialité. Le dossier de Gérard Philips sur la Nota Explicativa Praevia (Lumen gentium, Chap. III)*. Présenté avec introduction historique, annotations et annexes. Préface de G. THILS, 1986. 222 p. FB 1000.
73. A. VANHOYE (ed.), *L'apôtre Paul. Personnalité, style et conception du ministère*, 1986. XIII-470 p. FB 2600.
74. J. LUST (ed.), *Ezekiel and His Book. Textual and Literary Criticism and their Interrelation*, 1986. X-387 p. FB 2700.
75. É. MASSAUX, *Influence de l'Évangile de saint Matthieu sur la littérature chrétienne avant saint Irénée*. Réimpression anastatique présentée par F. NEIRYNCK. Supplément: *Bibliographie 1950-1985*, par B. DEHANDSCHUTTER, 1986. XXVII-850 p. FB 2500.
76. L. CEYSSENS & J.A.G. TANS, *Autour de l'Unigenitus. Recherches sur la genèse de la Constitution*, 1987. XXVI-845 p. FB 2500.
77. A. DESCAMPS, *Jésus et l'Église. Études d'exégèse et de théologie*. Préface de Mgr A. HOUSSIAU, 1987. XLV-641 p. FB 2500.
78. J. DUPLACY, *Études de critique textuelle du Nouveau Testament*. Présentées par J. DELOBEL, 1987. XXVII-431 p. FB 1800.
79. E.J.M. VAN EIJL (ed.), *L'image de C. Jansénius jusqu'à la fin du XVIIIe siècle*, 1987. 258 p. FB 1250.
80. E. BRITO, *La Création selon Schelling. Universum*, 1987. XXXV-646 p. FB 2980.
81. J. VERMEYLEN (ed.), *The Book of Isaiah – Le livre d'Isaïe. Les oracles et leurs relectures. Unité et complexité de l'ouvrage*, 1989. X-472 p. FB 2700.
82. G. VAN BELLE, *Johannine Bibliography 1966-1985. A Cumulative Bibliography on the Fourth Gospel*, 1988. XVII-563 p. FB 2700.
83. J.A. SELLING (ed.), *Personalist Morals. Essays in Honor of Professor Louis Janssens*, 1988. VIII-344 p. FB 1200.
84. M.-É. BOISMARD, *Moïse ou Jésus. Essai de christologie johannique*, 1988. XVI-241 p. FB 1000.
84A. M.-É. BOISMARD, *Moses or Jesus: An Essay in Johannine Christology*. Translated by B.T. VIVIANO, 1993, XVI-144 p. FB 1000.
85. J.A. DICK, *The Malines Conversations Revisited*, 1989. 278 p. FB 1500.
86. J.-M. SEVRIN (ed.), *The New Testament in Early Christianity – La réception des écrits néotestamentaires dans le christianisme primitif*, 1989. XVI-406 p. FB 2500.
87. R.F. COLLINS (ed.), *The Thessalonian Correspondence*, 1990. XV-546 p. FB 3000.
88. F. VAN SEGBROECK, *The Gospel of Luke. A Cumulative Bibliography 1973-1988*, 1989. 241 p. FB 1200.

89. G. THILS, *Primauté et infaillibilité du Pontife Romain à Vatican I et autres études d'ecclésiologie*, 1989. XI-422 p. FB 1850.
90. A. VERGOTE, *Explorations de l'espace théologique. Études de théologie et de philosophie de la religion*, 1990. XVI-709 p. FB 2000.
91. J.C. DE MOOR, *The Rise of Yahwism: The Roots of Israelite Monotheism*, 1990. Revised and Enlarged Edition, 1997. XV-445 p. FB 1400.
92. B. BRUNING, M. LAMBERIGTS & J. VAN HOUTEM (eds.), *Collectanea Augustiniana. Mélanges T.J. van Bavel*, 1990. 2 tomes, XXXVIII-VIII-1074 p. FB 3000.
93. A. DE HALLEUX, *Patrologie et œcuménisme. Recueil d'études*, 1990. XVI-887 p. FB 3000.
94. C. BREKELMANS & J. LUST (eds.), *Pentateuchal and Deuteronomistic Studies: Papers Read at the XIIIth IOSOT Congress Leuven 1989*, 1990. 307 p. FB 1500.
95. D.L. DUNGAN (ed.), *The Interrelations of the Gospels. A Symposium Led by M.-É. Boismard – W.R. Farmer – F. Neirynck, Jerusalem 1984*, 1990. XXXI-672 p. FB 3000.
96. G.D. KILPATRICK, *The Principles and Practice of New Testament Textual Criticism. Collected Essays*. Edited by J.K. ELLIOTT, 1990. XXXVIII-489 p. FB 3000.
97. G. ALBERIGO (ed.), *Christian Unity. The Council of Ferrara-Florence: 1438/39 – 1989*, 1991. X-681 p. FB 3000.
98. M. SABBE, *Studia Neotestamentica. Collected Essays*, 1991. XVI-573 p. FB 2000.
99. F. NEIRYNCK, *Evangelica II: 1982-1991. Collected Essays*. Edited by F. VAN SEGBROECK, 1991. XIX-874 p. FB 2800.
100. F. VAN SEGBROECK, C.M. TUCKETT, G. VAN BELLE & J. VERHEYDEN (eds.), *The Four Gospels 1992. Festschrift Frans Neirynck*, 1992. 3 volumes, XVII-X-X-2668 p. FB 5000.

SERIES III

101. A. DENAUX (ed.), *John and the Synoptics*, 1992. XXII-696 p. FB 3000.
102. F. NEIRYNCK, J. VERHEYDEN, F. VAN SEGBROECK, G. VAN OYEN & R. CORSTJENS, *The Gospel of Mark. A Cumulative Bibliography: 1950-1990*, 1992. XII-717 p. FB 2700.
103. M. SIMON, *Un catéchisme universel pour l'Église catholique. Du Concile de Trente à nos jours*, 1992. XIV-461 p. FB 2200.
104. L. CEYSSENS, *Le sort de la bulle Unigenitus. Recueil d'études offert à Lucien Ceyssens à l'occasion de son 90ᵉ anniversaire*. Présenté par M. LAMBERIGTS, 1992. XXVI-641 p. FB 2000.
105. R.J. DALY (ed.), *Origeniana Quinta. Papers of the 5th International Origen Congress, Boston College, 14-18 August 1989*, 1992. XVII-635 p. FB 2700.
106. A.S. VAN DER WOUDE (ed.), *The Book of Daniel in the Light of New Findings*, 1993. XVIII-574 p. FB 3000.
107. J. FAMERÉE, *L'ecclésiologie d'Yves Congar avant Vatican II: Histoire et Église. Analyse et reprise critique*, 1992. 497 p. FB 2600.

108. C. BEGG, *Josephus' Account of the Early Divided Monarchy (AJ 8, 212-420). Rewriting the Bible*, 1993. IX-377 p. FB 2400.
109. J. BULCKENS & H. LOMBAERTS (eds.), *L'enseignement de la religion catholique à l'école secondaire. Enjeux pour la nouvelle Europe*, 1993. XII-264 p. FB 1250.
110. C. FOCANT (ed.), *The Synoptic Gospels. Source Criticism and the New Literary Criticism*, 1993. XXXIX-670 p. FB 3000.
111. M. LAMBERIGTS (ed.), avec la collaboration de L. KENIS, *L'augustinisme à l'ancienne Faculté de théologie de Louvain*, 1994. VII-455 p. FB 2400.
112. R. BIERINGER & J. LAMBRECHT, *Studies on 2 Corinthians*, 1994. XX-632 p. FB 3000.
113. E. BRITO, *La pneumatologie de Schleiermacher*, 1994. XII-649 p. FB 3000.
114. W.A.M. BEUKEN (ed.), *The Book of Job*, 1994. X-462 p. FB 2400.
115. J. LAMBRECHT, *Pauline Studies: Collected Essays*, 1994. XIV-465 p. FB 2500.
116. G. VAN BELLE, *The Signs Source in the Fourth Gospel: Historical Survey and Critical Evaluation of the Semeia Hypothesis*, 1994. XIV-503 p. FB 2500.
117. M. LAMBERIGTS & P. VAN DEUN (eds.), *Martyrium in Multidisciplinary Perspective. Memorial L. Reekmans*, 1995. X-435 p. FB 3000.
118. G. DORIVAL & A. LE BOULLUEC (eds.), *Origeniana Sexta. Origène et la Bible/Origen and the Bible. Actes du Colloquium Origenianum Sextum, Chantilly, 30 août – 3 septembre 1993*, 1995. XII-865 p. FB 3900.
119. É. GAZIAUX, *Morale de la foi et morale autonome. Confrontation entre P. Delhaye et J. Fuchs*, 1995. XXII-545 p. FB 2700.
120. T.A. SALZMAN, *Deontology and Teleology: An Investigation of the Normative Debate in Roman Catholic Moral Theology*, 1995. XVII-555 p. FB 2700.
121. G.R. EVANS & M. GOURGUES (eds.), *Communion et Réunion. Mélanges Jean-Marie Roger Tillard*, 1995. XI-431 p. FB 2400.
122. H.T. FLEDDERMANN, *Mark and Q: A Study of the Overlap Texts. With an Assessment* by F. NEIRYNCK, 1995. XI-307 p. FB 1800.
123. R. BOUDENS, *Two Cardinals: John Henry Newman, Désiré-Joseph Mercier*. Edited by L. GEVERS with the collaboration of B. DOYLE, 1995. 362 p. FB 1800.
124. A. THOMASSET, *Paul Ricœur. Une poétique de la morale. Aux fondements d'une éthique herméneutique et narrative dans une perspective chrétienne*, 1996. XVI-706 p. FB 3000.
125. R. BIERINGER (ed.), *The Corinthian Correspondence*, 1996. XXVII-793 p. FB 2400.
126. M. VERVENNE (ed.), *Studies in the Book of Exodus: Redaction – Reception – Interpretation*, 1996. XI-660 p. FB 2400.
127. A. VANNESTE, *Nature et grâce dans la théologie occidentale. Dialogue avec H. de Lubac*, 1996. 312 p. FB 1800.
128. A. CURTIS & T. RÖMER (eds.), *The Book of Jeremiah and its Reception – Le livre de Jérémie et sa réception*, 1997. 332 p. FB 2400.
129. E. LANNE, *Tradition et Communion des Églises. Recueil d'études*, 1997. XXV-703 p. FB 3000.

130. A. DENAUX & J.A. DICK (eds.), *From Malines to ARCIC. The Malines Conversations Commemorated*, 1997. IX-317 p. FB 1800.
131. C.M. TUCKETT (ed.), *The Scriptures in the Gospels*, 1997. XXIV-721 p. FB 2400.
132. J. VAN RUITEN & M. VERVENNE (eds.), *Studies in the Book of Isaiah. Festschrift Willem A.M. Beuken*, 1997. XX-540 p. FB 3000.
133. M. VERVENNE & J. LUST (eds.), *Deuteronomy and Deuteronomic Literature. Festschrift C.H.W. Brekelmans*, 1997. XI-637 p. FB 3000.
134. G. VAN BELLE (ed.), *Index Generalis ETL / BETL 1982-1997*, 1999. IX-337 p. FB 1600.
135. G. DE SCHRIJVER, *Liberation Theologies on Shifting Grounds. A Clash of Socio-Economic and Cultural Paradigms*, 1998. XI-453 p. FB 2100.
136. A. SCHOORS (ed.), *Qohelet in the Context of Wisdom*, 1998. XI-528 p. FB 2400.
137. W.A. BIENERT & U. KÜHNEWEG (eds.), *Origeniana Septima. Origenes in den Auseinandersetzungen des 4. Jahrhunderts*, 1999. XXV-848 p. FB 3800.
138. É. GAZIAUX, *L'autonomie en morale: au croisement de la philosophie et de la théologie*, 1998. XVI-739 p. FB 3000.
139. J. GROOTAERS, *Actes et acteurs à Vatican II*, 1998. XXIV-602 p. FB 3000.
140. F. NEIRYNCK, J. VERHEYDEN & R. CORSTJENS, *The Gospel of Matthew and the Sayings Source Q: A Cumulative Bibliography 1950-1995*, 1998. 2 vols., VII-1000-420* p. FB 3800.
141. E. BRITO, *Heidegger et l'hymne du sacré*, 1999. XV-800 p. FB 3600.
142. J. VERHEYDEN (ed.), *The Unity of Luke-Acts*, 1999. XXV-828 p. FB 2400.
143. N. CALDUCH-BENAGES & J. VERMEYLEN (eds.), *Treasures of Wisdom. Studies in Ben Sira and the Book of Wisdom. Festschrift M. Gilbert*, 1999. XXVII-463 p. FB 3000.
144. J.-M. AUWERS & A. WÉNIN (eds.), *Lectures et relectures de la Bible. Festschrift P.-M. Bogaert*, 1999. XLII-482 p. FB 2400.
145. C. BEGG, *Josephus' Story of the Later Monarchy (AJ 9,1–10,185)*, 2000. X-650 p. FB 3000.
146. J.M. ASGEIRSSON, K. DE TROYER & M.W. MEYER (eds.), *From Quest to Q. Festschrift James M. Robinson*, 2000. XLIV-346 p. FB 2400.
147. T. RÖMER (ed.), *The Future of Deuteronomistic History*, 2000. VIII-240 p. FB 3000.
148. F.D. VANSINA, *Paul Ricœur: Bibliographie primaire et secondaire - Primary and Secondary Bibliography 1935-2000*, 2000. XXVI-544 p. FB 3000.
149. G.J. BROOKE & J.D. KAESTLI (eds.), *Narrativity in Biblical and Related Texts*, 2000. XXII-307 p. FB 3000.
150. F. NEIRYNCK, *Evangelica III: 1992-2000. Collected Essays*, 2000. Forthcoming.
151. B. DOYLE, *The Apocalypse of Isaiah Metaphorically Speaking. A Sudy of the Use, Function and Significance of Metaphors in Isaiah 24-27*, 2000. XII-453 p. FB 3000.
152. T. MERRIGAN & J. HAERS (eds.), *The Myriad Christ. Plurality and the Quest for Unity in Contemporary Christology*, 2000. XIV-593 p. FB 3000.
153. M. SIMON, *Le catéchisme de Jean-Paul II. Genèse et évaluation de son commentaire du Symbole des apôtres*, 2000. XVI-688 p. FB 3000.
154. J. VERMEYLEN, *La loi du plus fort*, 2000. Forthcoming.

155. A. WÉNIN, *Studies in the Book of Genesis*, 2000. Forthcoming.
156. F. LEDEGANG, *Mysterium Ecclesisiae*, 2000. Forthcoming.
157. J.S. BOSWELL, F.P. MCHUGH & J. VERSTRAETEN, *Catholic Social Thought*, 2000. Forthcoming.